Development in Karnataka

Development in Karnataka

Challenges of Governance, Equity and Empowerment

Editors:
Gopal K. Kadekodi, Ravi Kanbur
and Vijayendra Rao

ACADEMIC FOUNDATION
NEW DELHI

www.academicfoundation.com

The front cover photograph shows public in the backdrop of the imposing Vidhana Soudha building in Bangalore (Bengaluru).

Photograph, courtesy: Andrew C. Oliver

First published in 2008
by

ACADEMIC FOUNDATION
4772-73 / 23 Bharat Ram Road, (23 Ansari Road),
Darya Ganj, New Delhi - 110 002 (India).
Phones : 23245001 / 02 / 03 / 04.
Fax : +91-11-23245005.
E-mail : academic@vsnl.com
www. academicfoundation.com

Cataloging in Publication Data--DK
Courtesy: D.K. Agencies (P) Ltd. <docinfo@dkagencies.com>

Development in Karnataka : challenges of governance, equity and empowerment / edited by Gopal K. Kadekodi, Ravi Kanbur and Vijayendra Rao.
p. cm. Contributed articles.
Includes bibliographical references.
ISBN 13: 9788171886197
ISBN 10: 8171886191

1. Karnataka (India)--Politics and government. 2. Karnataka (India)--Economic policy. 3. Karnataka (India)--Social policy. 4. Local government--India—Karnataka. I. Kadekodi, Gopal K. (Gopal Krishna), 1943- II. Kanbur, Ravi, 1954- III. Rao, Vijayendra.

DDC 320.954 87 22

Typeset by Italics India, New Delhi.
Printed and bound in India.

10 9 8 7 6 5 4 3 2 1

Contents

Part II

Civil Society and Governance

Part III

Sectoral Perspectives and Interventions

List of Tables, Figures and Boxes

TABLES

FIGURES

BOXES

Editors/Contributors

Kripa Ananthpur is Assistant Professor at the Madras Institute of Development Studies, Chennai, India. Her broad area of specialisation is governance and civil Society. She has worked extensively in this area studying the dynamics of farmers' movements and organisations, voluntary organisations, village forest committees and their interface with formal local governments. She is currently coordinating a cross-country comparative research study with partners from India, Indonesia and Pakistan on informal institutions and state capacity, funded by the Centre for Future State, Institute of Development Studies, UK.

Timothy Besley is Professor of Economics and Political Science at the LSE and a Member of the Monetary Policy Committee of the Bank of England. He is a Fellow of the Econometric Society and the British Academy, and was a 2005 winner of the Yrjö Jahnsson award. His research interests are in development economics, public economics and political economy.

Asha George is a Research Consultant for the Gender and Health Equity Project at the Indian Institute of Management–Bangalore. She has a background in reproductive health and health systems analysis. Her recent research is on accountability in primary healthcare from the perspective of health workers. Her forthcoming publications include an international review of gender and human resources for health and an edited volume on health providers in India.

Ronald Herring teaches political economy and political ecology at Cornell University, where he is Professor of Government. His recent works include connections between aid and ethnicity (*Carrots, Sticks and Ethnic Conflict: Rethinking Development Assistance*) and genetic engineering in development studies (*Transgenics and the Poor*).

Anand Inbanathan is an Associate Professor, Sociology, in the Institute for Social and Economic Change, Bangalore. He has carried out research in areas such as occupational health in sericulture, decentralisation and political participation, and rural development, and has also published articles in these areas.

Aditi Iyer is a Research Consultant for the Gender and Health Equity Project at the Indian Institute of Management–Bangalore. Her research interests focus on gender and the political economy of health and health systems.

She is currently studying the intersections between gender, class and caste in relation to health in Koppal district, Karnataka.

Devaki Jain, a development economist, serves on the governing body of several research centres, and government committees in India. Her research interest is in women and governance, as well as feminist economics. She has published several books as well as articles which have appeared in leading journals and books, which explore and document women's engagement with development and politics.

Gopal K. Kadekodi was formerly Director of the Institute for Social and Economic Change (ISEC), Bangalore. He has been Research Professor at the Centre for Multi-Disciplinary Development Research, Dharwad for four years and a Professor at the Institute of Economic Growth, New Delhi for over 25 years. He was Visiting Professor at the Erasmus University, Rotterdam, and the Technical University, Twente. His areas of research include common property resources, energy, environment and economic development. He has been the President of the Indian Society for Ecological Economics. He was the Editor of *Journal of Social and Economic Development*, and has been on the Editorial Boards of *Environment and Resource Economics*, *The Pacific and Asian Journal of Energy* and *Journal of Quantitative Economics*. He has published over 12 books and more than 100 articles in national and international journals.

Ravi Kanbur is the T.H. Lee Professor of World Affairs and Economics at Cornell University. During 2004-05 he was the V.K.R.V. Rao Chair Professor at ISEC, Bangalore. He has previously served as the senior staff of the World Bank. His research interests span public economics and development economics and he has published articles on these topics in leading economics journals.

G.K. Karanth is a Professor of Sociology and heads the Centre for Social Change and Development in ISEC. He was formerly teaching in the Department of Sociology, Mangalore University. His work in the past has ranged from agrarian sociology, social mobility of the socioculturally deprived sections of society, to the working of new technologies for healthcare, and issues of child labour. Several of his papers based on work on these themes have appeared in leading journals and as books and monographs.

Neema Kudva teaches in the Department of City and Regional Planning at the Cornell University. Her research focuses on understanding institutional arrangements and organisational practices for local level planning and development; another research interest is secondary urbanisation. She is currently involved in a project that examines urban transformations in coastal South Karnataka.

S. Madheswaran is Associate Professor in the Centre for Economic Studies and Policy at ISEC, Bangalore. His research interest includes labour economics, economics of education and applied econometrics. He has published articles on these topics in refereed economic journals.

James Manor is the Emeka Anyaoku Professor at the Institute of Commonwealth Studies, University of London, and V.K.R.V. Rao Professor at ISEC, Bangalore. He focuses mainly on politics and state-society relations. He has previously taught at Yale, Harvard and Leicester Universities, and at the Institute of Development Studies, University of Sussex.

M.R. Narayana is a Professor at the Centre for Economic Studies and Policy at the ISEC, Bangalore. His current research areas include economics of information technology and telecommunications demand. His latest research on "Consumer Demand for Telecom Services in Karnataka and Goa" is sponsored by the Department of Telecommunications, Government of India. He has widely published on topics in general economics in journals and edited volumes in India and abroad.

Rohini Pande is the Mohamed Kamal Professor of Public Policy at the Kennedy School of Government, Harvard Unversity. Her research focuses on the economic analysis of the politics and consequences of different forms of redistribution, principally in developing countries.

Pamela Price is a historian, teaching at the University of Oslo. She began her career writing about the colonial period, but moved into the study of post-colonial political culture after moving to Norway. Since then, she has written on ideas and values of honour and authority in Karnataka, Tamil Nadu and Andhra Pradesh.

D. Rajasekhar, Professor and Head, Centre for Decentralisation and Development, ISEC, Bangalore, is a Development Economist with specialisation in decentralisation, micro-finance, social protection for unorganised workers, and rural development. He has published 17 books and over 50 research articles in various journals and edited books.

Ramesh Ramanathan is co-founder, Janaagraha, a civil society institution working on urban governance reforms in India. Their work focuses on deepening democratic processes by expanding political space for decision making, and strengthening key political actors—citizens and elected representatives—to use these spaces. He is the coauthor of a book on urban poverty in India, and his interests include financial inclusion in the urban areas.

Vijayendra Rao is a Lead Economist in the Development Economics Research Group of the World Bank. He received his BA from St. Xavier's College, Mumbai, his PhD from the University of Pennsylvania, and has held academic appointments at Brown, Chicago, Michigan and Williams College. His research—much of it based on fieldwork in Karnataka—integrates economic and anthropological methods to inform poverty-reduction policies in poor countries. He has published several papers in leading journals on the broad themes of decentralised local development, gender inequality, culture and economic behaviour and mixing qualitative and quantitative methods, and co-edited *Culture and Public Action*.

Gita Sen is Professor at the Centre for Public Policy of the Indian Institute of Management in Bangalore. She has worked extensively on gender and development, combining research and teaching with policy advocacy and civil society activism. Her current action-research project on gender and health equity in north Karnataka allows her to bring local level insights to her policy work as coordinator of the knowledge network on the same subject for the WHO's Commission on the Social Determinants of Health.

Dattathreya Subbanarasimha teaches law and social sciences at the Christ College of Law, Bangalore. He is also finishing a PhD in sociocultural anthropology (on issues surrounding the peasantry in contemporary Karnataka) at the Columbia University. He has written and published extensively in a wide range of areas, including human rights, Kannada cultural and literary criticism, the social sciences, psychotherapy, and the sociology and history of science; and in a wide range of fora, including books, professional journals, web journals and newspapers.

J.Y. Suchitra is a researcher with the Centre for Decentralisation and Development, ISEC, Bangalore. Her main areas of interest are labour and institutional economics and for the past two years, she has been undertaking research relating to social protection for the unorganised work force, microfinance as a tool to reduce vulnerability, and child labour. She has published books and papers on these topics.

G. Thimmaiah is currently Hon. Visiting Fellow at the ISEC, Bangalore. He was Professor of Economics since 1973 and Director (1984-1987) of the Institute. He was Economic Adviser to the Government of Karnataka (1987-1994) and Member, Planning Commission (1996-1998). He was also ICSSR National Fellow (1998-2000). His area of research has been in public finance.

Ananda Vadivelu is a Doctoral Fellow at ISEC, Bangalore and works as a Research Associate at the Centre for Interdisciplinary Studies in Environment and Development (CISED), Bangalore. His research interests span issues related to watershed development, common property studies, property rights issues in groundwater and the Food for Work Programme. He intends to work and colloborate with institutions working on action research projects.

V. Vijayalakshmi works for Oxfam International. Her research interests are in the areas of governance, decentralisation, and political participation, and she has published widely on these topics.

1

Assessing the "Karnataka Model of Development"[1]

GOPAL K. KADEKODI, RAVI KANBUR and VIJAYENDRA RAO

The Karnataka Model

Karnataka was founded 50 years ago and in those decades has embodied the challenges and contradictions that are faced by the rest of India—spectacular technology-led growth in Bangalore tempered with an abiding sense of the city's ungovernability, enduring gender inequity and regional disparities, and a visibly increasing gap between urban and rural areas.[2] Yet, Karnataka is also increasingly being seen as a model of development. Bangalore's metamorphosis from a noun to a verb is the archetypical symbol of an India 'unbound', and Karnataka's pioneering experiment with *Panchayati Raj* reform under the Hegde Government in the 1980s sparked the 73rd amendment and the consequent and continuing wave of devolutions in finance and power to *panchayats*. This emphasis on technology-led growth coupled with local government reform is, at least in theory, a singularly innovative strategy to address the challenge of generating growth with equity and can be described as the "Karnataka Model" of development.

---

1. This is the introduction to an edited volume, *Development of Karnataka: Challenges of Governance, Equity and Empowerment*, which grew out of a conference held at the Institute of Social and Economic Change, Bangalore. We thank Srilata Batliwala, Arjan De Haan, Jeffrey Hammer, Maitreyi Krishnaraj, Lant Pritchett, and other scholars for their help with this symposium. S. Madheswaran did a splendid job of supervising the conference logistics. We thank S.L. Rao, the Chairman of the Institute, and R. Rameshappa, Registrar, for their support. We would also like to thank Cornell University for financial support, and Sue Snyder for administrative and logistical support at Cornell throughout the process of the conference and production of the volume. Some of the papers in this volume (Chapters 2, 5, 9, 10, 11 and 15) appeared in a symposium in *Economic and Political Weekly*, "Governance and Development in Karnataka" (February 24-March 2, Vol XLII, No. 8). The introduction to this volume draws on the introduction to that Symposium.

2. Narayana (2006) and Sen (2006) for an analysis of the factors behind Bangalore's high-tech growth and the challenges of extending high growth rates to the rest of the state.

The Karnataka model should more accurately be called the "Mysore Model" because the strategy was not arrived at serendipitously. It has century-old roots in policy decisions taken by the princely state of Mysore. As Manu Bhagavan (2003) has shown, the then *Maharaja* of Mysore, Krishnaraja Wadiyar, advised by his *Diwan* cum Chief Engineer M. Visweswaraya, instituted several initiatives to improve the quality of higher education in the state, with a particular emphasis on technology and the sciences. Additionally, in 1905, the Government of Mysore persuaded J.N. Tata to locate the Indian Institute of Science in Bangalore subsidised by a land-grant, and an annual government subsidy of Rs. 50,000. These initiatives did two things—they produced generations of highly trained engineers and scientists in the state, and they encouraged an atmosphere conducive to scientific and technological innovation.[3] Both were, arguably, crucial elements in Bangalore's 'take-off'.[4]

As M.R. Narayana argues in this volume, these policies have had a demonstrable payoff. Karnataka's rate of economic growth in the last 15 years has been about 5-6 per cent higher than the rest of India. Much of this difference can be attributed to differences in the rate of growth of information and communications technology (ICT) firms, with the average growth of tertiary GDP in the state being about double than that in the rest of the country. This technology-led growth has been greatly facilitated by a large hinterland of institutions for technical education that provide a steady supply of trained employees for the industry. The industry has been largely Bangalore-centreed despite efforts by the state government to build technology hubs in other major towns in the state.

The Mysorean roots of *panchayati raj* also go very deep. The historian Christopher Bayly (2006) has recently stated that the terms *panchayat* and *sabha* in the context of village institutions were first

3. It is interesting to note another Wadiyar initiative that has had an international impact. The *Maharaja* of Mysore instituted excellent Sanskrit schools and a university that, along with instruction in texts, taught the theory and practice of *yoga*. BKS Iyengar and K. Pattabhi Jois were both students at the *yoga* school and Jois continued his studies at the Sanskrit university. They, of course, went on to spearhead the international *yoga* movement *via* the Iyengar and *Ashtanga* schools that they, respectively, founded.

4. Kadekodi (2006a) for more on Visweswaraya's vision.

articulated by Ram Raz, based on his experience as a 'native judge' in Mysore about 200 years ago. These were then adopted by North Indian writers and subsequently absorbed into the nationalist canon *via* Gandhiji's vigorous advocacy (Gandhi, 1962). 'Modern' Panchayati Raj Institution (PRI) reforms in Karnataka can be traced at least as far back as Krishnaraja Wadiyar's expansion of local self-government in 1902-03 which created 8 district and 77 *taluk* boards. Nataraj and Ananthpur (2004) document the subsequent history of *panchayat* reforms in Karnataka. In 1918, the Mysore Local Boards and Village Panchayat Act was passed which provided for the election of half of the representatives in district and two-thirds in *taluk* boards respectively. In 1926, a two-tier scheme with village *panchayats* and district boards was established, abolishing *taluk* boards, with both bodies provided with power and independent sources of revenue; and in the post-independence period several acts and bills were passed culminating in the 1983 Act under the Hegde government whose provisions were adopted, with a few modifications, by the authors of the 73rd amendment to the Indian constitution.[5]

Karnataka, of course, is not entirely Mysorean. It was constructed by merging Mysore State with the Kannada-speaking parts of Hyderabad, Bombay and Madras in 1956. In particular, the districts that came from old Hyderabad tended to have lower living standards and infrastructure than the rest of Karnataka at the time, and this lag persists to this day causing a high degree of regional imbalance in the state (Sen, 2006). This regional imbalance perhaps has as much to do with geography and climate as it does with policy, but the fact that it has prevailed for two centuries indicates important path-dependencies in government and social action.

In June of 2005, we organised an interdisciplinary conference at the Institute for Social and Economic Change in Bangalore that examined various aspects of development in Karnataka, and this volume gathers most of the papers presented in the conference. The research collected here shows that development in Karnataka remains a daunting challenge—the success of technology-led growth in the state has not translated into marked improvements in governance or living

5. Crook and Manor (1998) study the impact of the Hedge's *Panchayat* Reforms.

standards. The theory of the "Karnataka Model" has far surpassed its implementation. Challenges that remain beyond regional inequalities, include the slow, incremental, nature of changes in many parts of the state, continuing gender inequalities, several shortcomings in the implementation of the PRI reforms, and a lack of attention to urban governance. Since these concerns are shared by almost every other state in the country, the papers in this symposium have applicability well beyond the state's borders.

State and Local Politics

Karnataka has a long history of using political and deliberative means to deal with difference and hierarchy. Chamrajendra Wadiyar, Krishnaraja's father, established the Mysore Representative Assembly in 1881 which was designed to give Mysoreans a forum to air their differences (Bhagavan, 2003). While *Brahmins* dominated this body, the assembly helped increase the level of political awareness particularly among the two other dominant groups—*Lingayats* and *Vokkaligas*. By the first decade of the 20th century these two groups formed associations to better their living conditions and to lobby the state government. In 1919, a committee led by Leslie Miller—the Chief Judge of the Mysore high court—defined a category of 'Backward Classes' in the state recommending affirmative action for non-*Brahmins* in educational institutions and state administrative services, special schools, scholarships, and hostels, to promote living standards among non-*Brahmin* classes. These measures were quickly implemented and, subsequently, *Vokkaligas* and *Lingayats* have become potent social and political stakeholders in the state.

James Manor's contribution in this volume examines the contemporary implications of this by examining the political history of Karnataka since 1972. He finds that while several changes have occurred, they have been gradual. This is because, in his view, politicians in Karnataka tend to be tentative, even conservative. Two competing coalitions have contended for power, what Manor borrowing Muzaffar Assadi's coinage, refers to as MOVD (Muslims, OBCs, *Vokkaligas* and Dalits) and LIBRA (*Lingayats* and *Brahmins*). These group dynamics have made power sharing within rainbow collections a necessary condition for stable government. This has made individual politicians less important than institutions, with loosely structured political parties. Bureaucrats have, consequently, retained considerable power with greater autonomy compared to other states. This has resulted in better crafted technical policies and more policy continuity. But it has also directed political competition in a way that has led to a marked increase in corruption because of the need to satisfy different blocks of voters.

While caste has remained an important marker of identity it has increasingly begun to signify difference rather than hierarchy. The 'materiality' of caste has also decreased—caste is no longer as significant in determining an individual's access to tangible opportunities and assets, and high caste status offers fewer material advantages. *Panchayats* have become increasingly important, and this has brought group-based political competition to the lowest levels of government. Links between low and high levels of government have shown improvement, but, because of changes in the nature of caste and in local governance, village society has become less cohesive with individuals mattering more than groups.

G. Thimmaiah elaborates on the link between Karnataka's development and changes in its political leadership. In the period between 1947 and 1956, when Karnataka was still Mysore, and the Congress party dominated both state and central politics, the state government did not have much flexibility in determining policy but simply implemented national dictates. At the same time, corruption was also low and the construction of public works tended to be timely and efficient. All this changed after 1956 when the introduction of territories from Hyderabad, Madras and Bombay brought in increased political competition between regions and caste groups. Nijalingappa, who was the first dominant CM of the post-integration era focused on implementing hydroelectric and irrigation projects which have resulted in a sustained supply of electricity and water in the state. Thimmaiah argues that Devaraj Urs, the CM from 1972 till 1980, had perhaps the most significant impact on socioeconomic and political changes in the state. He was the first CM to seek his political base among disadvantaged castes and implement ceilings of land holdings which reduced the economic base of the dominant *Vokkaliga* and *Lingayat* communities. He also built on Nijalingappa's efforts to expand the irrigated area in the state by completing the Cauvery basin project. These efforts had the effect of not only raising the state's economic growth but also reducing poverty. Ramakrishna Hegde's *panchayat* reforms have already been alluded to and are another example of important changes that are implemented largely because of the personal vision of a CM.

Pamela Price's chapter focuses on the Hegde period and is an account of the personal rivalry between Hegde and Deve Gowda—his successor as CM. She uses this rivalry as a case-study on the discourse of honour, respect and humiliation among Indian politicians arguing that such 'personality clashes' are central to understanding political competition. The bitter rivalry between Hegde and Gowda, which transcended Karnataka to enter national politics during Gowda's short tenure as Prime Minister, represented more than opportunistic contrivance but at the time was a major driver of the political dynamic. This argument reminds us of the agency of the individual, overriding structural constraints of caste and region.[6] However, Price concludes that while "large efforts and reserves of energy were needed to participate in and manage rivalries they do not seem, on the surface at least, to have had much to do with the formulation and implementation of development policy."

Land reform has always been argued to be one of the major pace setters in the development process. Focussing on Devraj Urs' 1974 land reforms, Ron Herring (this volume) says that though extensive in their conception, they did not have a large impact.[7] One concern is that these impacts have not been adequately tested in Karnataka—with most of our understanding deriving either from data collected for a bureaucratic purpose or from very small one-village case-studies. However, despite their limitations, these data show that Karnataka's reforms have been relatively well-administered but have generally resulted in very small farms. They have also been rather limited in scope covering only 1.1 per cent of sown area. Some economists, including Thimmaiah, have argued that land reform should be scaled-back because they create high transactions cost and prevent the efficient allocation of land resources.

---

6. Mines (1994) for a more general discourse on this point.
7. Aziz and Krishna (1997) for an authoritative discussion on land reform in Karnataka.

Herring takes a strong position against this point of view arguing instead that shortcomings in scope and implementation have limited their impact which suggests that reforms should be expanded instead of scaled-back. Moreover, land reforms have several important indirect effects such as 'restructuring the fields of power within which bureaucracies function and positive externalities in governance' which gives them greater salience than other, more fashionable prescriptions for rural policy.

Local Governance

Tim Besley, Rohini Pande and Vijayendra Rao, turn the focus to local politics in an econometric examination of various aspects of political behaviour within *gram panchayats* (GPs). Their data come from a household and village survey covering 500 villages, and spread across all the four southern states, with over a third of the data from Karnataka. The data were collected between September and November 2002 and therefore, provide a snapshot of changes in *gram panchayats* about 10 years after the 73rd amendment. Most results in the paper are from regressions with GP or village fixed effects, thus controlling for sources of variation across GPs and villages that are unobserved by the econometricians. The paper reports that reservations for Dalits and STs work in the sense that households in GPs that have presidencies reserved for SC/STs are 7 per cent more likely to offer targeted benefits to Dalits and STs. On the other hand, the political geography of the GP seems to matter with the President's own village showing 10 per cent more investment activity than other villages in the GP.

Gram Sabhas are supposed to be lynchpin of the *panchayat* system, yet in these data it is found that only 77 per cent of villages held at least one *gram sabha* in the previous year. Holding a *gram sabha* seems to have an egalitarian influence with more effective targeting of below poverty line (BPL) cards to the poor and disadvantaged. Perhaps because of this, landless and illiterate households are more likely to attend, but, on the other hand, women are much less likely to attend. Finally, the authors examine the role of politician selection within *gram panchayats* finding that they come from elite groups within the village. Even in reserved categories, elites within these those categories are more likely to become politicians. Moreover, politicians are more likely to obtain BPL cards, controlling for their socioeconomic status and village level variation, which is evidence for political opportunism.

What about corruption within increasingly empowered *panchayats*? V. Vijayalakshmi's contribution to this volume delves deeper into this issue with primary data on perceptions of corruption from Gram *Panchayats* representatives in Mandya and Udupi districts. Beneficiary programmes apparently have a fixed rate of commission ranging from 10 to 20 per cent at the GP level, while at *taluk* and *zila* levels corruption largely manifests itself in the form of fictitious contracts and false billing. All the representatives saw corruption either as an activity without risk or a low risk activity—and attributed its high prevalence to patronage networks, high cost of elections[8], and political competition. Almost all saw the payment of commissions (known as *mamul*) as a normal practice needed to cover election expenses and other costs, and not as a form of corruption. They distinguished these from bribes used to influence particular outcomes—which they do see as corruption. Thus, like the anthropologist Akhil Gupta (1995), Vijayalakshmi uncovers the normality of corruption—it seems to be part of the ordinary business of life with not much evidence either of public outrage or efforts to counteract it.

Ananda Vadivelu moves to looking at how well a sustainable development project works with local communities on joint strategies for watershed management. His case-study focuses on five villages where he uncovers some common flaws in the project's design. First, even though the project was supposed to be participatory—it was not broad-based and consisted of a project assistance meeting with a key informant to identify watersheds and prepare treatment plans—usually based on one or two day visits to the village. Participation in self-help groups was low, as was participation in planning meetings. Rich farmers, who stood to benefit greatly from the project, tended not to contribute towards its costs which were largely borne by medium farmers. Generally, rich farmers found that they could gain benefits

8. Vijayalakshmi says that maximum election expenses in GPs was Rs. 50,000, Rs. 3 lakh in *taluk panchayats*, and Rs. 8 lakhs in *zila* elections.

from the project without participating, while poor farmers tended to be disgruntled with the project because it did not meet their needs for creating employment. The paper points out the challenges of conducting community development projects within local contexts, and shows that political inequality at the village level can play an important role in determining who gains and who participates.[9]

Kripa Ananthpur conducts a qualitative analysis of traditional rural institutions and village politics in 30 villages in Karnataka. She finds that, despite, the increasing prominence of *gram panchayats*, customary village councils (CVCs) continue to play an important role in village life.[10] CVCs include various categories of 'traditional' *panchayats* including caste *panchayats*, street *panchayats* and *nyaya panchayats*. They perform a range of useful functions including the organisation of village festivals, dispute resolution, social services, and informal development activities. Interestingly, they tend to be inter-caste institutions, and serve as deliberative forums with an emphasis on compromise. They interact closely with *gram panchayats*, in selecting candidates for *panchayat* elections, encouraging uncontested elections, and selection of beneficiaries. The leadership of CVCs and GPs tend to overlap and villagers tend to view them not as competitors but as complements to *gram panchayats*.[11] This raises a question that if the activities of CVCs translate into activism in parallel formal bodies, such as water user groups, and whether these formal institutions complement or compete with *panchayats*.

Gender and Governance

Poor governance can have a particularly adverse impact on women by enhancing conditions of patriarchy. Gita Sen, Aditi Iyer and Asha George demonstrate this in their study of gender inequity in health in Koppal district, which was part of old-Hyderabad state and therefore historically underdeveloped. They find women's health is affected by systemic failures in both public and private health facilities.

9. Mansuri and Rao (2004) for a review of the literature on this topic.

10. This echoes Krishna's (2003) findings in Rajasthan.

11. Note that aside from *Panchayat* officials and CVCs, there is a third category of people who wield power within the *panchayat* system—"fixers"—whose job it is to assist in the manipulation of the system (Inbanathan and Gopalappa, 2002).

Government facilities, despite increasing funding, lack specialists and supplies, while private providers are dominated by informal medical practitioners. In an emergency, women are forced to constantly shuffle between inadequate government facilities and poor quality private providers who are, respectively, plagued by poor accountability and lack of regulation. The adverse effects of this 'forced pluralism' are compounded by disjunctions in diagnoses due to discriminatory attitudes. Women tend to have quite high levels of health seeking behaviours, but preventable maternal mortality rates remain high because they are much less likely to be treated for their illnesses than men. Women's complaints are more likely to be listed as 'not serious' by medical practitioners reflecting a lower recognition of their needs. A combination of discrimination within the home, poor access to health services, and discriminatory attitudes results in a systematic disenfranchising of women in the health system.

Devaki Jain further explores the problem of how to best engender public policy, based upon her experiences as a Karnataka-based scholar-activist. She argues that the inherited knowledge-base of public policy is inherently gender-biased because it is constructed within a patriarchal system. Moreover, women continue to lack a voice in policy decisions that affect them despite several years of effort. To break this deadlock, women need to create a strategic 'space of their own' but should have a say in all issues of relevance and not just those related to 'women's issues.' The knowledge base should be engendered by mapping the social and economic location of women both within the household and outside. Participation in leadership and political life, perhaps *via* reservations, can provide the turning point in changing the gendered nature of decision making.[12] Women need to become economic and political agents instead of passive recipients of special ladders and safety nets. This she calls a 'bubbling-up' model as opposed to a 'trickle-down' theory of development.

---

12. Studies of the impact of this have been mixed but provide an optimistic picture. Chattopadhyay and Duflo (2004) find strong positive effects in West Bengal and Rajasthan, but Ban and Rao (2007) find that in the South Indian states the impact is tempered by institutional issues such as whether the village is upper caste dominated, whether the woman president has served in a previous term, and whether the state has a history of supporting *panchayats*.

Jain illustrates these points with examples from her work in Karnataka. To demonstrate the gender-bias in information she uses the examples of poverty and sericulture programmes in Karnataka. Poverty programmes were based on data that did not adequately capture the extent of women's work or the double-burden they faced in working at home and outside. Therefore, special studies and surveys were conducted to map gender inequalities within the home, and the extent of women's work outside. This led to a change in policy where programs were modified to allow for the direct targeting of women. Sericulture projects, assisted by the World Bank, were found to systematically deny the possibility that women were significantly involved in silk-rearing and farming activities. A targeted study done to examine this found that they were, in fact, deeply involved—largely within the home—in tending mulberry plants, feeding silkworms, and removing waste. Consequently the projects were modified to improve facilities for women to receive training in sericulture. Finally, Karnataka's pioneering efforts in reserving seats for women in *panchayats*, supplemented with training, have strengthened their hand in village decision making.

Health and Social Security

Anand Inbanathan examines another aspect of the sericulture industry—as a significant cause of health problems such as asthma and other respiratory illnesses. He focuses on the activity of reeling—where silk yarn is unwound from cocoons and stretched into a long silk thread, an activity where Karnataka leads the country in production. The vast majority of scheduled caste workers in this occupation reported health problems (mainly asthma, cough, and persistent headache), and close to 50 per cent of non-SC workers also had similar complaints. These complaints are more prevalent among labourers than with owners indicating that proximity to the actual work of reeling matters more than simple exposure. Women workers face particular risks in this industry because exposure to reeling is compounded by the smoke they inhale from cooking. These negative health externalities also result in a poverty trap because they adversely affect a worker's ability to save and move out of reeling into higher-skill occupations. Reeling, therefore, is almost never a source of social mobility.

D. Rajashekhar and his colleagues highlight the consequences of another hazard for workers—the lack of social security in the unorganised sector. When asked what their social security needs were, over 70 per cent workers in a sample of 900 identified old age pensions and steady employment as their most important needs. Their concept of unemployment benefits seemed to closely approximate the principles behind the National Rural Employment Guarantee Act suggesting that extending the Act to urban areas would fulfill an important need. Construction works highlighted compensation against work-related injuries which is an increasing concern given the recent boom in construction. Actual risks faced by workers did not necessarily correlate with their insurance requests: about half faced health emergencies, about 20 per cent had suffered the death of a close family member. Eighty-seven per cent of domestic servants faced health problems due to the nature of their work, along with 53 per cent of construction workers and 37 per cent of agricultural labourers. Sadly, only 18 per cent of respondents had any type of insurance coverage—including central schemes like the Janashree Bima Yojana. All this suggests that risk management in the unorganised sector is a vastly underserved problem that requires more attention from policy makers. With the high rate of urban growth in Karnataka—it is likely to become a more serious problem in the future.

Civil Society and the Public Sphere

For more than 20 years NGOs have had a strong presence in Karnataka have often played an important role in governance. Neema Kudva lays out the landscape of NGO activity in the state and argues that they are neither a collaborationist nor an oppositional force. On the other hand "organisations are often simultaneously involved in collaborative and conflictual relations with the state and walk a thin line between establishing pragmatic relationships even as they acknowledge the need to keep some critical distance from the state." However, NGO activity is centered in five districts—Bangalore, Kolar, Tumkur, Chitradurga and Dharwad. While many NGOs are privately funded, or supported by international groups, corporate-funded NGOs are becoming increasingly visible. Karnataka's NGOs are seeing "new cleavages created by the simultaneous movement of the state towards the market and political decentralisation."

Some of these points are brought into sharp relief by Ramesh Ramanathan who focuses on his experience with Janaagraha, an NGO working on urban governance issues—largely in Bangalore. He makes the important point that with all the talk about the 73rd amendment, the 74th amendment, on urban local government, is largely forgotten—an afterthought, ignored in national and state policy. Ramanathan argues that this is a mistake. Participatory planning, and increasing citizen's voice in cities is just as important in urban as in rural areas, and more challenging because of the large size of the population.[13] Janaagraha's work in Bangalore has attempted to do this by a variety of different initiatives which include verifying voter and BPL lists, proposing benefit-sharing schemes with communities who are willing to monitor their members in order to increase tax-compliance. Ramanathan proposes that a framework to adapt the spirit of the 73rd amendment in a manner that will have real impact: 1) Institute Ward *Sabhas* in a manner similar to *gram sabhas*, but also have a new tier of government below the ward level that will have a more manageable size; 2) Integrate the different tiers of city government with improved systems of accounting, accountability and monitoring; 3) Have sequential and well-defined planning process building from grassroots discussions on priorities and needs.

Dattathreya Subbanarasimha moves from NGO activity to asking whether it is possible to conceive of a 'public sphere' in Karnataka—rather like Bayly's (1996) notion of an Indian 'ecumene.' Habermas (1989) conceived of the public sphere as an arena of voluntary participation, independent of political and economic systems—but consisting of associations where people are engaged in equal discussion. This was greatly facilitated in Europe by the right to freedoms of association and free speech. Gradually this emerging public sphere functioned as a voluntary system of accountability that

---

13. There is evidence from Delhi that shows that squatter settlements spontaneously tend to form democratically elected *panchayat*-like governance structures even in the absence of any state-led initiatives (Jha, Rao and Woolcock, 2007) indicating that the potential for deepening democracy in urban areas has been unrealised.

acted as a check on the excesses of government. Subbanarasimha argues that Karnataka has a 'diversity of organs' that operate in the public sphere that range from the press and other media (including 241 Kannada language dailies), to literary and cultural fora (movies, *Saahitya/Saanskruthika balagagalu*), traditional story telling (*harikathey*), and caste and religious associations. However, the creation of an integrated public sphere is challenged by low levels of literacy, linguistic and religious diversity, and divisions in caste and social class.

Some Implications

The "Karnataka Model of Development" has two pillars—technology-led growth and improved governance, particularly at the local level. As Narayana shows, the state has done spectacularly well in ICT growth but with a severe regional imbalance. On governance, which has become the new buzzword of development (Kaufman, Kray and Zoido-Lobaton, 2002); it has made important efforts albeit under different labels for at least a century with distinctly mixed results. However, it is clear that path-dependencies generated by these efforts have made a difference—at least in the world of ideas.

The papers in this volume highlight a common theme of a gap between ideas and implementation, between *de jure* and *de facto* governance. Nowhere is this more evident than in the state's efforts at land reform, as Herring points out. Politics matter. Manor argues that the strong caste-based nature of political coalitions in the state have had the negative effect of politicising caste in the state in a manner that is perhaps more acute than the other South Indian states. At the same time caste-politics has also resulted in more cautious politicians who have, generally, avoided the excesses of some other states. Coalition politics as a compromise have led to more stable policies, partly because bureaucrats have retained relatively more power in the state. But, this argument should also be supplemented by examining this continuity within the context of the policies of the Wadiyar regime. Thimmaiah and Price show the salience of powerful individuals in driving the political process. Therefore, the selection of leaders can play an important role in the development process.

With increasing devolution to *panchayats*, Besley, Pande and Rao show political considerations have also begun to matter at the village level with village politicians acting in ways that protect their electoral base. Panchayati Raj institutions are not yet working in the manner envisaged by the 73rd amendment, particularly in the irregularities in holding *gram sabhas*. Corruption is to some extent being localised with evidence of political opportunism by village politicians. On the hand caste-reservations seem to had the desired effect of improving the lot of disadvantaged groups. Vijayalakshmi, furthermore, shows corruption is both pervasive and free of sanction which makes it entrenched and pervasive. Several concrete recommendations can be drawn from these results, including instituting a system to monitor effective and regularly held *gram sabhas*, and limiting the number of villages within each *panchayat* to reduce the extent to which political competition can influence intra-village disparities in *panchayat* investments, and instituting incentives—such as increasing the salaries of *panchayat* committee members—to reduce corruption within the PRI system.

Ramanathan demonstrates the utter lack of attention paid to governance in urban areas with the lackluster implementation of the 74th amendment. Civil society groups can play a valuable role in changing this by highlighting attention to the problem and by initiating collective action to solve it. Civil society groups, as Anantpur and Kudva demonstrate, are active also in rural governance. In villages—in the form of Customary Village Councils though, unlike urban NGOs, these have long historical roots. They do, however, interact closely with *gram panchayats* in selecting candidates, influencing village decisions and conducting important activities like dispute resolution that are outside the mandate of *gram panchayats*. Ramanathan, Anantpur, and Kudva therefore, identify the singular importance of civil society in improving governance. While the theory of democracy emphasises the central role of electoral accountability, Subbanarasimha, Ramanathan and Anantpur point towards another type of accountability that the political scientist Lily Tsai (2007) calls "social accountability." Organisations and movements outside government can hold the government to task and cooperate with it to generate better governance. This is true both at the local level as shown in Kerala (Isaac and Heller, 2003), but also, more generally

(Fung and Wright, 2003) to correct what can be described as 'civil society failure' (Devarajan and Kanbur, 2005). However, as Vadivelu points out, government programmes that actively attempt to generate participation can fail when they are not well designed and implemented—therefore building civil society cannot be done within traditional development modalities.

Sen, Iyer and George highlight two more important limitations in the 'Karnataka Model'. First, that the large portions of Karnataka that come from the *Nizam's* territories face challenges that are particularly daunting; Second, that systemic challenges in governance have particularly adverse consequences for women—who face neglect within the home and exclusion outside which has adverse consequences for their health. Jain fleshes out where and how gender bias occurs within systems of governance and points out two factors—in the gender-biased nature of how the state 'sees'; 1) In the kinds of data it collects and the analyses it conducts; 2) In the fact that women are systematically excluded from decision making processes, a point that is also demonstrated by Besley, Pande and Rao who show that women are much less likely to participate in *gram sabhas*. It is also implicitly brought out in Manor's political history which shows that a woman has never risen to prominence in the higher reaches of Karnataka politics. Rajashekhar *et al.* and Inbanathan point out yet another important challenge—that unorganised workers face health hazards and other risks that are not adequately insured which severely affects their ability to be mobile and lead productive lives.

What lessons can we draw from all this?[14] What can other states within India, and countries outside, learn from Karnataka's experience? First, that good ideas do not always translate into good practices. Second, that deliberative democracy can be nurtured by the state by actively instituting forums for deliberative interaction as in the case of the Mysore Representative Assembly and in *gram sabhas* in village *panchayats*. Third, that in order for civil society groups to play useful roles as agents of social accountability—states have to be supportive and responsive to such groups. Fourth, that despite good intentions pervasive forms of discrimination, particularly against

14. See Kadekodi (2006a and 2006b) for concrete policy recommendations for Karnataka.

women, can persist. Tackling this requires supplementing a gender-specific approach in data collection, with mechanisms that will broaden political participation. Fifth, that deepening democracy is a very slow process with lots of ups and downs, and fits and starts, constant innovation, an active public sphere, and resistance from active social movements. Good governance cannot be achieved overnight, but with persistent efforts it will bear some fruits. Hopefully, as time goes by, 'Karnataka's Model' of development will better reflect its reality.

References

Aziz, Abdul and Sudhir Krishna (eds.) (1997). *Land Reforms in India Volume 4: Karnataka Promises Kept and Missed.* New Delhi/Thousand Oaks/London: Sage Publications.

Ban, Radu and Vijayendra Rao (2007). "Tokenism or Agency: The Impact of Women's Reservations on Village Democracies in South India". *Economic Development and Cultural Change* (forthcoming).

Bayly, Christopher A. (2006). "Rammohan Roy and the Construction of Liberalism in India", unpublished *mimeo,* May.

———. (1996). *Empire and Information: Intelligence Gathering and Social Communication in India, 1780-1870.* Cambridge UK: Cambridge University Press.

Bhagavan, Manu (2003). *Sovereign Spheres: Princes, Education and Empire in Colonial India.* New Delhi: Oxford University Press.

Chattopadhyaya, Raghavendra and Esther Duflo (2004). "Impact of Reservations on Panchayati Raj: Evidence from a Nationwide Randomized Experiment", *Economic and Political Weekly,* February 28.

Crook, Richard C. and James Manor (1998). *Democracy and Decentralisation in South Asia and West Africa.* Cambridge: Cambridge University Press.

Devarajan, Shantanayan and Ravi Kanbur (2005). "A Framework for Scaling-Up Poverty Reduction, With Ilustrations from South India", *mimeo,* Cornell University, August.

Fung, Archon and Erik Olin Wright (2003). "Thinking About Empowered Participatory Governance", in Aarchon Fung and Erik Olin Wright (eds.), *Deepening Democracy: Institutional Innovations in Empowered Participatory Governance,* Ch. 1. London and New York: Verso.

Gandhi, M.K. (1962). *Village Swaraj.* Ahmedabad: Navjivan Press.

Habermas, Jürgen (1989). *Structural Transformation of the Public Sphere: An Inquiry into a Category of Bourgeois Societ* (tr. T. Burger and F. Lawrence). Cambridge Mass: MIT Press.

Gupta, Akhil (1995). "Blurred Boundaries: The Discourse of Corruption, the Culture of Politics, and the Imagined State", *American Ethnologist* 22(2): 375-402.

Inbanathan, Anil and D.V. Gopalappa (2002). "Fixers, Patronage, 'Fixing' and Local Governance in Karnataka", *Working Paper* 112. Bangalore: Institute for Social and Economic Change.

Jha, Saumitra, Vijayendra Rao and Michael Woolcock (2007). "Governance in the Gullies: Democratic Responsiveness and Leadership in Delhi Slums", *World Development,* forthcoming.

Isaac, Thomas T.M and Patrick Heller (2003). "Democracy and Development: Decentralised Planning in Kerala", in Aarchon Fung and Erik Olin Wright (eds.), *Deepening Democracy: Institutional Innovations in Empowered Participatory Governance*, Ch. 3. London and New York: Verso.

Kadekodi, Gopal K. (2006a). "Vision for Development in Karnataka", in *Karnataka Development Report: Trends and Future Directions*, Ch. 17. New Delhi: Academic Foundation.

———. (2006b). "Policy Directions and Drivers for Future Development", in *Karnataka Development Report: Trends and Future Directions*, Ch. 18. New Delhi: Academic Foundation.

Kaufman, Daniel, Aart Kray and Pablo Zoido-Lobaton (2002). "Governance Matters: From Measurement to Action", *Finance and Development* 37(2), June.

Krishna, Anirudh (2003). *Active Social Capital*. Delhi: Oxford University Press.

Mansuri, Ghazala and Vijayendra Rao (2004). "Community-Based and –Driven Development: A Critical Review", *World Bank Research Observer* 19(1): 1-39.

Mines, Mattison (1994). *Public Faces, Private Voices: Community and Individuality in South India*. Berkeley and Los Angeles: University of California Press.

Narayana, M.R. (2006). "An Overview of the Karnataka Economy", in *Karnataka Development Report*, Chapter 1. Planning Commission, Government of India. New Delhi: Academic Foundation.

Nataraj, V.K. and Kripa Ananthpur (2004). "Delegation to Devolution: Karnataka", *Working Paper No. 184*. Madras Institute of Development Studies, February.

Sen, Chiranjib (2006). "The Dynamics of Karnataka's Growth", in *Karnataka Development Report*, Chapter 2. Planning Commission, Government of India. New Delhi: Academic Foundation.

Tsai, Lily (2007). *Accountability without Democracy: How Solidary Groups Provide Public Goods in China*. Cambridge: Cambridge University Press (forthcoming).

Part I

Politics and Policy

2

Change in Karnataka over the Last Generation

Villages and the Wider Context

JAMES MANOR

Introduction

This paper examines social and political changes that have occurred since 1972—at the village level where most of Karnataka's residents live, and at higher levels when they affect villages.[1] Throughout this discussion, we encounter an oddity—important changes have occurred despite the tendency of nearly all state governments to proceed cautiously, concentrating almost exclusively on incremental change. Six major changes are worth noting:

- In 1972 Chief Minister Devaraj Urs broke the dominance that *Lingayats* and *Vokkaligas* had exercised over state-level politics since Independence. Since then, Karnataka's leaders have constructed broad 'rainbow' coalitions in which important cabinet posts were given to leaders from every numerically powerful social group.
- In 1983, the state's party system changed when the Congress Party lost a state election for the first time. Since then, the alternation of parties at state elections has (with one exception) been the norm.
- After 1985, Janata Government generously empowered and funded panchayati raj institutions (PRIs).
- Caste (*jati*) has increasingly come to denote 'difference' rather than 'hierarchy'.

---

1. The paper largely omits changes that have occurred in the urban sector and in the state's economy.

- Society at the village level has become much less cohesive (discussed in Part V).
- After the late 1980s, a boom in software and outsourcing occurred in greater Bangalore.

Only the first and the third of these changes were the result of leaders' decisions to induce dramatic change—and since 1985, no such decision has occurred.[2]

So change in Karnataka has mostly been gradual, because politicians there have tended to be tentative, even conservative—a word that they will not like. But to ease their discomfort, it should be added that much of what we have seen has been enlightened conservatism—a tendency to pursue incremental changes which anticipate future problems in order to defuse them before they become acute. That tendency is consistent with the traditions of government in former princely Mysore (roughly the southern half of contemporary Karnataka) since 1881. So is an accompanying tendency towards caution lest powerful interests become dangerously alienated. And yet incremental change has been pursued persistently enough to have a significant cumulative effect.

One result of politicians' enlightened conservatism has been that certain actions which might have served the interests of all rural dwellers—or of disadvantaged villagers—have not been taken. That is regrettable. But other actions have been—for the most part—beneficial. Karnataka has thus avoided the extremes of inaction seen in places like Orissa, and of brutish governance seen in states like Bihar and, recently, Gujarat. Anticipatory changes—beginning with the Miller Committee in the 1920s and accelerating with Devaraj Urs' mobilisation of disadvantaged groups—ensured that this state experienced little conflict during the Mandal Commission controversy in 1990. And incremental actions to promote communal

2. One change which might be included in the list but which has been left out was Devaraj Urs' land reform during the 1970s. It has been omitted because it was radical neither in its intent nor in its impact. As Urs himself recognised, it failed to address the issue of landlessness. It dealt only with tenancy, and that was a far less serious problem here than in other parts of India because owner-cultivators constituted a much larger proportion of Karnataka's rural population than in other regions.

accommodation prevented Hindu nationalists from producing the kind of polarisation that occurred in many other states after 1990.

We shall see that this enlightened conservatism can be traced to several strong, interrelated tendencies within state governments since 1972. Most governments have tended towards collective leadership in 'rainbow' coalitions—with leaders from a broad range of social groups exercising substantial influence. Power-sharing at ministerial level has helped make individuals less important than institutions—including the bureaucracy which has suffered less damage than elsewhere. Policies have therefore, been comparatively well crafted. And since rival parties have sought support from the same broad social base, policy continuity has been strong despite frequent changes of government.

Because changes have occurred incrementally in Karnataka, they have for the most part endured. They have not produced sufficient dislocation to allow opponents to muster the support needed to restore the *status quo ante*.

The rest of this paper is divided into four parts. Part II analyses changes at the state level, and Part III considers changes at the village level. Part IV addresses links between villages and higher levels, between which there is greater vertical integration. Part V considers social cohesion in Karnataka.

The State Level

Several changes at the state level need to be explored. Those examined below have impinged, at least modestly, upon rural arenas.

Deteriorating Standards?

In Karnataka today, people often say—rightly—that standards in public life have deteriorated. For example, in March 2005, a former Chief Secretary of the state stressed that when civil servants inform ministers (as they routinely do) that a potential action would be illegal, ministers increasingly disregard this advice.[3]

But while standards have slipped, we need to compare this state with others—and when we do, things look less discouraging. In many

3. Interview, Bangalore, 6 March, 2005.

other states, civil servants no longer warn politicians of potentially illegal actions because they have been thoroughly intimidated by their masters, and because they know that such comments would have no effect. In Karnataka, such advice is still conveyed regularly—and sometimes it is heeded. When institutions and the rule of law have suffered under certain leaders there, steps have repeatedly been taken to restore them. Three things help us to understand this comparatively modest slippage in standards. They are discussed in the next three sections.

Mercifully Few Destructive Chief Ministers

Since Independence, only two destructive Chief Ministers have held power in Karnataka—R. Gundu Rao (1980-1983) and S. Bangarappa (1990-1992).

Gundu Rao became Chief Minister because he offered Indira Gandhi the kind of abject loyalty that, by 1980, she demanded—and because he was a favourite of her son Sanjay. He centralised power in his own hands to an unprecedented degree and imposed 'civil servant *raj*'. This had one minor advantage—civil servants tend, for the most part, to maintain certain minimal standards when given their head. But it was outweighed by serious disadvantages. Corruption, which was centralised, soared. Legislators were unable to exercise influence on behalf of their constituents. They were often unable to get appointments even with middle-ranking bureaucrats. Democratic government was thus stifled. And grossly insensitive acts occurred. When farmers were late in repaying government loans, the police seized moveable property—which a sensible Chief Minister would have regarded as politically insane.[4]

Bangarappa did greater damage. He placed unprincipled civil servants in key posts, and exiled the best to obscure postings. Illicit 'fund-raising' was a central preoccupation. Bangarappa became the only state-level leader in the last 150 years to encourage parochial

---

4. His government is discussed in greater detail in Manor, J. (1984). "Blurring the Lines between Parties and Social Bases: Gundu Rao and the Emergence of a Janata Government in Karnataka"—which appeared both in the *Economic and Political Weekly*, 15 September, and in Wood, J.R. (ed.) (1984). *State Politics in Contemporary India: Crisis or Continuity?*. Boulder and London: Westview. pp.139-68.

conflict—between *Kannadigas* and *Tamils*. When this led to rioting in Bangalore, the Chief Minister's aides rushed to inform him, only to find that he refused to consider their pleas for action until he had completed his badminton game.[5] It was that sort of government.

Two destructive Chief Ministers is too many, but two is a smaller number than is the norm in several other states. And since neither of these leaders served a full five years, they were unable to institutionalise their damaging practices. In both cases, they were ousted—Gundu Rao by the voters, and Bangarappa by a revolt of legislators who rightly feared voters' wrath. So the system proved self-correcting, and in both cases, politicians' accountability to a sophisticated electorate provided the explanation. Once out of office, they were thoroughly discredited and their successors restored standards—something that has not always happened in other states.

Corruption and Criminalisation

Corruption—in terms of the amounts of money illegally diverted—has increased markedly since 1972.[6] No accurate measurements are possible, but knowledgeable sources consistently attest to this.[7]

Why? First, politicians believe that 'fund-raising' can enhance their influence and their chances of reelection. They have sometimes been right about the first of these ideas. If a leader distributes substantial funds among subordinates or even opposition politicians, he[8] can buy cooperation. If he provides money to potential groups of supporters (or their leaders), he may strengthen their organisational capacity and win their backing. This occurred under Devaraj Urs between 1972 and 1980 when corruption first took off. He used illicit funds to establish and then build up caste associations among disadvantaged groups that had previously been poorly organised or entirely unorganised. He felt

5. Interview with an official who took the news to Bangarappa, Bangalore, 9 March, 1999.
6. This refers to corruption at higher levels. Corruption at the local-level is discussed in Part IV.
7. Note that a Karnataka IAS officer has produced a useful book on corruption which was surely informed by his work in the state. See Das, S.K. (2001). *Public Office, Private Interest: Bureaucracy and Corruption in India.* Delhi: Oxford University Press.
8. Very few senior politicians in Karnataka have been women.

compelled to do this to prevent *Lingayats* and *Vokkaligas* from re-establishing their former dominance.[9]

But the notion that massive 'fund-raising' will help to secure re-election is baseless. Parties in power always have far more opportunities to amass illicit funds than do opposition parties. Ruling parties, therefore, almost always have more campaign funds than their opponents. And yet at the vast majority of elections in Karnataka and other states since 1983, ruling parties have lost. If money decided elections, this would not happen. Politicians pursue 'fund-raising', in the vain hope that it will win them reelection. (Because they know that reelection is unlikely, they tend to maximise personal profiteering while the opportunity exists, which also increases corruption.)

Illicit 'fund raising' for parties has also occurred because state-level leaders—especially in the Congress Party—have been required to provide national-level leaders with substantial sums. This process became well established early—in Devaraj Urs' time—to persuade his party's national leaders not to intrude unhelpfully in the state's politics.[10]

There are, however, certain important checks and limitations on corruption in Karnataka which are less evident in many other states. Most politicians know that excessive corruption damages their hopes of reelection—by undermining their reputations and their capacity to deliver goods and services. The successors of Gundu Rao and Bangarappa sharply curtailed their excesses because they were seen as politically suicidal.

These limitations have, however, been modest. When a well-informed official in an international development agency saw evidence suggesting that the former Andhra Pradesh government received kickbacks of more that $1 million dollars on more than 100 occasions, he replied that Karnataka had not lagged very far behind.[11] But

---

9. These comments are based on discussions with Devaraj Urs in Bangalore in 1978.
10. In interviews with this writer in 1978 and 1980, Devaraj Urs stated this explicitly.
11. Interview, New Delhi, 9 September, 2004.

kickbacks do not occur at every opportunity,[12] so the overall picture is ambiguous.

The criminalisation of politics in Karnataka is far less serious than in many other states. Consider the contrasts with two.

Fifteen years ago, 155 Uttar Pradesh legislators (out of a total of 425) had criminal records—and things have not improved since then.[13] Karnataka has seen nothing remotely like this. Why? Voters in UP (and certain other states) turn to criminals because (i) government institutions have become so degraded that criminals are seen to offer at least some of the responsiveness that those institutions do not provide, and (ii) political parties have undergone severe decay. In Karnataka, the formal institutions are patently imperfect, and parties lack great organisational strength, but they have suffered far less erosion than their UP counterparts.

Until the early 1990s, the only urban centre in South India with a well-developed criminal underworld was Vijayawada in Andhra Pradesh.[14] During the late 1990s, those criminal organisations extended their influence from the coast across the region extending to Hyderabad—because the economic boom in Hyderabad created opportunities, and because the ruling party there forged ties to them

12. For example, in the mid-1990s, private companies seeking a contract to build a sizeable utility sent representatives to Bangalore to make final presentations before those who would make the decision. After one company's spokesman had finished, he was told by a senior bureaucrat that to secure the contract, he would need to pass Rs. 600,000 through the bureaucrat to the authorities. The businessman made no response and immediately contacted an analyst of the state's politics to ask whether this sounded like a genuine overture. The analyst quickly checked with reliable contacts close to the government, and was advised that it was probably not a genuine demand, for two reasons. The figure of Rs. 600,000 seemed too low for such a substantial project. And this specific bureaucrat was probably not in a position to affect the decision. This looked more like a free-lance attempt by that bureaucrat to make some money for himself. The analyst was advised to tell the businessman to telephone the Chief Minister's office and explain what had happened. The businessman did this and his company then secured the contract without paying a bribe.

13. This emerged from this writer's discussions with Paul R. Brass, an authority on Uttar Pradesh politics.

14. Manor (1993). *Power, Poverty and Poison: Disaster and Response in an Indian City.* New Delhi, Newbury Park and London: Sage Publications. chapter 4.

since it considered them useful allies.[15] The economic boom in Bangalore has no doubt attracted the attention of some criminals. But recent interviews with knowledgeable Karnataka officials, policemen and journalists indicate that criminal activities still fall far short of levels found in Andhra Pradesh, and that Karnataka's politicians have done far less to develop links with criminals. Karnataka politics has experienced very little criminalisation.

Institutions Still Matter More than Individuals

In many Indian states, political institutions have taken a battering from powerful, self-aggrandising politicians since 1972. Personalised patronage networks predominate over impersonal processes. Bureaucrats have been so thoroughly browbeaten that they and the institutions which they inhabit retain little substance or autonomy. Supposedly independent institutions beyond the bureaucracy have been subordinated to the whims of potent leaders. We have seen far less of this in Karnataka than in many other states. And when such excesses have occurred there, they have usually been followed by efforts to regenerate institutions.[16]

This is mainly explained by three features of Karnataka's politics. First, the preference for 'rainbow' coalitions at the state level has ensured that collective leadership has usually predominated. This has prevented excesses by individual leaders, and limited damage to institutions.

Second, most senior politicians there have risen through the ranks of their parties, so that individuals do not loom larger than parties. It is thus unusual to find a party in Karnataka utterly dominated by one leader. We saw signs of this in the Congress Party under Gundu Rao and Bangarappa (but they were soon ousted), and recently in the Janata Dal(S). But the norm is collective leadership—which is institution-friendly.

---

15. These comments are based on a detailed, confidential and unpublished study of governance in AP undertaken by this writer in 2001, with the assistance of three of the best informed analysts in that state—whose evidence on this point was highly credible.

16. For more on this process, see Manor, J. (1996). "Political Regeneration in India", in A. Nandy and D.L. Sheth (eds.), *The Multiverse of Democracy: Essays in Honour of Rajni Kothari*. New Delhi, Thousand Oaks and London: Sage Publications, pp.230-41.

Third, the alternation of parties in power has meant that no leader has been so successful at the polls that s/he becomes more important than the party and can do whatever s/he pleases. This again has spared institutions the kind of damage which untrammelled leaders can do.

Karnataka has also experienced less brutish government than several other states. It has seen nothing remotely like the excesses witnessed under the present Gujarat government, in Haryana under Bansi Lal, in Maharashtra under the BJP-Shiv Sena government, or the surge in deaths in police custody under Naidu in Andhra Pradesh.[17] No Karnataka leader has gone that far.

It is also exceedingly unusual in Karnataka for senior politicians to browbeat civil servants—a common occurrence in some North Indian states and an occasional occurrence in Gujarat, Maharasthra, and Tamil Nadu. As a result, the bureaucracy in Karnataka has maintained greater autonomy, institutional substance, and potential for constructive action than in most other states. That has enabled successive Karnataka governments to develop more intelligently crafted policies than most other governments—including policies that affect the rural sector.[18]

---

17. Senior civil servants in Karnataka express astonishment at the "brutal" actions against alleged 'naxalites' under the Naidu government.

18. The importance of this institutional capacity can be illustrated by a brief account not of policy affecting the rural sector, but of the interactions between Karnataka governments and major international development agencies. In 2002, a World Bank official in Delhi told this writer that Karnataka was the only state government in India that with an impressive capacity to develop its own detailed negotiating positions in its dealings with the Bank. This required the government to generate complex socio-economic analyses and proposals on its own, without help from the Bank which routinely provided such assistance to other state governments—a process that compromised their autonomy. Karnataka could achieve this not because it had more good economists among its senior bureaucrats, but because it managed its bureaucracy in ways that enabled its economists to make crucial contributions to policy making. (The state government also sought advice from formidable analysts available within the state—not least at ISEC.)

By giving bureaucrats greater autonomy, and by providing them with an enabling environment, successive governments have enhanced their own autonomy in their dealings with major international development agencies. This has ensured that the state's finances have been prudently managed, so that Karnataka does not share the desperate need of some other states for donor funds—something which can lead state

Contd...

Policy Continuity amid the Alternation of Ruling Parties

Since 1983, the alternation of ruling parties at state elections has been the norm in Karnataka. In some states—most notably Uttar Pradesh since the early 1990s—when governments alternate, huge changes ensue. The policies of previous governments are uprooted and contemptuously discarded, and key administrative posts are systematically purged of civil servants who served the previous government. We have seen very little of this in Karnataka.

This is partly explained by the preference for incremental policy changes. This offers a striking contrast to Uttar Pradesh where dramatic policy shifts by one government, introduced with extravagant histrionics, are shredded when a new government takes over and introduces radically different policies with still more histrionics. It is also explained by Karnataka's parties' tendency to appeal to the same social base (see the section below).

...Contd...

governments into agreements which undermine their autonomy. Thus when the World Bank offered the J.H. Patel government substantial funds, he was able to take advice from sophisticated advisors and—when they and he found the attendant conditionalities unpalatable—he refused the offer.

The strength of these institutions within the Government of Karnataka has not always endeared it to international donor agencies. In recent years, Chief Ministers of Uttar Pradesh (Kalyan Singh) and Andhra Pradesh (Chandrababu Naidu) have gone to extraordinary lengths to cultivate major donors at a personal level. When teams from donor agencies arrived in their state capitals, they had extensive access to these Chief Ministers who played the dominant role in negotiations. By contrast, when such teams reached Bangalore, they dealt mainly with Chief Secretaries, Finance Secretaries and their teams of economic advisors. At best, they might be given a meal with Chief Ministers. (The use of the plural is crucial, since it indicates that these practices were followed under successive governments.)

This caused some dismay in donor agencies. Egos were not massaged so assiduously in Bangalore, and it inspired suspicions about whether the real leaders there were serious about development. At one point in the late 1990s, an analyst stressed to a major donor agency that when they negotiated with governments in places like Andhra Pradesh they were dealing with individuals, while in Karnataka they were dealing with institutions. This should have made Karnataka more attractive since it indicated that policy continuity when governments changed was more likely, but that message was not fully absorbed.

This account focuses on high politics and on events that do not bear intimately upon the rural sector, but the same processes—creating conditions in which civil servants can contribute constructively to policy making—have had positive benefits for rural development too. (Interviews since 1998 with senior officials of the state government and at the World Bank in Delhi.)

When a new government assumes power in Bangalore, it tends to sustain most of its predecessor's policies—with some adjustments but little uprooting. This has produced broad policy continuity which has enabled the incremental changes that nearly all governments have introduced to have—over time—a considerable cumulative effect that has often been felt at the village level.

Continuity in Social Coalitions Underpinning Ruling Parties

Nearly all state governments in Karnataka since 1972 have sought to construct a broadly inclusive 'rainbow' coalition of all numerically powerful social groups. Again Uttar Pradesh differs radically, with contending parties seeking votes from more limited and largely distinct sections of society. Those parties magnify the differences between social groups and encourage antipathy between them. Hence the dramatic changes in policy there. The politics of division and spite that have predominated in Uttar Pradesh for over a decade have almost never been pursued in Karnataka.

These comments about 'rainbow coalitions' refer to more than the representation of different social groups within the state cabinet. It is possible to have relatively fair representation while leaders from certain social groups receive only tokenism—unimportant posts, or inadequate influence over the ministries that they supposedly control. But governments in Karnataka since 1972 have provided leaders from a diverse social groups with genuine influence over reasonably important ministries. Indeed, governments have tended to construct state-level cabinets which are even more broadly representative than the coalitions which voted them into power.[19]

It has, however, become increasingly difficult to build and sustain extremely broad coalitions because tensions between various social groups have grown more acute. Consider Muzaffar Assadi's stimulating arguments that two competing social coalitions have

19. This has become especially apparent in the period since the mid-1990s when data from the National Election Study have shown that the social coalitions which elect governments have sometimes been less broad than the array of groups represented in cabinets. But it appears to have been true in earlier periods as well. On the 2004 election, see Shastri and Ramaswamy (2004). "Karnataka: Simultaneous Polls, Different Results", *Economic and Political Weekly*, 18 December, pp.5484-85.

contended for power in the state: MOVD (Muslims, OBCs, *Vokkaligas* and *Dalits*) and LIBRA (*Lingayats* and *Brahmins*).[20]

If those two coalitions held together coherently, MOVD would always defeat LIBRA. The former contains far more voters than the latter. In practice, most governments since the alternation of parties began in 1983 have tended to appeal mainly to the MOVD groups. But we have often seen variations in this trend.

Governments have reached out to *Lingayats* and *Brahmins* as well as to MOVD groups. One was headed by a *Brahmin* (Ramakrishna Hegde) and two were headed, for a time, by *Lingayats* (S.R. Bommai and Veerenda Patil). And those *Lingayats* came from both major parties—Bommai from Janata, and Veerendra Patil from Congress. Since 1983, both parties have given significant representation to all numerically powerful groups. All cabinets have been broadly representative. Both parties have had *Vokkaliga* Chief Ministers, and though only Congress has had OBC Chief Ministers, Janata has also given them prominence. All Chief Ministers have also sought to include leaders from the two numerically powerful groups that have not provided Chief Ministers—*Dalits* and Muslims (although there has often been a shortage of Muslim legislators).[21]

The BJP, however, which is no longer a marginal party, has focused mainly upon the LIBRA bloc. This became apparent after Hegde aligned his version of the Janata Dal with the BJP. He was a *Brahmin*, and *Lingayats* and *Brahmins* have loomed large in the leadership of the state unit of the BJP. But he and the BJP recognised that they needed support from other groups. The BJP has sought to mobilise MOVD elements around communal issues—with only limited success. And the BJP and Hegde, until the latter's death, appealed to regional

---

20. Assadi, M. (1998). "Muslims and Politics of Social Coalition: Some Experiments in the Electoral Politics of Karnataka", Social Action (April-June 2003) pp.145-58; and "New Political Alignments of Social Groups", *Economic and Political Weekly*, 21 February, pp.382-83.

21. The main reason for this is that Muslim voters are spread unusually evenly and thus thinly across the state. They form a very substantial bloc in only three of the 224 assembly constituencies (interview with E. Raghavan and Imran Qureshi, Bangalore, 9 March, 2005).

resentments in northern Karnataka. So here again, the dichotomy between MOVD and LIBRA blurs at the edges.

Growing tensions between social groups may end the tradition of 'rainbow coalitions' by making it impossible for politicians to sustain the broadly accommodative approach that has long prevailed. But that has not happened yet. It is also possible that the BJP will gain power after the next state election—because they are the only alternative to the coalition between the Congress and the Janata Dal (S). But if that occurs, it will not be because the LIBRA bloc brought the BJP to power—it lacks the numerical strength to do so. It will be because many MOVD voters turned to the BJP out of frustration with the coalition government. And that will impel a new BJP government to reach out to those people once it takes power—to pursue yet another broad coalition.

The Village Level

Karnataka's villages have experienced diverse social and political changes in the last three decades. Most of these have occurred gradually, but over time, many have had considerable cumulative effects.

Social and Economic Change in the Villages

In the years since 1972, agriculture has gradually declined in importance—both economically (as people turn increasingly to non-farm incomes), and socially (as the interdependence and hierarchical bonds anchored in old patterns of agricultural production have been eroded). Change in this sector has been incremental but persistent, so that in many areas, the old social order has substantially crumbled. This is apparent from studies by G.K. Karanth, V. Ramaswamy and others. These indicate that there is much less order in village society, and that old rituals—and the collective arrangements for the management of resources linked to them—have withered.[22]

---

22. See in particular chapters 11 to 14 in Baumgartner, R. and R. Hogger (eds.) (2004). *In Search of Sustainable Livelihood Systems: Managing Resources and Change*. New Delhi, Thousand Oaks and London: Sage Publications.

G.S. Aurora has explained the background to these changes.[23] He notes a decline in the number of larger landholdings and an increase in the number of medium, small and marginal holdings. The numbers of marginal farmers and landless labourers have increased. Many artisans have been "forced to join the ranks of the rural proletariat" as goods used by rural dwellers have come increasingly from urban industries.

The proportion of lands put to non-agricultural uses has risen from 4.2 per cent in 1956-57 to 6.7 per cent in 1997-98. The commercialisation of agricultural household economies has become a 'dominant pattern'. In former times, farmers concentrated on growing cereals, partly for payments in kind under the old *jajmani* system. Now, as that system has disintegrated, they cultivate other crops for the market and pay workers in cash—loosening the old, hierarchical social ties which also implied interdependence. As it has diminished, dependence on external market forces—which carries serious risks—has grown. The use of high yielding varieties has increased, and with it the need for costly inputs. To obtain these, farmers must take sizeable loans, and when crops fail, this has led to farmers' suicides. (Far fewer of these have occurred in Karnataka than in neighbouring Andhra Pradesh, but the total in the former—over 400—is still alarming.)

Four themes from Aurora's analysis are immensely important.

- The potency of hierarchy and interdependence within villages has declined.
- Links to and dependence upon external forces have increased.
- Individuals now count for more than collectivities within villages—which increases both the liberty and the vulnerability of individuals.
- The result is a society that is more open and democratic, but in which people face greater risks—since the old hierarchical order entailed not only injustices but certain collective protections against uncertainties.

---

23. Aurora, G.S. "Core Issues in the Agrarian Economy and Society of Karnataka", in Ibid., pp.247-64. His focus was on Kolar District of Karnataka, but his comment apply to nearly off of the state.

Changes in the Role, the Importance and the Materiality of Caste

Given these changes, caste (*jati*) has diminished in importance, especially in one crucial respect. It has increasingly come to denote 'difference' rather than 'hierarchy'. This has caused certain invidious practices to decline, but it has also inspired greater tensions and conflicts between caste groups. We see this in other states too.[24]

This monumental change has occurred gradually. When a visitor mentioned it to Krishna Raj, the late editor of the *Economic and Political Weekly*, the latter stressed that what surprised him was that "it took so long."[25] At present, we lack a full understanding both of why the change occurred and why 'it took so long'. M.N. Srinivas stressed the importance of the decline of the *jajmani* system that provided the material underpinnings of caste hierarchy,[26] and he was probably correct. The role of politics was ambiguous. Political mobilisation on caste lines tended to strengthen caste consciousness and at times reinforced hierarchies. But the post-1972 mobilisation of disadvantaged castes in Karnataka, and the egalitarian logic of one-person-one-vote undermined it.

Government policies also had an ambiguous impact. On the one hand, policies after 1972 favouring disadvantaged groups contributed to the decline of hierarchy. On the other, one reason that 'it took so long' has been the cautious, incremental nature of economic liberalisation in India. Its leaders have carefully avoided radical changes common in China and much of Southeast Asia—because in a democratic polity, they are unwilling to risk massive social dislocation. In China, around 200 million peasants have been induced or forced off the land. Many of them live precariously round major cities, seeking work. This poses serious risks of political disorder. The Chinese leaders, with their formidable coercive power, are prepared to countenance this. Nothing remotely like that, or like the "social

24. For evidence from Madhya Pradesh, see Mayer, A. (1997). "Caste in an Indian Village: Change and Continuity, 1954-1992", in C.J. Fuller (ed.), *Caste Today.* Delhi: Oxford University Press, pp.32-64. See also D.L. Sheth (1999). "Secularisation of Caste and Making of New Middle Class", *Economic and Political Weekly*, 21-28 August, pp.2502-10.

25. Interview, Mumbai, 27 September, 1998.

26. Interviews with him, Bangalore, in 1996 and 1998.

change in fast forward" seen in Indonesia,[27] has happened in India.

But despite the gradualism, immense changes have occurred. One key example is a decline in the material utility of caste. Two decades ago, this writer argued that caste (*jati*) in Karnataka existed not just at the level of ideas, sentiments or identifications, but that it possessed materiality. A villager's caste status and connections played a major role in determining whether s/he could gain access to tangible opportunities and assets.[28] Today, this remains true to some extent. But high caste status offers fewer material advantages, and low status offers at least somewhat fewer disadvantages than before. And other things have gained in importance in providing or denying opportunities to villagers (see below).

The Proliferation of New Channels Linking Local and Higher Levels

This topic is discussed more fully in Part IV, but it is important to note it here, since it alters dynamics within villages. Far more channels now exist to link individuals within villages to higher levels in the system. Some of these—the electronic media (especially satellite television,[29] but also telephones) mainly provide villagers with more information than they could obtain 30 years ago. But others—improved roads, transport, *panchayati raj* institutions, other government structures, and civil society organisations—enable individuals to develop links to the wider world, which they can sometimes use to access new opportunities.

Individuals Matter More, and Social Institutions and Groups Less...

As caste (*jati*)—a social institution—has gone into decline, villagers seeking opportunities have increasingly turned to individuals who can (in G.K. Karanth's words) "get things done."[30] And those

27. This phrase belongs to Anne—Booth, an Indonesia specialist at the University of London.

28. Manor, J. (1984). "Karnataka: Caste, Class, Dominance and Politics in a Cohesive Society", in F. Frankel and M.S.A. Rao (eds.), *Dominance and State Power in Modern India: Decline of a Social Order*. Delhi: Oxford University Press, Vol. 1, pp.322-61.

29. See in this connection Crawley, W. and D. Page (2001). *Satellites over South Asia: Broadcasting, Culture and the Public Interest*. New Delhi, Thousand Oaks and London: Sage Publication.

30. Interview, Bangalore, 9 April, 2005.

doing the seeking have also often operated as individuals rather than on behalf of the social groups from which they come. Thus, social institutions and groups matter less, and individuals matter more than before.

...But One Political Institution Matters More—Panchayati Raj

At the same time, however, the comparatively generous empowerment and funding of *panchayats* in Karnataka have given—the *gram* (village) *panchayat*—a political institution—considerable importance in most villages. This has had ambiguous implications on two fronts.

First, the growing importance of this democratic political institution has acted as a counterweight to what might be termed a tendency towards anarchy within villages—which might follow from the decline of a substantially undemocratic social institution—caste (*jati*). But since people interact with *gram panchayats* not just collectively but also as individuals, it has in part enhanced the growing importance of individuals.

Second, the empowerment of *panchayats* has sometimes enabled villagers to solve problems on their own. But since *gram panchayats* often need administrative assistance from higher-ups to implement some decisions—like construction projects—villagers must still reach out to higher levels. When that happens, individuals' connections with higher levels are important. So here again, the results have been ambiguous. (*Panchayats* are discussed further in the section just below, and again in Part IV.)

Corruption At and Near the Village Level

Corruption at lower levels presents a mixed, but somewhat less grim picture than at the state level. Here as at the state level, our evidence is limited. But the following, sometimes unproven, points are probably accurate: Corruption occurs at lower levels for diverse reasons. Even candidates seeking lowly offices feel compelled to spend substantial funds—and to take out loans that must be repaid out of money illicitly raised. The market in transfers impels low-level bureaucrats to find similarly large sums, with the same result. And when a nexus develops at the subdistrict level among a small number of government employees and elected politicians, development funds may be diverted into their pockets. We have, however, seen the emergence in recent years of significant correctives to this last type of malfeasance—as the result of the empowerment of *panchayats*.

In Karnataka, as a consequence of democratic decentralisation, the number of people involved in corrupt activities has increased. That was inevitable when the number of elected offices increased in 1987 from 224 (assembly seats) to over 50,000 (seats on *panchayats*). But the key question is whether the overall amount of money stolen has declined. Evidence from Karnataka clearly indicates that it has.

Before 1987, when development funds reached the subdistrict (*taluk*) level, four or five persons (the Block Development Officer, the Assistant Engineer and influential non-officials) often met behind closed doors, stole a substantial portion of that money—around 40 per cent, say people involved—and presented the remainder to ordinary people as 100 per cent of the development budget. After 1987, when the system became so transparent that hundreds of people in every *taluk* knew what 100 per cent of the budget actually was, such grand theft became impossible. Estimates in 1993 placed the overall amount of funds stolen under the new system at around 5 per cent.[31] That figure may have increased in the ensuing years, but even if it has, the picture is still substantially brighter than before the empowerment of *panchayats*.[32]

Links between Villages and Higher Levels

The number of channels that provide potential links between villages and higher levels has multiplied over the last 30 years. This

31. This is discussed in more detail in Crook and Manor (1998). *Democracy and Decentralisation in South Asia and West Africa: Participation, Accountability and Performance*. Cambridge: Cambridge University Press, Ch. 2.

32. It is worth adding that the computerised *Bhoomi* programme, providing land certificates—by-passing village accountants who took bribes for this service—is said to have reduced petty corruption by an estimated Rs. 895 million annually. Public Affairs Centre, *A Report Card on Bhoomi Kiosks* (Public Affairs Centre, Bangalore, 2004). Some readers may suspect that that figure is an exaggeration—and Narayana Gatty have found evidence to indicate that in northern Karnataka, villagers prefer to pay the traditional bribes rather than incur the inconvenience of travelling to computer kiosks within their *taluks*. But even if the actual figure were only half of that amount, it still represents a significant decline in corruption.

is the result of the emergence or growing importance of four institutions/actors discussed below.[33] Before we examine them, it is worth noting that two institutions do not qualify for inclusion here. First, the role of the police—who have become more responsive in urban Karnataka[34]—has scarcely changed in rural areas. Second, the capacity of political parties to penetrate into rural arenas has declined over the last three decades. But let us consider four more encouraging changes.

The Proliferation of Government Programmes and 'User Committees'

National and state governments currently implement a vastly greater number of programmes in rural Karnataka than in 1972—providing new channels between villages and higher levels. And since many of these programmes create 'user committees' to consult villagers or their representatives (on health, education, forestry, etc.)—and since in this state (unlike many others) *panchayats* influence those committees—fresh opportunities exist for local preferences to flow upward into the policy process.[35] It should be stressed, however, that rural Karnataka has not witnessed the dramatic increases in government responsiveness that occurred in Bangalore under S.M. Krishna during the late 1990s.[36]

Panchayati Raj Institutions

Panchayats were substantially empowered and funded in 1987, and since then—despite a decline in their powers—they have remained reasonably strong by Indian and international standards. This system

---

33. A fifth, market forces, might be added to this list. But that is best left to economists to analyse.

34. Independent Surveys by the Public Affairs Centre found public satisfaction levels with the city's police rose from almost zero in 1994 to 17 per cent in 1999, and then to 83 per cent in 2003. See, *Development Outreach* (March 2004) p.12; and J. Manor, "Successful Governance Reforms in Two Indian States: Karnataka and Andhra Pradesh", report to the World Bank, 2004.

35. By linking most 'user committees' to *panchayats*, Karnataka has avoided serious problems often found elsewhere. See Manor, J. "'User Committees': A Potentially Damaging New Wave of Decentralisation?", *European Journal of Development Research* (spring, 2004) pp.192-213.

36. See again, the Public Affairs Centre surveys and Manor, "Successful Governance Reforms...".

has proved more successful that most others across the world, partly because its accountability mechanisms are unusually reliable.[37]

Their role in providing links between villages and higher levels is ambiguous. In certain respects, it is limited. *Panchayats* exist at village, *taluk* and district levels, but this has not resulted in sustained interactions between elected members at different levels—partly because *panchayats* at the intermediate *taluk* level are comparatively weak. But information flows have increased massively, both upward and downward. Governments find it far easier to transmit information downward because elected *panchayat* members can interpret policies to villagers in ways that the latter comprehend. And officials at higher levels have experienced a massive increase in information flows from below—so they feel better able to perform their tasks.[38]

Political 'Fixers'

Comments above on the increasing importance in villages of people who can 'get things done' refer to the large number of local-level 'fixers' who seek to arrange things with persons in authority at higher levels. Two recent studies of 'fixers' in Karnataka[39] found that many of them do not come from the traditionally dominant landowning groups, and that those who do are usually not involved in cultivating patrimonial ties to clients. They develop different types of relationships from those associated with the old village hierarchies and with *Lingayat/Vokkaliga* dominance. They have tended to erode those hierarchies. Most 'fixers' are more accessible than dominant caste

---

37. Crook and Manor, *Democracy and Decentralisation in South Africa and West Africa: Participation, Accountability and Performance.* Cambridge: Cambridge University Press, Ch. 2.

38. Ibid., Ch. 2.

39. Manor, J. (2000). "'Towel over Armpit': Small-time Political 'Fixers' in India's States"—published in a shorter version in Asian Survey (September-October), pp. 816-35, and in a longer version in Varshney, A. (ed.), (2004). *India and the Politics or Developing Countries: Essays in Memory of Myron Weiner*, New Delhi: Sage Publication, Thousand Oaks and London, pp.60-86; and Inbanathan, A. and D.V. Gopalappa (2002). "Fixers, Patronage, 'Fixing' and Local Governance in Karnataka", *Working Paper 112*, Institute for Social and Economic Change. See also Anirudh Krishna's research on similar actors in Madhya Pradesh and Rajasthan, whom he calls naya netas in for example, *Active Social Capital* (New York: Columbia University Press, 2002).

leaders in the old hierarchies.[40] And they help the democratic process to work more effectively, and government institutions and actors to become more responsive.

Civil Society Organisations

Civil society organisations also provide villagers with more links to higher levels than three decades ago. Today, they can be found in most rural arenas. Local-level associations tend not to connect villagers with higher levels, but many which originate at higher levels seek to forge links to the grassroots. We must not, however, overstate the coverage of the latter. It is unlikely that more than a minority of villagers are reached by such organisations.[41] So most important links between villages and higher levels are provided by the other three institutions and actors discussed above.

How 'Cohesive' Is Society In Karnataka?

To conclude, let us consider the answers to this question that emerge at the village and higher levels. In 1984, this writer argued that Karnataka was a 'cohesive society'—not as cohesive as more homogeneous societies, but more cohesive than the societies found elsewhere in South Asia. This was true despite invidious hierarchies and injustices within it. The key to the explanation was the exceedingly low incidence of landlessness in former princely Mysore.[42]

This had two important implications. First, hierarchies and inequalities there were not as extreme as in other regions of South Asia—so that we encountered less of the harsh exploitation found elsewhere, and less severe alienation among the exploited. Second, since old Mysore set the political tone for the enlarged state after 1956, accommodative politics which offered at least something even to disadvantaged groups took firmer root there than in other Indian states.

40. Inbanathan and Gopalappa, Ibid., p.18.

41. In Bangladesh, where national-level civil society organisations are more formidable than state-level equivalents in Karnataka, they estimate that they reach only around 20 per cent of the rural population. Interview with the head of one of the two most formidable organisations, Dhaka, 7 March, 1993.

42. Manor, "Karnataka: Caste, Class...

Is society in Karnataka today still as 'cohesive'? The simple answer is 'no', but the details are complicated. At the village level, caste hierarchies have eroded. Since those hierarchies entailed objectionable practices, this change that can be seen as 'progressive'. But it has also undermined the limited sense of interdependence and mutuality, which offered certain protections against uncertainties. The old hierarchies proved remarkably durable because they adapted incrementally as conditions changed.[43] They bent without breaking—until recently.

Over recent decades, 'caste' has come to denote difference more than hierarchy. The bonds linking higher and lower status groups have become more tenuous. Villagers look for help less to neighbours who have high ascriptive status than to people who 'can get things done'. And those people are often not of high caste status.[44] Thus at the village level, Karnataka has become a much less 'cohesive' society.

People who can 'get things done' usually achieve this by using connections and channels to higher levels in the system. Such channels have proliferated over the last three decades. This has made villagers less inclined to try to solve problems through their own collective efforts and more inclined to look beyond the village for assistance.[45]

This proliferation of channels does not mean that society in Karnataka has become more 'cohesive' in another way—in terms of vertical ties between villages and higher levels. Society is more vertically integrated. But the bonds that connect the villages with higher levels are too impersonal, impermanent and unpredictable to yield anything like 'cohesion'. We have seen a decline in 'social

---

43. For evidence of this durability, consider for example a survey of social attitudes conducted in the early 1980s by K.C. Alexander. He questioned village respondents in Alleppey District of Kerala, Thanjavur District of Tamil Nadu and Mandya District of Karnataka. In the first two of those places, the old hierarchies had been so extremely unjust that they had broken down. In Mandya District, however, the old hierarchies were far less inequitable—so he found that the hierarchies lived on. K.C. Alexander, "Caste Mobilisation and Class Consciousness: The Emergence of Agrarian Movements in Kerala and Tamil Nadu" in Frankel and Rao, Ibid., Vol. 1, pp.392-400.

44. Interview with G.K. Karanth, Bangalore, 5 March, 2005.

45. See for example, the arguments of G.K. Karanth, V. Ramaswamy and others in chapters 11 to 14 of Baumgartner and Hogger (eds.) *In Search of.....*

cohesion' at the village level, and an increase in mostly 'political and economic integration' between the local and higher levels. But the latter does not suffice to compensate for the loosening of social bonds at the grassroots.

There are greater tensions between castes—although some analysts argue that this is substantially explained by better reporting of such matters. There is evidence of at least a modest increase in suspicion between Hindus and religious minorities—despite the failure of Hindu nationalists to elicit much popular response through campaigns about Ayodhya or in Hubli and Chikmagalur.[46] Retreats by recent state governments on the issue of land reform have inspired some popular anger over concessions to globalisation and private companies. Policy changes on common property resources have inspired some 'naxalite' activity.

We see more resentment in rural areas about state governments' urban bias than three decades ago, and greater exasperation in northern Karnataka over regional disparities. State governments are more preoccupied with ensuring that benefits flow to *Kannadigas* rather than to linguistic minorities. On each of these fronts, we see growing impatience within a specific group—rural dwellers, northerners and *Kannadigas*—with the grand political settlement that has emerged from state governments' pursuit of incremental change and broad accommodations embracing a large diversity of social groups. These three groups are vastly powerful. Rural dwellers and *Kannadigas* constitute huge majorities, and one perceptive analyst of Karnataka's politics argues that northerners often decide state election outcomes.[47]

Frustrations within such formidable groups raise serious concerns about the sustainability of two important themes in Karnataka over recent decades. The first is accommodative politics at the state-level, the tendency of leaders to construct broadly inclusive cabinets since 1972. The second is the 'enlightened conservative' tendency to

---

46. See for example, Assadi, M. (2003). "'Dargah Versus Peeta': Hindutva's Politics of Appropriating Syncretic Culture in Karnataka", *Indian Journal of Secularism*, July-September, pp.93-109.

47. This is E. Raghavan, editor of the *Economic Times*, Bangalore. His view is not shared by this writer.

undertake change in anticipation of potential conflicts—to defuse them before they become acute, in order to sustain accommodative politics.

Will the increasing frustrations and social tensions at lower levels undermine accommodation at the state level? Perhaps not, unless much greater antipathy develops between social groups than we have seen thus far—and maybe even if it does. State-level politicians are likely to cling to the view that their ambitions are best served by developing broadly inclusive accommodations. That persuaded leading *Lingayats* and *Vokkaligas* not to seek a restoration of state-level dominance after Devaraj Urs had changed politics in 1972. That persuaded successive Chief Ministers to include in their cabinets leaders even from groups that had given them little electoral support—because this maximised their appeal. Even if social tensions grow more acute, that logic may still apply. The main potential exception to this is the BJP, which might pursue communal polarisation if it came to power. But some leading analysts have long expected them to conform to the accommodative tradition if they take office.

In 2006, they finally managed to do so—in coalition with elements of the Janata Dal (S). The compulsions of coalition government have thus far prevented dramatic actions by BJP leaders that might prove polarising. Indeed, confusion and occasional conflicts within that government have prevented it from achieving much of anything during its first few months in power.

Whatever happens in the future, it should by now be apparent that certain important changes have occurred—mostly incrementally—over the period since 1972. Village society in Karnataka is less cohesive, but more integrated with higher levels, as a result of the proliferation of channels linking the villages to those levels. It is less self-regulating (as a result of the decline of the old social hierarchies), but (as a result of *panchayati raj*) somewhat more self-governing.

It is a less quiescent and orderly society, characterised by greater (caste, regional, linguistic, urban/rural and perhaps communal) tensions and, at times, conflicts. And the loosening of hierarchical social bonds has made it possible, for the first time, that class conflict may become important in rural Karnataka. State-level politicians' preference for broadly inclusive accommodations, and the incremental changes that flow from them, have provided inadequate responses to interest groups caught up in these tensions.

And yet despite that, government has become more responsive. That is partly the result of the reasonably generous empowerment of *panchayati raj* institutions. But it is also explained by the introduction of participatory mechanisms (mainly 'user committees' and self help groups) that promote at least some consultation in various developmental sectors. These have been introduced both by governments and by some civil society organisations.

These things are patent realities, but they and politicians' accommodative habits may not suffice to prevent greater tension and turbulence in the society and politics of the state. Karnataka has become more democratic—thanks in part to the decline of the old hierarchies—but it has become more difficult to govern. The instruments available to those doing the governing—mainly formal institutions, agencies and programmes, since party organisations lack strength—have not suffered the sort of damage seen in some other Indian states, and have increased in number and penetrative capacity. But this has not eased the long-standing difficulty of ruling parties at getting reelected, and if tensions continue to intensify, they could eventually bring an end to the accommodative tradition in state politics.

3

Political Leadership and Economic Development in Karnataka

G. THIMMAIAH

Background

Political leadership is a complex process by which persons in power influence their followers, civil society and wider public to accomplish societal goals. Political leaders are necessary for initiating as well as for hastening the process of change in any society. It may be social and/or economic change, constitutional change or political change. In all these processes of change, political leadership plays an important role. Political leaders carry out the process of change by applying their leadership attributes like politically relevant beliefs, socially adored values, generally approved character, wide knowledge and wisdom acquired through learning and experience.

Political leaders are supposed to understand the hopes and aspirations of the people and identify the goals of the society. They may formulate a vision of the country's future. They acquire or develop the capacity to mobilise the people to achieve the common societal goal. Further, the political leaders are expected to have certain attributes in order to be effective as leaders. They should have unimpeachable commitment to the cause or societal goal which they decide to fight for or achieve. They should be prepared to render self-less service to the people at large. They should have the quality of inspiring their followers and even the common people. They should have patience and perseverance in pursuing the society's goals, maturity and wisdom for taking sound and timely decisions and exhibit strength of character by setting example and mental toughness to face criticism when found wrong. These are all ideal textbook attributes. It is difficult to find all of them even in an ideal leader. The success or failure of a leader is determined by many circumstances to which lack of some of these attributes may also contribute.

Social scientists have advanced several theories of political leadership. Of them four theories are considered relevant as they explain major types of political leadership operating in the world. The first is the theory of traits, which explains that some personality traits may lead some persons naturally into leadership roles. I may quote the example of Subhas Chandra Bose who possessed some personality traits which ultimately made him a leader rather than a British Indian civil servant. The second theory is crisis or cause theory, which outlines that an important social or political event in a society may throw up an opportunity for a person or persons to rise to the occasion which brings out extraordinary leadership qualities in ordinary persons. I may quote the examples of Mahatma Gandhi, Jawaharlal Nehru and Vallabhai Patel whose leadership qualities were brought out by the freedom movement. The third theory is that given equal opportunities, people may choose to become leaders by learning leadership skills. This is called transformational leadership. This is widely prevalent in most of the democracies. The fourth theory is the dynastic theory of leadership which is easy to understand. Leaders who emerge under one or the other type of leadership mentioned above try to groom their sons and/or daughters to become leaders to succeed them. This is common in traditional societies and much more widespread in India. The pros and cons of dynastic theory of political leadership is also currently debated in the country. But it is not unique to traditional or pre-modern societies. It operates even in developed and stable democracies like the USA where Bush family has shown the characteristics of dynastic leadership. Under this dynastic theory, wives or sons/daughters or brothers/sisters may succeed the assassinated leaders or those who are dead under tragic circumstances. In India, Rajiv Gandhi succeeded his slain mother. In Indonesia, Megawati Sukarnoputri became president partly because of her father's name. In Pakistan, Benazir Bhutto, and in Bangladesh, Hasina Begum, the daughters of their slain fathers (who were political leaders) succeeded them on sympathy wave.

I have purposely left out another categorisation of political leadership into military and non-military political leadership as it is not relevant for my main theme. Also I have not raised the issue of female political leadership as again it has been absent in Karnataka. I have also not referred to the controversy whether democracy is conducive for rapid economic development or not as the debate is inconclusive and it is not relevant for us in India. Because, the day democracy vanishes in India, its disintegration will start and no economic development can take place in the absence of peace and order. So that it is a big issue which our political scientists and economists may debate. Since India and Karnataka have had the great fortune of enjoying a fair degree of political democracy, I am only interested in analysing how the political leadership in Karnataka contributed for the economic development of the state.

Relation between Political Leadership and Economic Development

Since I am interested in understanding the role of political leadership in economic development, I want to know how they are related? Is there a one way causation or at least correlation? International experience suggests that there seems to be some strong association between political leadership and economic development. Economic development requires mobilising a country's physical, human and financial resources and their deployment in productive activities. Further, since the main goal of economic development is to raise the standard of living of the people, what is produced by deploying the country's resources should be equitably distributed. Today mere creation of material wealth and resultant material welfare are not the only goals of economic development. The prime objective of economic development is not merely elimination of material poverty but more importantly to eradicate illiteracy, disease, environmental degradation, and through them establishing peace and tranquillity in the society. In other words, political leaders play an important role in good governance and good governance in turn plays an important role in pushing up the pace of economic development.

Realising the importance of governance in achieving growth in developing countries, World Bank experts (Kaufmann *et al.*, 2002), have studied the association between governance and growth in developing countries. For their purpose they identified 'voice and accountability', 'political stability', 'government's effectiveness', 'regulatory quality', 'rule of law' and 'control of corruption' as the main indicators of good governance. They found strong correlation between quality of governance and level of growth in a majority of these countries. Political leadership does influence to a large extent these indicators of governance.

The most important mechanism through which political leaders contribute for economic development is by choosing appropriate policies and programmes, implementing them effectively and by creating and adopting the required institutions for hastening the pace of development. For example, Lee Kwan Yew, former Prime Minister of Singapore, was instrumental for formulating the right type of economic policies which integrated that city state into the world economy in the sixties of the last century. Even in the absence of natural resources he initiated the development policies primarily in the public sector but encouraged the private sector also to operate in the free market setting. This strategy worked and raised the level of development of Singapore. Mahathir Mohamad, former Prime Minister of Malaysia, was responsible for the creation of world-class economy in Malaysia which has ensured higher standard of living, higher literacy and higher life expectancy to his people. Mahathir Mohamad was not an admirer of western values but not an anti-capitalist either. He understood the merits of market forces and their requirements to spur economic development in a traditional society. Accordingly, he implemented appropriate economic policies to encourage Malaysian enterprises to grow and expand by adopting latest technology and management practices and ultimately to compete globally. He faced an uphill task because of the wide disparity between the Malays and Chinese ethnic groups which resulted in bloody clashes in 1969. Therefore, simultaneously he implemented a set of affirmative (*Bhumiputra)* policies under which Malays were given preferential treatment in education, employment and even in equity ownership. Thus he combined free market policies with redistributive policies which minimised the ethnic disparities and ensured social harmony. Now his successor Abdulla Ahamed Bidwai is trying to encourage competition among Malays by abolishing the *Bhumiputra* policies some of which have come to be misused. The latest example of political leadership spurring economic development is in China. Former President of the Peoples' Republic of China, Jiang Zemin, has been credited with exposing a basically centralised communist economic system to capitalist market stimuli and achieving spectacular rates of growth of GDP in China. There is no need to narrate what is common knowledge now. What is important is that he and his comrades in Chinese communist party were bold enough to initiate policies which encouraged inflow of enormous foreign capital and technology into China and transform a poor economically oppressed economy into a manufacturing hub of Asia. Nearer home, Jawaharlal Nehru no doubt laid the foundations for the development of the Indian economy. But his policies were found to be inadequate to make India to achieve higher growth rate of its GDP. Though late by a decade, Narasimha Rao-Manmohan Singh duo took the risk of introducing required economic reforms like economic liberalisation, privatisation, and globalisation which enabled India to raise its GDP growth rate to a higher plateau, apart from integrating the Indian economy into the global economy. It is true that even after 15 years, some sections of the society including ideologically left oriented political parties have not accepted these economic reforms wholeheartedly. Therefore, the risk of diluting the economic reforms as for example in the power sector and delay in implementing the required reforms particularly in the fiscal sphere still remains.

Political Leadership and Economic Development in Karnataka

Against this lengthy background let us turn to the role of Karnataka's political leadership in the process of economic development of the state. For this purpose, I have identified political leadership of the state with the chief ministership. This is because the chief minister is the political leader of the party in power and all policy decisions relating to economic development and social justice have to be approved by the cabinet headed by him. Other leaders may influence economic development policies through their performance and advice to the cabinet and the chief minister. But the chief minister's role is crucial in influencing the pace and quality of development of a state.

It may be argued that it is futile to search for any association between chief ministership and the pace and quality of development of a constituent state in a vast country like India where major economic development policies are determined at the national level. Though there is an element of truth in this argument, it is necessary to remember that most of the development policies and programmes are implemented by the state governments. The degree of efficiency of utilisation of available natural and financial resources for implementing development programmes and projects explains the inter-state disparities in the levels of development in India. Political leadership does play some role in inter-state disparities. Even so, India's development experiment may be broadly divided into two phases. The first phase started with first five-year plan and ended with seventh five-year plan. The second phase started in the middle of 1991 with the introduction of structural economic reforms. While in the first phase the role of chief ministers in economic development of their states may have been dictated by the national economic policies, though they did make a difference in implementing those policies, their role in the second phase has been significant because of the political support they had to mobilise for the structural reforms in addition to effective implementation of the required economic and fiscal reforms. I have tried to examine the role of chief ministers of Karnataka in both the phases with available quantitative data. In a study like this, qualitative judgements cannot be avoided. But I have tried to be as dispassionate as possible.

Karnataka state has been administered by as many as seventeen chief ministers from 25-10-1947 to date. It may be observed from Table 3.1. that three chief ministers administered the former princely state of Mysore and 14 chief ministers presided over the destiny of the reorganised state of Karnataka. Many of them functioned as chief ministers for short periods which makes it difficult to assess their role and contribution to Karnataka's development. Even so their contribution to formulating and implementing appropriate policies at the right time cannot be ignored. Such efforts deserve appreciation particularly in the second phase when structural economic reforms were implemented.

Table 3.1

Chief Ministers of Former Mysore State and of Karnataka

	Chief Ministers	*From*	*To*
1.	K. Chengalraya Reddy	25-10-1947	30-03-1952
2.	K. Hanumanthaiah	30-03-1952	19-08-1956
3.	Kadidal Manjappa	19-08-1956	31-10-1956
1.	S. Nijalingappa	01-11-1956	10-04-1957
2.	S. Nijalingappa	10-04-1957	16-05-1958
3.	B.D. Jatti	16-05-1958	09-03-1962
4.	S.R. Kanthi	14-03-1962	20-06-1962
5.	S. Nijalingappa	21-06-1962	28-05-1968
6.	Veerendra Patil	29-05-1968	18-03-1971
•	*President's Rule*	19-03-1971	20-03-1972
7.	D. Devaraj Urs	20-03-1972	31-12-1977
•	*President's Rule*	31-12-1977	28-02-1978
8.	D. Devaraj Urs	28-02-1978	07-01-1980
9.	R. Gundu Rao	12-01-1980	06-01-1983
10.	Ramakrishna Hegde	10-01-1983	29-12-1984
11.	Ramakrishna Hegde	08-03-1985	13-02-1986
12.	Ramakrishna Hegde	16-02-1986	10-08-1988
13.	S.R. Bommai	13-08-1988	21-04-1989
•	*President's Rule*	21-04-1989	30-11-1989
14.	Veerendra Patil	30-11-1989	10-10-1990
•	*President's Rule*	10-10-1990	17-10-1990
15.	S. Bangarappa*	17-10-1990	19-11-1992
16.	M. Veerappa Moily	19-11-1992	11-12-1994
17.	H.D. Deve Gowda	11-12-1994	31-05-1996
18.	J.H. Patel	31-05-1996	07-10-1999
19.	S.M. Krishna	11-10-1999	28-05-2004
20.	Dharam Singh	28-05-2004	—

Note:*– Six Chief Ministers starting from Mr. S. Banagarappa presided over the destiny of Karnataka State after the introduction of structural reforms in the country.

Source: Government of Karnataka, Bangalore.

Development Performance of Chief Ministers of Karnataka

The political leadership of both K.C. Reddy and Kengal Hanumanthaiah emerged during freedom movement. But Kengal Hanumanthaiah's leadership was the product of that great political event which brought out his leadership potential. Nijalingappa was also thrown up by freedom movement. So were B.D. Jatti and S.R. Kanthi. However, Devaraj Urs' leadership emerged by a particular socio-political development which had evolved after the formation of unified Karnataka state. It was the outcome of a crisis of confidence. There was a general perception that the two dominant communities in the state had monopolised the political power and all the benefits which go with it. At that momentous time there was a split in the national congress party and Devaraj Urs joined Indira Gandhi congress. This set him against Congress (O) and *Garibi Hatao* slogan caught the imagination of the poor people. Devaraj Urs rode to power on that political wave. Though Ramakrishna Hegde had participated in freedom movement, his political leadership did not emerge from that political event. After 1983 Karnataka assembly elections, when two dominant community leaders were pitched against each other for the chief ministership, he emerged as a compromise candidate and continued for a considerable time. All other chief ministers were followers of other leaders who chose to become political leaders by acquiring leadership skills through experience. Through this process of transformation they emerged as chief ministers. They were transformational leaders and not thrown up either by their leadership traits or by great social and political events.

When the princely state of Mysore got integrated into the Indian union, the state had already achieved considerable economic progress thanks to the farsighted policies of the erstwhile *Dewans* particularly Sir M.Viswesvaraya and Sir Mirja Ismael. They invested government funds productively in irrigation dams, good roads, electricity generation, free public health and education. On top of developing these economic and social infrastructure, they had started public sector industries like iron and steel, porcelain factory, sandal oil factory, electrical goods manufacturing industry, etc. People were content with the development which was achieved. But their horizon got widened after princely state of Mysore became category 'B' state in the Indian union. When Kengal Hanumanthaiah became the chief minister, the first five-year plan of India was launched with all the fanfare. The five-year plan regime in India robbed the political leaders at the state level of an opportunity to formulate their own vision for the future of their states. Their vision had to fit into the wider vision prepared by Jawaharlal and his advisers in New Delhi. Kengal Hanumanthaiah clashed with Nehru on many occasions on this issue.

The first five-year plan of India gave priority for achieving self-sufficiency in food grains and the states were asked to give priority for those schemes which would increase food grains production. The first five-year plan of princely state of Mysore envisaged an outlay of Rs. 47.58 crores. Originally it was lower at Rs. 42.14 crores but because of the transfer of Bellary district from Hyderabad state in 1952-53, the plan outlay was enhanced. But the state government could not mobilise the required financial resources and the central government was not in a position to help the state to implement the total outlay. The state government could spend only Rs. 40.51 crores, a shortfall of about 15 per cent. Even so, the total income of the state increased from Rs. 199 crores in 1950-51 to Rs. 247 crores in 1955-1956 and the per capita income increased from Rs. 103 in 1950-51 to Rs. 127 in 1955-56, at 1950-51 prices. Please do not compare these rupee figures with the present rupee figures. State income data are hardly available for princely state of Mysore. The rate of growth of state income was 5 per cent per annum. This was what the Indian first five-year plan had envisaged. Kengal Hanumanthaiah's government fulfilled the national target of economic development with 15 per cent lower outlay. Indirectly it reflects the effectiveness of implementation. There were no contractor lobbies to inflict shoddy development works on the people of Mysore state. Kengal Hanumanthaiah never allowed any such lobbies near him. Even the huge construction work of Vidhana Soudha was entrusted to the state public works department. It should be remembered in this context that by spending 33 per cent of the plan outlay on irrigation and 29 per cent on power he laid firm foundation for future development of the state.

If we examine other indicators of development which have more relevance for the welfare of the people, we find that the net irrigated area which was 10.51 lakh hectares in 1951-52 increased to 17.80 lakh hectares in 1955-56. Consequently, food grains production which was 25.50 lakh tonnes in 1951-52 when Kengal Hanumanthaiah assumed the office of chief ministership, increased to 37.83 lakh tonnes in 1955-56 when he left the office.

The princely state of Mysore was reorganised by adding the kannada speaking areas of former Bombay, Hyderabad and Madras states to form Karnataka state. While *kannadigas* felt happy about this union, they hardly realised the enormous burden imposed on the political leadership and beauracracy to manage the disparate regions of the state which had joined together with high hopes and aspirations. The legacy of this past still hangs around the necks of Karnataka political leaders. The first chief minister of reorganised state was S. Nijalingappa, who was confronted with the problem of balancing the pushes and pressures of different regional political leaders within the state. During the first period of his chief ministership, from 1956 to 1958, he was preoccupied with administrative problems of integration. He was able to give attention to economic development only in his second stint from 1962 to 1968. But we do not have data for these subperiods and hence we have to use whatever available data for assessing the pace of development from 1956-57 to 1960-61. This period also coincides with the second five-year plan which was implemented for one year by Nijalingappa and for three years by Jatti. The state income for reorganised state shows that it increased from Rs. 416.50 crores in 1956-67 to Rs. 477.40 crores in 1960-61 and per capita income increased from Rs. 192.43 in 1956-57 to Rs. 204 in 1960-61 at 1955-56 prices. Here again the development goals were handed down from New Delhi though the state was free to choose its own priorities of development for allocation of state plan funds within the framework of national five-year plan. So irrigation, power and roads received top priority in that order. As a result the net area irrigated increased from 17.80 lakh hectares in 1955-56 to 18.76 lakh hectares in 1957-58.

During Nijalingappa's second term the state income grew at a modest rate of 2.6 per cent per annum and the per capita income increased from Rs. 310 in 1961-62 to Rs. 316 in 1967-68 at 1960-61 prices. However the net area irrigated did not increase though food grains production increased from 46.10 lakh tonnes in 1961-62 to 58.91 lakh tonnes in 1967-68. It is worth noting that this was achieved during the pre-green revolution period and after facing a very severe drought in 1965-66 and 1966-67. This was a remarkable recovery in the field of agriculture. It is also necessary to remember that Nijalingappa is credited with implementing Sharavathi hydroelectric project which made the state a power surplus state. He also conceived the Cauveri river basin irrigation projects from the state's own funds as non-plan schemes. He had foreseen the bellicose attitude of Tamil Nadu government and political leaders towards water sharing and therefore, he wanted Karnataka farmers to utilise most of the water flowing in Cauveri basin in Karnataka as the original agreement was to lapse in 1974. In the field of irrigation and power Nijalingappa showed economic foresight and political wisdom. However, poverty estimates showed that the percentage of rural people in Karnataka living below poverty line which was 45.14 in 1960-61 increased to 59.26 in 1967-68. In urban Karnataka it increased from 37.49 per cent to 53.27 per cent in 1967-68. Even so, because of the implementation of tenancy abolition legislation during this period, the inequality of landholdings came down as reflected in Gini-coefficients declining from 0.68 for operational holdings and from 0.69 for ownership holdings in 1960-61 to 0.67 and 0.59 respectively in 1961-1962. What is more, in 1960-61 the Gini-coefficient of state income was only 0.32 in rural Karnataka and 0.40 in urban Karnataka. Even the Gini-coefficient of consumer expenditure in rural Karnataka was only 0.30 though it was slightly higher at 0.41 in urban Karnataka.

Jatti was the chief minister from middle of 1958 to early part of 1962 during which he implemented the second five-year plan for four years. During that period, the state income (NSDP) grew by 5.8 per cent per annum and per capita income increased from about Rs. 265 in 1958-59 to Rs. 310 in 1961-62. Rural poverty was very high when he left power. But for these, one does not find any far reaching policy decisions or major achievements of his government. Further, the second five-year plan faced financial crunch during this period and as a result the size of the plan had to be pruned down. This had its own impact on the state plan.

Veerendra Patil assumed office of the chief minister in May 1968 and continued till March 1971. These were politically disturbing years in the country. Five-year plan was discontinued and annual plans were reluctantly implemented. Even then green revolution was initiated in the country. Veerendra Patil's good administration was able to harness the economic infrastructure base created by his predecessors in the past to achieve a very impressive growth rate of NSDP of 6.8 per cent per annum during his period as the chief minister. Per capita income increased from Rs. 316 in 1967-68 to Rs. 361 in 1970-71 (in 1960-61 prices). Food grains production increased to 69.62 lakh tonnes thanks to the effective dissemination of HYV technology in agriculture. As a result the per cent of people living below poverty line declined in 1970-71 to 51.63 in rural areas and to 51.51 per cent in urban areas. The inequality of income and consumer expenditure also showed a decline during the chief ministership of Veerendra Patil. The Gini-coefficient of state income in 1970-71 was 0.32 in rural Karnataka and it was 0.33 in urban Karnataka. The Gini-coefficient of consumer expenditure was also lower at 0.27 in rural Karnataka and 0.31 in urban Karnataka in 1970-71. Even the inequality of landholdings as reflected in Gini-coefficient declined to 0.56 in 1970-71 for operational holdings though for ownership holdings it increased to 0.60.

Now we come to the period of the chief ministership of Devaraj Urs. I have treated his tenure as a whole though he was chief minister from 1972 to 1978 and again from 1978 to 1980. His period is marked by not merely reasonably good pace of economic development but also by the far reaching socioeconomic and political reforms. In the field of economic development, his period witnessed 5.3 per cent annual growth of NSDP. Per capita income increased from Rs. 584 in 1972-73 to Rs. 729 in 1979-80 at 1970-71 prices. Net area irrigated in the state had declined in earlier years. It stood at 13.78 lakh hectares in 1971-72 which increased to 14 lakh hectares in 1979-80. He completed many Cauvery basin irrigation projects by allocating more funds. Consequently, food grains production increased from 60.67 lakh tonnes in 1971-72 to 73.73 lakh tonnes in 1979-80. The degree of income and consumer expenditure inequalities declined during his period. The Gini-coefficient of state income was 0.27 for rural Karnataka and 0.36 for urban Karnataka in 1974-75. The Gini-coefficient of consumer expenditure was 0.25 for rural Karnataka and 0.30 for urban Karnataka. In 1977-78 the per cent of people below poverty line declined to 48.49 in rural Karnataka and to 39.99 in urban Karnataka.

Devaraj Urs hit upon a political strategy of dividing the two dominant communities and uniting the nondominant backward caste people. He succeeded in both though not for long. He appointed Havanur Commission to identify socially and educationally backward castes in the state and to recommend reservations in admissions to educational institutions and in state government jobs. The commission retained one dominant community in the backward class list and removed other community which created a lot of political opposition. But Urs weathered it when the High Court upheld the recommendations. Then he implemented the ceilings on landholdings which reduced the economic base of both the dominant communities. Though the two dominant communities opposed the ceiling legislation, its implementation was timed during emergency period and hence they could not resist. So the economic backbone of the dominant communities was broken and reservation benefits were denied to one dominant community. He gave political opportunities to unheard of caste groups in the legislature and in political appointments. (See for further details Thimmaiah, 1994).

Gundu Rao succeeded Devaraj Urs as the chief minister of Karnataka and he was there for three years from 1980 to 1983. During his period the NSDP of Karnataka increased by 4.5 per cent per annum and the per capita income increased from Rs. 1520 in 1980-81 to Rs. 1663 in 1983-1984 at 1980-81 prices. The net area under irrigation increased from 13.60 lakh hectares in 1980-81 to 15.90 lakh hectares in 1983-84. The food grains production which had declined to 58.80 lakh tonnes in 1980-81 increased to 72.52 lakh tonnes in 1983-84. Was that the result of free supply of electricity to the farmers? Whatever may be the reason for this impressive increase in food grains production, the percentage of people below poverty line in 1983-84 declined to 30.26 in rural Karnataka and to 22.73 in urban Karnataka.

Ramakrishna Hegde's period of chief ministership was marked by continuous drought in the state and political tight rope walking. He served Karnataka state for a period of five years from 1983 to 1988. During his period the NSDP of Karnataka grew at an annual rate of

6 per cent which is a remarkable achievement judged against the background of successive droughts faced by the state. The per capita income increased from Rs. 1663 in 1983-84 to Rs. 1853 in 1987-88 at 1980-81 prices. The net area irrigated increased to 20 lakh hectares and food grains production increased to 71 lakh tonnes after recovering from drought years. Even so the percentage of people living below poverty line in 1987-88 showed an upward tendency by increasing to 31.10 in rural Karnataka though it declined to 19.83 in urban Karnataka. This is the effect of continuous droughts which affected the cereal intake of rural people.

A lasting contribution of Ramakrishna Hegde to the state of Karnataka has been the implementation of political decentralisation by enacting *Panchayat Raj* legislation. There were several novelties in the system created by Hegde—like making the elected representative as the chief executive, reservation for women, backward classes and SCs/STs in the elected seats, etc. These novelties attracted the national attention and induced Rajiv Gandhi to initiate efforts to enact 73rd and 74th constitutional amendments to give constitutional status to the Panchayati Raj institutions in the entire country.

Subsequently, Bommai's period was lacklustre in the sense that his term was short (eight months) and Veerendra Patil's second term was only for 11 months. Though Veerendra Patil tried to provide a responsive and clean administration, he had to leave because of his ill-health. Bangarappa and Veerappa Moily served for two years each. During the period of Veerappa Moily the NSDP of the state increased by 5.23 per cent and the per capita income increased by 3.30 per cent. The per capita income of the state stood at Rs. 9966 in the last year of Moily's term (in 1993-94 prices). Deve Gowda was supposed to serve the state as the chief minister for five years but left after two years to become the prime minister of India. During his period of two years NSDP increased by 5.29 per cent and per capita income increased by 3.35 per cent. The per capita income increased to Rs. 11478 in 1995-1996. J.H. Patel succeeded Deve Gowda and during his period NSDP of the state increased impressively by 9.18 per cent, 6.21 per cent and as much as 13.56 per cent respectively in 1996-97, 1997-98 and 1998-99. Per capita income also increased by 7.43 per cent, 4.73 per cent and 12.03 per cent respectively. The per capita income of the state increased from Rs. 13180 in 1996-97 to Rs. 16673 in 1998-99 (in 1993-94 prices). S.M. Krishna became the chief minister towards the end of 1999. During his period Karnataka faced successive droughts for three years and hence the development performance of the state was not as good as it was in earlier years. Even so, expansion of service sector in the wake of phenomenal growth of software industry in the state enabled the state economy to achieve 4.79 per cent growth of NSDP in 1999-2000 and 10.31 per cent growth in 2000-01. But the growth of NSDP declined by 1.58 per cent in 2001-02 though it recovered to achieve 4.21 per cent growth in 2002-03. Per capita income increased by 3.44 per cent in 1999-2000, 9.05 per cent in 2000-01 but declined by 3.23 per cent in 2001-02. It recovered to grow at 2.46 per cent in 2002-03. The per capita income which stood at Rs. 18332 in 1999-2000 declined sharply to Rs. 13335 in 2000-01.

I have presented the major economic indicators of economic development during the periods of successive chief ministers of Karnataka. I do not want to assert that the changes in these indicators were the direct result of the efforts of the chief ministers. They are the result of so many factors which operated simultaneously during those periods. Therefore, it would be more appropriate to review the policy initiatives taken by the successive chief ministers which might have created conditions conducive for the development of Karnataka.

Policy Initiatives of Chief Ministers

It should be remembered that most of the major development policies were formulated by the central government and the state governments were only expected to implement them. This was true even in regard to the subjects which were constitutionally reserved for the states like agriculture and land reforms. The required compliance was induced by carrot of financial assistance for state plans and also by the stick of one party rule both at the centre and at the state level for almost 20 years after independence. However, some enterprising chief ministers did take the initiative to make marginal changes in the nationally decided policies to meet the local exigencies.

The most important policy which was taken up for enacting legislation and effective implementation was abolition of various types of tenancies in the state (Thimmaiah and Aziz, 1984). Kadidal

Manjappa, who hailed from a tenant's family, took special interest when he became the chief minister, to get the *Inam* tenancy abolition Acts passed. But he could not remain in office for long to prevent evasion of the *Inam* tenancy abolition legislations by his own party leaders who owned tenanted land. After the reorganisation of the state, Nijalingappa turned his attention to expanding the cultivated area under irrigation. The Planning Commission of India was providing central assistance for state plans mainly on the basis of the quality of the projects submitted by the states. He used that opportunity to take up Cauvery basin irrigation projects by diverting state government funds for Cauveri basin irrigation projects on nonplan account and allocated substantial funds for their execution. He also took up Sharavathi hydroelectric project which on completion made the state power surplus though temporarily. Nijalingappa openly invited industrialists to invest in Karnataka by offering them cheap power at as low as 10 paise per kwt. Of course some power guzzling industries like aluminium industry established their production units in Karnataka.

Deveraj Urs made a difference in his policies to develop the state. Apart from devising a new political strategy to reign in the two power hungry dominant communities, he diverted substantial funds for the completion of all Cauvery basin projects started by Nijalingappa. This enabled the state to hoodwink Tamil Nadu which used to raise objections to Karnataka state starting of any new irrigation projects in the Cauvery basin area. Next he enacted a new land reforms Act in 1974 and completely abolished all forms of tenancies and made the tenants not only *de facto* but also *de jure* owners of the lands which they had cultivated. Besides he imposed ceilings on landholdings owned by all members of a family taken together. Further he barred non-cultivators from owning land. Furthermore, he imposed ceiling on urban land owned by individuals. Though he bestowed ownership right on tenants, he could not successfully implement the land ceilings. He also implemented a justifiable reservation policy for the backward classes in Karnataka.

His immediate successors did not bother about any new policy initiatives in the state. They simply implemented the plan programmes handed down to them from the Planning Commission except that Ramakrishna Hegde broke a new ground by introducing a well conceived democratic decentralisation scheme which was appreciated by even the Congress government at the centre. By the time Deve Gowda became the chief minister of the state, structural economic reforms were implemented at the national level. Deriving inspiration from those policies, Deve Gowda got a new agricultural development policy document prepared which advocated changes in land ceilings and land ownership by non-cultivators and encouragement for horticulture crops. Deve Gowda amended the land ceilings provisions to relax the ceiling limit for growing of commercial crops and also non-cultivators to own up to 106 acres of land to be used only for growing horticultural crops. He also got the urban rent control act amended to exclude commercial buildings from its purview. Deve Gowda found it difficult to fund the Upper-Krishna irrigation projects with the limited resources available with the state government. So he created an independent corporation (Krishna Bagya Nigama), to raise funds in the open market to complete the Krishna basin irrigation projects within the stipulated period. Later S.M. Krishna emulated this example and created another independent corporation (Cauvery Jala Nigama) to raise funds for completion and renovating Cauvery basin irrigation projects.

It should be mentioned here that every new government headed by new chief minister made it a practice to announce innumerable policies relating to industrial development, export promotion, dairy development, sericulture development and so on. Some of them were implemented seriously so long as the concerned chief minister was in power and were shelved or forgotten after the change of chief minister. Thus there has been absence of continuity in implementation of many policies. Another feature of policy making in Karnataka has been to announce innumerable policies with attractive names and high sounding words. Many of them were forgotten after the euphoria was over.

Amidst all such political publicity, there were some major policies which were seriously implemented. For instance, Kadidal Manjappa and Devaraj Urs were responsible for abolishing tenancy and giving land to the cultivators which not only helped improve productivity but also ensured social justice. However, land ceilings implemented by Devaraj Urs did not help Karnataka's agriculture. Land ceilings increased the proportion of marginal and small farms and made landholdings economically unviable. This is one of the reasons for the economic distress faced by the farmers particularly those dependent on dry land agriculture. All talk about consolidation of holdings has become an exercise in futility. Recent amendment to land ceiling legislation to allow non-cultivators to own land for growing commercial crops has encouraged horticultural crops on a large scale in the state and private industrialists have taken up this activity though in a small way. Exclusion of commercial buildings from rent control Act has encouraged commercial activity and also increased the earnings from real estate in the state. It may be noted that successive chief ministers who came to power after the introduction of structural economic reforms have endorsed them and have been striving to encourage private sector investment in the state by improving/expanding the physical infrastructure through public-private sector initiative.

Inter-State Comparison of Development Performance

Before concluding this paper, I would like to present an inter-state comparison of the development performance with a view to throwing up some light on the role of political readership in the relative performance of Karnataka state in economic development. I want to begin such an exercise with contrasts in inter-state variations in infrastructure development because the pace of economic development depends to a large extent on the adequacy of good infrastructure. Karnataka Development Report prepared by the Institute for Social and Economic Change (2005), has found that there is a strong correlation between NSDP and index of infrastructure across the states in India. What is interesting is that the value of correlation which was 0.668 in 1990-91 increased after the introduction of structural economic reforms to 0.806 in 1995-96 and further to 0.833 in 2000-01. This is mainly in a liberalised economy where private sector is called upon to play a prominent role in economic development when infrastructure facilities become more important. Since infrastructure facilities have to be developed by undertaking government investment, the role of political leadership becomes important. This is much more so at the state level.

The Confederation of Indian Industry (CII) and the World Bank conducted a survey of 1099 manufacturing companies spread over 10 states in 2000 to assess their opinion about the quality of infrastructure available in 10 major states of the Indian union. The infrastructure facilities included transport network, banking and financial network, power availability and technically trained manpower. The perceptions of the companies were ranked as shown in Table 3.2.

Table 3.2

Subjective Ranking of State in Terms of Availability of the Best and the Worst Infrastructure

States with Best Infrastructure	*States with Good Infrastructure*	*States with Medium Infrastructure*	*States with Poor Infrastructure*
Maharashtra	Tamil Nadu	Delhi	Kerala
Gujarat	Karnataka	Punjab	West Bengal
	Andhra Pradesh		Uttar Pradesh

Source: CII and World Bank (2000).

It may be observed that private sector companies ranked Karnataka as only having good infrastructure facilities and second even among the states having good infrastructure facilities.

Mitra *et al.* (2002) conducted a study of the effect of infrastructure on total productivity and technical efficiency of the manufacturing industries in Indian states. Their study used annual data from 1976 to 1992 for 17 industries and 15 states. They found significant disparities in physical, social and economic infrastructure facilities across states in India. By using the principal component analysis they developed a composite indicator of infrastructure availability and ranked the states as shown in Table 3.3.

Table 3.3

Ranking of States in Terms of Infrastructure Availability

Best Infrastructure	*Good Infrastructure*	*Poor Infrastructure*
Maharashtra	Tamil Nadu	Assam
Punjab	Karnataka	Uttar Pradesh
Gujarat	Kerala	Bihar
		Orissa
		Rajasthan
		Madhya Pradesh

Source: Mitra *et al.* (2002)

They found that wide disparities in infrastructure availability explained variations in total factor productivity and technical efficiency of these industries. Here again Karnataka ranked second among those states having good infrastructure facilities.

CII and World Bank conducted another survey in 2003 covering a large number of industries and across 12 states to find out whether there was any improvement in the perceptions of industrialists regarding the availability of infrastructure facilities in different states. They ranked the states as shown in Table 3.4.

Table 3.4

Subjective Ranking of States in Terms of Availability of Infrastructure Facilities

State with Best Infrastructure	*State with Good Infrastructure*	*State with Poor Infrastructure*
Maharashtra	Gujarat	Madhya Pradesh
Delhi	Andhra Pradesh	Kerala
	Karnataka	West Bengal
	Punjab	Uttar Pradesh
	Tamil Nadu	
	Haryana	

Source: CII and World Bank (2003).

It is interesting to note that the perceptions of industrialists did not change in regard to Karnataka state. Instead, its position even in the company of states having good infrastructure came down from second to third position.

It is true that these are subjective judgements based on the specific experiences of the industrialists though Mitra *et al.* study is based on reliable data. A similar exercise has been done by the Institute for Social and economic Change (ISEC), in its study *Karnataka Development Report* (2005). Table 3.5 is reproduced below. ISEC's ranking of major states based on an independently computed index of infrastructure.

Table 3.5

Rankings of States on the Basis of their Infrastructure Indices

State	*1990-91*		*1995-96*		*2000-01*	
	Index	*Rank*	*Index*	*Rank*	*Index*	*Rank*
Punjab	0.60	1	0.65	1	0.83	1
Haryana	0.42	2	0.46	2	0.59	2
Tamil Nadu	0.41	3	0.46	2	0.58	3
Gujarat	0.38	4	0.44.	3	0.59	2
Kerala	0.37	5	0.42	4	0.58	3
Andhra Pradesh	0.31	6	0.34	6	0.44	5
Uttar Pradesh	0.31	6	0.33	7	0.37	7
West Bengal	0.30	7	0.33	7	0.35	9
Karnataka	0.29	8	0.32	8	0.42	6
Maharashtra	0.28	9	0.35	5	0.47	4
Orissa	0.28	9	0.29	9	0.37	7
Assam	0.26	10	0.26	10	0.30	10
Bihar	0.25	11	0.26	10	0.30	10
Rajasthan	0.25	11	0.29	9	0.36	8
Madhya Pradesh	0.20	12	0.25	11	0.27	11

Source: ISEC (2005).

The data presented in the foregoing table have thrown up interesting results. It has become conventional knowledge to consider Maharashtra and Gujarat states as well developed in infrastructure and hence have attracted more industries. But the ISEC study shows that such an assumption was not based on reliable and relevant data. Further, Karnataka which used to be considered as having good infrastructure facilities if not the best, is now confirmed as a state having a modest level of infrastructure facilities. However, what is encouraging is that a majority of the states have improved their infrastructure development particularly in the wake economic liberalisation. Political leadership has played an important role in this improvement because it is the state governments which spend on infrastructure development under their plan outlays and the policy decisions of the political leaders to give top priority for infrastructure sectors like power and roads have come to yield reasonably good results in the form of improved infrastructure development in most of the states.

Finally, I want to refer to another important area of policy making at the state level which has got a bearing on the creation of positive investment climate at the state level. This relates to the climate of industrial relations. It is generally believed that Indian labour laws are more in favour of the labour and hence impose additional cost on the employers in the private sector. Further, politicisation of labour has done harm to the industry, labour and also to the society. Therefore, industrial peace is considered important for attracting private investment and also for the growth of the manufacturing and service sectors in the states. This depends upon the nature of labour regulations and the state governments' effectiveness in enforcing them in a fair manner.

Immediately after independence, the central government enacted Industrial Disputes Act in 1947. Indian constitution empowers the state governments to amend this Act as and when required to promote industrial peace. The Act provides for conciliations, arbitrations and adjudications. Many state governments have amended this Act several times. Besely and Burgess (2002), carefully studied these amendments from 1952 to 1992 and coded them to rank the states in terms of labour regulation. They have given a minimum of +1 to indicate the labour regulations to be pro-worker, -1 for pro-employer and 0 for neutral. I have reproduced in Table 3.6 their ranking of different states in terms of labour regulations.

Table 3.6

Index of Labour Regulations in Indian States
(Cumulative Scores for 1992)

Pro-Worker	*Score*	*Pro-Employer*	*Score*	*Neutral*	*Score*
West Bengal	4	Andhra Pradesh	-2	Assam	0
Maharashtra	2	Tamil Nadu	-2	Bihar	0
Gujarat	1	Karnataka	-1	Haryana	0
Orissa	1	Kerala	-1	J&K	0
		Madhya Pradesh	-1	Punjab	0
		Rajasthan	-1	Uttar Pradesh	0

Source: Besley and Burgess (2002).

It may be observed that two richer states are having pro-worker labour regulations and three middle income states are having pro-employer labour regulations to attract private investment. What is interesting is that of the two states ruled by communist party, one (West Bengal) is having pro-worker labour regulations and another (Kerala) is having pro-employer regulations. Karnataka is having pro-employer labour regulations with a view to attracting private investment. This situation has been created cumulatively by the successive state governments which amended the Industrial Disputes Act to protect the employers without harming the workers. This is a positive feature of the actions of political leadership in Karnataka. In other words, though it is difficult to relate the contributions of chief ministers to the pace of development in cause and effect manner, their role in creating required infrastructure and ensuring industrial peace cannot be denied.

The end result of the role of political leadership in the development of Karnataka is presented in the following Table 3.7 which summarises not only the contribution to the growth of NSDP but also for qualitative areas of social development of the state.

Table 3.7

Inter-State Comparison of Economic and Human Development

State	*Rank in Human Development Index*			*Per Capita NSDP Rank*
	1981	*1991*	*2001*	*2001*
Andhra Pradesh	9	9	10	8
Assam	14	14	14	12
Bihar	15	15	15	15
Gujarat	4	6	6	4
Haryana	5	5	5	3
Karnataka	6	7	7	6
Kerala	1	1	1	7
Madhya Pradesh	13	12	12	11
Maharashtra	3	4	4	2
Orissa	10	11	11	14
Punjab	2	2	2	1
Rajasthan	11	10	9	10
Tamil Nadu	7	3	3	5
Uttar Pradesh	12	13	13	13
West Bengal	8	8	8	9

Source: Compiled from various sources.

Thus, it may be observed that Karnataka has lost one rank in terms of human development index during the years of economic reforms. So also Andhra Pradesh, Maharashtra and Gujarat which are competing states for attracting private investment. They have also not improved their ranks in human development index. But Tamil Nadu has improved its rank in human development index. Even Rajasthan and Madhya Pradesh have improved their ranks in human development index which shows the positive impact of economic liberalisation. In other words, while Karnataka has done well in achieving overall development in terms of growth of NSDP, it has slipped in the sphere of human development thereby indicating that the political leaders have not paid the required attention to the quality of life in the state. There is also a valid charge that political as well as bureaucratic corruption has increased over the years in Karnataka which has been responsible for the poor quality of public services. This issue is a separate topic which cannot be analysed here.

References

Besley, T. and R. Burgess (2002). "Can Labour Regulation Hinder Economic Performance? Evidence from India", *CEPR Discussion Paper* No. 3260.

CII and World Bank (2002). *Competitiveness of Indian Manufacturing: Results from a Firm Level Survey*. New Delhi: CII.

ISEC (2005). *Karnataka Development Report* (Planning Commission, Government of India). New Delhi: Academic Foundation.

Kaufmann, Daniel, Aart Kraay and Pablo Ziodo-Lobaton (2002). "Governance Matters II", *Policy Research Working* Paper 2772. Washington DC: World Bank.

Mitra, A., A. Varoudakis and M.A. Veganzones-Varoudakis (2002). "Productivity and Technical Efficiency in Indian States Manufacturing: The Role of Infrastructure", *Economic Development and Cultural Change* 50(2): 395-426.

Thimmaiah, G. and Abdul Aziz (1984). *The Political Economy of Land Reforms*. New Delhi: Ashish Publishing.

Thimmaiah, G. (1994). *Power Politics and Social Justice*. New Delhi: Sage Publications.

4

Ideological Elements in Political Instability in Karnataka

Janata Dal in the Late 1990s

PAMELA PRICE

The political party which used to be known as Janata Dal has been notorious for splitting and fragmenting in a political landscape in which the splitting and fragmentation of political parties occurs relatively often. The focus of this paper is on instability in the party leadership in the state of Karnataka in the late 1990s.[1] I argue that there were ideological elements which helped to shape political rivalries and provide rationalisations for political action. I use the term ideology here as: a cultural form that gives shape to cultural patterns.[2]

A comprehensive study of the break-up of the Janata Dal in Karnataka in the late 1990s would take into consideration economic conditions and trends as well as changes in social bases among political parties. Harold Gould (2003) argues persuasively in his analysis of the Assembly and General Elections of 1999 that the compulsions of balancing contradictory demands of rivalrous caste clusters and regions created complex and difficult tensions; the management of relations among social groups which were in intense competition in itself made for instability in state politics. A politician in Karnataka, as elsewhere in India, usually builds his[3] early career as a spokesman and fixer for the community he comes from, at the same

---

1. The gracious assistance of Neelambar Hatti, James Manor, V.K. Natraj and Sandeep Shastri made possible much of the research upon which this study is based. In Hubli-Dharwad Ms. Kamalaxi G. Tadasad kindly served as a translator when necessary and accompanied me to meet informants.

2. Thanks to Katinka Frøystad for this formulation.

3. Research is needed to establish the extent to which women's strategies for a political career are similar to those of men.

time as he also tries to makes alliances with other caste, language, and religious communities. A complicating factor in Karnataka is that the two dominating, rival caste groups (*Vokkaligas* and *Lingayats*) are associated with regions in intense competition for state resources. *Vokkaligas* tend to come from the wetter, richer southern part of the state while *Lingayats* dominate the dryer, poorer northern part. No politician in Karnataka can escape complications which arise from these compounded rivalries.

Relations among Karnataka politicians, then, are affected by issues of one's own caste or religious identity and the demands of relating to the identities of a large number of competing other groups. The argument of this paper is that relations among politicians are also complicated by notions of personal status and prestige which are connected to caste, but which at the same time transcend caste. There are in elite politics in Karnataka concepts of status and authority which are associated with political transactions in rural society.[4] That some politicians and observors recognise this is suggested by references in newspaper reports and political discussions to '*panchayat* level politics' or '*palegar* politics' when criticising political behaviour. *Panchayat* refers to village governance and *palegars* were belligerent chiefs who ruled the Karnataka country side in the 18th and early 19th century. The complex of values and concepts which are my focus below revolve around notions of status that are best translated by the English words honour and respect and speak to personal or group achievement, authority and/or domination. Concepts of moral integrity are also included in the complex.

There are many words and values attached to concepts of status, honour, respect and self-respect in Karnataka. Notions of honour which are associated with achievement, authority and/or dominance, include *sanmana* (high honour which is displayed through giving in public) and *stannamana* (the honour which comes from holding a position). There is also a concept, *mana,* which is a more private quality relating to one's inner character. The meaning of these words and others in the complex alter according to context. The aim of this

4. For Karnataka, see Price (2005). I have found this to be the case as well in Tamil Nadu and Andhra Pradesh. See, for example, Price (2006).

study is to explain how political transactions at the state level in Karnataka can be related to notions of personal status, honour and self-respect.

It is common to associate honour in politics with warrior societies and their focus on heroism. The politics of honour in warrior society in pre-colonial South India included conventional patterns of action and reaction (Price, 1996: 9-38). Here one finds rivalry for authority and domination in which the status of rivals can be threatened by humiliating defeats and shows of disrespect. Revenge was a predictable response. For reasons which cannot be investigated in this piece, one finds in the politics of honour in Karnataka some of the same themes of humiliation and revenge.

Academic writers rarely analyse 'personality clashes' or the 'clash of egos' among politicians.[5] Such conditions are, however, the object of comment in English-language newspapers.[6] To phrase failures of cooperation in those terms can give the impression that emotions override reason in political transactions. While it appears that emotions can take control of events, some part of the rhetoric of splitting and fragmentation is contrived. Politicians on occasion appear to be phrasing their actions in a language which will make them explicable to their constituents and potential new supporters.[7] This is the language of honour, respect and humiliation. References to honour and respect are found throughout political discourse in India, from *Dalit* parties and groups to speeches in the Lok Sabha. The vocabulary associated with relations of honour is particularly brought into play when politicians explain to journalists or say in a statement why they are leaving one political coalition, party or faction for another. They often give as a reason that they have suffered humilitation in the former context. While this characteristic is found frequently in Karnataka (as elsewhere in India), the late 1990s illustrates the point well. We find this usage with reference to the Rashtriya Navanirmana

5. A noteworthy exception is Brass (1965).
6. For example, in *The Hindu*, 12 January 1998, P. Ramiah quoted Chief Minister J.H. Patel as attributing "most of the 'hiccups' of his party to personal prejudices and personality clashes", in "BJP's Stable-Govt Plea Won't Help: CM".
7. I elaborate on this point in Price (2006).

Vedike, a non-party organisation which former Chief Minister Ramakrishna Hegde formed after he was expelled from the Janata Dal in 1996 and started his own party, the Lok Shakti, in 1997.

The political language of honour represents more than opportunistic contrivance. While the contradictory claims of many social segments fuel political instability, relations among politicians can also be fraught and vulnerable because of strong emotions attached to perceptions of challenge to one's personal status and authority. The language of honour used in political rhetoric reflects preoccupations with status which are not universal among politicians in Karnataka, but which are common enough to affect the nature of many political competitions and the outcome of political transactions. Because of preoccupation with personal honour and shows of respect, competition often turns into powerful 'personal' rivalry. A strong element in this rivalry is suspicion that one's rival seeks to humiliate one. Narendar Pani of *The Economic Times,* said, when I asked him about political honour in Karnataka politics, "Self-respect is important for all Karnataka politicians. A politician in Karnataka cannot suffer having his self-respect challenged in public. His self-respect cannot be politically challenged."[8]

Revenge can be a response to public humiliation. In some political cosmologies in rural and urban Karnataka, rivalry and revenge are accepted as 'natural' forms of political engagement. While rivalry among heads of factions in village politics in India has been an object of scholarly attention, less is known about how rivalry and revenge operate in state and national level politics. In political competitions where participants are preoccupied with personal honour and status, revenge for public humiliation is a common principle for political action. From the point of view of the history of political culture, the form and content of conflicts are commonly shaped by what participants feel to be appropriate responses to the actions of others. Revenge can be appropriate, even when it has long-term destructive consequences.

---

8. Interview, 8 May, 1998, Bangalore. I conducted interviews in English when possible. I did not use a tape recorder for any of the interviews, but was permitted to take notes.

The language of honor is not only culturally appropriate usage in competition and conflict. The cultural dynamics of conflict in Karnataka party politics encompasses notions of one's worth in the eyes of others, as well as one's sense of self-worth. Focus on honour and shows of respect contribute to the fluidity of political relations in a context of weak organisational structures in political parties. My argumentation begins with characterisations of Karnataka party politics which I collected during an eight month stay in the state in 1997-98.[9]

A Brief Characterisation of Relationships in Intra-party Politics

The general aspect of party politics which is most relevant to the discussion presented here is the phenomenon of deinstitutionalisation, studied in detail by Atul Kohli (1990). This process refers to the disintegration of party structures, in the sense of a relative lack of elected or appointed posts with defined responsibilities and powers. Deinstitutionalisation refers, also, to increased focus on personal loyalty to powerful personalities as a major criterion for career advancement. Similarly, the roles which personalities, as opposed to policies, acquire as a focus for some political parties has been another aspect of deinstitutionalisation. The process has occurred unevenly in India, with the BJP and CPI(M), for example, experiencing some success with cadre organisation. Recognition of the pitfalls of weak party organisation has led to efforts of improvement, in, for example, the Janata Dal before its split in 1999 and in the Congress (I) under the leadership of Sonia Gandhi.

In the Janata Dal in Karnataka in the late 1990s, the failure of the party to institutionalise positions of trust and responsibility in its

---

9. Besides reading English-language newspapers and magazines, I carried out interviews with: four present MLAs, one each from the CPI(M), Congress, Janata Dal and BJP; and one Janata Dal MLC. I interviewed one former Janata Dal MLA and two former MLCs, one Janata Dal who had joined Congress and one BJP who had joined Congress. Among municipal, district and *mandal* level politicians, I interviewed six from Janata Dal, five from Congress, one Independent and one BJP. I received the names of politicians through academic contacts. Among academics and intellectuals I interviewed four sociologists, three anthropologists, one historian and three political scientists. Eight journalists obliged me with interviews. My thanks to all those who met and discussed with me.

organisation had resulted in demoralisation. K.H. Srinivas, the political secretary to Janata Dal Chief Minister J.H. Patel, related this failure to complaints among party workers of not being respected in the party. I had asked him about the concept, "*stannamana*", the honour which comes from having high political status and/or position. My notes from our discussion include the following:

> [Srinivas argues that] *stannamana*...[is] a concept that belongs to [what he calls] the spheres of competition within politics and will be used by party workers in complaining about their lack of capacity to accomplish anything in politics. Srinivas says that a major problem is a lack of definition of a political worker [meaning, it seems, the lack of specification of responsibilities and powers]. There is no definition of a party worker or a party cadre. So how can party workers get respect? [As things stand now] they are power-oriented and think that without a position they can't do anything. So they say that they have no *stannamana*. In this loose party structure it is hard to get respect; they feel that they are nobody (Interview, 11 May, 1998, Bangalore).

The failure of party discipline in the context of deinstitutionalisation made an elected official from a party vulnerable to challenges from his own party men. Srinivas continued:

> There is no sense of leadership. After one has won the position as MLA, others will begin immediately undermining [his] position as MLA. There is no sense of objectivity on the part of those who want to compete. It is a situation of "no holds barred". We have a "lottery-culture" in politics....There is no objectivity, no sense of leadership, no sense of politics as a career (Interview, 11 May, 1998, Bangalore).

I asked E. Raghavan from *The Economic Times* about the sense politicians can have of their status: "One has to study how politicians conduct themselves. I have yet to meet a politician who was not conscious of his position. They all want to grow, to enhance their image." (Interview, 11 May, 1998, Bangalore). Raghavan commented that if one has been an MLA for a long time and has been a minister, one "ought to command great respect": "If he is not given the respect that he deserves, that is humiliation" (Interview, 11 May 1998, Bangalore).

When I asked Raghavan about suffering humiliation as an excuse to defect from a political party, he reported that he found distinctions among different kinds of defection. He found three reasons for people to defect:

1. A person may leave the party to achieve a better deal, a higher position in the political hierarchy.
2. If I am no longer wanted in the party or somebody grabs the opportunities which come along, leaving me [on the sidelines], I may defect to another party.
3. I may want to leave...and give up a position to start out in a new party, starting all over again (Interview, 11 May, 1998, Bangalore).

Having suffered humiliation can work as a public rationale for an action because causing the humiliation of one's rival is a common perception of political play. In popular cosmologies acts of revenge in return for humiliation are considered appropriate. Some informants used political language which reflected strongly the context of combat, associated with tests of honour and strength. Politics as war occasionally entered into newspaper writers' complaints about the tenor of political interaction.[10] Anthropologist Shankaranaraya Rao argued that myths and the great epics played an important role in the reproduction of notions of honour, rivalry and revenge in contemporary politics. He cited a principle of political action with clear antecedents in the literature of heroic ages: "One man takes pride in ruining his rival. Others can see the ruin. You get honour by ruining the honor of somebody else" (Interview, 30 March, 1998 Bangalore). Shankaranaraya Rao felt that such preoccupations had became "frenzied":

> Indian tradition gives place of pride for rivalry and seeking revenge—and for bringing down one's rival by hook or by crook. In Indian tradition one triumphs over the enemy. It has become a social value. Humiliation of the enemy is one's triumph. In our society competition is not orderly; you must ruin your rival. The latest example is that of the rivalry between Ramakrishan Hegde and

---

10. For example, see an anonymous commentary in the *Times of India*, 22 February, 1998, in "Heads and Tales—The Indian Voter: The Thumb People": "That each election is increasingly assuming the jagged contours of a war is altogether another story".

> Deve Gowda. Ramakrishna Hegde must stay with the BJP to triumph over Deve Gowda. But what does he get in the meantime? Almost nothing at the centre. In the meantime the situation is unstable... Ramakrishna Hegde is an intelligent man. He must have seen these problems, but his heart ached to destroy Deve Gowda (Interview, 30 March, 1998, Bangalore).

Shankaranaraya Rao's interpretation of Ramakrishna Hegde's actions in the late 1990s was a popular one. Others with a closer view of the alternatives open to him might put more weight on Hegde's reasoning about his chance in politics, given Deve Gowda's implacable antipathy toward him. In this connection we have to consider, also, the possible influence of news media in forming popular interpretations of motives for political action. While granting the usefulness of Shankaranaraya's analysis, we can also consider that the popularity of the revenge motif in discussions about politics may have been partly a reflection of media discourse.

In the course of my interviews I sometimes encountered the opinion that journalists overemphasised the drama of humiliation in Karnataka politics. A former mayor of Hubli-Dharwad, Pandurage Patil, argued that the media played into the public's "weakness" for "gossip" and tales of rivalry, humiliation, and revenge in politics (Interview, 28 April, 1998). What politicians themselves have to say about the nature of preoccupation with honorific status is more reliable. The interpretation of an MLA from the CPI(M) is relevant in this context. His opinion was that both ordinary people and politicians had "feudal sentiments": "People honour any person who is in the power....Most politicians play into their feudal sentiments.... [Politicians feel] everybody should respect me" (Interview, 21 April, 1998, Bangalore).

Popular Conceptions of Political Motivation

English-language newspapers in the late 1990s contained many references to a ceaseless and amoral appetite for 'power' as the motivating force in the behaviour of politicians. Apart from evidence that politicians can also be trying to better the welfare of their constituents and the prospects of their state, as a historian of political culture, I find this analysis incomplete. Political anthropologists tend not to see 'power' as an absolute quantity without qualitative content. As anthropologist Shanta Pawadi Halagi noted in her study of factional politics in Karnataka: "The leader receives from his followers both direct personal admiration and indirect benefits of status in the society as a leader of a faction. Faction leaders in their external relations are often motivated more by considerations of prestige than by desires for power only" (Halagi, 1991: 276). Disaggregation of motives in political action adds to the capacity to understand political styles and the tenor of many political interactions. Recourse to 'power-seeking' alone cannot explain the nature of unstable relations in political parties.

A similarly nuanced view is needed in analysing the common comment in the late 1990s that people went into politics for 'money' and that only 'money' gave respect in Karnataka. Such observations can be understood in part with reference to changes in political culture in the state in the last half of the 20th century. Local societies had been organised in part around hierarchies based on caste status in which mutual shows of respect contributed to political integration (Tapper, 1987; Price, 2006). However, based on her research in Hassan District in 1966-1967 Suzanne Hanchett found ostentatious display being worked into the expansion of previously simpler ceremonies (Hanchett, 1975). She argued that the principles which guided these 'potlatch'-like ceremonial strategies, among kin and non-kin, included "generosity, ritual rank acknowledgement and rivalry" (Hanchett, 1975: 44).[11] She found a smooth transformation in socio-political values, involving strong continuity with the past, in the application of ceremonies, such as marriages, to new conditions of electoral politics and economic development.

In the midst of her analysis of ostentatious display Hanchett had found preoccupation with honour, which she argued was one of the "valuables" being exchanged on ceremonial occasions (Hanchett, 1975: 48):

> In the case of the traditional family celebrating a wedding, honor is the general standing of the family in the community of kinsfolk and caste-mates; and this standing is reflected largely in the network of

11. 'Potlatch' is the term used by anthropologists in describing the destruction of goods in status competition among Native American Indians on the Pacific Coast.

reciprocal caste and family ceremonies. In the case of the village patron, honour is a question of building up a local faction of followers through competitive generosity. In the case of the modern family involved in business, government, or industry, honour is largely a result of career progress.

Thirty years later meanings of terms in the language of honour were changing. In the 1990s, in particular, it appears that new spending opportunities, the expansion of access to television and, for some groups, new possibilities for wealth contributed to alterations in the constituents of status. The common discourse about 'money' indicated preoccupation with accelerated shifts to mobile and unstable status based on or expressed by the consumption of commercialised goods. The constituents of honour in this context were unstable.

Since Karnataka voters, as elsewhere in India, often vote against incumbents and since candidates commonly go into debt in waging their campaigns, there has been an incentive to make money fast, once one is elected. Many feel compelled both to pay off their debts and to make the most of financial opportunities which accrue, before they lose the next election. This is not the place for an extensive consideration of money, corruption and politicians, but issues of ostentatious consumption and having access to large sums of cash are relevant to a discussion of ideological elements in Karnataka politics. E. Raghavan indicated that the construction of respect both among and for politicians involved several elements, besides getting things done, achieving something in politics:

> What is more important is whether someone gets something accomplished before another and earns respect. Having a huge bungalow and ten dogs gives respectability...Respectability is what politicians want. Respectability comes from wealth, achievement and power. A politician often will have both wealth and power [if not achievement] (Interview, 11 May, 1998, Bangalore).

Interpretations of the Rivalry between Ramakrishna Hegde and H.D. Deve Gowda

The three main leaders of the Janata Dal in Karnataka in the early 1990s were H.D. Deve Gowda (a *Vokkaliga* from southern Karnataka), Ramakrishna Hedge (a *Brahmin* from the northern coast) and S.R.

Bommai (a *Lingayat* from the northwest). They had been periodically engaged in sharp factional conflict during previous decades and both Hegde and Bommai had served as Chief Minister of the state. Scholarship on Karnataka politics is in agreement that it was the willingness of especially Deve Gowda and Hegde to join forces for the Janata Dal in the Assembly and General Elections in 1996 which led to the success of the party at the polls. Hegde decided not to contest in the elections and Deve Gowda was chosen to be Chief Minister.

Hegde had played an important role in the formation of the Janata Dal as a third force in national politics in 1988 and appears to have expected to be rewarded with the position of Prime Minister for his services to the party, as well as for his intellectual and other capacities. However, the United Front, of which Janata Dal was a member, decided that the Chief Ministers of the winning alliance would chose the Prime Minister from among their number. Deve Gowda became, thus, Prime Minister of India. Upon Hegde's death Parvati Menon (2004) wrote: "The choice of Deve Gowda as Prime Minister came as a cruel shock for him, forcing him to speak out in anguish and a certain degree of anger against the decision."

Shortly thereafter Deve Gowda engineered the dismissal of Hegde, with several of his supporters, from the Janata Dal, on the charge of anti-party activities. Hegde responded with the formation of a new political party, Lok Shakti, which appeared to be mostly a vehicle for himself. There followed the establishment of a non-party organisation, Rashtriya Navanirmana Vedike, for members of Janata Dal who were allied with Hegde, but could not leave the party without breaking rules against defections. J.H. Patel, a *Lingayat* who became Chief Minister when Deve Gowda went to Delhi, was caught in the middle, trying to hold the party together.

Hegde decided to join in alliance with the Hindu nationalist BJP in the General Election of 1998. In the meantime, Patel and Deve Gowda had become enemical. Another division in the Janata Dal occurred before the General Election of 1999, when the party split into Janata Dal (U), of which Patel was the leader, and Janata Dal (S), led by Deve Gowda. Janata Dal (U) joined the electoral alliance with Lok Sakti and the BJP. Congress won the Assembly Election in Karnataka at least in part because the BJP rank and file were disheartened by the alliance with Janata Dal (U) (Gould, 2003). Not only had the party in general become discredited for its intraparty squabbles and mud-slinging, but Patel's administration had acquired the reputation of being incompetant.

In the late 1990s, the relationship which was the most important in destabilising the Janata Dal was the continuing rivalry between Deve Gowda and Hegde. Periodically Janata Dal politicians said that the party had been severely damaged with the ouster of Hegde.

Ramakrishna Hegde had built a reputation as a politician of principle and had associated himself in the early 1980s with 'value-based politics', as opposed to customary wheeling and dealing.[12] His reputation had taken a fall several times, including in 1988, when, as Chief Minister, he was accused of ordering the tapping of telephones of his partymen. He responded by stepping down from his post. Another embarrassment was the appointment of a Commision of Enquiry to investigate charges of corruption. Hegde's alliance with the BJP as the head of Lok Shakti was a disappointment to those who had trust in him as a politician with high standards. Earlier he had been critical of cultural nationalist principles of the BJP, but Hegde asserted now that under the leadership of Vajpayee the party had been moving away from extreme positions.

As a young party which was mainly associated with the person of its leader, the only hope for survival for Lok Shakti was electoral alliance with a greater party. It appears that Hegde refused to consider allying with the United Front. After Hegde died, former Prime Minister I.K. Gujral, a friend of Hegde, said that the latter had hoped to join up with the Congress Party and had turned to the BJP only when circumstances in the Congress made alliance there impossible (Prasannam, 2004). Since Hegde had spoken out against dynastic rule in political parties, observors argued that Sonia Gandhi was opposed to his reincorporation in the Congress fold.

In the late 1990s many people argued that, whatever expectations

---

12. James Manor discusses Hegde's period as Chief Minister in the early 1980s in Manor (1984).

Ramakrishna Hegde had of a desirable position at the centre by joining the BJP, his other agenda was the destruction of the Janata Dal, in revenge for his being expelled from the party. It seemed to many that more important than breaking the principled mold in which Hegde had cast himself was the destruction of the career of Dêve Gowda. H.S. Balram (1997), Resident Editor for *The Times of India* in Bangalore, stated the case in an article about Hegde's options in the run-up to the General Election:

> Hegde has already made up his mind to reject this suitor (Janata Dal). He is unable to forget the humiliation piled on him by Mr Gowda *vis-à-vis* the Dal. Rather, his main aim now is to decimate the Dal. Some Dal men, including Gowda's arch rival R.L. Jalappa, are said to be in touch with him to speed up the process. Hegde is, however, ready to reconsider his stand if Dal ditches Gowda.

The great rivalry between Deve Gowda and Ramakrishna Hegde played itself out, in 'gossip' and in print. Deve Gowda, rough-spoken and quick to anger, representative for farmers' interests, made a colorful contrast with the elegant and cultivated Hegde. Deve Gowda recognised the contrast when he told a press conference that, "having a good and cultured family background was not enough to be successful in politics. One should live amidst poor farmers, till land and tend cows and buffaloes."[13] The contrast was epitomised in the story which people told explaining Deve Gowda's dismissal of Hegde from the Janata Dal. When Hegde said in public that the latter was not fit to be Prime Minister, he elaborated on Deve Gowda's presumed deficiencies in a manner which highlighted his own wide knowledge. The dismission of Hegde, in popular renditions of the scenario, was Deve Gowda's revenge.

The well-known novelist Anantha Murthy was one of the persons who tried to arrange a reconciliation between the two men:

> [From my notes] Anantha Murthy is a friend of Ramakrishna Hegde and has been in politics himself. Hegde admits that he should not have said Deve Gowda did not know the map of India. In the meantime Deve Gowda says that Hegde, as a *Brahmin* was not

13. Anon (1998a). "UF Won't Need Cong Suppport [*sic*]: Gowda", *Deccan Herald*, 24 January.

prepared to see a dark-skinned farmer of a low caste become the Prime Minister of India. Murthy points out that this is Deve Gowda putting a personal quarrel into the discourse of the time, conflict between high caste and low caste groups.

Murthy tried to bring the two men together. He asked Hegde why he was still put off by Deve Gowda and Hegde responded that "When I put out my hand to congratulate him as Prime Minister, he did not take it." When Deve Gowda was asked about his response to Hegde, Deve Gowda replied, "But he did not come to my dinner party." Hegde reminded Murthy [when asked about the continuing conflict] that he is, when all is said and done, only a human being, capable of being hurt and offended (Interview, 8 May, 1998, Bangalore).

It may be questioned whether Ramakrishna Hegde, as a (*Havik*) *Brahmin*, was subject to notions of honour. The received wisdom is that *Brahmins* have been preoccupied with status based on caste membership, not with the more fluid status of honour associated with heroism in warfare. However, the *Havik Brahmins* I interviewed in Uttara Kannada were well familiar with honourific values, discussing with me the lexicon of honour.[14] The two local Havik Brahmin politicians I interviewed knew honour as dominance, while the emphasis of non-politicians tended to be on *mariyata* as rules of courtesy, *gaurava* as respect one earned and *mana* as inner character. G.S. Hegde Ajjibal, former MLA, journalist and confidant of Ramakrishna Hegde, was concerned to associate his friend with the moral connotations of honour, rather than 'undemocratic' dominance and plays of rivalry and revenge. Ajjibal said that supporters of Ramakrisha faulted him with being "too much concerned with his honour", for example, when he stepped down from his position as Chief Minister in 1984 and then again in 1988 (Interview, 26 December, 1997, Sirsi). Sociologist N. Jayaram, in a less sanguine frame of mind, suggested that this moral connotation was part of Hegde's construction of his image:

---

14. Interviews, among others, with Ramnath, Janata Dal member, former President of the *Mandal Panchayat*, Sirsi, 25 December, 1997; Bhat, areca nut plantation owner and Ramchander, priest, 26 December, 1997, Uttar Kannada. Thanks to Neelambar Hatti for arranging for interviews and interpreting when necessary.

> Hegde used his honour strategically in the telephone tapping case. He had instructed the police to tap the telephones of his own party-men, including Deve Gowda, and the opposition. When he was exposed, he owned up, having no way out, and resigned as Chief Minister. You made a claim when you are challenged that you are serving a moral principle. Thus you can save face, as did Hegde (Interview, 11 April, 1998, Bangalore).

As Parvati Menon (2004) observes, "these acts of resignation may not have impressed his critics, but they enhanced his status in the public perception." That Hegde was concerned with honour as more than as moral principle is suggestion in an interview he gave in New Delhi in January 1998:

> Asked if he still held rancour in his heart for the break with the UF [United Front], Mr. Hegde said he would have gradually retired from active politics once Mr. Deve Gowda became the premier, "had it not been for the arbitrary manner in which I was expelled...Then it became a question of saving my honour."

One way was to launch a party [he continued] since his followers wanted a platform (Ved, 1998).

Gopal Karanth of Institute for Social and Economic Change, Bangalore, reported that Hegde did not talk about being humiliated, not even when he was dismissed from the Janata Dal:

> Hegde did not respond by talking about how humiliated he was. He made his humiliation that of others. He made it everybodies' business by talking about how Deve Gowda was unfit to be Prime Minister, about how he couldn't speak two words of English together, how he did not know how to figure inflation...Hegde [tried to make] Deve Gowda lose his base, even among his own [*Vokkaliga*] caste....Hegde never talks about his humiliation. He let others talk about what Deve Gowda did to him. Hegde's men, not Hegde, are the ones that demand enquiries about Deve Gowda. Hegde's friends have filed suits against Deve Gowda (Interview, 9 March, 1998, Bangalore).

Observors of Deve Gowda found a more direct play on his part in the politics of rivalry and revenge. He was sometimes accused of doing '*panchayat* politics' (as when he expelled Ramakrishna Hegde) and behaving like a *palegar*. In a speech in January 1998, Hegde made much of the *palegar* image in discussing the style of politics in Janata Dal.

He was speaking on the occasion of welcoming to the Lok Shakti a former minister and president of the Bangalore City District Committee of the Janata Dal, Mr. M. Raghupathy:

> Without mentioning anyone of them by name, he said that there was no future for the Dal with a "*palegar* at the helm of affairs. There is *palegar darbar* in Karnataka." So far he had been considered to be a soft person. But he could also prove that he could strike decisively at the crucial moment. "Such a moment has arrived now. Till now I was only waiting but throwing hints."
>
> The atmosphere in the Janata Dal was stifling and leaders such as Mr. Raghupathy had felt it. It was no longer a democratic organisation with *palegarism* ruling the roost. There is one big *palegar*, he said alluding to Mr. Deve Gowda, and some small *palegars*. Like the *palegars* or chieftains of the past, who never cared for the people, the *palegars* of the Janata dal [*sic*] too were interested only about their families, friends and the sycophants around them.[15]

I asked Gopal Karanth about the meaning of '*palegar* politics'. He listed three characteristics:

1. You just insist on what you want and do not take others into consideration. You do not take into account past actions, but say what will serve your interests at a point in time. There are expressions such as a person 'walks like a *palegar*', arrogant and proud, or that a person talks like a *palegar*.
2. You use your family and kin. This we can call the dynastic aspect, but it refers to all close kin. They will be brought up with you.
3. Like Deve Gowda, you move very much within the orbit of caste. He has used caste the way few others have (Interview, 9 March, 1998, Bangalore).

When three Janata Dal ministers and three other party legislators joined the "nonpolitical" Rashtriya Navanirmana Vedike in January, 1998, they claimed that Deve Gowda had converted the party into his "personal fiefdom."[16] They engaged thereby in an implicit discourse on

15. Anon (1998b).
16. Anon (1998c).

the constituents of democratic behaviour, joining their voice in the chorus which described Deve Gowda as autocratic and dictatorial.[17] Ironically, they themselves acted to reproduce the modern politics of honour when, at the same time, they complained that in the Janata Dal they had been "humiliated."[18]

Deve Gowda's occasional outbursts of anger against the press indicated his frustration with common coverage of his speech and actions. He appeared to credit news media with blowing up incidents and details out of proportion to their importance. The *palegar* portrayal of his career in politics was at odds with his disciplined work habits and capacity for planning (Manor, 1996). The former Prime Minister's resentment may have been fueled by the relatively mild treatment given to Ramakrishna Hegde, whom the press tended to "like."[19] As he said on the campaign trail, Deva Gowda was proud of his record as Prime Minister, for what he had achieved for the nation and for his state:

> I have a sense of immense satisfaction in having fulfilled poll-eve promises, and in having resolved many vexed issues such as the Indo-Bangledesh dispute over the sharing of Ganga waters and agreements between India and Nepal on hydel power projects, that had been pending for long.[20]

Gowda campaigned saying that political parties in Karnataka had "never felt proud of him" and pointed out that parties in Punjab were not fielding a candidate against then Prime Minister Gujral as a "gesture" of "appreciation" for his coming from their state.[21] Deve Gowda had reason to believe that his rivals were out to humiliate him.

Conclusion

There are strenuous difficulties in managing competing social groups, segments and regions in the political landscape of Karnataka, as elsewhere in India. These difficulties have been accentuated in

---

17. See, for example, the comments of MLC K.B. Shanappa, Janata Dal's parliamentary board chairman, quoted in Anon (1998d).
18. Nivas (1998).
19. Sandeep Shastri argued that Hegde was "overprojected" in a generally friendly media, interview, 3 April, 1998, Bangalore.
20. Anon (1998e).
21. Ibid.

Karnataka, as elsewhere, by touchy issues of status, including preoccupation with personal honour and the desire for respect. Politicians, at either local or state levels, are not equally preoccupied and the preoccupations which exist play themselves out in different ways at varying levels of intensity.

In pointing to a complex of values and concepts in political action, I am not making an argument for a general lack of rationality among politicians. Sociologist N. Jayaram argued in an interview that there are "operational rules of the game which are limited by cultural elements in political action" (Interview, 11 April, 1998, Bangalore). He took the point of view of politics as a universal set of games. My approach is that, as far as competition among leading politicians is concerned, the rules of the game can be set according to assumptions which are specific to place, time and culture.

The management of these culturally specific interests took much time and energy in all the political parties, to greater and lesser degrees. This came out clearly in an interview with V.N. Torgal, former private secretary to the leader of the opposition in the Karnataka Legislative Council in 1998, Congressman H.K. Patil. Torgal reported that the demands on Patil were heavy in managing competition and conflict at the same time as he strove to accomplish tasks of governing and serving his constituency. Patil, he said, "works 14 hours a day and thinks only of his work" (Interview, 29 April, 1998, Hubli-Dharwad). As Congress Party politicians pointed out in the spring of 1998, Chief Minister J.H. Patel was neglecting administrative tasks in his difficult pursuit of holding his party together. Much of the electorate was not impressed by what was transpiring in Janata Dal and perceived failures of governance. The party suffered at the polls at the General Election that spring.

The issue to focus on here, however, is not so much winning and losing in elections, a necessary part of electoral politics. What we can consider are the costs of the politics of honour in terms of effective governance. In 1997-98 large efforts and reserves of energy were needed to participate in and to manage rivalries that do not seem, on the surface at least, to have had much to do with the formulation and implementation of development policy, if that was the overriding goal.

References

Anon (1998a). "UF Won't Need Cong Suppport [sic]: Gowda", *Deccan Herald*, 24 January.

———. (1998b). "Now, Hegde Sets Deadline to Dal Men", *The Hindu*, 2 January.

———. (1998c) "3 MLAs Follow Deshpande, Jigajinagi, Sarnaik", *Deccan Herald*, 21 January.

———. (1998d). "Dal Gets Another Jolt as Shanappa Joins Vedike", *The Times of India*, 5 February.

———. (1998e). "Gowda Sees Conspiracy by Congress, BJP", *The Hindu*, 10 February.

———. (1998f). "Heads and Tales—The Indian Voter: The Thumb People?", *The Times of India*, 22 February.

Balram, H.S. (1997). "Wedding Bells Ring, But Hegde Keeps Suitors Waiting", *Sunday Times of India*, 28 December.

Brass, Paul (1965). *Factional Politics in an Indian State: The Congress Party in Uttar Pradesh*. Berkeley: University of California Press.

Gould, Harold (2003). "Political Self-Destruction in Karnataka, 1999", Paul Wallace and Ramashray Roy (eds.), *India's 1999 Elections and 20th Century Politics*. New Delhi: Sage Publications, pp.94-140.

Halagi, Shanta Pawadi (1991). "Factions in the Political Parties of Karnataka", *Doctoral thesis*. Karnataka University: Department of Anthropology.

Hanchett, Suzanne (1975). "Hindu Potlatches: Ceremonial Reciprocity and Prestige in Karnataka", Helen E. Ullrich (ed.), *Competition and Modernisation in South Asia*. New Delhi: Abhinav Publications. pp.27-59.

Kohli, Atul (1990). *Democracy and Discontent: India's Growing Crisis of Governability*. Cambridge: Cambridge University Press.

Manor, James (1984). "Blurring the Lines between Parties and Social Bases: Gundu Rao and Emergence of a Janata Government in Karnataka", *Economic and Political Weekly* 19(37), 15 September. pp.1623-1632.

———. (1996). "Understanding Deve Gowda", *Economic and Political Weekly* 31(39): 2675-2678, 28 September.

Menon, Parvati (2004). "A Politician with Elan", *Frontline* (on line) 21(3).

Nivas, Gayathri (1998). "Afraid to Strike", *Deccan Herald*, 25 Janaury.

Prasannam, R. (2004). "Ramakrishna Hegde (1926-2004): A Brilliant Mind", *This Week*, 25 January.

Price, Pamela (1996). *Kingship and Political Practice in Colonial India*. Cambridge: Cambridge University Press.

———. (2005). "Ideological Elements in Political Integration in (South) India: Aspects of a Political Language", in Crispin Bates and Subho Basu (eds.), *Rethinking Indian Politics*. London: Anthem Press. pp.39-62.

Price, Pamela (2006): "Changing Meanings of Authority in Contemporary Rural India", Qualitative Sociology 29(3): 301-316, Fall.

Ramiah, P. (1998). "BJP's Stable-Govt Plea Won't Help: CM", *The Hindu*, 12 January.

Tapper, Bruce (1987). *Rivalry and Tribute: Society and Ritual in a Telugu Village in South India*. Delhi: Hindustan Publishing Company.

[illegible] can be traced [illegible] considerable [illegible]

dev[illegible] by a tandem [illegible]

posi[illegible] a movement segment of the

dem[illegible] the basis of each

proc[illegible] mainly the ego [illegible]

the [illegible] conventional paradigm and [illegible]

loca[illegible] but the voters and diverse

cast[illegible] reason of [illegible]

[illegible] three problems [illegible]

prod[illegible] already how can we have

cap[illegible] the success [illegible]

the[illegible] rates, [illegible]

scor[illegible]

expe[illegible]

challe[illegible]

speci[illegible]

5

To Be or Not to Be

Problems in Locating Women in Public Policy

DEVAKI JAIN

This paper discusses some of the problems women face in gendering public policy. It suggests that the impediments faced lie largely in the nature of women's location in the social landscape. It also suggests that despite considerable progress in the general understanding of this social landscape we now have, and despite women lobbyists' efforts at skillful strategies for a more responsive public policy, the value of these efforts have not been sufficiently recognised by policy makers. Nor have they made a significant dent on them. One may wonder whether this failure is due to our inadequate tools to enforce our voices. Knowledge is not enough. The paper elaborates on how women's collective identity can be forceful politically when backed by knowledge and gives examples of this from Karnataka. New developments in decentralisation of governance, have opened possibilities for women's agency at the local level. Paradoxically, developments at global level have the possibility of undermining this process. We can only therefore, confront this not by integrating into the existing development paradigm and attempting small changes at local level but by evolving a different development paradigm that will ensure justice for the majority of the poor and women.

Women face three problems in incorporating their concerns in public policy. Firstly, how can we have 'woman' as an exclusive category given the heterogeneity among women. Women, belong to all the classes, castes, religions, political ideologies, and cultures in society. Thus to project an identity of 'woman' as defined by feminine experience to represent a collective point of view or opinion, is a challenge. Yet a case can and has been made for taking 'woman' as a specific category (as an imaginary) on the fact that across these conventional divides, various forms of discrimination converge. Indeed it was this recognition, namely, the experience of discrimination against women across all social groups that led the pioneers on women's rights, the founding mothers of the UN's conventions, to craft the Convention on the Elimination of All Forms of Discrimination Against Women(CEDAW). The universality of discrimination against women gives them an identity across differences. But discrimination alone cannot overcome the other problems of gendering mentioned below.[1]

The second question arises from the flawed nature of inherited knowledge. Women Studies have demonstrated how knowledge of society and knowledge about women are constructed by patriarchal biases—that all knowledge is gendered.[2] A very typical example relates to women's work. What kind of work is called work, how work is valued, the measures used to determine the value of their work are all determined by the perception of women's work by society, official agencies, and men. As a result, women's work is undercounted, under-estimated and often is invisible. There are dichotomies such as public and private space[3] and hierarchies[4] embedded in language and practice. For example, the large space occupied by the majority of women workers is called 'informal' implying its secondary status to the so called formal sector. The non monetised sector is either accorded a lower value or no value compared to the monetised[5]—an approach totally invalid for a largely subsistence economy where the

---

1. Morrisson, C. and J.P. Jutting (2005). "Women's Discrimination in Developing Countries: A New Data Set for Better Policies", *World Development* 33(7): 1065-1081, July.
2. Jain, Devaki (2004). *Women's Participation in the History of Ideas: The Importance of Reconstructing Knowledge.* Bangalore: National Institute for Advanced Studies and Indian Institute of Science. February 6; Jain, Devaki (1986). "Power Through the Looking Glass of Feminism", Paper Presented in Symposium on *Gender of Power.* Netherlands: University of Leiden.
3. Jain, Devaki (2000). "PRI Impact on Private Structure (Domestic sphere): How Important is the Private Public Dichotomy: The Case of the EWRS". Seminar on *Women in Panchayati Raj.* 27-28 April. New Delhi.
4. Jain, Devaki (2001). "Valuing Women-Signals from the Ground", Opening Session for the University of Maryland broad theme: *Cultural Diversity and Universal Norms,* June 1.
5. Goldschmidt-Clermont, Luisella (1981). *Unpaid Work in the Household: A Review of Economic Evaluation Methods.* Geneva: ILO.

non monetised sector is substantial. Thus if a policy arises out of such inherited 'flawed' knowledge, women advocates would not want to participate in it. They would not like to engender it. They would like to deconstruct it or challenge it or reject it.

Thus integrating into an existing framework has problems. If the formulation of public policy, that arise out of the accepted theories and frameworks and out of given data and analysis are unacceptable to say a group, like women, or Dalits[6] then their integrating into that setup, sitting at committees or negotiating tables is surrender. In so far as we start from a premise that is inaccurate and flawed, it can lead to undesirable results. But this staying away, also has its negative effects, i.e. exclusion. This is one of the dilemmas. In the language of the feminists this is often posed as: "do we want a piece of the poisoned cake?"[7] or another way of raising the same question, "do we want to swim in the polluted stream?" Hence ideas like integrating, gendering, mainstreaming, used now in current discussions, for inclusion of women in policy making efforts do not achieve desired results.

The third problem arises out of women's unhappiness over constructing 'boxes', to contain phenomena within strict boundaries. To women, such boundaries are invalid especially where boundaries are fluid. They do not easily accept attempts at imputing a false identity and deriving judgements on that basis. If one defines the boundary of identity as women's ways of doing things it is rejected as 'essentialism'. If one suggests that waged work for women empowers them it is called 'instrumentalism'. There is a tendency, amongst the women advocates themselves to question every notion or concept which attempts an arrival at a boundary for identity fixing. I call this the '*nethi nethi* syndrome', borrowing from the *Upanishads*.

But such an over critical viewing of identity that negates any bounding, impedes the participation of women in policy as a political

6. Guru, Gopal (2002). "How Egalitarian are the Social Sciences in India?", *Economic and Political Weekly* XXXVII(51), December 14.

7. Jain, Devaki (1999). "The Role of Peoples Movement in Economics and Social Transformation", paper presented at the Opening Thematic Plenary for "Economic and Social Development", Seoul International Conference of NGOs—*The Role of NGOs in the 21st Century: Inspire, Empower, Act*. October 10-16. Seoul, Korea.

presence drawn from a collective identity. An identity tag, (based on some markings, bodily or through the experience of subordination and exclusion), is crucial for claiming rights and special attention.[8] Such a clear identity tag, which is more easily available to say Dalits, or to 'blacks' in Africa or other white nations, is difficult to forge for the woman-identity due to her presence in all these other categories with all their separate politics. Gendering public policy is intimately related to our answers to these questions.

In a book I have just completed called *Women, Development, and the UN—A Sixty-Year Quest for Equality and Justice,*[9] I have reviewed the historical struggle of women to be understood and included and given space and citizenhood on an equal basis in the international arena of justice. I found that whenever women did achieve some 'success' by breaking through the male bastions of knowledge and power, it was through strategising on collective identity as woman, as well as by inclusion of even one woman in a drafting committee. I call this strategising space a 'place of one's own'[10] or 'the women's tent'[11] While 'the place of one's own' is needed to develop self-confidence, to face the bigger world, it also made the 'outside' see the 'tent', as a separate entity. This perception perpetuates the 'Women for women by women to women syndrome', a syndrome which is excluding women not only from recasting and reordering development, but also denying the course of development to reflect the living experience of women. Policy issues are not only about women's issues. Women need a say in all issues as copartners in the development of society. Thus 'the place of ones own' can be a power house or a ghetto, or both.

The 60-year review referred to above does point to some useful directions for women's participation in social change. First, there is value

---

8. Jain, Devaki (2002). *Globalism and Localism: Negotiating Feminist Space, Rethinking Gender, Democracy and Development: Is Decentralisation a Tool for Local Ownership of an Effective Political Voice?* May 20-22. Italy: Ferrara University and Modena University.

9. Jain, Devaki (2005). *Women, Development, and the UN—A Sixty-Year Quest for Equality and Justice.* New York: Indiana University Press (to be released in August).

10. Woolf, Virginia (1977). *A Room of One's Own.* Granada (Originally published in 1929).

11. In many international conferences women organised a separate 'tent' where many activities were carried out with an autonomy not available in the genereal conference schedules.

and usefulness in bonding across differences on the identity of woman, and strategising in meaningful ways for inclusion in public affairs. Hence an organised voice represented by the women's tent, is a crucial brick in this effort. Such an inclusion is necessary for instance, if we have to stem militarisation. Then women's tent can also be a peace tent.

Secondly, we need knowledge that delineates concealed details regarding differences within households and families, between the sexes, and in the various processes of reproduction, production, exchange. We may call this mapping the social and economic location of women in the above landscapes. Knowing can be a first step.

Thirdly, power claimed through some semblance of a collective identity, a United Stand Power or flag. There has been much discussion on this issue,[12] of building a maintainable unity, a united stand. This continues to be a quest. However, it is suggested here that it is increasingly being argued that participation in leadership, in formal politics,[13] can provide the turning point. Bonding across difference on the identity of woman, and strategising for inclusion as a collective voice can redress all aspects of gender derived discrimination: whether it is the demeaning gaze, the mind set; the stereotypical perceptions of women's roles and capabilities, or the embedded discriminatory practices—all these are linked elements of gender relations. The recent conference in New York called Beijing+10[14] revealed again the continuing disjunction between the reality on the ground and the sense of progress created by the 'visibility'[15] level, achieved by gendered analysis.

This disjunction can be seen in two opposite trajectories relating to women and development. The first trajectory is the emergence of a

---

12. Longino, Helen E. (1993). "Feminist Standpoint Theory and the Problems of Knowledge", *Signs* 19(1): 201-212. Autumn.

13. UN Economic and Social Council (2000). *Assessment of the Implementation of the System-Wide Medium-Term Plan for the Advancement of Women 1996-2001; Report of the Secretary-General Commission on the Status of Women.* Forty-Fourth session. 28 February–2 March, 2000; *Report of the Fourth World Conference on Women.* 4-15 September 1995. Beijing; "Including the Agenda, the Beijing Declaration and the Platform for Action" (Extract), in *The United Nations and the Advancement of Women*, pp.649-735.

14. *Commission on the Status of Women.* Forty-Ninth session. New York. 28 Feb.-11 March 2005.

15. Jain, Devaki (2005). "Spaces and Hopes", *The Hindu*, April 3.

strong political presence in the national and international scene of the women's movement. There is now a widespread consciousness of the necessity of engaging in gendered analysis that recognises both difference and inequality and their implications for development design. The other trajectory reveals that the situation on the ground for many women, especially those living in poverty and in conflict-ridden situations, seems to have worsened, despite the fact that it has been addressed specifically by both the state and development thought.

The question that arises then is, why does this disjunction exist after decades of what appears to be a vibrant and ostensibly effective partnership between policy makers and the women's movement? How much of the oppositional trajectories can be attributed to the external atmospherics of global power politics and its attendant economics? How much can be attributed to other factors, such as the style of functioning and priorities of the women's movement or its experience of the gendered institutional architecture of governance?

Two examples from Karnataka of gendering policy will be discussed to illustrate these problems—the problem of differences between women, need not be a hindrance; one can address the common experience of discrimination and inequality by women as a group. We can build adequate knowledge of the social embeddedness of gender roles then intervene in policy by studying the impact of gender insensitive formulations and identifying areas where interventions are possible.

The first is drawn from an attempt made in Karnataka to *Integrate Women's Interest into a State Five-Year Plan (1983).*[16]

Before we discuss the actual study it is pertinent to recall the tremendous advances made in understanding women's work. Without this background knowledge one would not have been able to evaluate any policy or programme.

The field of women's work became one of the major research domains both nationally and internationally. It was one of the most

---

16. *Integrating Women's Interests into State Five-Year Plan*, submitted to the Ministry of Social Welfare, Govt. of India, September 1984; used in an article by Krishnaswamy, K.S. and Shashi Rajagopal. "Women in Employment: A Micro Study in Karnataka", based on the ISST Bangalore Report, in Devaki Jain and Nirmala Banerjee (ed.) (1985). *Tyranny of the Household-Investigative Essays on Women's Work, for the Workshop Women in Poverty*. New Delhi: Shakti Books.

creative pursuits, influencing international organisations like the ILO. This focus helped to underline the ground realities in the developing countries. Women's movement then began to address the core issue of survival security for the principal defender of the family, namely, the woman. This generated discussion on issues such as measurement and inclusion of invisible unpaid work of rural women work, discrimination in wages, job security and revaluing what was called the 'informal' sector.

This new research about women as workers entered the development discourse. They looked at practices of national data collecting agencies that list women engaged in domestic work as unemployed. Concern and analysis about unequal wages, discrimination of women in the workplace, women's double burden of work for wages and work at home, the role that the tasks women perform to make possible other members' involvement in marketable production or service, and the absence of social security for women who perform unpaid labour at home. From a more narrow and focused approach on women's status *vis-à-vis* men, this research broadened the scope of investigation to look at the broader implications of global and national economic, political, and social changes and their impact on women's lives in their entirety.

The study was initiated in the 1980s by Institute of Social Studies Trust (ISST) partly, because of the impetus of the overall 'ideology' that was developed in international fora, of bringing women into development; and partly due to our interest in finding ways to enable women move out of poverty. It should be recalled that it was around 1970s and 1980s that women's studies and women's advocacy were emerging as major players in the struggle for women's equality. There was now a recognition that the 'household' needed to be broken open—as it was not as believed, a 'benign' shelter for all its inhabitants.[17]

---

17. Jain, Devaki and Nirmala Banerjee (eds.) (1985). "The Household Trap: Report on a Field Survey of Female Activity Patterns", in *Tyranny of the Household*. New Delhi: Vikas, pp.215-246; Folbre, Nancy (1994). *Who Pays for the Kids? Gender and the Structures of Constraint*. New York: Routledge.

Individuals within households had highly disparate locations in power, apart from inequalities in occupations, health and education. This disparity amongst individuals seemed to be more enlarged the lower one went down in the asset/income scale. Inspired by the international efforts at documenting the disparate impact of development between men and women, the study focused on examining the reach of the anti-poverty programmes on women. What emerged was that the household was not benign and definitely not a level playing field for men and women. In the poor households women had a different source of income from men. The study came up with the idea that women within poverty households should be independently identified and reached out to, with anti-poverty programmes such as Integrated Rural Development Programme (IRDP). We found setting a target for women within such programmes was flawed on many counts, not the least by inappropriate development offers and false reporting by functionaries.

This was further corroborated during the process of preparing a report for the Karnataka State Planning Board called District Level Planning for Social Development.[18] For the report District Level Studies were commissioned—one from a backward district i.e. Gulbarga and one advanced i.e. Dakshina Kannada. Achieving a target of covering couples of reproductive age with contraceptive services was irrelevant in Dakshina Kannada (a district in Karnataka's west coast, known for advancement in social indicators) where the fertility rate had already reached one, and in some villages less than one, but the fund allocated to the district continued to be allocated only for that purpose and when its irrelevance was brought out nothing could be done to shift the funds from limiting contraception to more advanced healthcare.[19]

Planned development appeared, as it does even now, as blind rubber stamping of schemes. An even more significant lesson was, that the methodology being used did not reach poor men either. The process was completely flawed for men and women amongst the poor

---

18. District Level Planning for Social Development, Devaki Jain, Chairperson of Sub Committee, Karnataka State Planning Board (1994), Government of Karnataka.

19. Report from Dakshina Kannada by Shalini Rajaneesh, IAS.

or deprived. It transpires that method adopted for stimulating development was critical, even superceded the task of gendering or integrating women into development.

The second is a project undertaken in Karnataka by the World Bank[20] to improve the quality of the cocoon in the sericulture industry. The project did not use the available knowledge about women's work.

Sericulture was one of the dominant land based activities in Karnataka and the perception of the policy designers was that women were not an issue in this project. It was perceived that women were basically using thrown away cocoons which had holes in them to make garlands. They were seen as not engaged in the basic chain of production and the sale of cocoons. An actual investigation that sought to break down tasks in the chain of production revealed that while mulberry was grown by the farmers, the men, it was women who not only picked the leaves but looked after the trays in which the silk worms were nursed or nurtured. The silk worms are usually kept in trays called *chandrikes* in shelves inside the home and have to be fed mulberry leaves every three hours just like a child, and the offal has to be removed as frequently so that they do not get diseased. Women in the strong sericulture farming areas complained that not only were their houses completely cramped with silk worms leaving hardly any place for the kitchen or their children, but the silk worm was more demanding than the child as it had a compulsive demand for leaves every three hours. Thus they were awake most of the night and most of them had chronic illnesses due to the suffocating atmosphere in the hut and the unremitting labour of cocoon rearing.

Despite their being the main rearers of worms, the women were not at all brought into the project. They were not given the training on better rearing on what were the special characteristics of feeding and health for the new worms that were introduced, they did not receive information about the new fodder; not shown how to upgrade the quality of the yarn they spent time on. Thus women's contribution

---

20. Institute of Social Studies Trust (ISST) (1982). *Assessment of Women's Roles—The Karnataka Sericulture Development Project*. Task Force on Sericulture for a World Bank funded project. Government of Karnataka.

to the process of silk manufacture was unrecognised with consequences for policy. It appears that the old Ester Boserup[21] story of the 1970s where she bemoans the non-recognition of women as farmers continues.[22]

As a result of lobbying both in Washington and in Karnataka with the government, a task force on sericulture was set up by the Government of Karnataka with the principal secretary of agriculture as its chair. All the relevant agencies were around the table and the meeting was to show that there needs to be greater inclusion of women as workers in the sericulture development programmes. It was found that this classical invisibility of women workers, especially when the productive work is within the home had deprived them of being engaged in the training for improved rearing practices as well as marketing.

There was no hostel accommodation for women at the Sericulture Training Institute, a state government institution. A proposal was made, by the task force, to build a women's hostel using another government scheme called 'Hostels for working women'. However, the task force neither sustained itself nor did it make for any transformation in the lives and concerns of women in the sericulture project.

A similar experience is recorded of the matching study that ISST took up with the Tasar[23] industry in Maharashtra. Again women were major workers but unrecognised and nothing that was done. The report funded by the Swiss Development Corporation tried to change this perception but it had no impact. The studies undertaken by ISST in various parts of India, and in Karnataka.[24] presented information on women's productive roles, and argued that the projects were losing

---

21. Boserup, Ester (1999). *My Professional Life and Publications* 1929-1998, Copenhagen Press.
22. Jain, Devaki (2003). "Are We Knowledge Proof? Development as Waste". Speech delivered at *Lovraj Kumar Memorial Lecture*. 26 September. New Delhi (Reprinted in *Wastelands News* 19(1): 19-30, August-October 2003. New Delhi: Society for Promotion of Wastelands Development
23. ISST (1982). *Interstate Tasar Project*. Report on a Field Survey: Chandrapur District of Maharashtra, .
24. ISST (1989). *Impact of Sericulture Pilot Project in Karnataka: An Evaluation.*

out on success by not recognising this. While this resulted in gendered analysis, it did not change the project.

Some new opportunities are emerging in India, and more strongly in Karnataka. These may help us incorporate the lessons learnt from history, mentioned earlier in this essay. To reiterate, we had talked of: i) the usefulness and value of bonding across difference on the identity of woman, and strategising for inclusion; ii) the need for knowledge about women's various productive and other roles and their location within household, families and community and iii) power claimed through a collective identity.

An aspect of the Karnataka landscape of governance and development, which offers some niches, some conduits for affirming these views is the long standing, and politically well supported decentralised management of development, especially the economic and social justice agendas.

For example as far back as in 1994-95, Karnataka's State Planning Board (earlier called Economic Planning Council (EPC)) set up two subgroups in 1994, one for District Level Planning for Employment, and other for District Level Planning for Social Development. The main task of the subgroup was to provide effective social and economic security to the poor, improve the quality of administering these services, all at the district and subdistrict level of accountability. Interestingly, in 2005, the Planning Commission has set up an Expert Group, to draw up guidelines for the States on what they call grassroot planning for development, and the thrust is to reduce if not efface the state dictated schemes, the pre-packaged development bundles that are handed out, and leave planning to local communities to design the use of untied funds.

The subgroup working with secretaries to government of each sector and some CEOs or Chief Secretaries of Districts as they were called at the time, were able to rationalise the 75 schemes into 15 bundles. And suggested that instead of having 15 schemes coming out of 15 departments even these could be bundled into a Social Development Service, as one sector and the fund could be used for 'Provisioning of social development services to the poor', with the functionaries attached to the service coming under one nomenclature called social development services providers. Thus the departmental lines would be liquefied, and the multiple schemes, would be consolidated without losing the overall intention.

One of the suggestions made by the subgroup was that there should be social mapping of the state, to show variations in human development indices between districts in order to identify gaps in performance and to spot interdistrict variations, was not implemented. However this compliance came later. During 1995–1997, Karnataka developed a Human Development Report that put together district level indicators and indices (*Human Development in Karnataka 1999*, Planning Department, Government of Karnataka, 1999)—a first in State Level Human Development Reports in India.

In neither of the illustrations from Karnataka, given above did this opportunity for intervention yield a clear 'tool' to tell us what to do and how to intervene. However, there is now, as we write this article an opportunity to engage with politcal power due to the clearer, more legally and politically ordained devolution of economic planning power, and funds to the locally elected bodies, in Karnataka.

Significant changes have been brought about in the State fiscal 2005-06 policy (embodied in the State Budget). State sector schemes pertaining to the 29 subjects in Schedule XI of the 73rd amendment, have been merged in the district sector schemes to be implemented by the *panchayat* institutions. From 1st April 2005 about Rs. 3500 crore have been thus devolved to *panchayat* institutions at *grama*, *taluka* and *zila* levels. The Departments have been asked to amend and issue afresh all government orders, notifications, circulars, etc., in accordance with these charges.

Most importantly some of the negative features in administration have also been removed. Departments are directed not to establish parallel bodies which were scuttling devolution intended by the 73rd amendment. Existing parallel bodies are to be now reconstituted under the chairmanship of the *adhyaksha* of the *Zila Parishad*. Besides, World Bank or external aided projects are to be implemented through PRIs only.

Right from the beginning the Ramakrishna Hegde Government in Karnataka, in collaboration with Abdul Nazir Sab, the Minister for

Rural Development brought in legislation not only to set up elected local councils but also reservation for women. Women elected to Councils have been invited to meetings held by women's organisations and attempts are made to give them a collective identity and give them a sense of knowledge based confidence. As the *panchayati raj* movement grew and broadened with the introduction of the 73rd and 74th amendments by the then Prime Minister Rajiv Gandhi, the Singamma Sreenivasan Foundation, for example, got even more deeply engaged in strengthening those women who had been elected to serve on these councils.

One of the first initiatives that they took was to bring them under one organisation namely, "An Association of Elected Women Representatives". While this may look baffling since the representatives come from different parties, in Karnataka it was found that women were willing to join an association of themselves across party lines. They seemed to need that collective strength in order to generate the self confidence to bring voice into the meeting. The women's collectives and collectivities also have an additional glint, namely, they are united across class, where poor and non-poor women engage in issues which impact women like domestic violence or water, or reproductive health, especially in urban slums and rural areas.

Using the collectives especially at the level of *gram panchayats,* the Foundation then built three other programmes with these groups— The Foundation then initiated similar projects in three of the other southern states, Kerala, Andhra Pradesh and Tamil Nadu and is now co-ordinating a network of agencies in these four states all of which are engaged in creating collectivities of these elected women and enabling them to strengthen their technical skills as well as their political presence in the local self government institutions.

Rather than 'train' them they have been formed into groups and these groups engage with themselves to create their own space, debate among themselves and devise programmes instead of being in mixed councils. Women's capability for collective action, and to form collectivities are transforming many programmes, processes and outcomes.

Currently, many women's organisations are partnering with State governments, to strengthen the capability of women elected to these Local Self Governments to participate if not lead development in their areas. For example, Singamma Sreenivasan Foundation has made a novel endeavour, to enable Elective Women Representatives (EWRs) to construct budgets, such that the interest of women and other subordinated groups is safeguarded. It is not just a programme to raise awareness about budget amongst local women politicians but to enable women to direct the economy from a space available to them. This helps them to understand, participate and transform local budgets.

The design of this "effective participation" has been enabled by collaboration with Janaagraha—an urban NGO which uses three cornered stakeholders meeting—namely, the civil servant who is the commissioner of the municipality, the ward committee and the elected corporators to have a transparent process of understanding and influencing revenue collection and expenditures and monitoring outcomes. This method has been tried in two municipalities—Mysore and Tumkur. The municipalities have changed their budget allocations as a result of collective lobbying by the elected women corporators across party lines. Similar experience has been found in two other pockets of Karnataka—Bijapur and Bellary.

Another project that they were exposed to, was to use their kitchen gardens for growing medicinal plants. This has now caught the imagination of the *gram panchayats* and at least four districts will be engaged in a movement for environment security, health security and livelihood security through the growing of medicinal plants.

Today, the situation and character of the various actors in governance have shifted quite dramatically and in significant ways. The State is receding from its earlier role as being responsible to the citizens for their well-being especially provisioning of basic securities. Civil society including the women's movement is becoming stronger on the one hand but also paradoxically more fragmented. International configurations of power are changing, with the UN's influence receding and the other world organisations like World Bank and other multilaterals like the WTO occupying centre stage. The market economy, signified by the corporates are playing a larger role in national and international governance than before, including the provisioning of public goods. There is also a return to conservative politics, and various forms of fundamentalism, across the globe.

Simultaneously there are the usual paradoxes in women's domain. There is an increase in the political participation of women in governance, especially at the local level. There is an increase in the capabilities and power of the women's movement, in knowledge and organisational capacities in informal economy as workers and traders and to contest violence against women. There is a shift in the nature of employment opportunities. There is increasing absorption of female labour into the new opportunities for earning income like in export processing and simultaneously a decline in the opportunities for men. This arises because of the nature of the growth poles and the nature of the organisation of production and trade. Women are on the move, selling either their bodies or their time into earning income for their families. The UN report on women and development for the year 2004[25] shows how the largest group or proportion of workers uncovered by any protection are women, and women migrants. The demand for women as workers in the flesh trade has made the flow of women across borders jump by leaps and bounds. The value of the flesh trade is now greater than the value of the trade in narcotics.

At the very beginning, women's quest was for equality or for overpowering, if not efface inequality. The strategy of leveling the playing fields by bringing in laws, introducing the power of rights, and finding ways to move women out of what looked like disadvantaged positions seemed all right for several decades. But it was clearly not enough. There was deep, widespread, unimaginable, and invisible discrimination. The women's movement responded to this by making inequality visible but that did not take care of the ignorance and non-recognition of women's value as citizens, workers and providers. Their contribution to society is equal if not even richer in value than men. So the movement generated new knowledge to show the role of women in development—again with the expectation that revealing

25. Department of Economic and Social Affairs (DAW) (2004). *World Survey on the Role of Women in Development—Women and International Migration*. New York: UN. 2005.

truth would lead to women's equality with men. But that strategy still disabled them because they had no voice in the determination of their lives and its road map. Thus, the notion of equal participation, of equal power, of leadership was worked into the notions of ways to redress inequality.

What we have seen is that while knowledge has increased and been funelled to the policy spaces, the advice of women, their leadership in directing public policy has not happened to a corresponding extent. The old method of 'integrating' through women only packages, mainly social development package schemes for women continues.

The revelatory aspect of this story can be summarised in the importance of space not only in funds but at the level of the intellect, for the excluded to claim their rights. Decentralisation with a quota of $1/3^{rd}$ seats of women has opened a new gateway in India and especially in Karnataka. But it is not enough.

The first need is to reconsider the paradigm of development itself, the identification of the engines of growth. Instead of seeing the poor as a target group who need special ladders within a framework of economic development, enabling them to become economic and political agents could itself become the engine of growth. Thus, from a 'trickle down,' or social safety net approach, it would be useful to look at what can be called the 'bubbling up' theory of growth. This alternative theory argues that putting incomes and political power in the hands of the poor could generate the demand and the voice that would direct development. The purchasing power and the choices of the poor could direct the economy to a pro-poor or poverty-reducing economy. The review of the past seems to suggest some dramatic reversal of the current theories of where the engine of growth lies if the interest is in poverty eradication.[26]

Mahatma Gandhi in fact had designed such a theory and a proposal for its practice. To some extent it could even be said that such a theory is close to, though not the same as, Keynes's theory of

---

26. Jain, Devaki (2003). "Enabling Reduction of Poverty and Inequality in South Asia", in *Population and Poverty: Achieving Equity, Equality and Sustainability*. New York: UNFPA, pp.99-100.

stimulating an economy by generating effective demand. Here the further detailing is Whose effective demand? Whose purchasing power? Gandhi's talisman, his test for action, was this: "Whenever you are in doubt, or when the self becomes too much with you, apply the following test: Recall the face of the poorest and the weakest man/woman whom you may have seen and ask yourself if the step you contemplate is going to be of any use to him."[27]

A major fault line that runs through narrations of history and their knowledge base—whether it is political, economic, or social history, is the failure to take note of, to understand and respect and absorb, women's ideational and intellectual skills and outputs in the area of theoretical and analytical knowledge. While some of the values emerging from the understanding of poverty, inequality, discrimination, conflict resolution, deepening participation, method, politics that this interaction or partnership generated has been applied or followed upon belatedly, recognition of the intellectual and leadership powers of women has remained in the ghettos. The minds of men have not changed.

And for that to happen, it seems that it is necessary to recast the development framework, to come out with a treatise, a theoretically stand alone development model which satisfies the external world changes and yet women's quest. The movement did some of this 20 years ago, at Nairobi, through the Development Alternatives with Women for a New Era (DAWN), the third world network.[28] But another such framework is needed now and it can be done if women put their minds together. Women's brilliant struggles, need to be treated as a BODY of knowledge, chiseled into theory, into an intellectual challenge to what 'is' i.e. the currently dominant ideas for national and international advancement. The importance of an intellectual theoretical construct out of the ground experience, which can claim space in the world of theoretical discourse, cannot be

---

27. Jain, Devaki (1996). *Minds, Bodies and Exemplars: Reflections at Beijing and Beyond.* New Delhi: British Council. p.8.

28. *The Bangalore Report: A Process for Nairobi* at Development Alternatives with Women for a New Era. New Delhi: Institute of Social Studies Trust. 1984.

minimised. A new *Das Kapital* or *Wealth of Nations,* is the only bomb that can explode the patriarchal mind set and exclusion of the real agency of women in public policy.

Part II

Civil Society and Governance

6

Conceptualising NGO-State Relations in Karnataka

Conflict and Collaboration Amidst Organisational Diversity

NEEMA KUDVA

Across post-Independence India, including Karnataka, NGOs rose to prominence in the early 1980s. Since then, much of the NGO literature, regardless of which end of the political spectrum it comes from, legitimises (or attacks) NGO activity on two axes: the economic and the political. Claims are made (or countered) of NGO effectiveness and efficiency at providing relief and social services compared to the state or the market, and of their ability to initiate and support positive political and social change through their value-driven, community-based practice. Relatedly, NGO practices—particularly those rooted in organising communities—are read as either shaping opposition in this current era of globalisation, or as eliciting support for state and elite led models of development.

The debates on the role and effectiveness of NGOs continue, even as several commentators have pointed out that the sector, though large, is still small compared to the Indian state in terms of the amount of funding and support it brings to addressing development issues.[1] Equally important is the fact that the majority of Indian NGOs tend to be small, with annual budgets that are below Rs. 500,000 per year. For many observers, the quality of NGO impacts in the face of pervasive poverty are captured in Sheldon Annis' (1988: 209-218) frequently quoted comments on how small-scale can be synonymous

---

Over the years several people have provided useful comments and criticism on this work; most recently I would like to thank James Manor, D. Rajasekhar and Kripa Anathpur for their comments at the Bangalore conference.

1. Rajesh Tandon estimated the financial outlay for the entire voluntary sector (NGOs are a subset) as being Rs. 160 billion for the year 1999-2000. Direct funding and support received through bilateral and multilateral donors is left out of this calculation (Planning Commission, 2002: 40-41).

with insignificance, low-cost can simply mean underfunded and of low-quality, and political independence can signify powerlessness. Despite these reservations, observers seem to be in agreement that the growing NGO sector does have an impact and is becoming increasingly diverse. This diversity reflects not just regional differences and variation between State governments but also the influence of donors and the need for NGOs to demonstrate success.

This paper maps the organisational diversity of the NGO sector in Karnataka, a "middle order state" (Vyasulu, 1995), and demonstrates that conceptualising NGO actions *vis-à-vis* the state dichotomously—either as a close collaboration or as a conflictual, oppositional force—is problematic. The federalist structure of the Indian state provides numerous points of contact for NGOs. Bring that together with the interests of a diverse group of organisations, and we find that NGO relations with the state are best characterised as marked by uneasiness. Individual organisations are often simultaneously involved in collaborative and conflictual relations with the state and walk a thin line between establishing pragmatic partnerships even as they acknowledge the need to keep some critical distance from the state. The ability of NGOs to influence development outcomes then turns on how effectively they can negotiate this uneasiness while keeping their commitments and remaining accountable to the communities they work with.

A brief description of how we conceptualise NGO-state relations follows this introduction. The state's positions as regulator, funder and political force at multiple levels, provides various points of contact that allow several possibilities for conflict and collaboration with NGOs. The second section of the paper maps the NGO sector in Karnataka, which closely follows all-India patterns with some significant differences. One important difference being the active involvement of the state in the initiation of a range of NGOs along with the support of external donors and corporate entities. This section also describes NGO-state contact in some cases to illustrate the coexistence of collaborative and conflictual relations.[2] The paper concludes by making the point that capturing the organisational

2. The word "State" refers to an administrative unit, 28 (along with 7 Union Territories) of which make the Indian Union, while "state" refers to the abstract concept of a governing entity for any territory.

diversity of the NGO sector, and understanding the uneasy, complicated nature of NGO-State relations are key to understanding the possibilities that exist for a pragmatic, progressive NGO politics.

Situating NGOs and the State

The NGOs this paper is concerned with, work on development issues that in some manner, reduce poverty and have an impact on the livelihoods of those who are poor and marginalised.[3] It is estimated that there are between 20,000-30,000 such NGOs in India: some of these are voluntary in nature, others are membership-based, but most have employed staff. NGO actions are best understood through an organisational typology that includes 'issue/sector base' and 'modes of practice' where the issues may include poverty reduction, literacy, empowerment, infrastructure, health, child labour, land rights, or housing, and modes of practice span the range from service delivery, conscientisation and awareness building, to support and advocacy work. These issues are articulated in the context of the needs of particular 'target groups'—communities demarcated by various parameters including income, gender, age, occupation and caste—and often within 'spatial boundaries' as defined by the issues with which the NGOs engage (watershed development, forest management or resettlement for example) or by the scale of the place where they work (a village, district, region, or state). Figure 6.1 lays out this typology. It is important to emphasise that many NGOs work across sectors, simultaneously engage in different modes of practice, and work with target groups in different spatial boundaries, even as many change sectoral emphasis and modes of practice over time in the interest of organisational survival and/or effectiveness.

As mentioned earlier NGO activity is legitimised and critiqued on its claims of efficiency and effectiveness in both the economic and political spheres. The growing body of literature reveals a complicated, messy picture of organisations adjacent to, between and intersected by state, donor, market and civil society actors, with complex networks and relationships that span boundaries. Studies have shown that NGO claims to economic efficiency need to be tempered: they are not as

3. Definitions and categorisation have been a preoccupation of the NGO literature, see Vakil (1997).

cost-efficient or innovative, lack broadness of reach, rarely target as deeply as presumed or claimed, and tend not to locate in areas of highest poverty.[4] Political claims of supporting social justice and democratisation are as difficult to pin down. In organisations that achieve some measure of success—however defined—a complex picture emerges of participatory management and organisational practices in the context of progressive legislation and a strong engaged state.[5] As important are issues of NGO capability, representativeness, and accountability and how these in turn, shape an organisation's ability to effectively reach and work with people, in particular, those who are marginalised.

Figure 6.1

NGO Typology

	Issue/Sector	*Modes of Practice*
Target Group		
Spatial Boundaries		

In contrast to theorising on NGOs, which is still in its early phases, the Indian state, towering as it does over society, has been theorised and understood in many ways. To most NGOs the "monolithic, rent-seeking, turf-maximising" developmentalist state would seem to be a multi-headed, multi-armed giant that asserts authority even as it often loses track of what its various entities are doing. As important is the simultaneous movement of the post-liberalisation Indian state towards the market and political decentralisation. Understanding the nature of the state, however, is crucial to NGO effectiveness. It is important to grasp three aspects of state actions on NGOs: as a 'regulator' the state seeks to control NGOs and make them accountable to it by imposing registration, monitoring, and financial reporting requirements; as a 'funder' the

4. For more on these issues see, Tendler (1987), Ridell and Robinson (1992), Farrington and Bebbington with Wellard and Lewis (1993), Zaidi (1999), Edwards and Hulme (1996), Hulme and Edwards (1997), Fruttero and Gauri (2005), Gauri and Fruttero (2005).

5. For more on these issues see, Biekart (1999), Kamat (2002), Kudva (2001, 2005), Mohan (2002), Webster (2002).

state seeks to selectively support and collaborate with groups that can elicit people's participation and make government programmes more efficient and effective. For the state as 'political entity' however, a strong community-based NGO is a potential threat to the local power structure and it can expect to have a contentious relationship with both a cadre-based political party and other state functionaries. These aspects of state action take place at multiple levels.

Figure 6.2

Operationalising the State

Administrative Jurisdiction	*Actions on NGOs*		
	Regulator	*Funder*	*Political Entity*
Central			
State			
District			
Taluk/Village			

Yet, for many NGOs their relations with the state are best characterised through their relationships with individual state functionaries, the 'officials' who stand as proxies for the state. Reflecting this widely held view, Aloysius Fernandes (2004: 26-31) categorised three levels of state officials. Level A officials are senior representatives of government, administrators from the IAS, the IFS, and the State Administrative Cadres, who head programmes and projects, and are often "entreprenuerial, willing to listen and learn and to function in a situation that is continuously evolving...where such officials lead the government department, the synergy grows between Government and NGOs." Level B officers are drawn from the various line departments who visit the field rarely but maintain supervisory powers over projects and programmes. "The willingness and often the ability of officers at level B to take risks, decisions, and to manage staff diminish sharply...by and large officials at this level are uncomfortable with NGOs; this results in lack of mutual trust." Level C officials are those who are the interface between citizens and the state. They "normally relate well with NGO staff" one reason being that NGOs provide these officials "with some degree of support in terms of transport, stay and achieving targets given to them under different government programmes. Staff at this level, however, have little opportunity to upgrade their skills; besides there is no space for them to even consider innovative strategies" (Fernandes, 2004: 29-31).

Clearly, NGOs negotiate a crowded, complex arena of actors and institutions with particular interests and ideologies. While regulatory functions imposed through registration and reporting requirements tend to be concentrated at the Central level, the state as funder and political entity exists at all levels from the Centre down, particularly in States such as Karnataka where *Panchayati Raj* has (arguably) been in place for almost two decades. As important is the variability of NGO-state interactions not only because state-society relations are in flux but also because state officials, especially at level A, are regularly moved.

While the burdens imposed by the regulatory framework, particularly on small, community-based rural groups, are seen as inimical to good NGO-state relations,[6] another important factor in NGO-state relations in post-liberalisation India is the expanding role of the state as funder. This expansion is best illustrated by the growth in the Central Government initiated and funded trust, Council for Advancement of People's Action and Rural Technology's (CAPART) funding portfolio from over Rs. 545 million for about 4,000 NGOs in 1993-94, to about Rs. 3 billion to fund over 10,000 rural development NGOs working across a range of issues and with various target groups in 2002-2003.[7] Karnataka NGOs follow all-India trends in accessing state support. Table 6.1 summarises the numbers of state (Central Government)-funded NGOs across various sectors in Karnataka and India.

Even as the state seeks to control NGOs through its regulatory and funding regimes, NGO-state relations are mediated through the

---

6. A number of reports have explored problems created by government regulations, most recently see Mohanty and Singh (2001).

7. Figures for 1993-1994 from CAPART *8th Annual Report 1993-94* and for *2002-2003* from *Annual Report of the Ministry of Rural Development 2002-2003*, Government of India, Chapter 7, pp.49-55 (Also available at *http://rural.nic.in/anual0203/anualreport.htm.* Accessed April 2004).

Table 6.1

State Funded NGO Distribution by Sector, Karnataka and India, February 2004—June 2005[1]

	Rural Development Development	*Human Resource & Empowerment*	*Social Justice & Welfare*	*Health & Family*	*Environment & Forest & Sports*	*Youth Affairs Funding*	*State UT &*	*Tribal Affairs*	*NABARD*	*Others*[2]	*Total*
February 2004											
Karnataka											
Total Number	232	107	212	50	20	22	15	11		10	679
Per Cent of Total	*34*	*16*	*31*	*7*	*3*	*3*	*2*	*2*		*1*	*100*
India											
Total Number	6,467	2,074	2,944	1,038	649	589	795	262		627	15,445
Per Cent of Total	*42*	*13*	*19*	*7*	*4*	*4*	*5*	*2*		*4*	*100*
June 2005											
Karnataka											
Total Number	232	107	212	50	20	41	15	24	13	11	725
Per Cent of Total	*32*	*15*	*29*	*7*	*3*	*6*	*2*	*3*	*2*	*2*	*101*
India											
Total Number	6,541	2,074	2,944	1,343	649	853	795	509	367	722	16,797
Per Cent of Total	*39*	*12*	*18*	*8*	*3*	*5*	*5*	*3*	*2*	*4*	*99*

Notes:

1. Includes NGOs funded by the state, but does not preclude organisations receiving funding from several sources, including foreign donors.
2. "Others" includes Labour, Non-conventional Energy production, Textiles, Science and technology, Agriculture, Road Transport and Highways, Statistics and Programme Implementation in February 2004. By December 2004, it included three other categories: small-scale industries, computer & IT.
3. All percentages rounded off to nearest whole number.

Source: *NGO Database*, Planning Commission, Govt. of India, February 2004 (accessed June 2004); June 2005 (accessed August 2005)

ideological optic of the political party in power both at the Central and the State levels. The early alliance between Gandhian NGOs and the Congress fractured as the crisis of deinstitutionalisation grew, and many NGOs allied instead with the Janata Party, hoping, however, to articulate a non-party based opposition politics. Soon after the Congress returned to power and legislation was passed that enforced the separation between NGOs and party politics; by law registered NGOs may not be actively involved in party politics or have any of its members stand for election. Newer, professional, and avowedly apolitical NGOs began to occupy the public eye, and with the Constitutional Amendment of 1993 that brought back *Panchayati Raj* (PR), the relationship of NGOs to the state and to political spaces at the local level once again changed. Many NGOs support their members' attempts to contest local elections, just as they use funds from state and foreign donors to conduct training programmes in PR procedures, rules and responsibilities, for the communities they work with, and for elected representatives, particularly women who hold 33 per cent of all seats as a result of state-imposed quotas.

A NGO typology that takes into account sector, modes of action, target groups and spatial focus of the organisation, as well as operationalising the state as regulator, funder and political entity at multiple levels allows us to grasp the complexity of NGO-state relations more fully. The next section starts by mapping the evolution and organisational diversity of the Karnataka NGO sector, following which it explores the NGO-state relation briefly, through some examples (not necessarily exemplars of trends or organisational types).

Mapping the NGO Sector in Karnataka

Karnataka, like most Indian States, has considerable interdistrict variations. The two extremes within which all other districts fall, are Bidar which can be compared to Rajashthan, and Dakshina Kannada, which is closer to Kerala in terms of developmental indicators. Karnataka also suffers from an inadequate and unevenly distributed infrastructure that impacts unfavourably on economic development: there are chronic power shortages, and the railway and road network, while improving, is barely able to link the various districts. The State is dominated by its capital, Bangalore, a city that is five times larger than any other in Karnataka, and often described as the capital of India's rapidly expanding electronics, software, and biotechnology industries, as well as—using the measure of foreign funding—the NGO sector (Table 6.2-B).

Table 6.2-A

Foreign Funded Associations from FCRA Reports, Karnataka and India: 1999-2002

	1999-2000	*2000-2001*	*Per cent Increase*	*2001-2002*	*Per cent Increase*
India					
Number of Associations	13,986	14,518	*3.8*	15,618	*7.6*
Amount of Funding in Crores (INR)	3924.6	4535.5	*15.6*	4871.9	*7.4*
Karnataka					
Number of Associations	1,154	no data	-	1,192	-
Amount of Funding in Crores (INR)	411	486	*18.2*	534	*9.9*

Source: AccountAid, 2002; Benjamin, 2004.

Table 6.2-B

Top Foreign Funding Recipients by State and City, 2001-2002

	Amount of Funding in Crores (INR)	*Percentage of Total*
States		
Delhi	794.4	16.3
Tamil Nadu	695.5	14.3
Andhra Pradesh	559.6	11.5
Karnataka	534.0	11.0
All India	4,871.9	100
Cities		
Bangalore	362.2	7.4
Chennai	313.6	6.4
Mumbai	298.0	6.1

Source: AccountAid, 2002; Benjamin, 2004.

Karnataka's pluralist politics, where no one political party or mass movement has had a sustained influence, marks it as different from adjoining States. It also has smaller rural inequities (in part due to post-independence land reforms), as well as a tradition of a strong civil service, and R&D inputs into agriculture (from Mysore state). Most importantly, under the Janata Party, Karnataka was the first State to reinstitute a three-tier *Panchayati Raj* system. Karnataka's pluralist politics, its administrative traditions, and its distance from political and economic extremes make it a particularly interesting regional case.

Organisational Diversity

Karnataka has a fairly active and heterogeneous voluntary sector, though exact numbers of organisations are hard to locate.[8] The Planning Commission's NGO database indicates that the Central government funds 725 organisations (4.4 per cent of all Central Government funded NGOs) in the State, with a larger than average clustering of NGOs that work in the areas of social justice and empowerment (Table 6.1). The majority of development NGOs surveyed a decade ago tended to be district based, and varied in size from MYRADA (Mysore Resettlement and Development Agency) working across several States, with an annual estimated budget of over Rs. 200 million and a staff (permanent and temporary) of more than 400 to small action groups with no more than a couple of staff scattered across villages within a district. NGO location across districts is, however, uneven. Over 60 per cent of all Central government funded NGOs are in five districts: Bangalore Urban (26 per cent), Kolar (19.6 per cent), Tumkur (6.3 per cent), Chitradurga (5.7 per cent) and Dharwad (3.9 per cent), all of which, except for Bangalore Urban, are middle range districts. In contrast, the five poorest districts have less than 10 per cent of all Central government funded NGOs (Planning Commission, NGO Database, August 2004).

A survey of 102 social action groups and 215 activists by George Joseph (1995) provides a finer-grained picture of the NGO sector across Karnataka. Almost two-thirds of the groups had started work in the 1980s, following all-India trends closely. Three-fourth of the groups were registered as Societies, and only 15 had no registration

8. An important group of development organisations based in the voluntary sector are those linked to various *Lingayat* and *Brahmin mathas*, whose long standing and growing influence on civil society begs serious attention.

with the Home Ministry and received no foreign funds. The majority of organisations (75 per cent) claimed to have not shifted their work emphasis on community development (54 per cent), research and training (12 per cent), and health care (8 per cent).[9]

The number of development NGOs receiving foreign funds is also hard to pin down, though Government of India Foreign Contribution Regulation Act (FCRA) figures indicate that for the year 2001-2002, as many as 1,192 Karnataka based organisations (about 8 per cent of all organisations receiving funds, and about half of which are organisations with stated religious affiliations) received Rs. 53.4 million from foreign funding agencies (AccountAid, 2002; Benjamin, 2004).[10] As indicated in Tables 6.2-A and 6.2-B, Karnataka is the fourth largest recipient state of foreign funds, with organisations located in Bangalore receiving about 70 per cent of the funds. This clustering of foreign funded NGOs in Bangalore requires more investigation, though the numbers of faith-based associations (not necessarily involved in development activities as defined here) and the fact that several NGOs and networks have headquarters in the city may be part of the explanation.

The clustering of both state and foreign funded NGOs in Bangalore is also due, in part, to the location of support NGOs. Many urban NGOs provide training and managerial services to smaller NGOs and community-based groups in rural areas. Their activities, often targeted at particular sectors, help create informal networks of NGOs. Support NGOs range from well established groups like SEARCH or the Bangalore affiliate of Delhi-based Indian Social Institute (ISI), each with their own training centre and campus, to smaller organisations that operate somewhat informally and support individual organisers like the Mangalore based NGO, Development Education Society (DEEDS).

9. George Joseph's (1995) study also indicated that a third of the groups were small and worked in up to 25 villages, 23 per cent were mid-sized and worked in 26-50 villages, another 25 per cent worked in 51-100 villages and only 11 per cent were really large and worked in more than a hundred villages. Only 17 of the 102 groups worked in more than one district. This data is difficult to compare with data available on state-funded NGOs that are categorised by the size of their budgetary allocations.

10. FCRA regulations do not consider direct funds from UN agencies, m/b, or non-resident Indians (NRIs) as "foreign funds".

Karnataka is also fairly well known for its NGO networks. Dense informal networks exist in the NGO sector at all levels; line staff seem to move between NGOs (on a subregional basis) and several people in leadership positions know each other. However, Karnataka also has strong formal networks and federations of NGOs involved in rural development, and increasingly in the urban areas as well. The best known amongst these has been the State level Federation of Voluntary Organisations for Rural Development in Karnataka (FEVORD-K), which has been active at points in its long history (Ramaswamy and Prasad, 1990). District level networks also exist, as do several examples of issue specific networks such as TANK—the Tank Awareness Network in Karnataka—consisting of NGOs that work around Kolar's 4790 tanks or the Campaign against Child Labour which has brought together various groups that work on the issue of child labour in urban and rural Karnataka. A study of these formal networks indicated that NGOs saw various advantages in networks: it was a good platform to express solidarity, share experiences and expertise, and identify developmental problems (Rajasekhar and Nair, 1995). However, it was the areas of solving procedural problems and interacting with the government that were seen as crucial. Networks also provided support to new members in obtaining funds and preparing grant proposals. While the majority of formal networks seem to be donor or state-initiated, there are some that are initiated and supported by their members, such as the Tribal Joint Action Commmittee (TJA), which played a crucial role in bringing the situation of tribal communities in southern Karnataka to the attention of the state (Kudva, 2001).

The 1990s saw a rapid expansion of urban groups and initiatives that draw support from a middle- and upper-class membership pool, and illustrate the growing importance of NGOs in infrastructure-short, rapidly growing cities across Karnataka. Urban NGOs have emerged in response to specific problems, which include the lack of urban citizen engagement, the ignorance of the crucial role of media, deteriorating or nonexistent urban services, the lack of innovative educational materials for children, or the problems of low-income settlements and migrant communities. One of the first examples of a citizen led urban initiative was CIVIC in Bangalore, which started in 1992 as a loose group of interested citizens who came together with the initial support of the Max Mueller Bhavan in Bangalore to create public awareness of Bangalore's rapidly decaying urban structure; to make accountable and pressurise the concerned authorities; and, to proactively participate in the improvement of Bangalore's urban environment. It was registered as a Trust in 1996, and has stayed small. More recently, there are other examples of urban-based groups that use different strategies but are driven by a similar agenda of improving urban services and governance. These include Swaabhimana, a NGO that focuses on organising communities for effective waste collection, the Public Affairs Center that initiated the innovative idea of "holding the state to account through citizen report cards" (Paul, 2004) and Janaagraha, an organisation that does not use the NGO label, but seeks to promote citizen participation and participatory planning through a number of different programmes focused on service provision and infrastructure at the ward level, and demands for public agencies to publish accounts of their operations and finances.[11] What distinguishes some of these NGOs from an earlier generation of purely awareness-oriented or service delivery groups is their explicit focus on scaling-up their impact through selective collaborations and by influencing policy making networks.

Selective collaboration between NGOs and the state for effective implementation of government programmes is not new in Karnataka or in India, and continued through the decades when NGO-state relations were perceived as conflictual. Collaboration dates as far back as 1968 when MYRADA worked with the Government of Karnataka to resettle Tibetan refugees in three districts. The Government of Karnataka like most other State governments, has also always had a welfare component to its programmes, and funded organisations directly to establish and run hostels, schools, short-stay homes, maternal and child health programmes and so on. Karnataka NGOs are also known to have pioneered collaborations that involved the state, a bilateral or multilateral agency (m/b) and NGOs; MYRADA being the first organisation in India to implement a watershed development

---

11. For more information on the Public Affairs Centre, go to *www.pacindia.org* (accessed April, 2005); on Janaagraha, go to *www.janaagraha.org* (accessed April, 2005)

project near Gulbarga in collaboration with a bilateral donor and the state. Since then many NGOs have become partners in such collaborative projects, though several problems remain, including not being given sufficient autonomy to design or implement projects, and not being treated as an equal partner with the state and the m/b (Fernandes, 2004: 35-42).

The Government of Karnataka also has considerable experience in setting up NGOs starting in the mid-1980s.[12] The prominence in terms of size, spread and resource availability of these organisations has created additional cleavages in the sector, deepening the division between nationally and globally linked NGOs of (mostly urban) Karnataka, especially those in the larger cities like Bangalore or Mysore, and the smaller NGOs of the districts. It also feeds the shift from the service and awareness focus and inclined-to-be-oppositional organisational culture of the 1970s and 1980s, to the 'competence culture' of the newer, directed and more managerially focused NGOs of the 1990s and beyond.

Another notable recent development in the Karnataka NGO sector is the increasing visibility of corporate funded donor NGOs and trusts, and public private partnerships like the Bangalore Agenda Task Force (BATF) for supporting urban development and good governance.[13] BATF, a consortium of public agencies and elite citizens, was led by a prominent IT executive and gained a lot of attention before the current Chief Minister withdrew his support. Ian Scoones (2003: 7) describes

---

12. As a Level A bureaucrat said to me in 1995, "We are creating NGOs, and encouraging formation of groups in villages..." There are a number of GONGOs (Government Organised NGOs) in India. CAPART based in New Delhi, with regional offices across the country is perhaps the best known, though it only funds and does not implement rural development programmes. Another well-known GONGO is Mahila Samakhya, set up as a separate Trust headed by the Secretary of the Ministry of Education, and more recently, the Akshara Foundation in Bangalore, which was launched according to its Chairperson by the State government when it "saw the efficacy of the work done by Pratham [another GONGO] in the slums of Mumbai."Akshara brings in considerable corporate support (http://www.indianngos.com/issue/education/interviews/rohininilekani/fullinterview.htm Accessed, May 2005).

13. For more details on BATF, go to www.blrforward.com (accessed April 2005). See also, "CM Snubs Politicians for Opposing BATF" *Deccan Herald*, 25 February, 2001, and Solly Benjamin and Bhuvaneswari (2001). "Democracy, Inclusive Governance and Poverty in Bangalore", *Working Paper* No. 26, University of Birmingham.

the BATF as offering a "private sector led alternative to what is perceived as a poorly functioning urban authority, although many feel that as an unaccountable body it should not be the basis for providing public services in the city." Initiatives like BATF, and the policy changing agendas of the larger NGOs dominate donor attention and the public eye. But as the contours of the sector shift, a number of observers are voicing concern for the growing real and imagined distance of NGOs from the ground realities of the lives of the people they hope to support.

To summarise, Karnataka's diverse NGO sector is seeing new cleavages created by the simultaneous movement of the state towards the market and political decentralisation. As the numbers of organisations grow and agendas diversify, some organisations have grown larger, and more established. With this, norms of efficiency and measures of effectiveness are being professionalised and disseminated. Large NGOs are becoming adept at establishing and maintaining partnerships with a range of state and non-state based donors and people's groups. The situation for mid-sized and smaller groups remains more difficult. What interests us here, however, is the ways in which NGO-state relations are impacted by these changes.

Conflict and Collaboration, Uneasy NGO-State Relations

The complexity of the federalist governmental system can be seen optimistically, as providing "many points of access and many sources of remedy"; it can also be seen as providing as many sources of possible conflict. Take the case of NGOs A and B, two mid-sized organisations that work with four different tribal (*girijana*) communities in two *taluks* of Mysore district. By the late-1990s NGO-A had established active programmes in 31 of the 35 *girijana haadis* of the *taluk* where it worked. It had also built one-room schoolhouses in 17 *haadis*; the teachers that ran the nonformal education programmes were paid directly by the state but helped support meetings of NGO-initiated *haadi* level groups. Some of the schoolhouses had small herb and medicinal plant gardens, a programme started with funds from a donor and the state. At the time of my interviews in the late 1990s, over a third of the organisation's budget came from the Central Social Welfare Board, and the rest from a single foreign donor. In 15 years of operation in the area, NGO-A had taken various forms of support from the state including discounted land from the district administration to build a small campus, obtaining land for the *girijana* community from the Revenue Department, as well as funding from various programmes associated with education, health, microcredit, obtaining livestock, building housing, setting up sericulture units and so on from the Central and State governments, the Forest Department, and the Integrated Tribal Development Projects (ITDP) programme in the area. It also partnered closely with a Government-Organised Non-governmental Organisation (GONGO) that focussed on women's empowerment and awareness building in the district. Accessing state-promised entitlements was an important part of NGO-A's developmental strategy and they had positioned themselves well: they were one of the organisations in the *taluk* who were qualified to ratify documents that allowed *girijana* to claim scheduled tribe status. They also focused on organising and supporting *haadi* level groups that federated into a *taluk* level organisation and a larger district and state level apex organisation.

NGO-B, which had spun off from NGO-A, but worked in an adjoining *taluk*, was twice as large by the late 1990s, and had seen regular expansion and contraction in tune with donor funding priorities and pull-outs. It was also one of three field sites of a Bangalore-based NGO. Like NGO-A gaining access to state entitlements was an important organisational agenda, and like NGO-A, it met these priorities through educating the community about its rights, and through various service delivery functions—identifying beneficiaries for state programmes of immunisation, free lunches for children, widow benefits programmes, housing, land, or giveaways of saplings, livestock and other inputs. Both NGO-A and B closely monitored various state programmes that helped fund *girijana* communities and worked to actively access them (at my count, they were interacting with a minimum of six different departments as well as the *taluk* and district administration) though managing the various relationships often proved to be a strain on their limited resources. Supporting *girijana* leaders' entry into *panchayat* politics and helping train elected *girijana* and women representatives was also part of both NGOs' strategy to gain access to the state. Being active members of a 11-15 member NGO Network (membership varied), which they along with two larger organisations had been instrumental in initiating, helped them in these tasks.

The Network's regular quarterly meetings were important ground for sharing information on funding and other developmental practices that involved collaboration with the state. It also helped focus the NGOs' oppositional activities. It was under the banner of the Network and the Girijana People's group (the apex body of the NGO supported taluk level groups) that the NGOs became actively involved in supporting the struggle for reclaiming forests and the struggle for self-rule.

The National Front for Adivasi Self-Rule had been launched in response to the political space created by the deliberations and report of the government-established Bhuria Committee that advocated sub-state status and self-rule for tribal majority areas in the wake of the reinstitution of *Panchayati Raj*. Despite the intense debates and politics within the Karnataka NGO Network around the struggle for self-rule (which is beyond the scope of this paper) some NGOs became active supporters. The physical manifestations of the struggle at the local level, particularly the bamboo barricaded and postered *girijana haadis* demanding self-rule, and the organised processions into the forests provided a striking counterpoint to the collaborative stance of the NGOs *vis-à-vis* the state. These were accompanied by meetings and sit-ins in Mysore (the district headquarters), and in Bangalore outside the *Vidhan Soudha*. In all this time, the NGOs continued to access state support for their various programmes. Over time, a combination of factors including the very small numbers of *girijana* in Karnataka, muted the struggle for self-rule. The Network, however, barely survived the internal debates where it became clear that not all NGOs, and especially not the larger groups, were willing to negotiate this collaborative yet conflictual relation to the state.

The experiences of NGOs A and B are not unusual in Karnataka. A NGO that works with women for instance could interact with the Central and State Social Welfare Boards, with the Ministries for Rural Development, Health, and Education, with various Departments and Programmes specifically interested in particular programmes ranging from watershed development, maternal health to voter education, as well as development corporations like KARMANI, specifically set up to support women's economic development programmes. They could also be involved in agitating against government operated arrack shops in their villages at the same time. By the 1990s, several smaller regional NGOs that supported oppositional movements on an issue or at one moment in time (the agitation against Cogentrix in Mangalore for instance, or the earlier well known movement to Save the Western Ghats) often continued to interact with other state agents/agencies in their deliberate attempts to access and expand state entitlements. Understanding this simultaneous collaborative/conflictual stance opens up the possibilities for a pragmatic progressive politics built around ideals of equity and social justice. It also underscores a difference in the actions of larger and smaller groups—where smaller groups seem to escape the scrutiny to which larger groups are subject, even as they struggle more than larger groups to manage NGO-state relations and survive. Larger groups also seem to focus more on professionalisation and reach, trends that tend to negatively impact the possibility of NGO-state relations being simultaneously collaborative and conflictual.

Conclusions

This paper began by arguing that the complex nature of NGO-state relations is key to understanding the possibilities that exist for Indian NGOs to play a meaningful role in development. The conceptualisation is of an uneasy partnership between NGOs and the state, in which NGOs collaborate selectively with the state, even as they work to hold the state accountable to its poorest and most marginalised citizens is crucial in the overwhelmingly poor, yet diverse and vibrant 'noisy polity' that is India. NGOs—under certain conditions—can have an impact, even if that impact is most likely to be 'limited' and rarely as effective or possessing the reach of a strong progressive state. What is important, however, is for NGOs and their donors to understand the possibility of 'simultaneous' conflict and collaboration. This is not to say that organisations do not (or should not) stake out particular positions, either of opposition or of partnership with the state. But it does suggest that a conceptualisation of NGO-state relations based on the location and scale of the NGO and the state in physical and political space and as including a range of fluid and intersecting relationships from closely collaborative to openly conflictual and hostile, provides a more robust explanation (and vision for NGO actions) than the stark, antagonistic categories currently proposed.

References

AccountAid (2002). *Accountable Handbook, FCRA*. New Delhi. <*http://education.vsnl.com/accountaid/*> (June 2005).

Annis, Sheldon (1988). "Can Small-Scale Development be Large-Scale Policy?", in Sheldon Annis and Peter Hakim (eds.), *Direct to the Poor: Grassroots Development in Latin America*. Boulder; London: Lynne Rienner Publishers. pp.209-218.

Benjamin, Nina (2004). "Bangalore NGOs Hog Lion's Share of Foreign Funds", *Deccan Herald*, February 1.

Biekart, Kees (1999). *The Politics of Civil Society Building: European Aid Agencies and Democratic Transitions in Central America*. Utrecht and Amsterdam: International Books and the Transnational Institute.

Edwards, Michael, and David Hulme (eds.) (1996). *Beyond the Magic Bullet: NGO Performance and Accountability in the Post-Cold War World*. West Hartford, Connecticut: Kumarian Press.

Fernandes, Aloysius P. (2004). "NGOs and Government in Collaboration for Development", *MYRADA Rural Management Systems Series, Paper* 39. Bangalore: MYRADA.

Farrington, John and Anthony Bebbington with Kate Wellard and David J. Lewis (1993). *Reluctant Partners? Non-governmental Organisations, the State and Sustainable Agricultural Development*. London and New York: Routledge.

Fruttero, Anna and Varun Gauri (2005). "The Strategic Choices of NGOs: Location Decisions in Rural Bangladesh", *Journal of Development Studies* 41(5): 759-87.

Gauri, Varun and Anna Fruttero (2005). "NGOs in Bangladesh: Activities, Resources and Governance", *World Development* (forthcoming).

Hulme, David, and Michael Edwards (eds.) (1997). *NGOs, States and Donors: Too Close for Comfort?*. New York: St. Martin's Press.

Joseph, George (1995). *Social Action Groups and their Activists* (Unpublished Dissertation). Mangalore: School of Social Work.

Kamat, Sangeeta (2002). *Development Hegemony: NGOs and the State in India*. New Delhi and New York: Oxford University Press.

Kudva, Neema (2005). "Strong States, Strong NGOs", in *Social Movements in India; Poverty, Power and Politics*, edited by Raka Ray and Mary Fainsod Katzenstein. Lanham, Boulder, Oxford: Rowman and Littlefield Publishers Inc., pp.233-266.

———. (2001). *Development and Democratisation/A Contextual Critique of NGO Behavior and Practice through the Case of the Tribal Joint Action Committee in Karnataka, India* (Unpublished Dissertation). Berkeley: University of California, Department of City and Regional Planning.

———. (1996). "Uneasy Partnerships? Government-NGO Relations in India", *Working Paper* No. 673. Berkeley, CA: University of California, Institute of Urban and Regional Development.

Mohanty, Manohar and Anil Singh (2001). *Voluntarism and Government: Policy, Programme and Assistance*. New Delhi: Voluntary Action Network India (VANI).

Mohan, Giles (2002). "The Disappointments of Civil Society: The Politics of NGO Intervention in Northern Ghana", *Political Geography* 21(1): 125-54

Paul, Samuel (2004). "Holding the State to Account through Citizen Report Cards in India", Paper presented at the *Scaling up Poverty Reduction Conference* in Shanghai, May. Washington, DC: The World Bank.

Planning Commission (2004). *NGO Database*. Government of India. *<http://164.100.97.14/ngo/default.asp>*

———. (2002). *Proceedings, All-India Conference on Role of the Voluntary Sector in National Development*. New Delhi: Voluntary Action Cell, Government of India. <http://*planningcommission.nic.in/data/ngo/vac_prced.pdf*> (Accessed January 2004).

Rajasekhar, D. and Linin Nair (1995). "Networks among NGDOs in Karnataka", in Rajasekhar, D., M.K. Bhat and Neil Webster (eds.), *People Central Rural Development NGDOs and Decentralised Government*. Bangalore: ISEC, CDR, BCO and NOVIB.

Ramaswamy, S.R. and G.N.N. Prasad (1990). *An Experiment in Working Together*. Bangalore: FEVORD-K.

Riddell, Roger, and Mark A. Robinson (1992). The Impact of NGO Poverty Alleviation Projects: Results of Case-Study Evaluations. *Working Paper Series* No. 68. London: Overseas Development Institute.

Sanyal, Bishwapriya (1994). *Cooperative Autonomy: the Dialectic of State-NGOs Relationship in Developing Countries*. Geneva: International Institute for Labour Studies.

Scoones, Ian. (2003). "Making Policy in the 'New Economy'; The Case of biotechnology in Karnataka, India", *IDS Working Paper* No.196. Sussex: Institute of Development Studies, Brighton.

Tendler, Judith (1987). "Whatever Happened to Poverty Alleviation?", A Report Prepared for the Mid-Decade Review of the Ford Foundation's Livelihood, Employment and Income Generation (LIEG) Programs. Ford Foundation, New York (*mimeo*).

Vakil, Anna C. (1997). "Confronting the Classification Problem: Toward a Taxonomy of NGOs", *World Development* 25(12): 2057-70.

Vyasalu, Vinod (1995). "Management of Poverty Alleviation Programmes in Karnataka: An Overview", *Economic and Political Weekly* 30(41&42): 2635-50.

Webster, Neil (2002). "Local Organisations and Political Space in the Forests of West Bengal", in *In the Name of the Poor: Contesting Political Space for Poverty Reduction*, edited by Neil Webster and Lars Engberg-Pedersen. London and New York: Zed Books, pp.233-254.

Zaidi, Akbar, S. (1999). "NGO Failure and the Need to Bring Back the State", *Journal of International Development* 11: 259-71.

7

Communication, Democracy and Evasive Silences

A Preliminary Report on the Public Sphere in Karnataka

DATTATHREYA SUBBANARASIMHA

Introduction

Any agenda for a project of emancipation in the 21st Century must necessarily have at its core the object of democratisation. If there is one notion that has managed to survive unscathed the constantly shifting sands of the intellectual uncertainties of our times, it is perhaps the idea of democratisation (or further democratisation). In societies across the world—in the face of the continuation of post-colonial domination of the non-Western world by Western and Westernised middle classes, and in the face of the disintegration of old certainties such as Soviet communism—cultures have continuously demanded that their voices be heard. Often these voices do not appear to follow conventional modes of articulating and recording dissent, and are therefore, beyond the range of audibility of the dominant structures and classes. This has not, however, stopped the non-Western cultures from speaking out and going about their lives as they have done for centuries previously.

My objective in this paper is quite straightforward. I will look at one of the most important conditions that defines democracy as a system of self-governance. This condition is that all individuals in a society must have the right to communicate freely with any other individual or group of individuals in the society. This is the fundamental condition of all democratic processes in a society. It is thus that the idea and practice of communication is at the heart of a democratic society. Without communication, or with a truncated practice of communication, the practice of democracy can become deeply flawed. Thus the idea of communication may even be described as a *sine qua non* for the practice of democracy.

The public sphere of any society determines the space available to its democratic praxis. The public sphere is the space in which all citizens of a democratic society are assumed by democratic theory to be entitled to interact with one another as equals. They are also assumed to be entitled to contest and debate one another on any issue of concern to them. The public sphere is also assumed by democratic theory to be, more specifically, the space where the authorities of the state are monitored by an alert, rational and interested citizenry. The public sphere may thus be described as a realm of discourse and debate located between the domain of the civil society and the domain of the state. According to democratic theory, it is the sanctity of this realm that guarantees the integrity of the institutional framework of the rule of law and democratic governance.

Note here that I am describing the public sphere purely in terms of the assumptions of a democratic theory. There are of course obvious differences in the coneptualisation of a public sphere between a liberal theory of democracy on the one hand and a social democratic theory of democracy on the other. I will return to these differences at a later point in this paper. Here I wish merely to note that at the least the concept of a democratic theory provides the necessary ground on which to locate our analysis and examination of the public sphere in Karnataka.

As the title of this paper clearly indicates, this paper has no greater ambition than to be a 'preliminary' report on the public sphere in Karnataka. The reasons for this are the following: (a) The theoretical dimensions of a public sphere in Karnataka, or in India in general for that matter, have not, as yet, been elaborately worked out. It is therefore, the task of my paper to sketch out, albeit in a very rudimentary form, the elements of what such a theory might look like. (b) The historical accounts of the public sphere in Karnataka have not, as yet, been written in full. To be sure, histories of the press in particular, both in India and in Karnataka, have certainly been available for quite sometime now. But this is not the same as a history of the public sphere as the conceptual and sociological categories of a public sphere are largely missing from such specific press histories.[1] Consequently it has been the task of my paper to list many of the important elements of the history of the public sphere in Karnataka and India. (c) My accounts of the specific empirical entities that constitute the public sphere in Karnataka are by no means exhaustive; they are schematic and seek only to be representative of the diverse forms of entities that prevail in the public sphere in Karnataka today. (d) Finally, and perhaps most importantly, it is preliminary in the sense that it is not a full-fledged and exhaustive report on the public sphere itself, but, rather, a report that is more concerned with describing the preliminary stages of the necessary interrelationship between, on the one hand, the elements of the public sphere, and, on the other, the social-critical imperative of the democratisation (or further democratisation) of social institutions.

There is one important caveat I need to make before I move on to the next section of this paper. I am not, as a scholar and a thinker, beholden to the idea that a set of Western 'theoretical' texts or models is readily available to be applied in the empirical 'laboratory' of India. This was, as most of us will recognise, the dominant pattern of governmental thinking in India for over a hundred years of the latter part of British rule in India.[2] I need not emphasise the fact that in post-independent India too most social science has generally tended to follow the belief that there is a set of Western theoretical texts that one may apply in the Indian empirical setting. My own work, on the contrary, assumes that in order to meaningfully engage with and reflect on our realities, our theory has to use the humanistic terms and language of our own cognitive systems. There is no point in strictly applying or transposing theoretical texts from elsewhere to Indian realities. Against such unthinking application of theory we may hold up here Mohandas Gandhi's mode of active theorising. The one hundred volumes of Gandhi's collected works have, for instance, innumerable precious jewels on how to theorise and actualise a public sphere in India. After all, what were Gandhi's *charkha* and *khadi* if not

---

1. For histories of the Indian press over the last two centuries see: Barns, 1940; Boyce, 1988; Khare, 1964 and Natarajan, 1962.
2. One important statement of this aspect of the history of governance and social science in India may be found in Kaviraj, 1991.

the semiotic accoutrement of a distinctly Indian mode of communication?

The Sociological Theoretical Salience of the Public Sphere

As described in my previous section, the primary phenomenon that is assumed to take place in the realm of the public sphere is undistorted communication. All individuals are assumed to be able to communicate in this space both as equal public citizens and also as private individuals. So not only may they conduct business transactions, fight disputes with others, form associations, etc., they may also publicise their most intimate thoughts and feelings to any reading public of their choice. The assumption is that with such completely undistorted communication all issues and disputes among the citizens may be settled reasonably and publicly, within the legal and institutional framework of the state.

The classic liberal theories of the social contract, the legalistic institution of the state and individual rights necessarily distinguish between public and private. The public is related to the domain of the maintenance and accountability of political institutions, primarily the institutions of the state. The public sphere here thus monitors the legally constituted authorities of the state and ensures that individual citizens may continue to be able to demand compliance from such state authorities to the constitutionally agreed social contract between the parties. The private is related to the domain of civil society in general. The latter includes everything from the economy (for-profit corporate entities of all kinds), to professional associations, cultural institutions, the family, and all other social and cultural institutions that do not fall into the first category. In the classic liberal-theoretical scheme of things, it was strictly only the institutions of the state that needed to be accountable to the citizenry. The individuals, associations and institutions of civil society were to be accountable only to the specific extents to which they had obligated themselves to other citizens by private contracts; beyond this limited degree of accountability, they had, theoretically, a free reign in social life.

Social democratic theories about the public sphere are more sensitive to the historical careers of the structures of the public sphere. Thus, for instance, they do not think of the economy as being the pace-setting system for all other domains of social life. They are acutely conscious of the distortions—the invisible modes of domination that Karl Marx included under the term 'ideology'—that characterise the domain of the economy, distortions that negate claims of it being a domain of human freedom. In their democratic theories social democrats account for such distortions of the possibilities of human freedom, and reformulate their democratic theories in such a way that they may yet meaningfully pursue a democratic politics.

Moving away from this theoretical dimension now, the empirical reality of today's public spheres is a very complex one, not always, or even usually, approaching anywhere near its oft-desired perfection. There are many factors that are responsible for this failure. Among these is the fact that reading publics are almost always split in multiple ways. There may be, for instance, linguistic barriers, or literacy barriers, that do not allow for all members of the public to communicate as equal citizens. There are also more fundamental structural barriers, for instance, the arrival of the new forms of mass media (television, radio, etc.) and the functional and technological exigencies of this segment of the public sphere. Then there is the brute barrier of power exercised arbitrarily and without the victim being able to access succour and recompense. Domestic violence can silence women in the household, for instance, or child abuse can silence children for a long time over their lives. There are of course many more such barriers. These barriers tend to render truly undistorted communication in such a public sphere a seemingly difficult objective to achieve.

While these are some fundamental problems in any public sphere, there have been other factors at play that have had just as decisive an impact on the public sphere. The cultures of the old traditional communities are now gradually being transformed, irrevocably, by newly acquired patterns of consumption. While this process has already been completed in the Western world, it has now also become conspicuous in significant parts of the non-Western world. The culture industry in the Western world today has features that are no longer recognisable to the cultures of the old traditional communities. The extent of the commodification of cultural practices is a topic of considerable debate and controversy. One of the more influential contributions in this area has been the work of the late German sociologist Theodor Adorno.[3] Adorno argued that the contemporary culture industry had rendered the products of such an industry as nothing but manipulative and reificatory products. Even the seemingly unreachable cultural domain of aesthetics had been affected beyond repair by the deliberate application of the laws of the economic system in the domain of culture. For Adorno, high modernist artistic creativity represented the last mode of truly free and meaningful activity available to human beings in contemporary Western society.[4]

Allied to this commodification of cultural practices is the modern phenomenon of the consumption of the products of the mass media. Together these processes of commodification in the cultural sphere have resulted in the unthinking and uncritical acceptance of structures of domination by the populations of societies. Political elites at the helm of modern nation-states have learnt to thrive on such a commodification and the means that it provides them with to manipulate their own people. This is of course to ensure the peoples' legalistic consent to their continuance in power. The public sphere is the uncertain scaffolding on which all these different processes are working themselves out.

If we now turn to the history of the actual reality of the public sphere the first thing that strikes us is that this history has been enormously complex, wishful liberal theories notwithstanding.[5] There are important differences between Western Europe and India here. I will venture a rather brief comparison between the two here just in order for us to better appreciate the larger contours of the world-historical processes at work here, especially those affecting the fate of diverse social classes and structures.

The most famous account of the history of the public sphere in

---

3. Adorno, 2001.

4. Many read in Adorno's arguments a bias against mass culture read positively, i.e. 'mass' in the sense of the people-at-large. Thus, many of Adorno's critics contended that his argument was nothing but an elite European's high cultural arrogance in the face of the practical mass culture of the new and fully industrialised America.

5. Most liberal social and political theories (for e.g. social contract theories and theories grounding the human rights discourse) simply and naively 'assume' the real existence of an ahistorical and fully established and efficient public sphere in a society.

Western Europe has been the one that the German sociologist Jurgen Habermas has had to offer.[6] This account covers the entire gamut, from the emergence, through the transformation and, finally, the disintegration, of the bourgeois public sphere in Western Europe. The bourgeois public sphere as a necessary realm of discourse and debate first emerged in the 18th and 19th Centuries in Western Europe with the primary object of demanding accountability from the authorities of the state. Its emergence and institutionalisation during this period was integrally connected with the developments in the realm of the economy and technology, especially communication technologies. The bourgeois public sphere emerged out of a literary public sphere that had preceded it genealogically. It was the literary public sphere that had first allowed for private bourgeois citizens to articulate their private thoughts and feelings in the literary and cultural fora of the day. Subsequently, the demands from the bourgeoisie for the accountability of state authorities made use of the spaces of discourse and debate that had been made available through the literary public sphere. This then resulted in the classic bourgeois public sphere of Western Europe. But by the middle of the 20th Century—by which time the domains of social and cultural life had been overtaken by (a) what Habermas calls refuedalisation[7] and (b) the production and consumption of the products of the capitalist mass media and the culture industry—the bourgeois public sphere had disintegrated and no longer served its original purposes. Specifically, it had now lost its ability to act as a check against the arbitrary exercise of state power.

When one looks at the history of the public sphere in India, the most relevant historical facts stand out glaringly. Evidently, it would be impossible to even conceptualise the contemporary Indian public sphere without looking at the historical facts of British colonialism in India. Although there were pan-Indian languages—Samskrita, Prakrit, etc., and Hindustani to a lesser degree—before the arrival of the British into India, none of these languages was equipped to be a

---

6. Habermas, 1989.

7. Habermas is referring here to the blurring in 20th Century Western European societies of the difference between the state and society and the public and private, and the return of aspects of representative publicness, all of which hark back in part to feudal concepts and practices.

language of global trade and commerce in a new commercial world. By coming together of circumstances—some fortuitous, most scandalous—English gradually became under the British colonial state a lingua franca for the new upper and middle classes that participated in the British state and economic institutions. However, this was yet only a tiny percentage of the total Indian population. If one were to use Habermas' terms for the historical structures of the public sphere in Western Europe in the context of the history of the Indian public sphere[8], the British colonial state could be described as the domain in which 'representative publicness' operated.[9] Subsequently, as the new bilingual/anglophone Indian upper and middle classes gradually replaced the British rulers at the helm of the Indian state institutions by the middle of the 20th Century, it was in 'the constitutional state' that they sought to link their domain of activities and discourse to the idea of law. Thus 'the constitutional state' in India has come to represent these specific classes. And it could very plausibly be argued that in relation to the rest of the population of the country it is 'representative publicness' that continues to operate in the domain of the constitutional state.

Starting from around the middle of the 19th Century there emerged a very serious literary and cultural creative output in the various Indian 'regional' languages. There emerged in most of these linguistic regions specific literary and cultural fora that could approximate 'the literary public sphere' that Habermas describes. Acting in opposition to 'the representative publicness' of the British Indian and,

---

8. Note that I am not trying to apply European theory in an Indian empirical setting here, but, rather, only trying to see how the history of the Indian public sphere might look in light of what Habermas has to say about the history of the public sphere in Western Europe. Habermas' account—which is itself completely historical rather than prescriptive in any way—does not therefore become here a prescriptive account for the Indian empirical setting in any way. It is important to state these caveats, as, obviously, I have many fundamental problems with Habermas' work, including his (i) understanding of world-history, (ii) positing of an allegedly hyper-sensitive and hyper-self-reflexive Western (Euro-American) community, (iii) vision of global democracy, etc. For instance, Habermas, perhaps because he is, after all, a parochial German, has nothing meaningful to say about the violent colonialisms that a great portion of the rest of the world experienced at the hands of European peoples for 500 years. Habermas' is still the same old lie about European and Euro-American exceptionalism, again allegedly in the domains of science and capitalism.
9. See for one version of this part of the story Cohn, 1988.

subsequently, bourgeois Indian, constitutional state, 'the literary public sphere' heralded the emergence of the public spheres of the non-English speaking Indian middle and lower middle classes. These classes had had some form of formal education and conducted all their critical cultural discourses and debates in the numerous Indian 'regional' languages. In Karnataka, for instance, they are represented by, amongst others, the *Navodaya*[10] (Renaissance) writers of the late 19th and early 20th Centuries. In recent years, what Robin Jeffrey has called India's 'newspaper revolution'—the explosion of media entities and products in India's regional languages—has come to represent the gradual transformation of this 'literary public sphere' into a full-fledged political public sphere.[11] So that today, accountability may be demanded of state authorities not only by traditional bilingual or anglophone elites, but also by the great numbers of middle and lower class citizens that are literate and participate in the new media fora in the regional languages.

My rudimentary schematic for a sociological and historical account of the public sphere in Karnataka has become necessary because very little has formally been written on the nature of the public sphere in contemporary Karnataka. Karnataka is today experiencing unprecedented transformations in the economy, society and the socio-cultural practices of its people, many of which have been highlighted in the introductory note to this conference. These transformations have resulted in the formation of extraordinary tensions within society along various faults, *viz.*, social-structural, economic, and cultural. These tensions cannot but be reflected in the public sphere as a whole, for what is the public sphere if not a reflection of these phenomena in the society as a whole? It has therefore, become necessary to study the empirical reality of the public sphere in Karnataka for two basic purposes: (a) as a diagnostic study of the nature of this public sphere, and (b) as facts that need to be looked at for any meaningful engagement with the state's democratic processes, and for the task of the further democratisation of society.

---

10. *Navodaya* is usually translated from Kannada as 'Renaissance' or 'Rebirth'. This literary cultural movement included such writers as Shivarama Karanth, Dattatreya Ramachandra Bendre, B.M. Srikantaiah, Pu. Thi. Narasimhachar and others.

11. See Jeffrey, 2000.

The Major Organs of the Public Sphere

I will here describe briefly a few of the major organs of the contemporary public sphere in Karnataka. Before I do that I want to clarify, in case it is not clear to the reader already, that the public sphere is not merely a single place or institution or instrument. It is an entire domain of different kinds of socio-cultural activities that are oriented to a publicness.[12] Thus the public sphere includes debates, discussions, writing and publication; the places where these activities are carried out, such as a restaurant/hotel, a coffee shop, etc.; and the institutions and instruments through which these activities are carried out, such as the newspaper, theatre, etc. The following listing of the major organs of the public sphere in Karnataka is not, and is not meant to be exhaustive. It is indicative, as I have said before, of the diversity of organs that operate here.[13]

(i) Literary and cultural fora (in this category I include both the places as well as the literary and cultural activities that are organised in these places): the theatre; literary and cultural organisations patronised by private citizens—such as the *Saahithya/Saamskruthika balagagalu*—that one can find in virtually all towns and cities of Karnataka; literary, movie and cultural review sections of newspapers, etc.

(ii) Traditional practices of story-telling: *harikathey*, *yakshagaana*, etc.

(iii) *Kattegalu*: Places/shops in the neighbourhood or by the streets, where people meet and discuss different issues over a cup of coffee, etc.

(iv) Other public meeting places: The barber's, hotels, *bars*, etc.

(v) Festivities: Neighbourhood community celebrations for *Ganesha Chathurthi*, *Ramnavami*, etc.

(vi) "Secular" festivities: Activities on occasions such as *Kannada Rajyothsavas* organised by the neighbourhood *geleyara balagagalu* and other such associations.

---

12. Habermas uses the term 'critical-rational' to characterise the interest this publicness has in monitoring state power and evaluating all aspects of the socio-cultural world.

13. I have one caveat here. The fact that there may be some overlap or repetition among the various items I list here should not be any cause for concern as the overlaps and repetitions are not of much consequence.

(vii) Places of worship: Neighbourhood temple, mosque, church, *arali katte*, places for the delivery of *pravachanas* (homilies).

(viii) Caste associations/religious associations: *Akhila Bharatha Veerashavia Mahasabha, Vokkaligara Sangha, Akhila Karnataka Brahmana Mahasabha*, Ramakrishna mission, etc. These become part of the public sphere only to the extent that they do not deliberately exclude the discussion of politics or any other topic from their fora altogether.

(ix) Political parties: These are the associations that, according to democratic theory, legitimately bridge the divide between the public sphere and the state.

(x) New urban public spaces: pubs, restaurants, music concerts (for the westernised upper and middle classes); music concerts (orchestras), humour festivals, etc. (for the Kannada middle and lower classes).

(xi) The press/media/new media:
- (a) Print Media:
  - (i) Newspapers.
  - (ii) Magazines.
  - (iii) Journals.
  - (iv) Book publishing industry.
- (b) Electronic Media:
  - (i) Television/Cable.
  - (ii) Radio.
- (c) New Media:
  - (i) Web portals for news, business, government, etc.
  - (ii) Web portals for personal communication/blogs.

A few comments about this list now need to be made. Firstly, while a few of these organs are receding from significance (e.g. *harikathey*, *yakshagaana*), others (e.g. web-based fora such as thatskannada.com, kannadasaahithya.com) are gaining in it. Secondly, not all of these organs are totally unbiased. Indeed, I would even say that a significant proportion of them have an explicit bias of some nature (e.g. the

Akhila Karnataka Brahmana Mahasabha will not necessarily entertain Idigas in their fora, or the newspaper *Vijaya Karnataka* will not publish anything critical of the *Kannada Naadu* political party, etc.). That being said, on the whole, despite these biases, these organs do allow for the articulation and discussion of views on politics and other aspects of the sociocultural world.

Thirdly, certain of these organs of the public sphere, especially the print and electronic media, have become organised on completely commercial lines, where the pursuit of profit drives all dimensions of the production of the product, be it a newspaper or a television news programme. So much so that if, for instance, a particular newspaper has already established a certain kind of readership, the newspaper will seldom be critical of that section of the population that forms its readership. Instead, it will direct all its criticism at the ubiquitous state and all the other sectors of the population. A good example of this is the *Deccan Herald*—whose readership comprises mainly the newly bilingual/anglicised upper and middle classes in the new economic sectors of Bangalore—continuously writing stories, investigations, doing surveys, etc. from the point of view only of the 'new techies'. Few of the other sectors of the state's population, e.g. the urban slum dwellers, landless agricultural labourers, etc., will find their point of view represented in such a newspaper.[14] Such organs therefore, represent not successes but failures of the public sphere.

Finally, those organs of the public sphere where technology plays an especially important role serve ambivalent functions within the public sphere. For instance, the internet-based fora seem on the one hand to democratise the processes of citizens articulating their views. On the other hand, this also leads to such a surfeit/glut of information that it becomes very difficult for anyone to discriminate among the varieties of views that are being expressed.

---

14. While I am very confident that, for instance, a statistical word count will bear this out, anyone familiar with the narrativising habits of this newspaper will recognise this straightaway.

The Main Constituents and the Multiple Splits of the Karnataka Public Sphere

In this part of the paper, I will run briefly through the various segments of the population of Karnataka that constitute the Karnataka public sphere. The public sphere that prevails in a region of the kind of population characteristics that I describe here cannot but be split[15] along the various axes that those population segments represent. I will discuss a few of the important splits here.

The latest Indian census, carried out in the year 2001, counts the population of the state of Karnataka at approximately 52.85 millions (5.28 crores).[16] Taking this number as our base figure, we can start to derive the various specific constituents of this population.

One of the first categories of distinction amongst the population is that of the extent of urbanisation of the peoples' habitats. The percentage of population that is described as urban is 30.9 per cent, which means that the great majority of the people in Karnataka (69.1 per cent) are still based in their traditional rural habitats.[17] A corollary of this is the fact that the great majority of the people in Karnataka still depend directly or indirectly on agriculture for a living.

The second category of distinction amongst the population is that of language. As we all know, the reorganisation of the states of India in 1956 was done on the basis of language. This has meant that Karnataka as a federal constitutional unit has been marked out as the region where people speaking primarily the language of Kannada reside. The breakdown for the different important languages spoken in Karnataka today is as follows:[18] Kannada (66.22 per cent), Urdu (9.96 per cent), Telugu (7.39 per cent), Tamil (3.84 per cent), Marathi (3.65 per cent), Hindi (1.97 per cent), Malayalam (1.69 per cent) and Konkani (1.57 per cent). It must be mentioned that most of those that speak a language other than Kannada (say Urdu or Konkani) usually also speak Kannada in numerous everyday social settings that cannot

---

15. I have borrowed the term "split public" from Rajagopal, 2001.

16. *The Census of India, 2001.*

17. The latest figures available on this subject are from the 1991 census.

18. *The Census of India, 2001.*

be successfully negotiated with just their mother tongues. However, there are two exceptions to this. Firstly, in the border districts of the region—for instance, in the northern parts of Belgaum district, the southern parts of Dakshina Kannada district, and the eastern parts of Bellary district—people may or may not speak both languages. Secondly, in the new urban centres of the city, primarily in Bangalore, there are pockets of people that only speak Hindi and English and not any of the other languages listed for the state.

The second split of the public sphere takes place along the axis of language. There are 241 Kannada dailies[19] that are published in the state and it is safe to assume that the Kannada language dailies do represent the great majority of the Kannada speaking people in the state. In addition to these Kannada dailies, there are also dailies that are published in Karnataka in at least five other languages, *viz*. Urdu, Telugu, Tamil, Malayalam and Hindi. These newspapers, although published in Karnataka, are produced for distinct sets of non-Kannada speakers. The result is a distinct splitting of the public in multiple ways. The newspapers of each language become the unique—usually exclusive—fora for the articulation of the views of each set of language-speakers—with little communication across these linguistically split publics. Predictably enough, this is often a prescription for misunderstandings, polarisations and uniquely different—and occasionally dangerous—ways of representing the same factual stories. If anybody has followed much of the dubious coverage[20] in some of the Kannada language newspapers of the Kannada-Tamil Cauvery riots in 1991, they will be left with little doubt that the Kannada language dailies cannot be expected to fully reflect the thoughts and experiences of the non-Kannada speaking peoples in the state. Possibly, this goes for the other language newspapers as well.[21]

---

19. Gunasekera and Holaday, 1998.

20. By dubious coverage I refer here to the readiness with which some of the Kannada newspapers turned the issue into a simplistic "Kannada *versus* Tamil" issue, in which, by the mere fact of your being a member of the Kannada-speaking and newspaper consuming community, you get coopted into a "us *versus* them" demagoguery. See, for instance, some of the issues of *Sanje Vani*, a Kannada evening newspaper, from the last fortnight of December 1991.

21. See for an account of the consequences of the split public based on linguistic differences in northern India, Rajagopal, 2001.

A third category of distinction of the population is that of religion. The percentages for the main religious denominations listed for Karnataka are: Hindus (83.86 per cent), Muslims (12.23 per cent) and Christians (1.90 per cent).[22] It is worth noting that most Muslims in Karnataka speak both Urdu and Kannada. The next category of distinction amongst the population is that of caste. For reasons that are well understood, the castes that constitute the Karnataka population are not counted by the census operations. The Scheduled Castes (SCs) and Scheduled Tribes (STs) are an exception to this. Our numbers for the non-SC/ST population are therefore, derived from other sources. The most significant of the caste numbers for Karnataka are as follows: *Lingayatha* (*Veerashaiva*) (15.34 per cent), *Vokkaliga* (10.80 per cent), *Kuruba* (6.28 per cent), *Brahmana* (3.46 per cent), *Maratha* (2.90 per cent), *Bestha* (2.54 per cent), *Beda* (2.49 per cent) and *Idiga* (2.30 per cent).[23] There are numerous other castes as well, but my point does not require the listing of all of them here. The percentages of Scheduled Castes (SCs) and Scheduled Tribes (STs), who are counted in the census operations, are as follows: SCs (16.2 per cent) and STs (6.6 per cent). For reference we may note that the percentages of these for the Indian population as a whole are: SCs (16.2 per cent) and STs (8.2 per cent).[24] The third split of the public sphere is along the axis of religion and caste. Although this might seem like a potentially explosive split of the public, in actual reality this tends to be less so. Except for the occasions when Hindu-Muslim riots are being commercially engineered by people specialised in these vocations, these split publics have some sense of their own limits. Each of these split publics usually knows already where it stands in relation to the other religions and castes around it; so seldom do these splits by themselves lead to any difficulties or dangers. On the other hand, it is also true that many of the participants in publics split along these axes are actively interested in monitoring and influencing the domain of organised state politics. Thus a *Veerashaiva Mahasabha* or a *Vokkaligara Sangha* will not only reflect on and discuss the latest political developments in the context of their impact

22. *The Census of India, 2001.*

23. These percentages are taken from the Chinnappa Reddy Commission Report, cited in Thimmaiah, 1993.

24. Gunasekera and Holaday, 1998.

on their own communities, they will also negotiate and bargain with politicians of different political parties for specific promises in relation to their own communities. This has long been the tacitly accepted mode of doing politics in India.

Another very important parameter that the census operations consider is the rate of literacy in all the different states of India. Here, against the national literacy rate of 64.8 per cent, Karnataka's literacy rate is 66.6 per cent.[25] This literacy rate implies that the 33.4 per cent of the population that is illiterate experiences a substantial exclusion from participation in the 'processes of the state'. The inability to read or write imposes on them a significant handicap in their efforts to participate in the state's processes in a meaningful and consequential manner. This is all the clearer when one realises that the constitutional state in India requires a citizen to be able to read and write in order to participate in any of its institutional processes. However, this does not of course detract from the fact that illiteracy does not stop them from participating—as interested citizenry—in the reflective and critical debates conducted in the various specific organs of the public sphere.

The fourth split that may briefly be considered here relates to the extent of the urban-rural divide. When 69.1 per cent of the population is rural, depends overwhelmingly on agriculture for a living and is largely poor, and the rest of the population is urban, part of the industrial or service sectors and much better off, there are bound to be splits of consequence. The principal distinguishing factor between these two publics concerns their modes of consumption. Because the rural masses are so much poorer than the urban citizens they are left out of most of the products of the media and the culture industry. Being left out of the latter may not have much consequence, but being left out of the former certainly does. It means that except for the few television channels that are interested in tapping that market, the rural masses are completely left out of the anglophone or bilingual organs of the media controlled and moderated by the urban upper and middle classes.

25. Ibid.

Finally, in India in general and in Karnataka in particular, the split of the public sphere along the axis of class is of great consequence. As I have discussed elsewhere in this paper, the emergence of the lower-middle and lower classes into a public sphere that had previously been dominated by the anglophone and bilingual urban upper and middle classes has been a recent phenomenon. Indeed, it is still occurring as we speak.

The publics split this way are still in conflict with each other and there is a great deal at stake in this battle for both parties, including primarily the control of the Indian constitutional state. However, although the latter classes are conscious of their class location—partly because this is now under threat—the former classes do not really have a consciousness of themselves as belonging to a single class. The former are split also along the lines of language, religion and caste.

Conclusion

Democratisation, Communication and Evasive Silences

I began the substantial part of this paper with the stated objective of looking at the empirical reality of the public sphere in Karnataka for two basic purposes: (a) as a diagnostic study of the nature of this public sphere, and (b) as facts that need to be looked at for any meaningful engagement with the state's democratic processes, and for the task of the further democratisation of society.

Our study has revealed that the public sphere in contemporary Karnataka is an enormously rich and variegated domain of socio-cultural and political life. While some elements in this sphere are in a state of recession/disintegration, others are well established and efficiently functional, and yet others are still in a state of emergence. But together they offer significant opportunities for any citizen wishing to participate in the processes of the public sphere to do so.

The nature of the organisation of the different organs of this public sphere determines to a great extent their efficacy as truly functional units of an ideal public sphere. Thus a small-scale non-profit neighbourhood association such as the *geleyara balaga* might in fact be more effective as an institution of the public sphere than a full-fledged for-profit corporate media institution producing newspapers and television news programmes. The continuing presence of multiple organs in the public sphere that sustain the practises of debate, discourse and discussion is a great asset. This is so especially when the spaces for the meaningful representation of the full spectrum of voices in society in the products of the corporate media are diminishing with every passing day.

The multiple axes along which the public sphere is split has had a profound impact on the nature and quality of democratic participation available to citizens. As we have seen in this paper, the multiple splits usually—though not always—have seriously detrimental consequences for the functioning of a public sphere. The splits introduce formidable obstacles in the path of efficient, meaningful and undistorted communication amongst all the citizens of the society. Often such obstacles have the effect of pulverising communication altogether, and breaking it down completely. The roles of the different media entities during the Kannada-Tamil Cauvery riots in 1991 demonstrated this with telling force.

If one is serious about the idea of politics as an essential human activity and engage seriously the issue of the structures of domination that operate in our contemporary society, one must be willing to work through the public spaces that are available for this active engagement in the organisation of our own political and social lives. Citizenship requires that we voice our thoughts and opinions, and the public sphere facilitates the communication of those thoughts and opinions to fellow citizens involved in this same exercise.

Despite the limits of the public sphere as it currently operates in Karnataka today—and there are many and important limits as we have seen in this paper—it is yet possible to promote certain elements and aspects of the public sphere as more conducive for fair and undistorted communication. By "undistorted communication", I mean communication that is not distorted either by the exercise of arbitrary and brute power or by the structures of capitalist organisation. We need to reflect on ways of promoting those elements and aspects of the public sphere that might reflect the population's diversity more meaningfully. It is possible, for instance, to promote the idea of minimum required diversity in content in different organs of the media that could be implemented by bodies such as the Press Council and *Prasar Bharathi*. Measures could be put in place that would ensure minimum coverage of 'local' legal and social issues in all the different organs of the media. These could make sure that the different specific organs of the public sphere don't turn too parochial. The different organs of the public sphere could also be encouraged to promote dialogue amongst the members of various communities in situations of tension and those organs could also specifically be discouraged from practising any form of brinkmanship in such situations. It would also be helpful to encourage the organs of the public sphere to develop long-term relations with the officials of the local governmental machineries so that they always have channels open through which they may be able to communicate in relation to any issue with the officials of the local governmental machineries.

We also need to look at ways of making sure that the most vulnerable and at-risk individuals and groups are protected from any failures of the public sphere to do its job. This is a complex job and requires a wide-range of responses. Minimum standards could be set, for instance, for the organs of the public sphere to respect and provide space for issues concerning the disabled, domestic violence, child-abuse, etc. Other dimensions could prove to be a bit more difficult. For instance, when one thinks of people that are illiterate, what are the measures that could possibly help their cause in the context of the public sphere? A great deal of creativity would be required to think through appropriate ways of responding to these challenges. All these would rightly be the subject of a fuller engagement with issues concerning the public sphere in contemporary Karnataka.

References

AMIC (2000). *Media and Democracy in Asia: An AMIC Compilation*. Singapore: Asian Media Information and Communication Centre.

Adorno, Theodor W. (2001). *The Culture Industry: Selected Essays on Mass Culture*. Edited by J.M. Bernstein. London: Routledge.

Barns, Margarita (1940). *The Indian Press: A History of the Growth of Public Opinion in India*. London: Allen and Unwin.

Boyce, Merrill T. (1988). *British Policy and the Evolution of the Vernacular Press in India, 1835-1838*. Delhi: Chanakya Publications.

Brooker, Will and Deborah Jermyn (eds.) (2003). *The Audience Studies Reader*, London: Routledge.

Chan, Joseph M. and Bryce T. McIntyre (eds.) (2002). *In Search of Boundaries: Communication, Nation-States and Cultural Identities*, Westport, Connecticut: Ablex Publishing.

Cohn, Bernard (1988). "Representing Authority in Victorian India", in Bernard Cohn, *An Anthropologist among the Historians and Other Essays*. Delhi: Oxford University Press. pp.632-82.

Crigler, Ann N. (1996). *The Psychology of Political Communication*, Ann Arbor. Michigan: The University of Michigan Press.

Escobar, Arturo (1995). *Encountering Development: The Making and Unmaking of the Third World*. Princeton: Princeton University Press.

Golding, Peter and Graham Murdock (eds.) (1997). *The Political Economy of the Media*, Two Volumes, Cheltenham, UK: Edward Elgar Publishing Co.

Gunasekera, Anura and Duncan Holaday (eds.) (1998). *Asian Communication Handbook 1998*. Singapore: Asian Media Information and Communication Centre.

Jalbert, Paul L. (ed.) (1999). *Media Studies: Ethnomethodological Approaches*. Lanham, Maryland: University Press of America.

Jeffrey, Robin (2000). *India's Newspaper Revolution: Capitalism, Politics and the Indian-Language Press, 1977-99*. London: Hurst and Co.

Habermas, Jurgen (1989). *The Structural Transformation of the Public Sphere: An Inquiry into a Category of Bourgeois Society*, translated by Thomas Burger. Cambridge, Massachusetts: MIT Press.

Kaviraj, Sudipta (1991). "On State, Society and Discourse in India", in James Manor (ed.), *Rethinking Third World Politics*. London: Longman, pp.72-99.

Khare, P.S. (1964). *The Growth of Press and Public Opinion in India, 1857-1918*. Allahabad: Piyush Prakashan.

Luhmann, Niklas (2000). *The Reality of the Mass Media*. Translated by Kathleen Cross. Stanford, California: Stanford University Press.

MacBride, Sean (2004). "Commission (UNESCO)". *Many Voices, One World: Towards a New, More Just, and More Efficient World Information and Communication Order*. Maryland: Lanham, Rowman & Littlefield, (1980).

Mosco, Vincent (1996). *The Political Economy of Communication: Rethinking and Renewal*. London: Sage.

Natarajan, S. (1962). *A History of the Press in India*. New York: Asia Publishing House.

Rajagopal, Arvind (2001). *Politics After Television: Hindu Nationalism and the Reshaping of the Indian Public*. Cambridge, UK: Cambridge University Press.

Rao, Vijayendra and Michael Walton (eds.) (2004). *Culture and Public Action*. Stanford: Stanford University Press.

Sachs, Wolfgang (ed.) (1992). *The Development Dictionary: A Guide to Knowledge and Power*. London: Zed Books.

Sankhdher, B.M. (1984). *Press, Politics and Public Opinion in India: Dynamics of Modernisation and Social Transformation*. New Delhi: Deep and Deep.

Slack, Jennifer Daryl and Fred Fejes, (eds.) (1972). *The Ideology of the Information Age*. Norwood, New Jersey: Ablex Publishing Corp.

Steinberg, Charles S. (1972). *Mass Media and Communication*. New York: Hastings House.

Thimmaiah, G. (1993). *Power Politics and Social Justice: Backward Castes in Karnataka*. New Delhi: Sage. pp.134-140.

8

Corruption and Local Governance

Evidence from Karnataka[1]

V. VIJAYALAKSHMI[2]

The possible impact of decentralised governance on corruption has generated considerable interest and debate. Local governance is considered more responsive and accountable to citizens. The assumption is that localisation of authority, and decision making being closer to the people would contribute to an increase in citizens' involvement in planning and budgeting. Further, electoral accountability would be higher at the level of local government, as citizens are better informed about the performance of representatives and will decide on their continuance in the next term. All these are means by which elected representatives can be made accountable, and in ensuring transparency in public actions. While decentralisation can enhance accountability and responsiveness in governance, it needs to be emphasised that the one does not lead to the other unless certain conditions are met. These include adequate checks and balances, specific measures to effect accountability and transparency, and the active role of opposition parties.

In India, institutions of rural local government or Panchayati Raj Institutions (district and below) have been revived through the efforts of both the Central and State Governments. Local governance was conceived not only as a means for people's participation, but also to

---

1. This paper is based on a study of *panchayats* in Karnataka, financially supported by Ford Foundation.

2. The views expressed in the paper are that of the author and not of the organisation she represents.

enhance the quality of governance and development outcomes.[3] The 73rd Constitutional Amendment (1992) provided certain guidelines in the basic structure of the institutions of local government, though the actual devolution of powers to these institutions is left to state governments. In the manner that decentralisation is actually implemented in different states, there is an asymmetry in various areas of decentralisation, (i.e. fiscal, political and administrative decentralisation). There is no uniformity among the states in the devolution of powers to these institutions, or of incorporating mechanisms of transparency and accountability in institutions of local governance.

Corruption is one of the most important problems facing the *panchayats*. In the case of Karnataka, which has had institutions of local government for nearly two decades estimates indicate that large-scale corruption involving commissions paid through public works and procurement deals was up to 65 per cent of the total cost. Karnataka had introduced decentralisation reforms in the 1980s (by the Janata government), even before the enactment of the 73rd Constitutional Amendment.[4] Following the Constitutional Amendment, the Karnataka Panchayati Raj Act 1993 was enacted, which brought about changes in the Panchayati Raj Act to conform to the Constitutional Amendment. Devolution of powers in Karnataka has been to greater extent in the political sphere and less of fiscal and administrative decentralisation has been effected. As events have shown, accountability and transparency, have not got sufficient importance and adequate emphasis in the Karnataka Panchayati Raj Acts (both 1983 and 1993), or the subsequent amendments.[5] The existing

---

3. From the development perspective, decentralisation can be an effective means through which programmes related to poverty reduction are better implemented (Bardhan and Mookherjee, 2000; also see Seabright, 1996).

4. Karnataka has had a longer history of quotas for women in the institutions of local government. For the first time in the country, 25 per cent of the total seats in the panchayats were reserved for women through 'The Karnataka *Zilla Parishads, Taluk Panchayati Samithis, Mandal Panchayats*, and *Nyaya Panchayats* Act 1983. This Act provided the design for the 73rd Constitutional Amendment. The panchayats based on this Act started functioning in 1987.

5. When the 1983 Act was formulated, the *grama sabhas* (village assembly) included in the Act were ahead of what then existed, in terms of the expected participation of rural people.

measures of accountability are *gram sabhas, jamabandhi* (has been in existence from 2001) and accounts audit. *Gram sabhas* were envisaged as where the constituents meet and indicate their preferences and needs on development activities. They are the only institution of direct democracy where people communicate with elected members and officials, and assess the performance of the representatives and the activities of the *panchayats*. *Gram sabhas* must be convened at least four times a year in every village (earlier it used to be twice a year). *Gram sabhas* were expected to enhance transparency, accountability and, most importantly, people's participation. Subsequent years have shown that *gram sabhas* have not served this purpose. *Jamabandhis* were introduced in the year 2001 and are an assessment of the functioning of the *gram panchayat* by the electorate, conducted on one day in a year.[6] They are mainly intended to provide citizens with access to documents and files of the *gram panchayats*. All three-tiers of *panchayats* have accounts audits and in the upper tiers the audits are conducted by the Comptroller and Auditor General. Accounts audits at the *taluk* and *zilla panchayats*, however, have been irregular, often only once in three years, and their effectiveness in checking the misuse of funds has been limited.

The utilisation of *panchayat* funds assumes importance considering that most of the central government and a few state government rural development programmes are implemented through the *panchayats*. Prior to the devolution of powers to institutions of local government, the decision making powers were with MLAs, MPs and the Deputy Commissioners. The political space following the 73rd Amendment (after 1992) is denser, with MLAs and MPs laying claims over the same space through overlapping constituencies, and intervening in the functioning of the *panchayats*.

---

6. *Jamabandhis* are meant to enhance citizens' accessibility to information. The objective was not achieved in the *panchayats* that we studied, as the citizens were not aware of the programme. Conducted once a year, and for just one day between 15 August-15 September the method of public audit of the *gram panchayat* financial records has several limitations. The *Jamabandhi* is conducted by the officials at the *taluk* level, and the executive officer has the responsibility for preparing the report of the public audit. Citizens were informed about the contents of the public audit report as there is no provision for public discussion, for example in *gram sabhas*. (See Sivanna, N. and Devendra Babu, 2004).

Using micro data the paper examines corruption in the *panchayats* of Karnataka. First, existing literature and perceptions on decentralisation and corruption are examined, with a brief discussion on the issues in *panchayats* which have a bearing on corruption. Second, the attitudes of elected representatives towards corruption are examined. Representatives were asked to respond to statements on rent seeking, election expenses and the factors that lead to corruption. Third, the perceived levels of rent seeking in *panchayats* are used to arrive at the corruption level score, and factors contributing to rent-seeking are analysed. Finally, the corruption networks and the practice of *'mamul'* are discussed.

Decentralisation, Utilisation of Public Resources and Corruption

Decentralisation has been viewed as a useful means of public service delivery, and for the implementation of programmes related to poverty reduction (Bardhan and Mookherjee, 2000). Through an *ex-post* argument it is also considered as more responsive to local needs. The assumption has been that since citizens have an opportunity to interact with the functionaries of the institutions of local government, the accountability of representatives is enhanced (Seabright, 1996; Rose-Ackerman, 1999; Persson *et al.*, 1997; Laffont and Meleu, 2001). Citizens have access to information on the performance of the local government. It was also suggested that administrative and fiscal decentralisation reduced corruption (Wade, 1997; Huther and Shah, 1998). According to the governance index constructed by Huther and Shah (1998), which contains indicators such as citizen participation, government orientation, social development and economic management, fiscal decentralisation is one of the explanatory variables. They also indicated that fiscal decentralisation has a significant impact on good governance.

Devolution of powers to institutions of local government for local expenditure, and revenue collection, was considered essential for effective governance. Fiscal decentralisation was expected to reduce the centralisation of political power, and the favourable effects from democracy will percolate, towards improving the rule of law and smaller government consumption. The rationale of the political economy explanations is that decentralisation will increase bureaucratic accountability from what it was under centralised governance (Wildasin, 1995).

Political and administrative decentralisation were seen to be effective in reducing corruption (Crook and Manor, 1998; Wade, 1997).[7] Electoral and political competition brought about innovative leadership, which in turn, enhanced the quality of governance (Bird and Fiszbein, 1997).[8] Wade (1997) points out from evidence of corruption in irrigation service delivery in India, that centralisation was a major factor in bureaucratic rent seeking. Crook and Manor (2000) concluded that decentralisation reduced the diversion of public funds by politically powerful individuals.

A contrary view is that political and administrative decentralisation contributed to the localisation of corruption. While there is evidence of bureaucratic rent seeking in the centralised system, the influence of local elites over public resources in local governance is also visible (Bardhan and Mookherjee, 1998), Prud'homme (1994), Tanzi (1995), Brueckner (1999), Blanchard and Shleifer (2000), Treisman (2000), consider political decentralisation as contributing towards corruption. If local vested interests are powerful, and in the absence of local accountability, decentralisation increases corruption (see, for example, Blanchard and Shleifer (2000) and Bardhan and Mookherjee (1998). Tanzi (1995, 1996) was of the view that corruption may be more common at the local level and pointed to the limitations in the provision of services by the institutions of local government, that may prevent the realisation of benefits from decentralisation. Also, increased interaction between officials and citizens reduces professionalism and arms-length relationships, and furthers personalism. Prud'homme (1994) had argued that the scope for corruption increases with localisation because of the greater influence of interest groups at the local level.[9] He also indicated that the discretion available to local officials (a point argued in support of decentralisation as a means of

---

7. This was pointed out in the context of Bangladesh, India (Karnataka state), Cote d'Ivoir and Ghana; and Wade, 1997.

8. These observations were mde in the context of Columbia.

9. Prud'homme's views are based on observations in France and Italy.

reducing corruption) and long tenure of local officials in the same place, contributed to rent seeking coalitions. With respect to the delivery of public service, institutions of local government can be inefficient because of poorly trained local bureaucrats, and a similar inefficiency of elected representatives (Tanzi, 1996).

Data

The analysis included information from Mandya and Udupi districts. A few case studies from Bangalore Rural district were also used. Two *zilla* (district) *panchayats*, four *taluk* (subdistrict) *panchayats*, and 12 *gram* (village) *panchayats* were included in this study. The data were collected from interviews with 266 elected representatives, 64 officials, 25 contractors and 400 citizens.

Corruption is broadly defined here as the misuse of authority and public resources for private gains. It is a deviation from the 'formal duties of a public role because of private-regarding (family, close family, private clique) pecuniary or status gains; or violates rules against the exercise of certain types of private-regarding influence,' (Nye, 1967: 966). Most of the political corruption studies used expert opinion to measure corruption (for example, Fisman and Gatti, 2000; Treisman, 2000; Johnson, Kaufmann, Zoido-Lobanton, 1998; Mauro, 1995). In the present study we use the views/perceptions of the representatives on the extent of corruption in *panchayats*. Representatives were asked about the level of corruption in *panchayats*, areas of corruption, corrupt acts, and their attitudes toward corruption. They were willing to state their views on the corruption in *panchayats*, involvement of other representatives, and in some cases their own involvement.[10] To get a wider perspective of corruption processes we interviewed officials and contractors of public works and those who received or applied for procurement deals. An earlier study on the *panchayats* in Karnataka

10. While there is a risk that representatives may not want to reveal their involvement or the money they received, and overstate the involvement of others instead, we checked the information through other sources (such as officials, contractors, political party workers who are well informed about *panchayats*). What is important in the context of seeking information from the elected representatives is that our response rate for most questions was high, as over 85 per cent of the respondents answered most questions; and we could interview almost all the representatives in the panchayats which we had selected as our sample.

which we carried out prior to the one on corruption helped in developing rapport with the representatives.

Description of the Variables

The Perception of Corruption is the Dependent Variable

Perception of Corruption Level

The level of corruption in *panchayats* was assessed based on the perception of elected representatives to a set of twelve questions, on a three-point measure of 'high', 'medium' and 'low'. The questions included—level of corruption in *panchayats*, frequency of rent seeking, political corruption, bureaucratic corruption, perceived risk, role of middlemen, percentage of commissions, minimising competition in awarding contracts and procurement (where 1 indicated high, and 3 was low), effectiveness of transparency measures, effectiveness of accountability measures, redressal mechanisms (where 1 indicates not effective, and 3 is effective), and development and public works for which commissions and bribes are paid (where 1 indicates all and 3 was nil payment). An aggregate score was constructed which indicates the corruption level in the *panchayats*. A corruption score of 12 indicates high level of rent seeking, 13 to 24 indicate medium corruption, and 25 to 36 are low corruption.

Explanatory Variables

The explanatory variables are classified into four categories *viz.*, structure (levels) of local government, institutional, political and others. The first consists of levels of local government, *viz.*, *gram panchayat*, *taluk panchayat*, and *zilla panchayat*. Second comprises effectiveness of transparency and accountability measures, corruption cases filed, action taken on corruption cases and perception of risk. The third category comprises party composition, role of the opposition parties, election expenses and corruption as election issue. Finally, the factors such as attitude towards corruption, *de facto* politics, first time representatives, and reporting of corruption in local news papers and number of times a representative was elected to *panchayats* were examined. For each of these variables (except the ones with scores) in the analysis, one category has been selected as reference category.

Research Findings

The analysis indicates that corruption levels are high in the institutions of local government (Table 8.1). The representatives were asked about their overall perception about corruption in *panchayats,* where 1 indicates that corruption is high, 2 suggested that corruption is moderate, and 3 that corruption is low. Comparatively higher levels of corruption were perceived in *taluk* and *zilla panchayats* as compared to *gram panchayats*. The number of corrupt representatives was also seen to be higher among *taluk* and *zilla panchayat* representatives (Table 8.1). A marginally lower level of corruption was perceived in Udupi district compared to Mandya district. A similar difference was suggested about representatives who were corrupt.

Table 8.1

Corruption in Panchayats
(N=266)

Corruption in Panchayat	*Gram Panchayat*	*Taluk Panchayat*	*Zilla Panchayat*
High	70 (54.3%)	65 (77.4%)	46 (79.2%)
Moderate	50 (37.7%)	16 (19%)	10 (18.9%)
Low	9 (7%)	3 (3.6%)	1 (1.9%)
Proportion of Corrupt Representatives	42	78	92

The most common corrupt practises are found in the management of public funds in *panchayats* and are listed in Table 8.2. According to the elected representatives corruption is highest in public works and in procurement deals.

A means of siphoning off funds was through lowering the quality of public works compared to the requirements of the design. For example, in road surfacing if the estimated cost was for three layers, only two layers were actually laid. Additionally, funds for public works were taken off through over estimation of costs, and false bills. Officials were candid in admitting that false billing was the most common practice as they have to account for the various payments made for the personal expenses of the representatives (which also includes paying for the political party related activities). They also reported instances where bills were ready even before the work was carried out. The other practices include *benami* contracts, reducing quality and quantity of work, and circumventing procedures in the tendering process.

Table 8.2

Areas of Corruption in Panchayats–Perception of the Representatives (N=266)

	High	*Medium*	*Low*
Public Works	92.4	6.6	1
Procurement	89.7	9.1	1.2
Awarding Contracts	64	32.6	3.4
Tendering	31.1	36.8	32.1
Beneficiary Selection	59.3	32.6	8.2

It was also common in the *gram panchayats* for bribes and commissions to be paid to get beneficiary grants. The responses of the beneficiaries of programmes indicate that frequency of the payment of bribes and commissions was high (Figure 8.1), while the responses of the representatives indicated a moderately high rate of frequency.

There was a fixed rate of commissions for some beneficiary programmes. For example, in the case of the housing programme, 10 per cent of the grant is paid as commissions. In other programmes (such as house electrification—bhagya jyothi, construction of toilets, loan for the purchase of cattle, bullock cart, sericulture equipment, smokeless traditional stove, and house repair) the commissions ranged from 2 per cent to 25 per cent. A majority of the representatives indicated that the commissions were in the range of 10 to 20 per cent for most of the beneficiary schemes (Figure 8.1). Our interviews with the citizens indicated an even higher per cent of commissions (Figure 8.2).

The difference in commissions paid for beneficiary schemes between the two districts was not significant, although the method adopted to receive commissions varied. In Mandya district, the

Figure 8.1

Frequency of Payments Made by Beneficiaries

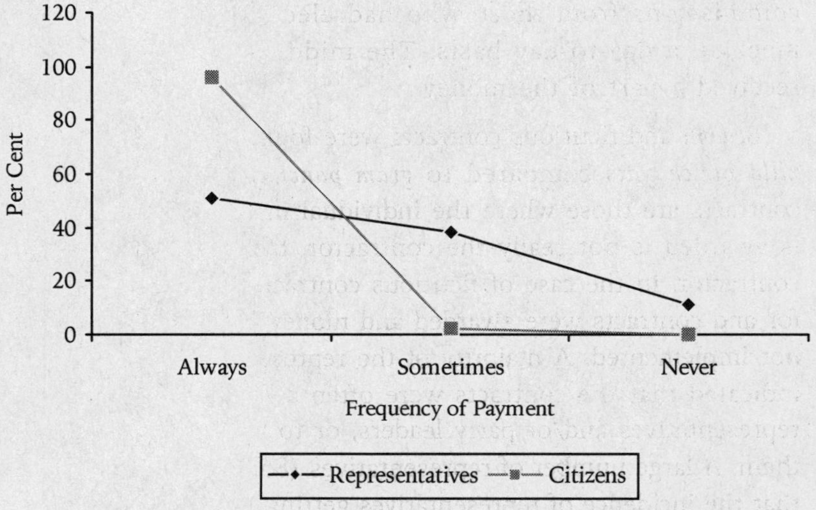

Figure 8.2

Bribes/Commission Paid in Beneficiary Schemes

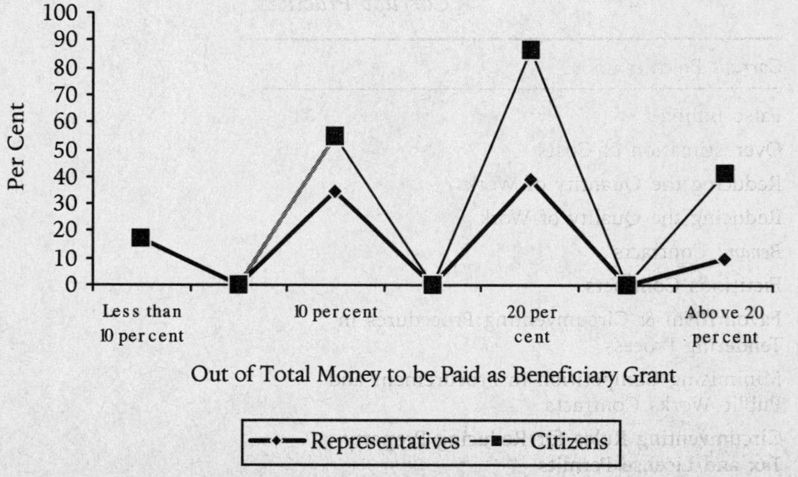

representatives negotiated commissions directly with the beneficiaries. In Udupi district, the deals were through middlemen. The representatives considered it inappropriate to directly ask for commissions from those who had elected them and whom they meet on a day-to-day basis. The middlemen who fixed the deal received a part of the money.

Benami and fictitious contracts were found more often in *taluk* and *zilla panchayats* compared to *gram panchayats* (Table 8.3). *Benami* contracts are those where the individual in whose name the contract is awarded is not really the contractor, but acts as a proxy for the contractor. In the case of fictitious contracts, the tenders were called for and contracts were awarded and money paid but the contract was not implemented. A majority of the representatives (165 out of 234) indicated that the contracts were often awarded to the proxy of the representatives and/or party leaders, or to those who were known to them. A large number of representatives (85.9 per cent) also indicated that the incidence of representatives getting the contracts in the name of their family members was widely prevalent. *Benami* contracts were more common when the contracts were awarded to the family member of representatives. Lack of transparency in awarding contracts contributed to the practice of *benami* and fictitious contracts.

Table 8.3

Corrupt Practices

Corrupt Practices	*High*	*Medium*	*Low*
False Billing	75	14	11
Overestimation of Costs	91	7	2
Reducing the Quantity of Work	63	21	16
Reducing the Quality of Work	87	9	4
Benami Contracts	22	34	44
Fictitious Contracts	21	34	43
Favouritism & Circumventing Procedures in Tendering Process	55	35	10
Minimising Competition in Procurement and Public Works Contracts	90	9	1
Circumventing Rules for Reducing Property Tax and License Permits	59	30	11

The representatives were asked about the risks involved in corrupt acts, particularly about the risk of prosecution or the possibility of legal action. A majority (62 per cent, i.e, 135 out of 234) were convinced that there was no risk at all in indulging in corruption, while the remaining 38 per cent perceived corruption acts as involving low risk. No one said there was high risk. Factors that contributed to low or no risks (Table 8.4) were frequency of reporting corruption, filing of corruption cases, and action taken, all of which were low/negligible. Accountability and transparency through forums such as *gram sabhas* were not effective. Although corruption was discussed in *panchayat* meetings it was more to settle personal scores. The discussions on corruption were not pursued and were not even recorded in the minutes of the *panchayat* meetings. The reservation of seats, to a certain extent, contributed to corruption not being considered as an election issue, as the incumbents (who may have been seen as corrupt) were often not eligible to contest elections. Opposition parties too did not consider corruption as an election issue at the level of local government. Corruption was also reported only occasionally and did not get adequate publicity in the print media. This only added to the perception of low risk. Representatives who were illiterate or functionally (barely) literate did not read even what was reported in the papers.

There was a mixed response to whether institutions of local government reduced corruption. Most representatives (41.5 per cent) did not see any difference in the corruption levels prior to the decentralisation reforms in the state in 1983 when the officials had more powers and the later situation under *panchayats*, 25.2 per cent stated that corruption has increased after the *panchayats* were formed, 16.2 per cent felt that there was a reduction in corruption, while the remaining did not have any opinion. On the prevalence of political and bureaucratic corruption, the opinion was that both are widely prevalent in *panchayats*. The elected representatives (89.3 per cent) were of the view that the officials played a significant role in rent seeking transactions.

Several reasons were given for the widespread prevalence of corruption (Table 8.5). Election expenses, patronage, and crowding of the political space with too many people wanting to have a say in how funds are spent were the most common reasons that were given by the representatives. Patronage was seen both as a reason for high corruption and also as a facilitating factor.

Table 8.4

Factors Contributing to Low Risk Perception

Factors Contributing to Low Risk	*Always/Frequently*	*Sometimes*	*Never*
Frequency of Cases Reported	11 (4.7)	90 (38.5)	133 (56.8)
Frequency of Cases Filed	—	7 (3)	227 (97)
Action Taken	—	—	234 (100)
Discussion of Corruption in *Gram Sabhas*	6 (2.6)	8 (3.4)	220 (94)
Discussion of Corruption in *Panchayat* Meetings	45 (19.2)	25 (10.7)	164 (70.1)
Is Discussion on Corruption Recorded in Minutes of *Panchayat* Meetings	—	6 (2.6)	228 (97.4)
Reporting of Corruption Cases in Print Media	18 (7.7)	60 (25.6)	156 (66.7)
Is Corruption an Election Issue	11 (4.7)	25 (10.7)	198 (84.6)
Do Opposition Parties Make Corruption a Governance Issue	25 (10.7)	45 (19.2)	164 (70.1)

Table 8.5

Reasons for Corruption

Reasons for Corruption	*Per Cent (Multiple Responses were Given)*
Lack of Effective Mechanisms to Check Corruption	58
Low Prosecution Rates	62
Election Expenses	89
Political Culture	85
Indifference of Citizens	76
Patronage Networks and Support Received During Elections	94
Crowding of Political Space with too Many People Wanting to have a Say in How Funds are Spent	74
The System is Corrupt	69

Attitudes Towards Corruption

Representatives indicated their opinions to a set of statements on corruption and rent seeking behaviour (Table 8.6 for the statements) depicting different types of situations, which could possibly occur in any *panchayat*. The statements included definition of corruption, acts of corrupt behaviour and their acceptability, range of situations which involved rent seeking, and on reporting corruption. These have been analysed on a three point measure of 'least agreement' to 'full agreement', where 3 indicates that the behaviour can be fully justified/ acceptable/fully agreeable, and 1 that it can never be justified/not acceptable/disagree. An aggregate score of opinions was constructed where 23 to 33 indicates that corruption is justified, 12 to 22 indicates a tendency towards corruption, and 11 that rent seeking can never be justified.

The responses to the attitude statements varied from subject to subject. The way representatives perceived what constitutes corruption was situational and hence was not in agreement with the widely accepted definition. Although the representatives in general considered corruption in public life unacceptable, their attitude on specific issues in *panchayats* that actually amounted to corruption varied significantly. For example, the representatives did not consider accepting commissions as corruption. There was also justification for awarding contracts to relatives, the role of middlemen in carrying out development activities, and accepting commissions to cover election expenses (Table 8.6). These situations were more commonly reported in *panchayats*, and there was greater likelihood that the representatives were a part of these at some point of the time or other. There was a significant difference in the articulation of attitudes between the representatives of two districts that were studied, with the justification of corruption being lower in Udupi district compared to Mandya. There was only a marginal difference based on gender in the attitude towards corruption (Vijayalakshmi, 2005).

The response to statements on corruption that were more general in nature (such as 'politician accepting bribes', 'Officials accepting bribes/ gifts to speed up bureaucratic procedures' and for carrying out official work') was one of disagreement. At the same time, statements on payment/receiving of commissions in *panchayats* were justified. A majority were of the view that commissions did not constitute corruption (when elected representatives are involved), while at the same time the commissions paid to officials was seen as bribes. Representatives made a distinction between 'corruption/accepting bribes' and 'accepting commissions' although both amounted to rent seeking. While accepting bribes in general was considered as corruption, accepting commissions or *mamul* while carrying out the functions of the *panchayats* was viewed as acceptable. Although the representatives held the view that corruption can never be justified, their responses to the statements on the corrupt practices in *panchayats* involving elected representatives was one of justification. What was most striking was that only a small section of the representatives were of the view that corruption should be reported (Table 8.6).

Table 8.6

Attitudes Towards Corruption
(N=234)

	Attitude Towards Corruption (Justified/Acceptable/Agree) (Per cent)
	Men and Women
Accepting Commissions (*Mamul*) is Not Corruption	82.9
Commissions and Bribes are Accepted to Cover Election Expenses	94.2
Politician Accepting Bribes	14.7
Bribing Politicians and Officials for Government Benefits for Which One is Not Entitled	6.1
Spending Money during Elections to Buy Support	94.8
Role of Middlemen and Intermediaries in Carrying out Development Work	89.4
Awarding Contracts to Relatives and Friends	77.4
Officials Accepting Bribes/Gifts to Speed up Bureaucratic Procedures or for Carrying Out Official Work	9.2
Any Case of Corruption Should be Immediately Reported to Authorities Concerned	17.5
Paying Bribes	3.9
Overstatement of Cost Estimates	91.4

Accepting commissions was seen as a legitimate means to recover expenses incurred during election campaigns. It was claimed that getting elected to *panchayats* involved a considerable amount of money. Elections to executive positions involved expenses on two occasions, i.e., to get elected as members and later, to the executive positions. Contesting executive positions involved money to buy supporters, and sometimes to pay off those from their own party who were potential competitors for the post. The ability to raise funds during elections was crucial in getting the party ticket. A lower capacity to raise funds meant that the party may not support their candidature. Getting party tickets often entailed paying high ranking party functionaries to mediate in the process of candidate selection. The representatives considered spending various amounts of money during elections as an acceptable practice. There were several instances where contractors and the political party paid a part of the election campaign expenses.[11] Recovering election expenses was only a means to justify what can be clearly seen as corruption. It would, in any case, be extremely unlikely that they would classify their own activities as corruption.

Among the representatives who disagreed with the statement on corruption as a means of recovering election expenses, a large section belonged to the *gram panchayats*. These representatives did not spend money during elections. There was a difference in the attitude score of the representatives between the Mandya and Bangalore (Rural) and Udupi districts. In Mandya district and Bangalore (Rural), there was more openness in expressing an attitude that favoured accepting bribes and commissions, when compared to Udupi district. The justification for accepting commissions, and holding the view that *mamul* is not corruption was higher in Mandya. In Udupi, the representatives were more discreet in expressing their views. The literacy levels, as well as civil society participation of citizens in Udupi district, were much higher, and the representatives were conscious about expressing their views. Justifying corrupt practices was also considered politically harmful, and the responses were subdued.

11. The maximum election expenses reported in the *gram panchayats* in Karnataka was Rs. 50,000, in *taluk panchayats* it was 3 lakhs; and in district *panchayats* it was 8 lakhs. The election expenses were on a lower scale for women contesting the Scheduled Castes seats, and seats reserved for women in *gram panchayats*; and where elections were unopposed because of the intervention of local elites.

The rank ordering of the responses to the statements show that there was clustering on different types attitude statements. While there was less justification for politicians and officials accepting bribes, at the other end of the continuum of attitude statements there was justification for accepting commissions, overstatement, and favouritism in awarding contracts. The overstatement of estimates of public works expenditure was not only justified by a large section of representatives but was considered acceptable for various reasons. One of the reasons given was also that there was a large gap between government specified prices (for labour, and material) while the actual prices were much higher. The overstatement was to make up for this difference. In most cases however, overstatement of estimates was one of the means of paying commissions.

Multiple Regression Analysis of Perception of Corruption

The perception of corruption is considered here as an indication of corruption and is used as a dependent variable. We examined factors influencing corruption in *panchayats* using multiple regression analysis. Table 8.7 presents *beta* estimates and t values. The R^2 is 0.641 indicating a reasonable good fit of the model. The factors that were robust in explaining the incidence of corruption are examined below.

Institutional Factors

Levels of Local Government

The results show that there is a significant relationship between the different tiers of *panchayats* and level of corruption. The *gram panchayat* was used as the base group. It was found that the corruption in the *gram panchayats* was lower than in *zilla panchayats* and *taluk panchayats* as indicated by the coefficients of these tiers. While such a difference cannot be interpreted as low corruption in *gram panchayats,* such a perception is related to the magnitude of corruption and that the actual funds that the lower tier received were much lower than in the *taluk* and *zilla panchayats. Gram panchayats* receive only five per cent of the total allocation to the institutions of local government, while the remaining is shared between *taluk* and *zilla panchayats,* which is 55 and 40 per cent respectively.[12] The magnitude of the payments was higher in *taluk* and *zilla panchayats*, and the representatives associated it with the high corruption level in these tiers.

Transparency and Accountability Mechanisms and their Effectiveness

Gram sabhas, Jamabandhi, and accounts audits are accountability measures in local governments in Karnataka. A set of questions on a three point scale on effectiveness of the functioning of accountability and transparency mechanisms, the availability of information to the citizens on budgets, procurement, and money spent on public works, and the procedures used in allocations, selecting investment projects was used to arrive at the score on effectiveness of accountability and transparency mechanisms. The score reflects the assessment of the elected representatives of accountability and transparency in their *panchayats*.

The coefficient of effectiveness of accountability and transparency is high indicating a robust relationship with corruption level. The existing participatory mechanisms such as *gram sabha, Jamabandhi*, were limited to *gram panchayats*. The accounts audit at the *gram panchayats* was carried out once every year and was regularly conducted. At the upper tiers the accounts audit was the only accountability mechanism, and it was not effective. Further, the accounts audits look more at procedures and accounting and not at the quality of development works. Interaction with the electorate was minimal in the *taluk* and *zilla panchayats*, although representatives were of the view that they had access to citizens' perspectives through party networks and were responsive to their needs.

One of the factors hindering the enhancement of the transparency and accountability has been the sheer number of development programmes. The information on the allocations for these programmes is not easily available to the citizens and sometimes even to the elected representatives. A few individuals who had access to this information also had greater possibility of extracting bribes and commissions. The other consequence is also that the dependency on

12. The state government increased the funds devolved to *gram panchayats* from the current year 2005-06.

the bureaucracy is far greater when information is not easily available, thereby strengthening corruption networks.

There was a close relationship between elite dominance, lack of accountability and rent seeking in the *panchayats*. The political networks showed a central core of elites perceived as influential in the political and local community affairs. The elites were from locally dominant caste groups who occupied leadership roles (such as community elders) and belonged to prominent political families of the area and who had access to and control over various structural resources. They had a political base and occupied important party positions, and had contacts with prominent politicians, MLAs and MPs. By virtue of their social, economic, and political positions, these individuals wielded considerable power. The elites at each level of *panchayats* usually had more than one of these characteristics. While elites controlled the activities of the *panchayats*, there was a difference in the perception of who among the elites influenced the functioning of the *panchayats* at different levels. The social, political and economic power enabled the elites to influence the functioning of *panchayats* whether or not they were representatives. In the cliente list networks in Karnataka, elites played a major role even when they were not elected to *panchayats*. This was not objected to as they played a significant role in the selection of the candidates, mobilising support for them during elections and in keeping the election competition under their control.[13]

Corruption Cases Filed

When there is widespread corruption, the filing of corruption cases or seeking legal recourse is an indication of public awareness of corruption and their trust in the rule of law. The relationship between number of cases filed and corruption level was examined and the magnitude of coefficient is high. Similarly, the low perception of risk contributed to higher levels of corruption. Of the three alternatives for the question on number of cases filed, there was no one who stated that the incidence of filing corruption cases and seeking legal course has been high. Of the remaining two alternatives 'cases were filed

13. Vijayalakshmi, 2003b.

sometimes' is considered here as a reference category. Only a few corruption cases were filed despite the general awareness about rent seeking in *panchayats*. No legal action was taken on these cases. The environment from the point of view of representatives and officials was risk free and more favourable for rent seeking.

Table 8.7

Multiple Regression Analysis of Level of Corruption

	Standardised Coefficients	*t*
	Beta	
Constant		8.820*
Institutional Mechanisms		
Accountability and Transparency Mechanisms	-.096	-1.941**
Number of Corruption Cases Filed	-.178	-3.767*
Tiers of Local Government		
Zilla/District *Panchayat*	.207	3.468*
Taluk/Sub-district *Panchayat*	.088	2.051*
Political Factors		
Composition of Political Parties	-.025	-.478
Opposition Parties Raise Corruption Issues	-.010	-.226
Election Expenditures and Contribution to Party Funds	-1.37	-2.221***
Corruption a Election Issue	-.107	-2.545*
Others		
De facto	-.702	-9.005*
No. of Times Elected to *Panchayats*	.000	.005
Involvement of Middlemen	-.071	-1.728***
Risk Perception	-.160	-2.445**
Attitude Towards Corruption	-.006	-.142
Corruption Reporting in Local News Papers	.383	1.599
R^2 .641		
N=234		

Notes: * Significant at 1 per cent
** Significant at 5 per cent
*** Significant at 10 per cent

In the two districts, petitions of misappropriation of funds were filed only in 11 cases, out of which three in Mandya and one in Udupi had been filed with the *Lok Ayukta*. The representatives were emphatic that no legal action followed. In one of the cases, a senior official who was involved was transferred, and there was no follow up action on that case. The enormous delay in taking action on the cases that were filed discouraged citizens and representatives from reporting on corruption. The representatives who had earlier acted as whistle blowers (out of personal reasons as was seen in Mandya district where these representatives were dissidents within their own party, and also did not get 'their' share of commissions,) were also discouraged by extended legal procedures. In one of the cases in Udupi district, 11 months had passed after the *Lok Ayukta* filed a report on the misappropriation of funds in the Engineering Department. No legal action had been taken even after one year and the report was not available.

Political Factors

Role of Opposition and Composition of Political Parties

As in the higher levels of government, in the *panchayats* too the expectation is that the opposition party plays an important role in making corruption an issue within and outside the forums of *panchayats*. The coefficients has been weak indicating that opposition parties were not effective in raising issues of corruption. One of the reasons for the failure to take up corruption issues is the involvement of opposition party representatives as well in misappropriating development funds.

The composition of the major political parties, both the ruling and the opposition, influences accountability and rent seeking in the *panchayats*. The assumption is that opposition parties can play an effective role in ensuring accountability if their numerical strength is closer to that of ruling political parties; and that the marginalisation of the opposition parties is greater if they are a small number in the local government.

We had included in our sample the *panchayats* that had a close numerical composition of the members from at least two major parties. In both the districts, the *panchayats* where the seats occupied by the opposition and the ruling party was close there was more responsiveness compared to the *panchayats* where a single party was dominant. The coefficients of *panchayats* where there was close composition of the political parties was not significant indicating that numerical strength of the political parties did not act as a checking mechanism in the prevalence of corruption. Despite having significant numbers, corruption was not a major issue for the opposition parties. The opposition did not make corruption in public funds an issue because most of the members received payments for the work implemented in their constituencies. The negotiating power in the payments was high for members of the opposition when the composition was close in number to that of ruling party/parties.

Corruption as an Election Issue

The relationship between representatives perception of corruption as an issue in winning election was examined. The coefficient has a significant result. This indicates that corruption not being an election issues influenced rent seeking practices. Our study also found that corruption was never an electoral issue during *panchayats* elections.

Election Expenses and Contribution to the Party Funds

The magnitude of coefficient is high in the case of expenses incurred by the representatives during elections and the contribution they made towards party funds and the corruption in *panchayats*. This was found to a greater extent in the case of district and *taluk panchayats*. The other dimension of election expenses in *panchayats* is the favours received during elections. This also includes contributions of cash and kind from contractors and other individuals, and sponsoring by the political parties.

Other Factors

The relationship between the level of corruption and the representative's attitude towards corruption, number of times elected to *panchayats*, and risk perceptions were examined. The results show that the attitude of representatives on corruption did not have any significant influence on the level of corruption in *panchayats*. The results also show that the participation of representatives in civil society associations did not have any significant influence on corruption. However, *de facto* politics and risk perception were significantly related to corruption levels. *De facto* politics is a situation where functions of the *panchayats* are carried out by individuals other than the elected representatives.

De facto Politics and Number of Times Elected to Panchayats

There were high levels of *de facto* politics in both the districts, and between the districts it was comparatively higher in Mandya district. In the case of high levels of *de facto* politics the magnitude of coefficient is high. A related factor in *de facto* politics is the reservation of seats. The undesirable aspects of representation through reservation of seats and rotation of seats is that it significantly reduced political accountability as it was not possible for most *panchayat* representatives to be elected for a second term. It curtailed accountability, since in the case of women and Scheduled Caste members, it was often party functionaries and/or elites and family members who carried out the functions of the representatives.

In *panchayats,* because of the rotation of seats, there was a high percentage of representatives who were elected to the *panchayats* for the first time. There are two possibilities if a majority of elected representatives are elected for the first time. Being new to politics would mean that exploring rent seeking opportunities and establishing rent seeking networks takes a longer time. The possibility of *de facto* politics was high particularly among women who hold the seat for one of the male family members. The higher the *de facto* politics, the higher was the level of corruption as the number of claimants for commissions will be higher. The other reason for the significant result when the number of first time representatives was used as an explanatory variable is that since the representatives are not likely to contest again the profiteering tendency was greater. There is also no risk of electoral accountability.

The representatives (including women) were drawn into the 'practise of commissions' in *panchayats* earlier in their career as *panchayat* representatives than into other responsibilities or development of their skills. It was also evident that over 85 per cent of the representatives being first timers did not have any significant impact on the level of corruption. Part of the reason for this was the entrenched corruption network comprising officials and contractors. While the institutional structure is clear about the accountability of elected representatives to the people, and the officials to the representatives, the reality is different. The inexperience of the representatives, their lack of awareness about the rules and procedures and the paucity of information on development activities contributed to a dependence on the officials. This largely reduced the accountability of officials to the elected representatives. Although it cannot be justified, officials were of the view that their accountability to the elected representatives was low because of the poor administrative capability of the representatives. Such a view cannot be generalised as some of the representatives in the *taluk* and district *panchayats* in Karnataka had higher levels of administrative and political skills.

Risk Perception

The perceived risk of engaging in corrupt act includes the perception of representatives of the possibility of getting caught and legal action being taken. The low risk of getting caught had corresponding effect on the rent seeking tendencies in *panchayats*. The results show that the relationship between risk perception and the corruption level is significant.

Considering that political and institutional mechanisms of accountability are weak the risk perception of representatives is considerably low. The analysis also indicate that other factors that increase the risk perception of representatives had a significant impact on corruption. These include opposition parties acting as a checking mechanism, electoral accountability and number of corruption cases filed and number of cases where action was taken.

Commissions or *Mamul*

Mamul in local parlance is the rate of bribe paid to get work done and for commissions (or payments) made in carrying out development activities. It is used, rather loosely, for both bribes and commissions. *Mamul* in the case of bribes was paid to get land records changed, reduce property tax, obtain electricity connections, get transferred to a place of one's choice, to settle police cases, and for official documents of any kind. Representatives did not make any distinction between bribes and commissions and also referred to the commissions paid for awarding public works and procurement contracts as *mamul*. This is a percentage of payment that was made for different slabs in all the development and public works activities carried out in the *panchayats*.

While bribes paid by the citizens for getting work done can be categorised as petty corruption, the going rate paid in the case of public works and procurement deals was large scale corruption involving commissions up to 65 per cent of the total cost in Karnataka. There were fixed rates of payments. For example, in a procurement deal in *zilla panchayats* which cost 65 lakhs, the president of the *panchayat* received a proportion of up to 10 per cent, the chairperson of the committee received 15 per cent, officials shared 20 per cent and the key individuals (which also included the representative in whose constituency the work was implemented i.e., if it is not a procurement contract) shared 20 per cent. While there were indications that the entire commission amount was not retained by the representative alone and was shared with politicians at higher levels, there was no means to verify this information.

'Fixing' activity by middlemen in *panchayats* was the crucial link in the payment of bribes. Among the representatives who carried out activities of middlemen, there were two types—elected representatives who as party workers were engaged in these activities and continued to do so; and representatives who started this work after their election to *panchayats*. Both these categories of representatives did not consider themselves as middlemen. Although the services of middlemen were widely used, they did not have respectability and the representatives did not like to be referred to as middlemen. It was much easier for representatives who were fixers to influence officials, and more so if the representative was also the president. Although representatives at the three levels carried out activities as middlemen, the visibility was far greater in the village *panchayats* than at the district and *taluk* levels. While we did not come across women representatives who acted as fixers (all middlemen were men), there were instances where the husbands of the representatives acted as middlemen, using their wife's position.

The fixers were actively involved in petty corruption in *panchayats*. Considering the active presence of fixers in *panchayats* and their own involvement in the same kind of activity, the support expressed by the representatives is not surprising. The representatives considered fixing as being responsive to the needs of their constituents. Citizens often approached the elected representatives for getting work done for which they were willing to pay the going rate. In Karnataka, the most common work that citizens sought included—to get license permit, transfers to a place of their choice, settling of police cases, and changing land documents. The elected representatives used their position and political influence to get the work done. It needs to be noted that not all representatives were politically influential to accomplish these tasks. The people approached the representatives who could get their work done. In the case of women representatives the constituents did not approach them for any help. They sought either the intervention of the politically powerful male representatives or the husbands of the women members if they were politically influential.

Citizens were content if the work that they wanted done was actually accomplished, and did not consider it as corruption even if they had paid a fee to get it done. From the perspective of the citizens a bribe is not problematic if the money paid is commensurate with the savings in time and effort, that they would otherwise have spent in getting the work done by themselves (and without the bribe). The acceptability of *mamul* was high in Karnataka as the public pressure against corruption was weak. Among the citizens we had interviewed, 62 per cent said that they paid bribes on more than one occasion. They considered the officials and representatives who completed the work helpful, and not corrupt, even if they accepted the bribe. Having said this, it should also be noted that citizens' experience and interface was usually with petty corruption.

Conclusion

Corruption in *panchayats* exists in various forms. As with its manifestation in most other institutions, it is not easy to measure the full extent of corruption in the *panchayats*. Our study indicates that pay offs and commissions are in the region of 65 per cent of the development funds. The wide spread prevalence of corruption has serious implications for development at the levels below the district, and to the villages. At the outset, it should be stated that the institutions of local government have not succeeded in reducing corruption, though this was one of the anticipated outcomes of decentralisation and the functioning of the *panchayats*. According to politicians and officials, the scale of payments and commissions has also increased considerably over the years, and particularly after the formation of panchayats. A reason for this is the increase in the number of individuals who have a role in decision making at the local level. Also, while individuals from different social groups are elected as representatives, elites who have had a longer presence in politics continue to dominate the political and development space at the local level.

The virtues of liberal democracy, *viz*., electoral politics, citizens' voice, opposition party and a vigilant media, have not made any significant impact in reducing corruption in *panchayats*. Participatory forums have not been effectively used by citizens, and they do not function as measures of accountability and transparency. There is still a considerable gap in what citizens know about *panchayat* funds and resources, and what perhaps they ought to, if principles of accountability had been adequately fulfilled. There is, however, a general awareness of the corruption that prevails in the *panchayats*, though ordinary citizens think cases against corruption have very little chance of meeting with success, or that any action would be taken against erring officials or representatives.

Access to information and the quality of information are factors that may contain rent seeking. Here, however, the poor reporting systems of *panchayats* impede such a possibility. For example, there are no uniform standards for the accounting of expenditure, that would enable the assessment of public expenditure. There is also a lack of information on the unitary costs of public works. A lack of a proper budgeting system also provides additional opportunities for rent seeking. The collusion of elected representatives and officials furthered the reluctance to share information on the utilisation of public funds with the public. The large number of government schemes/ programmes (various central and state grants) and the paucity of information about them increased the scope for rent seeking.

Accounts audits, which are an accountability measure at all the levels of *panchayats*, are not effectively managed, and no regular audits conducted particularly at the *taluk* and *zilla panchayat* levels.[14] There are no effective mechanisms to check clientelist networks, and to ensure quality in the implementation of the development works. Adequate vigilance mechanisms are not present, to follow up the functioning of the elected representatives and officials, particularly in areas of procurement, awarding contracts for development work, and on the quality of work. Although the present *Lok Ayukta* in Karnataka is active, clearly that is not on a sufficient scale to monitor the functioning of the *panchayats*.

Opposition parties did not make corruption an important issue in the provision of development services. While there were discussions on the misappropriation of development funds in *panchayat* meetings, it was not an important issue for the opposition, and few cases were filed. Even when opposition parties had a significant presence in the *panchayats*, corruption was not a governance issue, as they were more interested in negotiating for payoffs. The risks for the political parties engaging in corruption is also minimal, and there is not much of difference between political parties. The local press occasionally reports on acts of corruption, but usually no action is taken, though on rare occasions, some limited action is taken at least to avoid further publicity. Such actions, though, are few and far from adequate.

Institutions of local government provide an opportunity to introduce measures to further governance that is more responsive and accountable. Without adequate and effective institutional mechanisms to monitor the use of public funds, the institutions of local governments will only add to the layers of clientelist networks and claimants for commissions and payoffs. The continued dominance of traditional patterns of patronage has blurred the notion of accountability in *panchayats*. There are no checks on the activities of powerful individuals interfering in the functioning of *panchayats*.

Finding corruption on the scale that we have observed should not be construed as an argument against local government. Sufficient need

14. In one of our study districts, the *zilla panchayat* accounts were not audited for three years. However, *gram panchayats* appear to be better managed and have an annual audit.

has been recognised for the establishment and functioning of the *panchayats*. However, greater participation in governance should not be a means of greater participation in corruption, where the benefits of development are diminished by the leakages of resources towards private enrichment, rather than for the benefit of the community and the people.

References

Bardhan, Pranab and Dilip Mookherjee (2000). "Decentralising Anti-Poverty Program Delivery in Developing Countries", University of California, Berkeley, *Working Paper. http://econ.bu.edu./dilipm/wkpap.htm/wkbpaphmpg.html.*

———. (1998). "Expenditure Decentralisation and the Delivery of Public Services in Developing Countries". Berkeley: Department of Economics, University of California. *mimeo*.

Besley, Timothy and Stephen Coate (1999). "Centralised versus Decentralised Provision of Local Public Goods: A Political Economy Analysis", *NBER Working Paper* No. 7084.

Bird, R. and A. Fiszbein (1977). "Fiscal Decentralization in Colombia: The Central Role of the Central Government", in R. Bird and F. Vaillancourt (eds.), *Fiscal Decentralization in Developing Countries*. Cambridge: Cambridge University Press.

Blanchard, Olivier and Andrei Shleifer (2000). "Federalism with and without Political Centralization: China versus Russia", *NBER Working Papers* 7616. National Bureau of Economic Research.

Crook, Richard, James Manor (1998). *Democracy, Decentralisation in South Asia & West Africa: Participation, Accountability & Performance*. Cambridge: Cambridge University Press.

———. (2002). "Democratic Decentralization" in N. Hanna and R. Picciotto (eds.), *Making Development Work*. World Bank Series on Evaluation and Development. Volume 4. New Brunswick and London: Transaction Publishers.

Fisman, Raymond and Gatti, Roberta (2000). "Decentralization and Corruption—Evidence across Countries", *Policy Research Working Paper Series* 2290. The World Bank.

Huther, Jeff and Anwar Shah (1998). "Applying a Simple Measure of Good Governance to the Debate on Fiscal Decentralization," *Policy Research Working Paper Series* 1894. The World Bank.

Inbanathan, Anand and D.V. Gopalappa (2003). "Fixers, Patronage, 'Fixing', and Local Governance in Karnataka", *Sociological Bulletin* 52(2): 164-185.

Johnston, Michael (1979). "Patrons and Clients, Jobs and Machines: A Case Study of the Uses of Patronage", *American Political Science Review* 73(2): 385–98.

———. (1993). "Political Corruption: Historical Conflict and the Rise of Standards", in Larry Diamond and Marc F. Plattner, (eds.) *The Global Resurgence of Democracy*. Baltimore: Johns Hopkins University Press.

———. (1998). "What can be Done about Entrenched Corruption?", in Boris Pleskovic (ed.), *Annual World Bank Conference on Development Economics 1997*. Washington, DC: The World Bank. pp.149-180.

Johnson, Simon, Daniel Kaufmann and Pablo Zoido-Lobaton (1998). "Regulatory Discretion and the Unofficial Economy", *American Economic Review* 88(2): 387-92, May, American Economic Association.

Knack, Stephen, and P. Keefer (1995). "Institutions and Economic Performance: Cross-Country Tests Using Alternative Institutional Measures", *Economics and Politics* 7(3): 207–27.

Laffont, Jean-Jacques, and Mathieu Meleu (2001). "Separation of Powers and Development", *Journal of Development Economics* 64 (2001): 129-145.

Manor, James (2000). "Small-Time Political Fixers in India's States: 'Towel over Armpit'", *Asian Survey* XL(5): 816-35.

Mauro, Paolo (1995). "Corruption and Growth", *Quarterly Journal of Economics* 10(3): 681-712, August.

Nye, J.S. (1967). "Corruption and Political Development: A Cost-benefit Analysis", *American Political Science Review*, Vol. LXI, 2. Reprinted in Heidenheimer, A.J., M. Johnston and V.T. Le Vine (eds.) (1990). *Political Corruption: A Handbook*. New Brunswick, New Jersey: Transaction Publishers. pp.963-981.

Persson, Torstein, Gérard Roland, and Guido Tabelini (1997). "Separation of Powers and Political Accountability", *Quarterly Journal of Economics* 112(4): 1163-1202, November.

Prud'homme, Remy (1994). "On the Dangers of Decentralisation", *World Bank Policy Research Working Paper* 1252. Washington: World Bank.

Rao, Govinda (2000). "Fiscal Decentralisation in Indian Federalism", *Working Paper No. 98*. Bangalore: Institute for Social and Economic Change.

Reddy, G. Ram and G. Haragopal (1985). "The Pyraveekar: 'The Fixer' in Rural India", *Asian Survey* XXV(11): 1148-62.

Rose-Ackerman, Susan (1999). *Corruption and Government: Causes, Consequences, and Reform*. Cambridge: Cambridge University Press.

Seabright, P. (1996). "Accountability and Decentralization in Government: An Incomplete Contracts Model", *European Economic Review* 40: 341-356.

Sivanna, N. and Devendra Babu (2004). "Panchayat Jamabandhi in Karnataka: A Case of Transparency and Accountability in Good Governance", *Working Paper 142*, Institute for Social and Economic Change, Bangalore.

Tanzi, Vito (1996). "Fiscal Federalism and Efficiency: A Review of Some Efficiency and Macroeconomic Aspects", in M. Bruno and B. Pleskovic, (eds.), *Annual World Bank Conference on Development Economics 1995*. Washington DC: World Bank.

———. (1994). "Corruption, Governmental Activities and Markets", *IMF Working Paper* 94/99.

Tiebout, Charles (1956). "A Pure Theory of Local Expenditures", *Journal of Political Economy* 64: 416-24.

Treisman, Danierl (2000). "The Causes of Corruption: A Cross National Study", *Journal of Public Economics* 76(3): 399-457.

Vijayalakshmi, V. (2003). "Accountability and Governance: Local Government in Kerala and Karnataka", *Working Paper* No. 125. Bangalore: Institute for Social and Economic Change.

———. (2005). "Rent Seeking and Gender in Local Governance", *Working Paper* 164. Bangalore: Institute for Social and Economic Change.

Wade, Robert (1997). "How Infrastructure Agencies Motivate Staff: Canal Irrigation in India and the Republic of Korea", in Ashoka Mody (ed.), *Infrastructure Strategies in East Asia*. World Bank.

Wildasin, David (1995). "Comment on 'Fiscal Federalism and Decentralisation'", *Annual World Bank Conference on Development Economics*, pp.323-328.

9

Dynamics of Local Governance in Karnataka

KRIPA ANANTHPUR*

Introduction

Governance discourse tends to focus strongly on formal political institutions. This is particularly true at the local level where decentralised governance has become synonymous with local governance. Given this strong focus on formal decentralised structures of governance, the role of customary village councils in local governance often gets overlooked. There are two reasons for this. It is generally believed that formal institutions are (a) quite distinct from the customary institutions and are relatively free of 'traditional' influences that bear on them; and (b) more powerful than the customary ones, and so tend to 'drive them out'. However, the extent to which these assumptions are in consonant with local reality is debatable. Decentralised local government structures such as *Gram Panchayats* (GPs) coexist with customary village councils and often interact with them. Development outcomes, either positive or negative, at the local level are often determined by these interactions.

Karnataka has a fairly long and impressive history of decentralisation. Democratically elected local government structures were institutionalised and political space created for marginalised groups long before the 1992 amendment that made Panchayati Raj Institutions (PRIs) constitutionally mandatory.[1] Despite this, local governance in Karnataka has not become fully formalised. At the

---

* This paper is the product of an ongoing research project "Formal and Informal Local Governance in India" supported by the Centre for the Future State, Institute of Development Studies, Sussex, U.K. Data analysis is in progress and the findings reported here are preliminary and tentative.

1. The 1992 constitutional amendment (73rd) established an elected three-tier government structure at the sub-state level known as Panchayati Raj Institutions.

village level, elected GPs continue to coexist with customary village councils (CVCs), which are rooted in traditional practices, values and power relations. It is widely believed that customary institutions are instruments of caste dominance, oppressive in nature and shrinking in face of modernity, especially with the introduction of formal, elected, local GPs. While these perceptions are not completely wrong, the research indicates that the picture is more complex.

In reality, CVCs:

- generally are inter-caste institutions consisting of caste leaders of different caste groups represented in the community and act as forums of deliberation with an emphasis on compromise rather than simple rule enforcement.
- in addition to enforcing 'traditional' rules and norms, also perform a range of useful functions at the village level often in a non-repressive manner.
- rather than disappearing in the face of modernity, often interact in a positive manner with the 'so-called' modern, formal local institutions that are said to be replacing them.

This indicates that local governance in Karnataka is a complex and contested site where formal and informal local governance institutions complement each other in some instances and are in conflict at others.

The objective of this paper is to unpack the dynamics of local governance in Karnataka by studying the interaction between two sets of rural institutions, (a) the formal, elected GPs, mandated by the 73rd amendment to the Indian Constitution in 1992, that typically cover a group of natural villages; and (b) the informal, long standing, village level CVCs, which undertake dispute resolution and a wide range of other activities at the level of the individual natural village. On the basis of field research in 30 villages in Karnataka, this paper tries to present a more holistic picture of CVCs, including their role in village governance and service delivery (Section 2) and the ways in which they interact with GPs (Sections 3). The concluding section analyses the implications of this interaction and its influence on local democracy in Karnataka.

Local Governance in Karnataka

Karnataka is one of the better-developed states in India. Land reforms and other developmental initiatives and opportunities aimed at backward classes and Dalits in the 1980s has created a society that is not as polarised as some of the other states in India. This has led to the formation of a fairly cohesive society (Manor, 1997). A less well-known fact about Karnataka relates to its long experimentation with decentralisation. Attempts to devolve powers to local bodies had been initiated even before independence (Natraj and Ananthpur, 2003). A serious effort to decentralise its political structures in Karnataka came about in the 1980s. The first major landmark in Karnataka was the 1983 Act, which introduced a two-tier, elected sub-state level governance structure. A notable feature was 25 per cent reservation for women in these bodies even before this was mandated by the Constitution. Elections under this Act were held in 1987. The 1983 Act was substituted by a new law in 1993 (the Karnataka Panchayat Raj Act, 1993) to accommodate the mandatory provisions brought in by the 73rd and 74th amendments to the Constitution. The 1993 Act provides for a three-tier structure—*Zilla Panchayat* (district level), *Taluk Panchayat* (Block level) and GPs (village level).

Gram Panchayats

Of the three tiers of PRIs, GP is the most important tier as it is directly involved in local governance specially given its proximity to the rural population.

Some of the key features of GPs in Karnataka are as follows:

- Democratically elected bodies.
- Elections conducted once in five years.
- Constituted for a group of villages (5-7000 population) with one representative for every 400 population.
- 33 per cent seats reserved for women and 33 per cent seats reserved for OBCs.
- Reservation of seats for SCs & STs in proportion to their population.
- Reservation for the post of president and vice president.

- Tied and untied funds from the state and central governments.
- Vested with powers of taxation.

Given that GPs have become institutionalised and influential, one would expect that customary village councils(CVCs) at the village level in Karnataka to become defunct and faded away. In fact, it is generally believed that the 'traditional' *village panchayats,* studied and documented by Ishwaran (1968), Srinivas (1987) and others no longer exist in Karnataka. Village elites, instead of the *village panchayat,* are now seen as mediators of power relations and influencing the process of local governance (Inbanathan, 2000). But field research in 30 villages from three different districts[2] of Karnataka indicates that CVCs are not only prevalent but also quite active in all 30 villages. Rather than declining CVCs continue to be ubiquitous and influential.

Customary Village Councils[3]

CVCs are one among a variety of local institutions, structured mainly around caste, that exist in Indian villages. This is true of Karnataka also. The type of local institutions range from caste *panchayats,* street *panchayats* to CVCs. Of all these local institutions, CVCs are the most important category of institutions from a democracy and governance perspective mainly because intra-village caste *panchayats* and/or street *panchayats*[4] (for a single street or a group of streets) operate at sub-village level and have limited authority—restricted to a caste group in the case of caste *panchayats* or limited to the population of a street or few streets in case of street *panchayats.* But the CVC is an apex body with jurisdiction over the entire village. They are not formal political institutions, which have a set of clearly delineated responsibilities. Rather they are better comprehended as a 'pattern of dialectic, decision and action' (Mandelbaum, 1970). CVCs play a central role in village governance by maintaining social order and ensuring community harmony and thus fostering village solidarity.

2. Ten villages each from Mysore, Dharwad and Raichur districts were chosen to study the interaction between the formal and informal local governance institutions.
3. For a detailed description of CVCs, see "Rivalry or Synergy? Formal and Informal Local Governance in India", *IDS Working Paper* No.226, June, 2004.
4. I came across street *panchayats* in only one big village where the ILGI was relatively weak.

CVCs are long-standing institutions that draw their legitimacy from 'traditions' and customs and are quite distinct from the modern associations that are formed as part of external interventions such as user committee groups, micro-credit groups etc for a specific purpose. However, leaders of the CVC are often found represented in 'modern' local bodies such as watershed committees, water and sanitation committees, forest committees etc.

Customary Village councils go under a wide variety of local names in Karnataka. In southern part of the state, particularly in Mysore district, CVCs are known locally as *"panchayati" (Council), "Halli panchayati"* (Village Council), *"nadu"* or *"nadu panchayati"* (Regional Council), *"nyaya panchayati"* (Justice Council) or even *"nyaya samiti"* (Justice Committee). In northern Karnataka particularly in the area covered by the former Dharwad district, the terms *"pancharu"* or *"Hireru"* (village elders) are prevalent, while in one village the CVC is known as the "Civic Board". In Raichur district the normal term is *"Daiva"* (God). However, for the purpose of this paper I will refer to them as "customary village councils" (CVCs).

Unlike GPs, CVCs function at the village level and have authority only over the 'natural' village within which it operates. Typically a single *Gram Panchayat* may include several CVCs. In contrast to GPs, the basic structure of CVCs is rooted in 'tradition' and customs. Srinivas describes 'village councils' (CVCs) as being 'informal and flexible' bodies with 'no hard and fast rule about who should constitute them'. He has also observed a variation in membership over space and context (2002: 81). Mandelbaum's (1970) detailed study of 'village *panchayats*' from different parts of the country indicates a similar flexible pattern of representation. Basically there are two types of CVCs based on the caste composition of the village. (a) In a single caste village the caste *panchayat* also operates as the CVC, (b) but in village with multi-caste population, the CVC is a broader forum that includes the caste leaders of all caste groups. Essentially all CVCs have a core set of leaders of various caste groups represented in the village. However, the variation is visible in the extent of inclusion of other members such as SC leaders, GP members and new leaders. Caste leaderships tend to be hereditary titles but the inclusion of new members is based on more modern criteria such as education, mobility, their political linkages, ability to interact with government officials and so on. There are instances of corrupt or discriminatory CVC leaders being replaced with those that have the respect of the entire village community (Ananthpur, 2004).

CVCs broadly have a similar pattern of representation—a set of members or *panchas* headed by a leader- *Yajamana*. The membership to CVCs is intrinsically embedded in caste and gender. Virtually all *panchas* are men and are usually the caste leaders[5] of individual caste groups present in the village. The size of a CVC is broadly proportional to the number of caste groups present in a village. Although headed by *Yajamanas*, CVCs are rarely, if ever, *controlled* by a single, dominant caste leader or big landowner of the village. It is perceived as a more deliberative forum, where decisions are arrived at after discussions and consensus. This 'egalitarianism' is not unique to Karnataka CVCs but also found in the village councils of Rajasthan where '*panchas*' (representatives) of all caste groups sit as equals on the central platform'. (Krishna, 2002: 136).

A major criticism against CVCs is that they reinforce caste and gender hierarchies. The pattern of representation in the CVC, to a certain extent, confirms this view. This is particularly visible in the marginal representation, in CVCs, of Scheduled Castes[6] (SC) in some villages to complete exclusion of women in all the 30 villages. However there is evidence that many CVCs are adapting to the changing sociopolitical context. For instance, there is a better representation for SCs in villages with dominant SC population (at least in three villages SC and Scheduled Tribe members were the *Yajamanas* of the CVC) and in a couple of villages, female elected members of the formal GP sometimes were invited to join in the deliberations of the CVC for specific purposes.[7] Krishna finds that in

5. Some caste groups in a few villages have a leadership, usually hereditary but at times elected, and accounts (of funds collected by that particular caste group for religious and other purposes) that are checked by the people belonging to that particular caste group around every Hindu New Year. Caste *Panchayats* have jurisdiction over all families belonging to that caste in the village. These organisations are often quite formal and institutionalised.

6. Those belonging to caste groups previously considered as 'untouchables'.

7. Specially disputes related to women.

Rajasthan, 'though representatives of the scheduled castes (previously known as untouchables) sit some distance apart or even at a lower level from other *panchas*, they have equal say in the decision, particularly when a person from their own caste group is involved as a party' (Krishna, 2002: 136). In Karnataka, particularly in some villages of Mysore district, SC leaders sit together on the same platform with other caste leaders while resolving disputes. This ability to adapt has made CVCs more pluralistic (with limitations) and also able to project a more modern image to outsiders.

Many CVCs have also begun to widen their base of representation in an attempt to adapt to local democracy. Apart from the core membership (caste based), CVCs include other members many of whom are members of the elected GPs. and their membership in the formal GPs. The emergence of new and parallel leadership at the village level is not a new phenomenon and is commonly found in most rural areas (Bailey, 1960, Beteille, 1971, Krishna, 2002). But Karnataka seems to differ in that the 'new leaders' often find a place on CVCs and play active roles there (Ananthpur, 2002).

CVCS do not have any permanent source of income. Donations collected for religious activities and fines imposed on villagers found guilty during the dispute resolution purpose are the two main sources of income. CVCs ability to raise local resources is reported in greater detail elsewhere. In Karnataka CVCs perform a wide range of useful, collective activities. With the formal elected GP taking care of the development needs of the villagers, CVCs have not become redundant as they provide valuable services to the rural citizens that are not offered by the formal GPs. The following is a list of activities/ functions that CVCs generally perform at the village level. CVCs may perform some or all these functions depending upon their influence and degree of activism.

1. All 30 CVCs were involved in religious activities, such as organising religious festivals, rituals and processions (*Jathre*), temple construction, repairs and maintenance. In some villages a separate temple committee is constituted to oversee the preparations for the Village *Jathre*. Such temple committees tend to be much more broad based and consist of leaders of the CVC

along with other village notables. Most CVCs collect donations—cash or kind—from the villagers for these activities.

2. CVCs were involved in dispute resolution in all 30 sample villages. They not only arbitrate disputes but also help maintain local law and order and thus play a key role in the internal regulation of villages. The types of disputes that come before the CVCs include petty disputes, thefts, encroachment issues, minor property disputes, drunken brawls and marital problems. Criminal cases are handed over to the police. Villagers do not necessarily see dispute resolution by CVCs as an end point, but rather as the first opportunity for justice because it is quick, affordable and accessible.[8] In most villages, villagers have the option of approaching the police station or the formal legal system if disputes are not satisfactorily resolved there. On an average 80 per cent of local disputes are resolved by the CVCs in these 30 villages. There are also a few instances of pending disputes being brought back from the law courts to the CVC for resolution.
3. CVCs also provide social services and support to those in need. There are a number of cases of CVCs helping destitute or widowed women to get a share of their husbands' property, helping widows in the village to get widow pension and/or ration cards, collecting funds from the villagers to help accident victims (generally from poor families), arranging funeral rites for the insolvent people, organising mass marriages for the poor, donating stationery to local school children, or supporting the education of gifted students. CVCs have also played a significant role in maintaining communal harmony in villages with substantial Muslim populations. CVCs in 24 out of 30 sample villages were involved in providing various forms of social support to the villagers. However these activities are not part of their regular functions and are taken up as and when required.
4. Some CVCs have also taken up development activities using

8. While in most cases villagers respect the ILGI as an institution capable of delivering fair judgement, there are instances where ILGIs have been accused of being biased and corrupt.

their own initiatives and resources. CVC members have donated or solicited donations of land from villagers or neighbouring villagers for building roads, schools, *anganwadis* (pre-schools), community halls and/or living quarters for village government functionaries such as local nurses, teachers, doctors. CVCs in 23 out of 30 sample villages were involved in some sort of development activities but the degree of activism varied significantly. CVCs are not always successful in mobilising cash resources for development purposes but are more influential in soliciting donations of land or labour from the villagers for development purposes. This is mainly because there is a general feeling among the villagers that development activities are the responsibility of GPs and should be funded by the government. However, a couple of CVCs have managed to raise resources for own development projects. Some of the innovative activities of the two CVCs are listed below:

- Constructed an approach road to the village. Villagers also donated tractors, labour and some adjoining land to widen the road.
- Purchased 4 acres of land for the construction of a high school building in the village, ensuring that female students had easier access to higher education.
- Purchased land for building a small hospital in the village.
- Built a community hall which is available free of charge for local weddings
- Organised health camp in the village.
- Repaired and modernised the local school by donating T.V., sound system.
- Organised a legal awareness camp in association with *Gram Panchayat* members, local youth club and women's groups[9].

9. One of the CVC leaders in this village, who is also a practicing lawyer, initiated this legal awareness camp by linking up with the district legal cell, which gives free legal aid to the citizens. A range of issues such as Hindu personal law, Muslim personal law, legal aspects related to land revenue, vehicles, property rights and others were discussed. The villagers not only participated in large numbers but also were interested in making this an annual event.

- Concerned with the receding ground water table in the village, one of the CVC has purchased 1.5 acres of land, for Rs. 50,000/- from their own contributions, for constructing a tank. Subsequently, the CVC collected funds from higher tiers of local governments and local MLAs[10] and MPs [11] and further extended this tank by another 2.5 acres. This tank has not only regenerated the water table in the village but also provides a regular source of water for the villagers.

These two are rather exceptional cases as not all CVCs exhibit the same level of innovativeness in initiating development activities. But reports from different parts of the state indicate that CVCs do play a significant role in local development activities and either substitute or complement formal development initiatives.

5. Another area where the CVC is becoming an important actor in local governance, relates to informal resource mobilisation. CVCs, in all the villages studied, were involved in some form of informal resource mobilisation. The amount raised per year may range from a minimum of Rs.1000/- to a maximum of Rs.1,00,000/-. Informal resource mobilisation may include donations or contributions in cash and kind. Many CVCs maintain bank accounts and submit the expenditure statement to the villagers once a year. Apart from raising resources for religious purposes, CVCs also play an important role in mobilising resources for development projects. Increasingly a number of development projects initiated through GP now require matching contributions from the villagers. It is here that the CVC's ability to raise local funds comes into play. One such programme is the rural water and sanitation programme, which requires 10 per cent matching grants to be raised by the community. While in a few villages, CVC has been successful in raising this matching grant, in others the project was not initiated, as the CVC was not involved in the process. Some

---

10. Each Member of Legislative Assembly (MLA) is given Rs. 40 lakhs as constituency development fund.
11. Each Member of Parliament (MP) has access to 20,000,000 million rupees for development activities in his/her constituency.

> CVCs have also donated money collected through fines (from the process of dispute resolution) and additional or left over funds collected for religious festivities for this purpose. However, as mentioned above, there were just two cases of CVCs mobilising local resources on their own for village development.

How are CVC decisions enforced? The CVC leaders I interviewed agree that their decisions, particularly regarding dispute resolution, are not absolutely enforceable. One or other party to the dispute has the option of accessing formal police or judicial channels. CVCs still manage to enforce most of their decisions through social pressure. For example, a person who has openly violated the dictates of the CVC does not find support in the village in times of need or distress unless he or she openly tenders an apology to the CVC for violating its dictates. However, the legitimacy of CVCs and the extent to which they are able to enforce their decisions are somewhat contested. There is a general perception that they no longer enjoy the influence they once did when formal local institutions were relatively weak. But they remain very influential. Villagers, especially women, believe that in a context where they are still distant from the formal law and order mechanisms like the police and the judiciary, there is a need for locally-rooted institutions that provide justice and maintain local law and order.

While the institutional structure of CVCs embodies an inherent contradiction to the democratic principles, their functional characteristics complement the functions of local democratic institutions. But despite their progressive and functional aspect, as an institution dominated by the village elite, CVCs are largely seen as vehicles for 'elite capture' of local democratic institutions and processes. The extent to which this proposition is valid is tested in the next section where I explore the different ways in which CVCs interacts and influences GPs.

Interaction with *Gram Panchayats*

In India, the Constitutional amendment that mandates local governance has remained silent on the role of 'Informal/customary institutions' in local governance. It does, however, make provision to accommodate the tribal laws and customs for tribally dominated regions. In fact special Constitutional provisions have been designed to protect the tribal governance structures by bringing the tribally dominant regions under the Vth schedule of the Constitution and providing them a central role in local governance. In 1996, a national level legislation—"The Provisions of the *Panchayats* (Extension to the Scheduled Areas) Act 1996"—allowed for the accommodation of the tribal laws and customs in tribally dominated regions.[12] This development came in the wake of objections and protests that formal, local governance structures as mandated by the Constitution would impede and destroy the tribal ways of life (Mahi Pal, 2000). CVCs do not get similar recognition in the Constitutional amendment mandating local governance. This makes the role of the CVCs in formal, local politics in the Indian context somewhat unique, as they do not have any legally or formally assigned role to play in the process of local democracy. The interaction between CVCs and GPs has remained largely un-explored as these two institutions occupy different spaces, mainly state and non-state spaces. They also operate at different levels—formal and informal levels. This makes the interaction almost invisible not only to the outsiders but also to the villagers.

CVCs interact and influence GPs various ways. I've grouped these interactions into two main categories:

a) Influence over GP Elections (IGPE)

b) Involvement in GP Activities (IGPA)

a) Influencing GP Elections (IGPE)

CVCs try to influence the GP elections by:

1. Trying to influence the choice of candidates for GP elections—in 29 out of my 30 research villages, CVCs have played a role in influencing the selection of candidates for GP elections held

12. India has a significant tribal population. It is estimated that they constitute about 8 per cent of the total population. Quotas are provided for the tribal population in various spheres to make the governance and development process more inclusive.

during years 2000 and 2005. However, the data reported here pertains to 2000 GP elections. The process of influencing the choice of candidates for elections may take place either before nominations are filed or when they are being finalised. There have been instances of CVCs asking some candidates to withdraw in favour of their candidates. However, the dictates of the CVC may not always be accepted as contesting local elections has become a 'prestigious' issue to the villagers. This is especially true of the village youth. The CVC, as a village forum, not only exhibits caste and gender monopolies but also has an inherent age-ist bias. Village youth, while allowed to participate in the CVC meetings, are not permitted to speak unless permitted by the CVC leaders. Thus the village youth, traditionally excluded from the CVC, have begun to use the GP elections and membership to establish their influence in village politics while the CVC tries to utilise GP elections to extend its sphere of authority. These tensions rather than dissipating are likely to exacerbate in the future. But in situations where contested elections have taken place, villagers admit that most of the successful candidates were those originally chosen by the CVCs.

2. Trying to contest elections themselves or through their relatives thus leading to overlap of leadership in both institutions—In 26 out of my 30 villages, some form of overlap of leadership exists. For example, the *Yajamana* of the CVC in one village is also the president of the *GP*. In another village, a CVC leader was the previous president of *Gram Panchayat*. In the same village, the son of the CVC *Yajamana* is presently a member of the *Gram Panchayat*. In a number of villages, *panchas* are also members of the *Gram Panchayat*. The extent of overlap of leadership for all 30 villages is around 32 per cent of all GP seats. Overlap of leadership also occurs with higher tiers of local governance such as *Taluk Panchayats* and *Zilla Panchayats*. However this aspect has not been included in our research as elections to *Taluk* and *Zilla Panchayats* are contested on the basis of party politics and I have not investigated the influence of party politics on the choice of candidates.

3. Ensuring that their candidates hold the positions of president or vice president of GPs where possible—CVCs has played an important role in ensuring that elected GP members from their village get access to the positions of president or vice president of GP. Even in cases where CVCs have not been fully successful in influencing the choice of candidates for GP elections, they have played a decisive role in ensuring that the position of president or vice president is allocated to their village. However this is mainly dependant upon the type of reservation that is applicable to that particular GP. In 13 out of 30 sample villages the CVC had played a role in securing the position of president and/or vice president to the candidates from their village. Overall, about 28 per cent of positions of president or vice president were held by either CVCs leaders or candidates selected by them in 30 sample villages.
4. Trying to control election outcomes by encouraging uncontested elections—CVCs have tried, where possible, to concretise their choice of candidates by trying to ensure 'unanimous' (uncontested) elections. In 18 out of my 30 sample villages 'unanimous' elections took place in 2000: in four cases all the seats were uncontested, and in 16 villages at least one or more seats were uncontested and a total of 38 per cent of GP seats were filled up through uncontested elections in the 30 research villages This appears to be in accordance with the general trend in Karnataka. In the 2000 *Gram Panchayat* elections, 26 per cent seats of all GP seats in Karnataka were filled by 'unanimous' elections (*The Hindu*, 1st March, 2000). However CVCs' influence in controlling election outcomes by ensuring unanimous elections is not absolute but subject to a range of factors both external and internal. Involvement of political parties, reservation of seats, village youth aspiring for leadership positions, and increased awareness in local political participation and representation have all contributed to a visible decrease in the percentage of unanimous elections. A preliminary look at the results of the 2005 GP elections reveal that the number of seats filled up through uncontested elections in these villages have come down significantly.

(b) Involvement in GP Activities (IGPA)

In almost all the villages I studied, the CVC leaders play an important role in negotiating with the formal, local representatives and institutions for benefits to the village even where they have had little involvement in the selection of formal local representatives. CVC leaders and members play an important role in the (a) implementation of development projects and (b) selection of beneficiaries for anti-poverty schemes.

a) *Implementation of development projects*: By and large the CVC supports its GP members in ensuring that development projects allocated through the GP are delivered to the village. Consultations with the local leaders, regarding the implementation and location of development project in the village, by the GP members are most common. Often the CVC influences decisions related to the location of roads, streetlights, water taps or drainage. The CVC leaders constantly put pressure on the elected members for development projects such as construction or repairs of school buildings and community halls, provision of drinking water, roads, and drainages. This was evident in all 30-study villages. CVC leaders also monitor their performance and erring or inefficient elected representatives are often pulled up.

In addition, the CVC also try to improve the village infrastructure by soliciting donations, in cash or kind, for village development as mentioned above. The involvement of the CVC in the implementation of development projects can be a positive feature of local democracy as it encourages local participation and decision making in the development process. But this intervention assumes negative undertones if these decisions are biased in favour of the village elite as it has an adverse implications for the welfare of the village poor.

b) *Selection of beneficiaries for anti-poverty schemes*: An important aspect of the influence deals with decisions impacting directly on the poor. The process of selection of beneficiaries for anti-poverty schemes takes place in the *Gram Sabha*—the village assembly. All adults in the village are members of the *Gram Sabha* and are allowed (and expected) to participate in this process. Those representing the CVC often use this formal space to influence decisions regarding the selection of beneficiaries. The CVC leaders feel they are better placed to identify beneficiaries as they are better attuned to the local reality. The involvement of CVCs in this process often makes it more transparent. But this democratic decision making process gets subverted when it is used to strengthen the CVC's position in the village, by favouring those that support them. Field research indicates both these two types of outcomes.

A comparison of the interaction between CVCs and GPs in 30 sample villages indicates a wide inter-village variation in the level of interaction. CVCs also seem to be more active in more developed districts like Mysore and Dharwad compared to Raichur, which is one of the backward districts. However my sample is too sparse to analyse this statistically.

Villagers' Perceptions of CVCs' Interaction with GP

The field data depicts a rather a negative view of CVCs as institutions undermining local democracy. People representing the CVC, it appears, not only influence the choice of candidates, but also try to control elections outcomes by ensuring uncontested elections and where possible attempt to occupy formal positions. The impact of this influence is especially visible in women's 're-election' to GPs (Ananthpur 2002). By denying rural citizens a chance to participate in free and fair elections, CVCs seem to be subverting the process of democracy and capturing local democratic institutions. This view, by implication, perceives rural citizens as mute, passive recipients of this process.

In order to assess the awareness and perceptions of villagers regarding the interaction between CVCs and GPs, a perception survey was carried out in all 30 villages. Based on random sampling, a total of 2183 villagers (of which 51 per cent were males and 49 per cent were females) were interviewed. Villagers' awareness regarding the role played by CVCs in influencing GP elections as well as their involvement in GP activities was assessed. A series of cross-tabulations was carried out to study the levels of knowledge of different groups of people regarding the interaction between CVCs and GPs. Variables such as gender, caste, occupation, age and literacy were cross-tabulated with levels of knowledge. In general, cross-tabulation indicates that independent variables such as literacy, occupation, caste, and landholding make little difference to the levels of knowledge. Perception survey of villagers from 30 villages indicates that villagers are quite aware of the role played by the CVC in local elections. Nearly 74 per cent of the surveyed villagers were aware that CVCs were involved in selection of candidates for GP elections. Villagers were not only aware of the CVC's role in local elections but also, at times, supported and at others, opposed the CVC's influence over local elections. The role played by CVCs in election process is perceived by the villagers in different ways: as making the democratic process more efficient; as reducing unnecessary expenditure on election campaigning; or maintaining community peace as elections are seen as fostering factionalism within villages. Even the overlap of leadership is not perceived as 'elite capture' by the villagers but a way of choosing effective and efficient leaders; those capable of performing and serving the village better by bringing development to the village. Unanimous elections where effected and accepted is seen as reducing costs (campaigning expenses), time and effort by the villagers.

Equally the influence of the formal processes and institutions on the informal cannot be disregarded. As GPs have become institutionalised and influential, villagers have begun to consider contesting local elections as being important and prestigious. This has led to an increased interest in local political participation and representation. Consequently a slow resistance to CVCs' influence over local election processes is emerging. In a couple of villages, the CVC *Yajamanas* who belong to the dominant caste groups, have little interest in controlling nominations as all the seats in the village are reserved for Scheduled Castes and Scheduled Tribes. In another case, there was opposition within the village to the list of 'consensus candidates', as there were a number of villagers interested in contesting elections. In yet another village, some people did not accept the unanimous choice of a CVC *Yajamana's* son as the candidate for *Gram Panchayat*, and nominated another candidate. Although the CVC *Yajamana's* son went on to win, the show of dissension itself indicates the changes that reforms from above, in the form of reservation of seats and the process of democratic decentralisation, have initiated in the rural regions. This view is further substantiated by the fact that there are at least couple of instances of *panchas* or their kin losing the elections to candidates who were not part of the CVC. This indicates the increasing importance of creating formal spaces as it has the potential to act as a counter to the local political monopolies that CVCs often represent.

Villagers do not view these two institutions as competitive but as complementary , each serving different purposes and needs. This view is clearly reflected in their institutional preferences.[13] Cross-tabulation of different variables such as gender, age, caste, and education with preference shows some interesting results. In general, there is a clear gender difference in preference. (a) Women prefer CVCs more -36 per cent as compared with 17 per cent to men. (b) 40 per cent Men prefer GP more than CVC—but a slightly lesser percentage of men—35 per cent—want both CVC and GP.

Two of the main reasons cited for wanting 'both CVC and GP' are that: (1) the CVCs offer useful services not offered by GPs, and (2) the CVCs make the formal process more transparent and accountable. Women prefer CVC as they feel that it provides local law and order at the village. Women's clear preference for CVCs, despite the fact that they find no representation in CVCs, and the general shift towards wanting both institutions with increase in literacy indicates that the important role played by CVCs in local governance is often not recognised by the 'outsiders' who view them as oppressive and moribund institutions.

---

13. I'd asked an open-ended question as to which institution people preferred and why. Based on the answers given I categorised them into 5 groups: (a) Don't know (b) Only CVC, (c) Only GP, (d) Both CV and GP (wanting both the institutions) and lastly (e) Neither.

Table 9.1

Villagers' Attitudes to Local Governance Institutions: Respondents' Preferences for Customary Village Councils (CVCs) and/or Gram Panchayats (GPs)

(*Per Cent*)

	CVC Only	*GP Only*	*Both CVC and GP*	*Neither*	*Don't know*	*Total*
All respondents	27	32	27	9	5	100
Female respondents	36	25	20	12	7	100
Literate respondents	22	36	34	5	3	100
Illiterate respondents	30	29	22	12	7	100

Source: Open-ended question about adult villagers' preferences were asked in the baseline survey conducted in 2002-03. We have interpreted and grouped the responses.

In addition, qualitative and other data collected through interviews and focus group discussions illustrate the impact of formal processes in not only reforming CVCs but also producing better development and governance outcomes. For instance,

- CVCs with high and synergistic interaction with GPs are also engaged in initiating own development activities and engaging in public-private partnerships with formal institutions for development projects. CVCs are taking on new roles that involve interaction with formal institutions. Some do more than work with and through elected GPs: in relating to higher levels of government and electoral politics, they have become significant actors in their own right. CVCs are supplementing and complementing formal development initiatives.
- The constructive interaction between CVCs and GPs has also positive implication for local governance. Focus group discussions with poorer groups in the villages were carried out to assess their awareness and opinion about the programmes of the *Gram Panchayat* and the involvement of the CVC leaders in this. Awareness and satisfaction with *Gram Panchayat* programmes and activities was high in villages where there was high interaction between CVCs and GPs compared to others. In these villages, the villagers also reported that corruption, an important indicator of governance, was less because of the

involvement of the CVC leaders in *Gram Panchayat* activities. Villages with low interaction between CVCs and GPs' had high reports of corruption by *Gram Panchayat* members and less satisfaction with the activities of the GPs.

Concluding Comments

Research in Karnataka indicates that CVCs play an important role in local governance not only as social institutions but also as agencies that impact development process. In a context where local governance is being formalised and decentralised up to the village level, these institutions assume importance as they play a significant role in local governance.

Two key findings that stand out from this research are:

a) CVCs co-exist, interact with and influence GPs and this influence is not always negative. What we see in Karnataka is a 'hybrid' situation. Villagers are not only aware of this interaction but also seem comfortable with this hybridity of having access to both institutions. Rather than conflicting, CVCs in Karnataka seem to complement the initiatives of GPs.[14]

b) CVCs are more active in interacting and influencing GPs in better developed districts compared to less developed districts. This indicates that CVCs are not disappearing but reinventing themselves with development and modernity.

The notion that development or progress is associated with defined patterns of institutional change has a long history. The modernisation theory of the 1950s and1960s was but one highly articulated version of that general pattern. So too has been the recent insistence by most international aid and development agencies that 'good government' in developing countries is in large degree of matter of adopting certain standard political and legal institutions. These assertions of the value

14. Preliminary regression analysis indicates that CVCs are most active and interactive where GP headquarters are located in the same villages as CVCs and where these GPs are effective and efficient. Here GP efficiency is measured by their revenue raising as assessed thorough their Total Own Revenue collection and their outcomes/outputs assessed through people's awareness and satisfaction with GP performance and activities.

of what is sometimes termed a form of 'institutional monoculture' inevitably generate counter-reactions. Some of the most productive counter-reactions are based on empirical research. They demonstrate (a) that dichotomous notions of bad (= old) versus good (= new) institutions often leave us unable to explain effective institutional performance; and (b) that it is generally very important not to confuse the form of institutions with the functions that they carry out. Effective institutions can often be characterised in terms of 'institutional dualism': the combination of putatively 'traditional' (= old) with 'modern' (= new) norms, relationships and practices (Brinkerhoff and Goldsmith, 2005). CVCs in Karnataka could be viewed as an example of institutional dualism, and, for practical policy purposes, treated in the same way that Brinkerhoff & Goldsmith (2005: 2) enjoin us to think about the treatment of dualistic institutions generally: to distinguish those that "serve, or at least do not contradict, the majority's needs and aspirations, from similar looking organisations that block or even reverse improvements in economic performance and social welfare"; and to recognise "the hidden positive functions of certain dualistic practices, such as giving poor people access to resources or allowing them an informal voice in the political system."

The purpose of the paper is to present a clearer understanding of the local institutional arrangements in Karnataka and the ways in which they interact with each other. Evidence from the field indicates that the CVCs influence local democracy in many ways and this merits further enquiry, especially in the context where policy makers, donor agencies and NGOs have been investing resources, both financial and human, to strengthen formal, elected local institutions. For this investment to be productive a better and deeper understanding of the dynamics of local governance is essential.

This research was supported by the Centre for the Future State.

References

Ananthpur, K. (2002). "Interfaces in Local Governance in Karnataka", *Economic and Political Weekly*, Vol. XXXVII(42), October 19-25.

———. (2004). "Rivalry or Synergy? Formal and Informal Local Governance in Rural India", *IDS Working Paper* No. 226, June.

Bailey, F.G. (1960). *Tribe, Caste and Nation: a Study of Political Activity and Political Change in Highland Orissa.* Manchester: Manchester University Press.

Beteille, A. (1971). *Caste, Class, and Power Changing Patterns of Stratification in a Tanjore Village.* Berkeley, Los Angeles and London: University of California Press.

Brinkerhoff D.W. and Goldsmith A. (2005). "Institutional Dualism and International Development: A Revisionist Interpretation of Good Governance", *Administration and Society* 37(2):199-224, May.

Government of Karnataka (2002). *High Power Committee for Redressal of Regional Imbalances*, Final Report.

———. (1993). *Karnataka Panchayati Raj Act, 1993.*

Inbanathan, A. (2000). "Power, Patronage and Accountability in the Panchayats of Karnataka", *Working Paper* No. 68. Bangalore: Institute of Social and Economic Change.

Ishwaran. K. (1968). *Shivapura: A South Indian Village*. London: Routledge & Kegan Paul Ltd.

Krishna, A. (2002). *Active Social Capital.* New York: Columbia University Press.

Leftwich, A. (ed.). (1996). *Democracy and Development.*

Mahi Pal (2000). "Panchayats in Fifth Scheduled Areas", *Economic and Political Weekly* XXXV(19), May 6-10.

Mandelbaum, D.G. (1970). *Society in India.* Bombay: Popular Prakashan.

Manor, J. (1997). "Karnataka: Caste, Class, Dominance and Politics in a Cohesive Society", in Sudipta Kaviraj (ed.), *Politics in India.* Delhi: Oxford University Press.

Natraj, V.K. and K. Ananthpur (2003). "Delegation to Devolution: Karnataka", *MIDS Working Paper* No. 184, February.

Srinivas, M.N. (1987). *The Dominant Caste and Other Essays.* Delhi: Oxford University Press.

———. (2002). *The Collected Essays.* Delhi: Oxford University Press.

The Hindu (2000). "Gram Panchayats Election Results Declared", *The Hindu*, 1st March, Bangalore.

10

Federalism, Urban Decentralisation and Citizen Participation

RAMESH RAMANATHAN

The Context: An Institutional Perspective

Federalism and Urban Decentralisation in India

With all the focus on Panchayati Raj institutions in India, urban decentralisation has received far less attention in the country, suffering for long from policies that saw urbanisation as a trend that needed to be slowed if not stopped altogether.

With the 73rd and 74th Constitutional Amendments in 1992, we completed the federal puzzle in our country, creating units of local self-government at the rural and urban levels. While there are still enormous challenges in implementing the legal provisions with regard to rural decentralisation, tremendous energy is being expended within many state governments to solidify this process. Issues such as untying of funds, streamlining of programmes, capacity building and training of *Gram Panchayat* members are among the hottest potatoes being tossed around in state legislatures.

So, in this journey towards a healthy federalist governmental arrangement, the patient incrementalism of policy makers seems to be working fairly well. While there are gaps in intergovernmental institutions that can oversee and regulate the interchanges, given the magnitude of the local government initiative in the last decade to expand the base of the third level, it seems that enough is going well. As George Mathews says, "The *Panchayats*—Districts and below are now treated as third stratum of governance...Today in India if there is a strong Centre it is not by virtue of its powers over other units but because the lower units—States, Districts, Blocks, Villages—are powerful. This is exactly opposite of what India started with. Thus, one can say that strong regional and state level political parties have strengthened India's democracy and federal character."[1]

Unfortunately, these statistics hide an uncomfortable truth: the base of the pyramid is expanding only for rural local government. Such leadership is sorely lacking in urban decentralisation. Caught in the penumbra of the spotlight on their rural brethren, urban dwellers are finding themselves in a governance vacuum, with all signs of the situation worsening. Consider the following statistics for Karnataka:[2]

Political Representation Ratios, 2000

Rural Karnataka			*Urban Karnataka*		
Population	*3.2 Crores*		*Population*	*1.7 Crores*	
Level	*No. of Units*	*No. of Reps.*	*Level*	*No. of Units*	*No. of Reps*
Zilla Panchayat	27	890	City Corporations	6	410
Taluk Panchayat	176	3,255	City Municipal Councils	40	1,308
Gram Panchayat	5,659	80,023	Town Municipal Councils	81	1,919
			Town *Panchayats*	89	1,373
Total No. of Elected Reps.		84,168	Total No. of Elected Reps.		5,023
Citizen: Rep. Ratio 380:1			Citizen: Rep. Ratio	3,400:1	

The representation ratio between citizens and their elected representatives is almost ten times larger for urban areas. In a city like Bangalore, the ratio is 42,000 citizens for 1 Elected Representative. One possible interpretation of this could be that government is more than 100 times further away for the resident of Bangalore than the average rural dweller.

In addition to this, the idea that every registered voter is a member of a *Gram Sabha*, and should participate in decision making through

1. Mathew, George (n.d.). *Democracy at Work: Evolving Federalism Through Political Representation in Socio-Cultural Pluralism.* Institute of Social Sciences.
2. Urban Development Department, Government of Karnataka, and Department of Panchayati Raj Institutions, Government of Karnataka.

this vehicle is one that at least has formal sanction in rural decentralisation, if not much track record.

In contrast, urban areas have the concept of the Wards Committees, which are meant to be constituted for the City Corporations. In Bangalore for example, there are meant to be 28 (recently revised to 31) such Ward Committees, which are fatally hampered by the combination of a debatable nomination process, limited citizen representation and an ambiguous mandate.

So, while it may seem reasonable to believe that decentralisation is now only an implementation challenge in India, the reality is that we have an extremely skewed federalist structure at the third tier. And this situation is getting worse, because while India was 28 per cent urban at the turn of the century, it is projected to be 46 per cent urban by 2030.[3]

This failure to have a coherent rural-urban approach to decentralisation is a big lacuna in Indian federalism. Indeed it is astonishing that—despite the general rigour that has characterised India's approach to democratic institutionalisation, often correctly placing due process at a premium to short-term outcomes—there has been such an intellectual vacuum with respect to urbanisation, with very few champions of the cause.

This lopsided approach can be traced even to the drafting of the two seminal pieces of legislation that have given rural and urban local governments their current positions—the 73rd and 74th Constitutional Amendments respectively—and perhaps explains the difference in attitude that people in government have towards these two forms of local government even today. The 73rd Amendment was the culmination of over four decades of struggle and intense debate by a range of players: three generations of Gandhians, advocates of rural self-government, and champions of three-tier federalism. This saw numerous initiatives at promoting Panchayati Raj institutions as well as two national committees separated by two decades—the Balwantrai Mehta Committee in 1957, and the Ashok Mehta Committee in 1977.

---

3. United Nations (1996). *World Urbanisation Prospects: The 1996 Revision*. Department for Economic and Social Information and Policy Analysis, Population Division.

Associated with this energy—possibly because of it—there is also a great deal of documentary evidence on the evolution of rural decentralisation in India. Unfortunately, this richness of material is absent when it comes to urban decentralisation. There were some noises about urban challenges through the early decades of our Independence with the constitution of an All India Council of Mayors which consistently demanded greater urban autonomy. The mid-1980s saw the crystallising of some of this energy: for example, one of the recommendations of the National Commission on Urbanisation (NCU) was to suggest that Article 40 of Directive Principles of State Policy—requiring states to organise *Panchayats* as units of local self-government in rural areas—be expanded to include urban areas as well.

In discussions that this author has had with some of the key actors in the drafting of the 74th Constitutional Amendment, this is the picture that emerges on how this amendment came about: even as the original Amendment (64th CAA for *Panchayati Raj* was being drafted during Rajiv Gandhi's tenure as Prime Minister in the late 1980s amidst much debate, one of the senior Congress Party members asked the Prime Minister what was being done about municipalities. Until this issue arose, no protracted debate on this subject had occurred across the country, and no advocates of urban self-government had as yet emerged on the Indian political landscape—at least none who had national impact. At this point, given the urgency in passing the laws, an urban decentralisation amendment (65th Amendment) was drafted within a period of a few months, mirroring in some ways the structural aspects of rural decentralisation, capturing in others the unique needs of urban areas, but missing the essential spirit of the rural amendment—the centrality of the citizen and the bottom-up nature of local self-government.[4] Both amendments failed to pass, and were eventually passed in 1992 as the 73rd and 74th amendments respectively.

---

4. Conversations on the subject that the author has had with Mani Shankar Aiyar and Mr. Sivaramakrishnan, both involved in drafting the original 66th Constitutional Amendment that dealt with urban decentralisation. Both the rural and the urban bills were defeated in parliament, and were only re-introduced after Rajiv Gandhi's death in 1993, under Narasimha Rao's tenure as Prime Minister, eventually passing as the 73rd and 74th Amendments to the Constitution.

This gap, created at the very genesis of the 74th Amendment, continues to plague urban decentralisation even today: our cities and towns do not have bottom-up structures that create more proximity between the citizen and their urban local government. And without citizen participation, federalism is like a batsman without a partner at the crease: decentralisation of what is called the 3 'F's—funds, functions and functionaries—needs to be accompanied by accountability as well. This accountability ought to be directly to citizens, rather than to some other level of government. One form of such accountability is to provide formal opportunity for citizens to participate in local governance. Citizen engagement is one of the critical success factors for federalism.[5] Indeed, some would claim that citizen participation is at the heart of democracy itself.[6] The absence of the opportunity to participate has other consequences beyond poorly functioning urban local governments, and these are related to the political education of the urban Indian. In a young democracy such as India's, local governments act as a political kindergarten to educate the citizen. In the absence of this, the urban voter is not only disconnected from government, but also illiterate about the politics of change. So today, when we are often confronted with a cynical citizenry, it begs the question: what comes first, the indifference or the disempowerment?

The Context—A Citizen Perspective

Our cities and towns in India provide many comforts: livelihood opportunities; relatively better infrastructure than rural areas; access to choice in education and healthcare, and so on. While the quality compares poorly with developed countries, conditions are superior to what is available even a few miles outside the urban boundaries.

However, viewed in a different sense, our urban centres do not have an essential 'rooting', an organic connection between the urban

---

5. Hosp, Gerald (2003). *Fiscal Federalism for Emerging Economies: Lessons from Switzerland*? Publius.

6. Drèze, Jean and Amartya Sen (2002). *India: Development and Participation*. OUP. In the 3-pronged framework that the authors use to assess democracy in India—ideals, institutions and practice—the only element that finds place in all three prongs of the framework is the participation of citizens.

citizen and the government. From the point of view of the individual citizen, there are significant gaps in urban living. Examples abound: there is no opportunity to participate in decisions on local development, no mechanism to stop the illegal violation of the local park, no system to prevent the neighbour's residence from being converted into a hospital that could soon dump toxic waste in the storm water drains, no grassroot answer to manage the voter roll errors which are upwards of 40 per cent in urban areas, no space to even vent one's frustrations. While the urban resident can see herself as a producer of urban goods and services, or as a consumer of urban comforts, she cannot so easily see herself as a citizen. In fact, her identity as a citizen in urban India is one that is minimally developed, if at all.

These gaps exist for everyone. For those within government, be it a Supreme Court judge, a Cabinet Secretary or an employee of the railways, they know all about the empty edifice of citizenry and often come to terms with their civic emasculation by leveraging their positions and titles. Even for the elite, this same sense of disconnection prevails: the industrialists, the writers, the media, the film-makers, the intellectuals, even the activitists. None of them can individually survive in the city without the coping mechanisms that their particular position offers them: their networks, their identities. Strip away these identities, and the hollow shell of basic 'citizenry' will provide cold comfort. Imagine if this is true for the 'empowered' urban Indian, what it could be doing to the 35 per cent and more of the urban dwellers who are the urban poor. They are twice forsaken, once because of their state, and once by the State.

The fabric of any society begins with the individual, her sense of empowerment, her belief in her own agency. In a society that is static or changing at a leisurely pace, most challenges can be addressed at a similar pace. However, in a society that is urbanising rapidly, the changes are faster: old identities are being wiped clean and being replaced with an aching vacuum, where the underlying rules of engagement are increasingly transactional. And this is what is happening in our urban areas. Alienation is the underbelly of urban living in our country.

It sounds odd to be talking of urban residents needing to be treated in the same vein as the rural citizen, when one compares the quality of life in urban India with the rural areas. However, in this context, the comparison is not about roads or water supply, education or health care, employment opportunities or gender equality. It is about the fundamental right to be treated equally as a citizen fully engaged in the democratic process, with the same rights and responsibilities.

Summary of Janaagraha's Experiences

Against the backdrop of a state that has not provided enough toeholds for the urban resident to assert his identity as a citizen, grassroot work continues to show that people do not stay still, they react to this reality. It is not that people don't care, or don't want to address this. Across the length and breadth of this country, local communities sprout like wild grass, bringing groups of people together to address their local problems. Whether it is in the form of Resident Welfare Associations (RWAs), neighbourhood groups in urban slums, or even less formal community-based groups, these display an energy for change that in many cases has tremendous potential.

And in the study of these communities, one discovers remarkable stories of self-help: of cleaning their streets of garbage, of procuring water supply in their slums, of community policing and so on. But equally striking will be the observation that these demonstrate either a complete detachment from the state, or at best an ad-hoc, situational arrangement with the government. They will also show the power of collective action, rather the empowerment of an individual citizen.

In Bangalore, over the past few years, we have attempted to right this ship of decentralised urban governance through a citizen-led initiative for participatory democracy called Janaagraha (meaning *Jana Agraha*, or the moral force of the people). During this time, we have accumulated piece after piece of evidence to suggest that while the urban resident cares, and wants to take part, the state has not only denied her the formal spaces to engage, but often actively thwarts this desire.

Examples of work that we have been involved with over the past few years in Bangalore are detailed below:

- A ward works campaign was Janaagraha's launch, between December 2001 and May 2002: getting citizens to participate in the allocation of ward-level funds for local development. This was the first campaign of Janaagraha, and marked our approach: a collaborative one, emphasising partnership between citizens, their Corporators, and the city administration. Done for the financial year 2002-03, citizens from 65 wards took part in this exercise; in 32 of these wards, citizens came together in strong numbers, and actively negotiated with their Corporators and BMP administration; in 22 of these wards, citizens were happy with the final works list that was produced. This represented a total of Rs 10.7 crores of works, out of a total ward works list of Rs. 50 crores. A total of more than 5,000 citizens took part in the exercise, and hundreds of volunteers were involved in conducting the training programmes, and providing the engineering, technology and support activities. Since there was no formal space for such citizen participation in ward-level planning, each ward success was the result of one or more of a unique set of conditions: a resolute citizenry, a willing elected representative, a supportive administration. Where these enabling conditions did not exist, the results were marginal or non-existent. The experience demonstrated that citizens are willing to engage, take the trouble, and even compromise on their own needs, so long as they perceive the process as scientific, transparent, and fair. Institutionalising this engagement would increase citizen participation manifold.
- In the 2004 national elections, many citizen communities wanted to be involved in increasing voter registration and voter turnout. There is sketchy documentary evidence to suggest that urban voter rolls have error rates that are 40 per cent-45 per cent,[7] arising primarily from non-registration of valid voters, and bogus entries in the list. Rural voter lists also have errors, but these are less than half the urban error percentages. Also, several initiatives in various states have had significant

7. Lok Satta Study in Andhra Pradesh, available on their website: *www.loksatta.org*. Also confirmed by Janaagraha in a sample study of 2 polling booths in Bangalore during Elections 2004.

impact in correcting voter lists in rural areas. To name one successful exercise, the Mazdoor Kisan Shakti Sangathan (MKSS) exercise of getting the CEC to have the voter list read out formally at all rural ward *sabhas* (80-100 households) in Rajasthan resulted in a CEC notification (order 23/2003-PLN-II), resulting in the correction of over 7 lakh voter entries. Unfortunately, the CEC provision for the urban voter was a much-diluted one, requesting that the list be read out in *mohalla* committees or Resident Welfare Association meetings; this is because there is no similar politically legitimate platform for such an exercise, there is no ward *sabha* or *grama sabha* for the urban voter.

The only alternative for communities is to conduct door-to-door verification of the voter list. This suffers from two weaknesses: one, it is not a formal exercise of the government machinery; and two, it is extraordinarily time and people intensive. In spite of this, a pilot exercise was conducted in two polling stations, which showed that the error rates were in the region of 45 per cent. Unfortunately, there could be no institutional redressal of the matter, since the entire election machinery by this time was occupied with other pressing matters like Electronic Voting Machines (EVMs), candidate disclosure and the rest.

Hence, the urban voter list continues to be error-prone, due to the lack of equality in treatment of the urban voter. Is it any surprise that voter turnout is low and tending to become lower in urban areas, across all elections in our federalist system?

- A 'Ward Vision' campaign conducted between June to December 2003, where citizens at the ward level got together to prepare a vision for their ward. In 10 of the city's 100 wards, over 2,000 people attended 5 workshops to prepare detailed documents for their wards, including the expenditure requirements, and the sources of funds. After analysing the funding sources, they discovered that the city was only collecting 30 per cent of the potential property tax revenues at the ward level, and hence suggested an innovative plan to raise compliance. Called Ward RECI-P (Revenue Enhancement with Citizen Participation), they suggested that citizens would support the city administrators to increase revenues, with the condition that a portion of the increased revenues be allocated for local ward development.

Hailed as an innovative public finance solution to help local governments by eminent economists and public policy experts, this proposal is still awaiting a response from the local government. The actual citizen plans would have done any government department proud: detailed, prioritised projects, with estimated costs. However, because there was no formal mechanism for these plans to be produced in a participatory process, they are lying in cold storage. The result is that the citizen participant is fast becoming an activist, demanding their rights: while some are willing to trudge this path, it is too large a burden to place on all citizens.

- While all Janaagraha's campaigns encouraged citizens across the spectrum to participate, the experiences in the first campaign showed that the poor needed additional focus to bring them to the governance table. With this in mind, an exclusive campaign was undertaken, focused on the urban poor. Swarna Jayanti Shehari Rozgar Yojana (SJSRY) is a Government of India urban poverty alleviation programme. Unfortunately, the record of implementation of this programme was less than satisfactory in the Bangalore area.[8] In 2002, Janaagraha conducted a survey in respect of loans sanctioned under Swarna Jayanthi Shahari Yojana and produced a report titled "Case Studies on Delivery of Loans to the Urban Poor."[9] This led to the creation of ANKUR (Alliance for Networked Kinship of Underprivileged Residents), a platform which envisaged participation of all the stakeholders of SJSRY i.e. Government, NGOs, Beneficiaries and Banks. A pilot project steered by the Karnataka Government's Department of Municipal Administration was undertaken over a period of 12 months, with the following features:

---

8. Supriti, Sharon Barnhardt and Ramesh Ramanathan (2002). *Urban Poverty Alleviation India.* Ramanathan Foundation.

9. Janaagraha report submitted to Directorate of Municipal Administration, Government of Karnataka.

- Bringing all the stakeholders on a common platform
- Identification of Nodal branches for disbursal of loans
- Standardisation of loan application forms
- Joint identification of beneficiaries by the community, bankers & NGOs
- EDP training for beneficiaries mandatory before release of loan
- Participation of NGOs in the formation & nurturing of Thrift & Credit Groups

The performance under the pilot project was as follows:[10]

Components of SJSRY	*No. of Groups*	*Coverage of BPL families*	*Loan amount (Rs. in Lakh)*
USEP Loans (ME)	0	341	78.72
DWCUA	3	45	3.75
TCGs	234	3656	125.00
Total	237	4042	207.47

While the results on improving the bank linkage through the SJSRY pilot were promising, Janaagraha's purpose for improving the functioning of the SJSRY programme in Bangalore was a different one, related to the structural presence of community groups in the scheme: a pyramidal clustering of neighbourhood groups (NHGs), neighbourhood committees (NHCs) and Community Development Societies (CDS), representing over 1 lakh BPL families in Bangalore.

The SJSRY programme not only provided a single platform through which to link to what was supposed to be a readymade community structure of the poor at the grassroots, but also one that was empowered to demand development outcomes from various arms of government that worked in the area of urban poverty (slum improvement boards, housing boards, city corporations, etc.) through the Articles of Association of the CDS, which were registered societies.

However, the experience was that the city-wide SJSRY platform

10. SJSRY Pilot Project documentation reports submitted to GoK, and available with Janaagraha.

provided little tangible benefit to the poor in terms of public service outcomes, or governance outcomes. There were several impediments to this process:

1. The formal mandate to demand outcomes was only with the CDS, the apex institution, and not with the lower-level community structures like the NHC and NHG. The six CDS's that were established for the entire city meant that each CDS had a massive coverage area of 1/6th of the city, covering approximately 15,000 urban poor families.
2. There was little social connection among the members of the CDS, since they came from different parts of the city, with no prior inter-personal contact.
3. Very little capacity-building effort had been expended for the CDS members, who were officially vested with a fair-degree of authority to demand the presence of various government agencies, and pass binding resolutions for actions by these agencies, but little real use of these powers.
4. CDS meetings did not take place within the geographic boundaries of each CDS (itself a vast geographic stretch), but at the nodal SJSRY office. Members did not get travel compensation or any pay for the time and cost in participating in the CDS meetings. As a result, few of the CDS meetings were well-attended, and often did not even have quorum.

Janaagraha's efforts, over an 18-month period, in attempting to make an exclusive, legitimate, government-authorised platform for the poor, work to bring them better local services were less than successful due to a variety of reasons: one, grass root resistance from the administration despite senior-level leadership; two, the limited duration of the pilot; three, the inherent structural considerations of the programme that the CDS was too large and removed a platform to provide meaningful engagement for the poor.

While the first two issues are part of any social change process, the third issue gave us pause to see if it was even worthwhile to make the CDS work. This resulted in an effort to work with the local neighbourhood communities. The responses at this level were far greater, with poor residents willing to engage on issues that mattered to them locally: water supply, sanitation, electrification of lanes, health concerns and so on. It was interesting that the poor were willing to engage at a neighbourhood level that did not have any formal legitimacy, while not using a platform like the CDS that had power, but was somewhat removed from their specific concerns.

There was one additional positive experience: given the reasonable level of middle-class involvement in other campaigns of Janaagraha, they expressed interest in knowing more about the SJSRY campaign, and working with local community clusters of the poor in their wards. This resulted in Janaagraha linking the middle-class with the urban poor at the ward-level, with many interesting positive outcomes.[11]

- One of the significant issues that arose in the SJSRY campaign was the choice of beneficiaries, and the veracity of the BPL list. There were many claims by NGOs that the list had many flaws in it, and even by other government departments (the Food and Civil Supplies Department refused to use the SJSRY list for the release of its BPL ration cards).

  Arising out of this, Janaagraha undertook a separate exercise to verify the BPL lists across 3 government agencies: Food and Civil Supplies (F&CS), Directorate of Municipal Administration (DMA) and Karnataka Slum Board. A detailed report prepared jointly by Janaagraha and these 3 agencies has been submitted to the Government of Karnataka (Gok).[12] The key finding of the study was that the list of common BPL names among all three agencies was less than 6 per cent. Given the startling nature of the statistic, it was clear that substantial work needed to be done to improve the quality of the BPL list. The proposal submitted to government suggests the creation of a Common BPL List (CBL) that could be used by all government agencies. While no action has been taken on the report, it must be admitted that this process would only eliminate multiple lists, and not necessarily address the issue of the authenticity of the list itself.

---

11. Documentary examples of middle-class and poor interactions available with Janaagraha.

12. Food and Civil Supplies, Municipal Administration, Karnataka Slum Board and Janaagraha (2004). *Common BPL List Report.* A joint report submitted to GoK. Available with Janaagraha.

There were several learnings that emerged out of these experiences for Janaagraha:

1. While the myth of the cynical urban citizen is not without merit, there are still sufficient numbers of urban residents willing to participate. Over the past three years, more than 1 lakh citizens have participated at some level in one or more of Janaagraha's activities.[13] And this is when there is no formal sanction for citizen participation. Robert Putnam writes of the level of citizen participation in Portland, Oregon at 10 per cent, where citizen participation was actively encouraged by the city government.[14] Clearly, these are large proportions at the grassroots, numbers that could ensure robust participatory outcomes. There is nothing to suggest that they cannot be achieved in urban India when formal roles are given to citizens.
2. Even though the CDS platform for the poor provided a great level of political legitimacy to the poor, there were several lacunae that prevented it from being used appropriately. One possible explanation could have been that real political legitimacy needed to come at a level that was much more personal, much closer to home for the individual to feel empowered. Also, the CDS platform was a parallel form of political legitimacy, which—in the long run—would only undermine the legitimate political structures of local government. It could be argued that the demands of the poor are best achieved within the institutional framework of governance, rather than establishing structures outside it.
3. The lowest level of political representation is the unit of the ward, one that has a reasonable limited geographic boundary, a political representative, and the possibility of a grass root platform for direct political participation. It seems that the ward ought to become the unit of all endeavours, with the establishment of additional structures within it, to ensure organised citizen participation.

---

13. Janaagraha campaign documents.

14. Putnam, Robert D. and Lewis M. Feldstein, with Don Cohen (2003). *Better Together. Restoring the American Community.* Simon & Schuster.

This hypothesis has some merit to it, when looking at the Kerala experience with poverty alleviation (including SJSRY), through a programme called Kudumbashree. The SHG members of Kudumbashree have secured many outcomes for themselves outside of the Kutumbashree programme, through their participation in the *Grama Sabhas* of the participatory planning campaign that the state has established.[15]

4. The BPL list experience demonstrated that while administrative reforms are critically needed to ensure proper targeting of beneficiaries, there also needed to be a grassroot component, where beneficiary identification could be done at a locally legitimate level itself.

   Interestingly, the study on the effectiveness of *Grama Sabhas* also found that "targeting of landless and illiterate individuals is more intensive in villages that have held a *Gram Sabha* meeting. Moreover, these effects are economically significant with an 8-10 per cent increase in the probability of receiving a BPL card in a village that held a *Gram Sabha.*"[16]

   The correlation between the conducting of *Grama Sabhas*, and the improvement in the quality of the BPL list in such areas, suggests that similar outcomes could be likely with urban *sabhas* as well.

5. Voter list issues are somewhat similar to the BPL list issue, in that there are concerns with the quality of the list, both in terms of inclusion and exclusion. Even if there were a one-time clean up of the list, it begs the question of how this can be done consistently over time. A structural solution to this question would be one where there is a politically legitimate platform for the voters in a polling booth; given that the numbers involved (approximately 1000-1200 voters), compare with those of *grama sabhas* in the rural areas, there could some merit to this argument.

---

15. Several documents on the convergence of the People's Planning Process in Kerala, and the Poverty Alleviation Programme called Kudumbashree.

16. Besley, Tim, Rohini Pande and Vijayendra Rao (2005). "Participatory Democracy in Action: Survey Evidence from South India". *Journal of the European Economic Association* (forthcoming).

Institutionalising Citizen Participation—A Proposal

From a constitutional standpoint, there has always been a bias towards the rural voter, whether it be the Directive Principles of State Policy or the 73rd Constitutional Amendment.[17] While the voter was a central figure in the 73rd Amendment, in the 74th CAA on urban decentralisation, there is no mention of the phrase "a body consisting of persons registered in the electoral rolls." Even in Article 243S, which discusses the Ward(s) committee, the Amendment is still engaged with institutional arrangements rather than recognising the centrality of the registered voter, as in the case of rural decentralisation.[18]

These Constitutional Amendments have percolated down to State laws for rural and urban decentralisation that mirror these biases. Two reports were prepared to assess urban decentralisation—the National Commission to Review the Working of the Constitution (NCRWC), and the Sen Committee Report to review Decentralisation in Kerala. However, these reports, while making incisive observations about the poor functioning of urban decentralisation and the need for greater citizen involvement, did not go far enough to fill the fundamental gap in the architecture of decentralisation to give a clear and formal picture to every urban voter.[19]

---

17. Directive principles of state policy: Article 40, which states "Organisation of village *panchayats*. The State shall take steps to organise village *panchayats* and endow them with such powers and authority as may be necessary to enable them to function as units of self-government." Article 243b of the 73rd CAA which states "*Gram Sabha*" means a body consisting of persons registered inthe electoral rolls relating to a village comprised within the area of *Panchayat* at the village level."
18. Article 243S which states "(ii) The Legislature of a State may, by law, make provision withrespect to: (a) the composition and the territorial area of a Wards Committee; (b) the manner in which the seats in a Wards Committee shall be filled."
19. National Commission to Review the Working of the Constitution (NCRWC Report): One example is suggestion 1.62 c, which only requires "knowledgeable residents" of a ward to be included. If this were suggested for rural decentralisation, there would have been howls of protest, with justified accusations of elite capture of political institutions. Similarly, in the Sen Committee Report for Kerala, the concept of the Ward Sabha is not thought of as mandatory, but rather as a vehicle that can be used only in smaller municipalities (population less than 1 lakh). In 1991, there were 296 Class 1 cities with a population greater than 1 lakh, out of the 3,610 urban centres in the country. They contained over 65 per cent of the total urban population in the country, meaning that over 150 million Indians are living in cities and towns that would be considered too large for them to exercise their fundamental rights as citizens.

Janaagraha's experiences in Bangalore are not unique—they reflect those of many other civil society and community-based organisations across the country. Collectively, they provide substantial evidence that urban residents—even in large metros—care deeply about their city, and wish to participate. Indeed, the amount of social energy that can be harnessed is extraordinary, if the appropriate structures are made available to the citizen.

Urban local governments also face a range of other challenges that require changes in law, jurisdiction, administrative streamlining, decision-support systems etc. Credible, realistic solutions are available for these issues as well, so that a holistic governance environment can be created in urban India. We cannot adopt an 'either-or' approach to resolving issues of urban governance: all reforms are required, and we need to find the intellectual bandwidth and institutional energy to push for all necessary reforms.

The suggestions for reforms in municipalities being made here will concern themselves only with two aspects: one, ensuring that the urban citizen has access to a platform for full freedom of expression; and two, that this mechanism also functions as a platform of accountability from the local government. Both these aspects are being clubbed together under the broad heading 'Institutionalising citizen participation in urban areas'.

Any response to such a demand for citizen participation needs to address the following issues:

1. The creation of a mechanism for every registered voter to participate in issues of local government, in a meaningful manner. This means creating an appropriate tier below the ward-level.
2. An unambiguous role for these ward-and sub-ward platforms, so that there is a seamless integration between their role, and that of the municipality. This role should be comprehensive, extending from planning to budgeting to oversight and financial authority, and possibly also to spatial planning issues like zoning, change in land use and comprehensive development plans that can be built bottom-up.
3. The integration of the internal systems of the municipality to support such a decentralised architecture: appropriate

accounting and budgetary systems; administrative support; establishment of necessary bank accounts; ward maps and GIS systems; data collection mechanisms at the ward-level on issues like building starts and other such economic activities; voter rolls and BPL lists, and so on.

4. A calendar of activities that define clearly how these grassroot decision making systems are linked to the processes at the municipality. For example, the municipality budget is to be placed before the Taxation and Finance Committee at a certain time of the year, normally around January. It is then placed before the Council within a few weeks, for approval. In any proposed system decentralisation, full teeth to their roles can only be provided if they have a say in the budgeting process. This means that a calendar of their budgeting process needs to be created, to synchronise with the overall municipality calendar.

In fulfilling the above requirements, the first is the most critical: the establishment of the appropriate legitimate political and accountability 'spaces'. Once these are done, then these spaces can be mandated with functions, roles and responsibilities, with appropriate support systems, to fulfil these responsibilities.

This document concerns itself only with the first issue: the structure of decentralisation that links urban governance to the last citizen. The other issues of functions duties and responsibilities are addressed separately in a separate document. Figure 10.1 illustrates the solution being suggested and describes the proposed structure in detail. It can be understood in terms of 'Platforms' and 'Participants'.

Platforms

There are three, at the level of the Municipality (A), at the level of the Ward (B), and at the level of the Polling Station, called the Area *Sabha* (C). There shall be a Ward Committee in every ward, irrespective of the size of the Ward or the Municipality. While the first two are well-known, it is the Area *Sabha* that is being newly introduced. The footprint of every polling station could be the smallest unit in such an architecture; this could be called an Area *Sabha*. Each of these is a legitimate, formal space, which will be defined in terms of constitution, composition, functions, duties and responsibilities.

Figure 10.1

Proposed Urban Decentralisation Structure

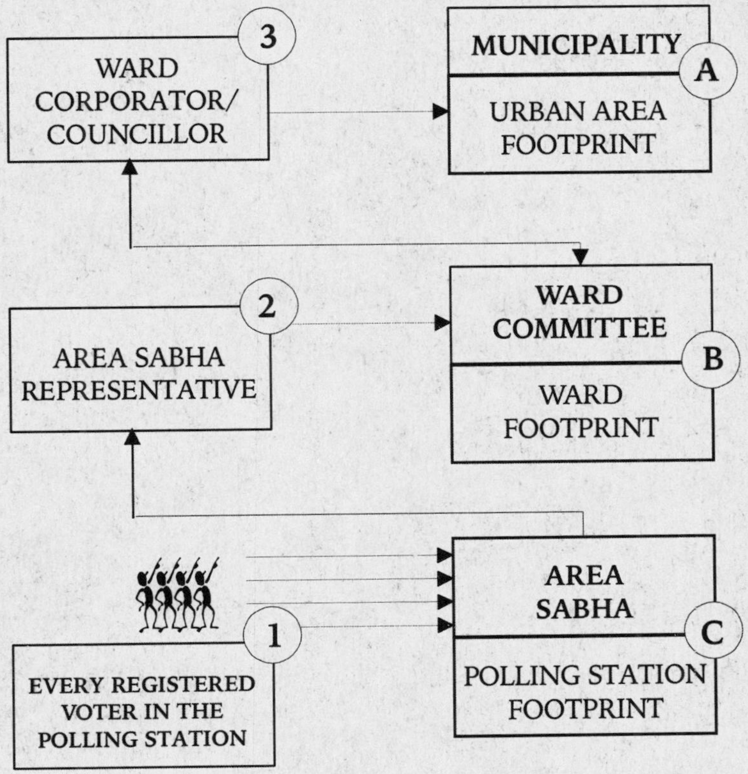

Participants

Every registered voter of a polling booth (boundaries of the polling booth will be defined by the Election Commission) shall be a member of that Area *Sabha*. This creates an urban equivalent of the *Grama Sabha*, retains a reasonable level of intimacy, and recognises the unique features of urban dwellings.

At the next level of the Ward Committee, the current practice of nomination to the Ward Committee can be replaced by a nomination of an Area *Sabha* Representative from the Area *Sabha*. The benefit of this structure is that it automatically adjusts for the size of a municipality or ward, rather than have a prescribed single size being defined for a Ward Committee. Large municipalities would have wards with greater population, more polling booths, and hence more Area *Sabhas*, resulting in larger Ward Committees. Smaller municipalities would have smaller population in each ward, hence fewer Area *Sabhas* and fewer members in each Ward Committee.

The elected Councillor of the Ward shall be the Chairman of the Ward Committee, and continue to represent the Ward in the Municipal Council.

Role of informal structures: The presence of a formal structure of decentralisation to the citizen will create the appropriate participatory and accountability mechanism for the citizen. However, this does not mean that informal community structures like local resident associations, neighbourhood groups and ward-level federations will become less important. If anything, these structures can now become more effective beyond their social role, by linking their public issues at the grassroots into the appropriate platform, either the Area *Sabha* or the Ward Committee. The lessons from rural decentralisation indicate that while informal structures are important, parallel power structures should not be created.

Janaagraha has prepared a draft 'Nagara Raj Bill', embedding the above structure into a legal document, with details like the constitution, composition, functions, roles and responsibilities of the Area *Sabhas* and Ward Committees. This document has emerged out of the examination of the platform that was provided with the 74th Amendment, the good work already done by some selected states like West Bengal and Kerala, and also the grassroot experiences from a citizen standpoint. The drafting has been done in a manner that would allow the Bill to be passed separately, or included as an Amendment to the Municipalities Acts of States as a chapter exclusively dealing with Institutionalising Citizen Participation in Urban Governance. Some sections of this Act could require other parts of a state's Municipality Act to be modified, such as the budgeting process mentioned above.

The structure above solves many problems of urban governance described in the earlier sections of this document, as detailed below:

1. It will give formal voice to every voter to participate in issues of local governance, removing the lopsided treatment of the rural

and urban voter that has prevailed since the 73rd and 74th Constitutional Amendments were passed.

2. This 3-tiered municipal governance structure will also create accountability of the municipality directly to the citizen herself. Issues of transparency, decision making, and so on can be addressed at the level of the Area *Sabha*, rather than creating complex processes of reporting to State Government bureacracies.
3. These platforms will also expose citizens to the need to participate, rather than stand on the sidelines and complain. While participation cannot be expected to be widespread, this process of political engagement will bring citizens closer to government, and seek solutions to public issues from our public institutions rather than outside them. In some sense therefore, Area *Sabhas* are as much about government accountability to citizens as they are about citizens' accountability to themselves.
4. The creation of local engagement allows for localised solutions to emerge, as well as a flexibility and dynamism that are healthy attributes for any institution.
5. Other institutions could also use these platforms to integrate into their requirements: even a small handful of Area *Sabha* members can verify membership rolls to the voter lists, and maintain the accuracy of the voter lists. The Election Commission, in turn, could formally use the Area *Sabha* to update the voter lists. Similarly, departments of government that require BPL lists could have these verified at the level of the Area *Sabha*, much like the *Gram Sabha* experiences in rural India. The Police department could use the Area *Sabhas* for community policing initiatives. Disaster management situations will have a readymade, widespread grassroot platform for information dissemination and coordinated action.
6. Given the nature of the Area *Sabha*, its composition will be heterogeneous, cutting across caste, community and economic lines. Engagement at the Area *Sabha* could therefore have significant social implications, in generating social capital in ways that are otherwise unlikely to occur.

7. A few important findings with respect to *Gram Sabha* functioning warrant some discussion here, in light of the potential implications for Area *Sabha* functioning:

   a. Literacy levels and *Gram Sabhas*: the positive correlation between literacy levels and *gram sabha* functioning holds positive implications for Area *Sabha*, given that urban literacy levels are higher than rural.

   b. The evidence suggests that *Gram Sabha* meetings "seem to a be a forum used by some of the most disadvantaged groups in the village—landless, illiterates and scheduled castes/ tribes. This suggests that these groups find the *Gram Sabha* useful and that *Gram Sabha* meetings may play some role in moving policy in a direction favoured by these groups." The same could be true of urban Area *Sabhas* as well, possibly solving an issue of elite capture in urban planning and public expenditure.[20]

   c. The study finds correlation between levels of awareness of the *Gram Sabha*, and levels of participation. A case can be made that given the density of urban settlements, and more powerful tools of communication, coupled with higher literacy rates, the likelihood of greater awareness of Area *Sabhas* could also be greater, thus leading to potentially greater participation. This higher awareness also has another possible effect: how it changes the mental attitude, from emasculation to empowerment. Irrespective of whether a voter participates or not, she now has the knowledge of the opportunity to participate. This needs to be measured as well, in terms of what voters begin to feel about 'empowered', irrespective of their actual participation.

   d. The *Grama Sabha* findings also observed that participation from women is lower in rural areas. Here again, Area *Sabhas*

---

20. Jha, Rao and Woolcock (2005). *Governance in the Gullies: Democratic Responsiveness and Leadership in Delhi's Slums*. World Bank Paper. July. The study shows the presence of "informal leaders (who) are accessible to all slum dwellers, but (that) formal government figures are most accessed by the wealthy and the well-connected." This highlights the need for legitimate participatory spaces in urban areas, open to all voters across the social spectrum.

could be more powerful as a forum for women, given higher levels of literacy and emancipation of women in urban areas.

8. If anything, the hypothesis could be that not only will the *sabha* concept work well in urban areas, and generate socially equitable outcomes, but that these could also be a more significant presence in local governance issues than rural areas, and possibly more successfully address universal participation issues across caste, economy and gender.

The proposed benefits of citizen participation in urban areas are in the realm of hypotheses. These need to be urgently tested, not only for their own reasons, but also the positive and normative impact they can have on rural decentralisation, and the cross-fertilisation of successful practices and learnings. Such common platforms across rural and urban centres could also create mechanisms for rural and urban citizens to reach out to each other directly, rather than only through removed political processes. This has major significance in peri-urban areas, and the fringes of urban growth, where deep schisms are being created everyday due to the damaging consequences of jurisdictional schizophrenia.

Conclusion

India stands at the inflection point of two critical trends: the increasing importance of local governments, and a critical mass of urbanisation. Both these have significant implications for governance outcomes on a range of important quality-of-life issues for citizens. Citizen participation is not just a moral argument, it is a strong accountability mechanism for local governments. While rural participation is imbedded in the Constitution, citizen involvement in urban areas is still very indirect. This needs to be urgently corrected. This paper describes the context of urban decentralisation, the need for citizen participation, and also offers a solution that can be imbedded into law at the State and Municipality levels, without having to change the Constitution. There are credible reasons to believe that substantial benefits can accrue by creating institutional mechanisms for citizen participation in urban areas.

11

The Political Economy of *Gram Panchayats* in South India

TIMOTHY BESLEY, ROHINI PANDE
and VIJAYENDRA RAO

Introduction

The Indian experiment in local village democracy—galvanised by the passage of the 73rd amendment in 1993—is among the most ambitious in history. Moreover, the experiment with *Panchayats* in India is of global interest given the array of similar policy experiments going on around the world.[1] It comes at a time when economists are reengaging with political economy issues in their thinking about policy.

It is unsurprising, therefore, to find that *Panchayats* have attracted significant academic attention.[2] Since 1993, village governments in India, *Gram Panchayats* (GP), have been responsible for maintaining local amenities such as village roads and drinking water facilities, and for identifying beneficiaries for federal and state poverty alleviation programmes. A key motivation for the 73rd amendment was the belief that local governments may be better placed (than, say, centrally appointed bureaucrats) to identify and respond to villagers' needs. It was also held that villagers may find it easier to monitor local politicians. Democratisation of the public service delivery system has, thus, been a central element of the Indian decentralisation experiment.

This paper reviews findings from a research project on the political

---

1. See Bardhan (2000) and Crook and Manor (1998) for background discussion.
2. Shortage of space precludes us from surveying the extensive emerging literature. Recent contributions include Bardhan and Mookherjee (2000), Chattopadhyay and Duflo (2004a; b), Foster and Rosenzweig (2001), Chaudhuri and Heller (2004), Manor (2004).

economy of Indian *Gram Panchayats* in four states in South India. The research is based on a household and village survey covering 522 villages in Karnataka, Andhra Pradesh, Kerala and Tamil Nadu. The decentralisation experience of these four states shows significant variation (Matthew and Buch, 2000). Karnataka was one of the pioneers of the *Panchayat* movement, and was the first Indian state to mandate regular *Panchayat* elections. Fiscal decentralisation has advanced the most in Kerala, with forty per cent of state expenditures allocated by *Panchayats*. Kerala *Panchayats* are characterised by high levels of villager participation and regular villager meetings. Andhra Pradesh took a different route and, till recently, sought to energise a political alternative to the *Panchayat* system—the *Janmabhoomi* programme. Finally, Tamil Nadu continues to have relatively weak *Gram Panchayats* with limited devolution of policy powers.

We examine how features of the *Panchayat* system, in particular the design of political institutions affect how it target resources towards economically and socially disadvantaged groups in the village. We also examine politician selection. One of the striking features of the *Panchayat* experiment is how it has led to a new political class, many of whom had never held public office previously. We examine how selection mechanisms in Indian villages affect politician outcomes.

The paper is organised as follows: In the next section, we discuss survey design. Section three discusses some background institutional issues. Section four reviews some concrete findings from the research while section four pulls together the policy implications.

Survey Design

Our data come from a village-and household-level survey conduced in Andhra Pradesh (AP), Karnataka (KA), Kerala (KE) and Tamil Nadu (TN). The survey was conducted between September-November 2002. Sampling occurred in multiple stages, and consisted of purposive sampling up to the level of blocks and random sampling within these blocks. Our final sample consists of 527 villages belonging to 201 elected GPs.[3]

---

3. See Besley, Pande, Rahman and Rao (2004b) for an extended discussion of the project.

For each pair of states, we selected two districts (one per state) that shared a common boundary.[4] The district pairs were selected, with one exception, to focus on districts that, prior to the linguistic reorganisation of states in 1957, had belonged to same administrative unit. Our sample consists of nine districts—Bidar (in KA) and Medak (in AP) from the erstwhile Hyderabad, Pallakad (KE), Coimbatore (TN), Kasargod (KE), Dakshin Kanada (KA), Dharmapuri (TN), and Chithoor (AP), all from erstwhile Madras Presidency. In KA, we also sampled Kolar district which was a part of erstwhile Mysore.

For each pair of districts which shared a common boundary three pairs of blocks were selected (that is, 3 blocks in each of the two districts).[5] Two blocks form a pair if they lie in different states but are 'linguistically similar'. Using 1991 census block level data we defined two blocks to be linguistically similar if, of all the blocks in the district, they have the highest fraction of households with the same mother tongue. The top three matches entered our sample. Linguistic similarity is a good proxy for shared cultural history, given the prevalence of caste and linguistic endogamy. Hence, language matching provides a partial control for 'unobservable' sociocultural differences. The historical and administrative similarity of linguistically matched blocks was checked using princely state maps and the Report of the States Reorganisation Commission (GoI, 1955).

In AP, KA and TN we randomly sampled 6 GPs per block and within a GP all villages if the GP had 3 or fewer villages. If it had more than three villages, then we selected the *Pradhan's* village and randomly selected two other villages.[6] To account for the much higher GP population in KE we sampled 3 GPs per block and 6 wards per GP in KE. This procedure gave a total of 201 GPs and 527 villages. Our

4. One district in KA (Kolar) that shared boundaries with both AP and TN entered the sample twice. The same holds for one district in AP (Chithoor).

5. If one district was matched with 2 different districts then 6 blocks were chosen from it (three per match). In one block in KE an additional block was sampled as a check on our language matching. This gave us a total of 37 blocks (12 in KA, 9 in AP and TN and 7 in KE).

6. We excluded all villages with less than 200 persons from our sampling frame. All hamlets with population over 200 were considered as independent villages in drawing the sample.

survey used four different questionnaires to collect data at the village, politician and household level.

We conducted household surveys (20 per village) in a random sub-sample of 259 villages giving us a sample of 5,180 households. The household questionnaire obtained information on household's socio-economic status, household structure, views and use of public services in the village, private government benefits. Respondents were also asked to rank order problems in the village. Since the sample is divided between male and female and SC/ST and non-SC/ST respondents this provides yet another source of information on gender and caste differences on preferences about village problems.

We also surveyed an elected member of the GP in every village (with precedence given to the GP head if he/she lived in that village) —this gives us a household sample of 544 elected officials. In addition to all the questions on the household questionnaire politicians were also asked a series of questions about their conduct of GP activities.

At the village level we administered a questionnaire using Participatory Rapid Appraisal (PRA) techniques (Chambers, 1994) to a group of men selected to represent different caste groups in the village. The PRA questionnaire assessed villager views on problems in the village, the work done by the GP and prevalence of political oligarchy. For the last, we asked respondents to list the extent to which the *Pradhan*, former *Pradhan* and the Vice-*Pradhan* controlled prominent activities in the village. We also obtained a detailed listing of castes within the village, and land distribution both within and between castes. The PRA-based questionnaire was separately fielded to a: (i) group of women, and (ii) group of SC/ST individuals. These PRA obtained separate measures of women's and SC/ST problem ranking *vis-à-vis* public service delivery.

Finally, we undertook an audit of all public goods in the village. This was conducted by an independent enumerator who visually assessed the quality of schools, clinics, roads, drinking water, and sanitation. The enumerator was also asked to identify the extent of GP involvement in improving these facilities.

Background

It is important to begin by engaging with the details of the *Panchayat* system and its operation. Schedule XI of the Indian Constitution defines the functional items for which states may devolve responsibility to *Panchayats*. While states vary in the extent to which they devolve policy powers to the *Gram Panchayat*, most *Gram Panchayats* have responsibilities of civic administration in the village together with limited independent taxation powers. On average, roughly 10 per cent of a GP's total revenue come from own revenues with the remainder consisting of transfers from higher levels of government.

While the ambit of GP policy influence varies across Indian states, GPs typically perform (at least) two distinct policy tasks. The first is beneficiary selection for central and state welfare schemes. These are 'low spillover' public goods because the benefits are likely to accrue to individual households. These include a variety of transfer programmes such as schemes that provide beneficiary households with funds to acquire housing, private electricity and water supply. Eligibility for these schemes is usually restricted to households below the official poverty line. Most schemes also require that a minimum fraction of beneficiaries be SC/STs.

An important part of a GP's job, and one on which we focused in our research, is identifying households which are 'Below the Poverty Line', or BPL households. Possession of a BPL card makes the household eligible for an array of government schemes, ranging from subsidised food through the public distribution system to free hospitalisation. The GP, in collaboration with state government officials, is supposed to identify (*via* a census) households with income below the poverty line, and prepare the list of BPL households. This list, and subsequent selection of beneficiary households under various schemes (from among the BPL households), is supposed to be ratified in *Gram Sabha* meetings. All BPL households are eligible for a BPL card, also often provided by the government. This procedure makes the allocation of BPL cards highly political and the success or failure in targeting needy households a key issue. Eighty-seven per cent of the politicians in our sample stated that elected GP politicians were responsible for BPL card allocation.

The second area of GP policy activism is the construction and maintenance of village public goods such as street lights, roads and drains. These are 'high spillover' public goods since the benefits accrue more broadly across members of a village. The GP decides the distribution of these public goods within the village and across villages within a GP. It also determines the quality of provision.

Two important institutional features of the *Gram Panchayat* which are specific to decentralisation in India are political reservation and village meetings (*Gram Sabhas*). The 73rd constitutional amendment mandated political reservation in favor of SC/ST for the *Pradhan*[7] position, and required that the extent of such reservation in a state reflect the SC/ST population share in that state. It also required that no GP be reserved for the same group for two consecutive elections.

Panchayat legislation also requires that the *Pradhan* consult with villagers and ward members in deciding the choice of beneficiaries and allocation of public goods. This is supposed to be done *via* village meetings, or *Gram Sabha* meetings, called by the elected local government to discuss resource allocation decisions in the village. Seventy-six per cent of the villages in our sample reported have at least one *Gram Sabha* meeting in the last year. However, final decision making powers in a GP are vested with the *Pradhan*.

Findings

In this section, we discuss some of the results from the research under three headings. We first study how the *Panchayat* system is targeting resources across households and villages. We then discuss political participation and the operation of *Gram Sabhas*. Finally, we will discuss the selection of politicians and its consequences. Table 11.1 gives the basic data from our sample of households and villages from which the following analyses are drawn.

Targeting

One of the key problems in targeting public resources is to get them to those who need them most. One key hope for the *Panchayat*

---

7. Also known, depending on the state, as President or *Sarpanch*.

Table 11.1

Descriptive Statistics

	Mean
Household Data	
SC/ST household	0.23 (0.42)
Illiterate	0.27 (0.44)
Landless	0.38 (0.48)
Wealthy	0.29 (0.45)
Ever Attended *Gram Sabha*	0.20 0.40
Possess a BPL Card	0.22 (0.43)
Received Private Good	0.06 (0.24)
Politician	0.09 (0.292)
Village Data	
Literacy Rate in 1991	0.42 (0.182)
Fraction of Villages which had a *Gram Sabha* in last year	0.77 (0.41)
Pradhan's Village	0.39 (0.48)
GP Headquarter	0.31 (0.460)
Pradhan Reserved for SC/ST	0.20 (0.403)
Public Good index	0.45 (0.30)

Notes: All variables based on Survey data, except the village literacy rate which is from the 1991 Census of India. Wealthy is a dummy=1 if household possesses a watch, a fan and either a TV or radio.

system was that it would use the political process to create more effective targeting to needy households and villages. Our data allow us to look at these issues at both levels as we have detailed data on which transfers households receive and which villages are favoured. We focus on the targeting of scheduled caste and scheduled tribe households (SC/ST). SC/ST households have suffered from significant historic social and economic disadvantage, leading to worse contemporary outcomes for this group. An important aim of the Indian state's welfare policy has been to target resources towards this group (Pande, 2003).

In Besley, Pande, Rahman and Rao (2004a), we use our household survey data to measure the provision of household public goods. Here we used only 4059 households of which 981 were SC/ST spread across 193 villages.[8] We measure a household's exposure to low spillover public goods by a dummy which equals one if it had a house or toilet built under a government scheme or if it received a private water or electricity connection *via* a government scheme since the last GP election. Approximately 7 per cent of the sample households fall in this category.

We also examine the activity of *Gram Panchayats* at the village level. For our key measure—an index of GP activity on high spillover (i.e. village-level) public goods—we use information from our audit of village facilities. Specifically, we used an index based on whether the GP undertook any construction or improvement activity on roads, drains, street lights and water sources within a village since the last GP election. (The index is normalised to lie between 0 and 1.) Roughly 79 per cent of our sample villages experienced GP activism on at least one of these public goods.

We were interested in investigating whether the activity at the household or village level is related to reservation status. To capture a village's reservation status, we constructed an indicator variable equal to one if the village belongs to a GP where the *Pradhan* is reserved for an SC/ST. We used two different variables to measure the political influence of a village—the first equals one if the *Pradhan* resides in that village, and the second equals one if the GP headquarters are in that village.

The results are reported in Table 11.2. Column 1 reports results from a regression where the left hand side variable is a dummy

8. We did not use data from Kerala in this study as the process of allocation in Kerala was very different.

Table 11.2

Effect of SC/ST Reservation on Resource Allocation

	Private Good		*Public Goods*
	Household Data		*Village Data*
	(1)	*(2)*	*(3)*
SC/ST Household	0.048*** (0.016)	0.041 (0.025)	
SC/ST Household*—*Pradhan* Reserved for SC/ST	0.071** (0.031)	0.071** (0.031)	
SC/ST Household*—*Pradhan* village		0.03 (0.025)	
SC/ST Household*—GP Headquarters		-0.019 (0.025)	
Proportion SC/ST Households			0.041 (0.042)
Pradhan Village			0.048** (0.023)
Pradhan Reserved for SC/ST			-0.003 (0.039)
Pradhan Village*—*Pradhan* Reserved for SC/ST			0.003 (0.051)
GP Headquarter			0.041* (0.023)
Fixed Effects	Village	Village	Block
Observations	4059	4059	395
R-squared	0.11	0.11	0.67

Notes: "Private good" is a dummy variable which equals one if the household's house or toilet was built under a government scheme, or if it received a private water or electricity connection *via* a government scheme, all since the last GP election. "Public good" is an index of whether the GP undertook any construction or improvement activity on roads, drains, streetlights and water sources after the last GP election. The SC/ST Household dummy equals 1 for SC/ST households. The Pradhan village dummy equals one if the Pradhan resides in the given village. The GP headquarter dummy equals 1 if the GP headquarter is located in the village. Robust standard errors in brackets. *: significant at 10 per cent; **: significant at 5 per cent; ***: significant at 1 per cent

variable denoting whether the household benefits from a government scheme. The regression includes village fixed effects to account for any factors that differ between villages and affect the extent of targeting. The main finding is that SC/ST households are more likely than non-SC/ST households to receive household transfers suggesting that these groups are targeted within villages. In column (2), second row, we examine the interaction between being from an SC/ST group and having a *Pradhan* from a GP that is reserved for an SC/ST. We observe a positive coefficient indicating that SC/ST households living in a reserved GP are 7 per cent more likely to receive a transfer under government schemes relative to living in non-reserved GPs.

The column (2) regression explores whether this effect is robust to controlling for whether the household lives in the *Pradhan*'s home village. Here we find that there is no benefit to an SC/ST household from either living in the *Pradhan*'s village or from living in the village where the GP headquarter is located. Thus, it appears the improved targeting of SC/ST households is generated from reservations.

Our results suggest that having a reserved *Pradhan* does indeed further the end of getting better targeting towards SC/ST households. This complements the results on targeting towards women by female *Pradhans* found by Chattopadhyay and Duflo for Rajasthan and West Bengal and the evidence on state level targeting of SC/ST households by SC/ST politicians reported in Pande (2003).

Another important aspect of targeting concerns resource allocation across villages. To examine this, we look at measures of village activism at the village level as measured by the GP activism index. We find that this index is on average 0.05 points higher in the *Pradhan*'s village. This is equivalent to a 10 per cent increase in village activism by *Panchayats*. There is no advantage to being in the GP headquarters. Moreover, having a reserved *Pradhan* has no consequences for village level targeting.

As Table 11.1 shows, 39 per cent of our sample villages have *Pradhans* drawn from them. These also tend to be the larger villages within a GP. We interpret the result in column (3) of Table 11.2 as a consequence of political geography, though we cannot rule out the possibility that larger (and potentially richer) villages both house the

Pradhan and are more successful at lobbying for public goods. States that have only one village per GP are clearly not going to create an advantage for any particular village whereas those with many villages per GP face a distributional issue. If the *Pradhan* is from a particular village on a repeated basis, then our results suggest that this may create a serious distributional bias.

Gram Sabhas

The *Gram Sabha* has often been considered the lynchpin of the *Panchayat* system. It has the potential to structure democratic institutions to ensure fair and efficient allocation of public funds. The idea that encouraging citizen participation can improve the workings of a democracy is also echoed in the political science literature. One role for participation emphasised in that literature is to improve the flow of information into the political process beyond that available by electing representatives. Thus, Verba *et al.*, (1995) characterise political participation as 'information rich' acts and observe that:

> "From the electoral outcome alone, the winning candidate cannot discriminate which of dozens of factors, from the position taken on a particular issue to the inept campaign run by the opposition..., was responsible for the electoral victory." (page 10).

There are two main ways in which such meetings may improve the workings of government. First, relative to elected representatives, these meetings may better reflect citizens' preferences on issues such as how to target resources to the neediest groups. Second, by providing a forum for monitoring the actions of elected representatives they may reduce agency problems in politics, and the extent of corruption.

While holding *Gram Sabhas* is compulsory, their frequency and content owes a lot to the discretion of elected officials. Officials from the State or District administration can also have a role in this by choosing not to attend, and therefore making the *Gram Sabha* less attractive to hold. It is also the case that a well-attended meeting may have no bite on policy decisions. We exploit our household and village surveys to examine the determinants of participation in *Gram Sabha* meetings, and whether having a *Gram Sabha* meeting affects beneficiary selection for welfare programmes.

In our PRA survey, we asked about whether a *Gram Sabha* meeting had been held in the past six months. The household survey also asked individuals about *Gram Sabha* attendance. Table 11.1 show that only 77 per cent of villages held *Gram Sabhas* in the last year. This suggests a considerable degree of non-compliance with the law. In our household data, Table 11.1 shows that only around 20 per cent of our sample households report having attended a *Gram Sabha* meeting.

Besley, Pande and Rao (2005a) looks at the probability of holding a *Gram Sabha* meeting at the village level and find evidence that this is related to village literacy with more literate villages more likely to hold meetings. Quite why this is true is hard to discern in these data. However, it parallels a larger literature emphasising the civic benefits of greater education.

In Table 11.3 (based on Besley, Pande and Rao (2005a) we use household data to examine who attends *Gram Sabha* meetings, and whether holding *Gram Sabha* meetings is correlated with needy households access to public welfare as measured by receipt of BPL cards. All specifications include village level fixed effects which control for variation at the village level.

In column (1) the dependent variable is whether the household respondent attended a *Gram Sabha* meeting in the past year. We observe that illiterates are less likely to attend a *Gram Sabha* meeting than others. However, this effect is somewhat offset if the household lives in a village with greater overall literacy. This reinforces the idea that literate villages have stronger civic cultures. It is also interesting to observe that SC/ST households and landless are also more likely to attend *Gram Sabha* meetings in villages that have a greater number of literate households. Note that this is not a Kerala specific effect since the regressions control for variation at the village level using fixed effects.

These findings are notable for two reasons. First, there is some suggestion of a political externality from living in a more literate community. Second, *Gram Sabha* meetings seem to be a forum used by some of the most disadvantaged groups in the village—landless and scheduled castes/tribes. This suggests that these groups find the *Gram Sabhas* useful and that *Gram Sabha* meetings may play some role in moving policy in a direction favored by these groups. Indeed, a key function of *Gram Sabhas* is to target resources to poor households. We now look for evidence of the latter.

Table 11.3

Gram Sabhas: Participation and Resource Allocation

Dependent Variable/ Village Characteristic	*Attended Gram Sabha Literacy Rate*	*Received BPL Card Gram Sabha*
	(1)	(2)
Illiterate	-0.103***	-0.042*
	(0.028)	(0.026)
Illiterate* Village Characteristic	0.183**	0.091***
	(0.078)	(0.030)
SC/ST	-0.029	0.094**
	(0.040)	(0.042)
SC/ST* Village Characteristic	0.139	0.062
	(0.097)	(0.047)
Landless	-0.073**	0.018
	(0.029)	(0.030)
Landless* Village Characteristic	0.232***	0.067*
	(0.066)	(0.035)
Female	-0.086***	-0.009
	(0.030)	(0.010)
Female* Village Characteristic	-0.242***	
	(0.076)	
Upper caste	-0.007	-0.028*
	(0.018)	(0.016)
Wealthy	-0.027*	-0.079***
	(0.016)	(0.014)
Fixed effects	Village	Village
Observations	5240	5364
R-squared	0.25	0.4

Notes: Standard errors in brackets are clustered at village level. Regressions also include respondent age and age squared as controls.

In column (2) we estimate a household regression which exploits within village variation in individual characteristics to examine whether the targeting of BPL cards differs depending on whether the village had a *Gram Sabha* in the last year. The results show that illiterate households in villages that have held *Gram Sabhas* in the past year are more likely to have a BPL card. There is also evidence of greater targeting of BPL cards towards landless households. In Besley, Pande and Rao (2005a) we interact the characteristics that represent disadvantage—illiteracy, landlessness and schedule caste/tribe—with the village literacy rate instead of whether the village had a *Gram Sabha* meeting. All three of these interactions are also significant. This does raise the possibility that holding a *Gram Sabha* meeting is correlated with other village characteristics that are important in shaping the way in which public resources are targeted. Therefore, we cannot say that holding a *Gram Sabha* has a causal effect on targeting. This is not an issue we can resolve with the existing data. However, these encouraging results on *Gram Sabhas* clearly deserve further careful investigation.

Our results contribute to a wider debate on how institution design can shape public resource allocation and how the poor can increase their voice in public institutions. It is frequently remarked that poverty is much more than material deprivation and that the poor may receive much less voice in the political process. Moreover, a good deal of cynicism attends initiatives to strengthen that voice.

While the context is very specific, our results sound a more optimistic note. The illiterate, landless and SC/STs are significantly more likely to attend *Gram Sabha* meetings than other groups. Moreover, there appears to be more targeting towards these groups where *Gram Sabha* meetings are held. The results are also suggestive of some externalities from literacy in the political process at the village level.

On a less optimistic note, we find that women are less likely to attend *Gram Sabha* meetings than men. Women respondents are around 20 per cent less likely to attend a *Gram Sabha* than men. Whether this has significant consequences for public resource allocation needs further investigation. But it is clear the representativeness of *Gram Sabhas* is likely to be affected by this. Other tools such as gender reservation in *Panchayat* representation may go some way towards remedying this (Chattopadhyay and Duflo, 2004a).

Political Selection

By the year 2000, the 73rd amendment led to the institution of 227,698 new village governments, *Gram Panchayats* (GP), staffed by over two million elected representatives. Whether these individuals have different skills and motivations from those who previously made political decisions is hard to discern. However, there is a growing body of evidence that political selection is an important consideration in political systems and the current context is an excellent one to think about this.

The Downsian model of politics, which has dominated political economy for over a generation, has no role for political selection. The role of politics is to seek out the policy position of the median voter, and not to examine who implements that policy. But there is now increasing attention paid to the role of political selection in reforming and improving politics.

Little is know in general about characteristics of politicians and how they differ from the general population. Table 11.4 gives some insight into this in the current context. It compares the sample of 540 politicians with the household sample in our data. We report two sets of comparisons. First, we use our entire sample to compare politician and non-politician households, and report the t-test for differences in means across these two populations in column (3). Second, we restrict attention to SC/ST households and examine whether within this group politician and non-politician households differ (columns (4)-(6)). In all cases, we weigh the non-politician sample by the population share of SC/ST households in the village to account for our purposive sampling of SC/ST households.

Looking across columns (1)-(3) an immediate finding, which is not particularly surprising, is that politicians are an elite group. Politicians, on average, own 5 acres of land which is more than twice the average landownership of non-politician households. The likelihood that a politician comes from a household with a history of involvement in politics is 25 per cent, as against a mere 6 per cent for non-politician households. Most politicians in our sample do not report politics as their primary occupation. This, in part, reflects the fact that most of them are first time entrants into politics. While both politician and non-politician households tend to rely on agriculture, politicians are significantly more likely to be cultivators than agricultural labourers. Politicians are also much more likely to be educated, enjoying an advantage of around three years of education per capita. They are also much more likely to read a newspaper which reflects greater literacy in the population group.

Table 11.4

Selection of Politicians

Sample:	*All*			*SC/ST*		
	Politician	*Non-politician*	*t test for Difference of Means*	*Politician*	*Non-politician*	*t test for Difference of Means*
	(1)	*(2)*	*(3)*	*(4)*	*(5)*	*(6)*
Landownership	5.705	2.025	10.118	2.374	1.055	3.862
	(0.353)	(0.086)	[0]	(0.296)	(0.170)	[0]
Family Political History	0.258	0.065	9.874	0.213	0.060	3.900
	(0.019)	(0.005)	[0]	(0.037)	(0.010)	[0]
Agricultural Labourer	0.066	0.237	-12.660	0.161	0.460	-7.880
	(0.010)	(0.008)	[0]	(0.033)	(0.019)	[0]
Cultivator	0.481	0.217	11.533	0.315	0.145	3.830
	(0.021)	(0.008)	[0]	(0.042)	(0.014)	[0]
Years of Education	7.276	4.750	11.860	6.161	2.880	7.180
	(0.186)	(0.103)	[0]	(0.421)	(0.174)	[0]
Newspaper Readership	0.692	0.342	15.810	0.613	0.220	8.280
	(0.019)	(0.010)	[0]	(0.044)	(0.018)	[0]
BPL Received	0.253	0.230	1.170	0.363	0.340	0.460
	(0.018)	(0.007)	[0.23]	(0.043)	(0.016)	[0.64]
Public Works Programme	0.091	0.040	3.904	0.121	0.084	1.170
	(0.012)	(0.003)	[0]	(0.029)	(0.010)	[0.23]

Notes: The non-politicians means are weighed by fraction SC/ST households in the village to account for purposive sampling of 4 SC/ST households per village. The p-values for the t test are provided in square brackets.

Columns (4)-(6) show that reserved politicians who belong to SC/ST also tend to be elites compared to their comparison group (non-politician SC/ST households). Both SC/ST politician and non-politician households are, however, economically disadvantaged relative to the general population. Thus, while reservation is bringing wider participation in politics, it tends to do so by picking elites from among traditionally disadvantaged groups.

Whether having a political elite that is also an economic elite is moot. It may reflect concerns about village politics being dominated by a set of narrow interests. However, it may also be the case that the more educated and knowledgeable citizens are better placed to run the village and to provide citizens with what the public goods and transfers that they need.

The last two rows of Table 11.4 show, however, that the political elite is more likely to claim BPL cards and to participate in public works programmes in spite of them appearing less disadvantaged in economic dimensions. This is evidence of political opportunism. While the difference in unconditional population means for politician and non-politician households receiving a BPL card is insignificant, in Besley, Pande and Rao (2005b) we saw that within villages this effect is statistically significant. However, there is evidence that the effect is diminished when politicians are more educated.

Overall, these results reinforce the need to have a good understanding of the process of political selection and its consequences in village government.

Policy Implications

The mainstream economics literature now engages with political economy issues in trying to understand what makes government work. The study of *Panchayats* provides an excellent basis for thinking how the insights of modern political economy can contribute to our understanding of public service delivery in India. While the *Panchayat* system has many specific features, there are potentially general lessons for experiments in democratic decentralisation elsewhere.

The mantra of decentralisation is that it will achieve policies that better reflect the needs of citizens living in villages of India. Our results on *Gram Sabhas* and their link to targeting provide some support for this idea. The fact that reserved politicians target differently in three of our states also reinforces earlier findings that reservation in the *Gram Panchayats* can achieve policy change.

But there are important unresolved issues. Politicians remain opportunistic undermining the most romanticised view of village government. The fact that this may change with selection of politicians suggests that there needs to be further focus on methods to draft an honest and competent political class. Policy measures that are worth debating include enhanced training for village politicians and use of wage incentives.

The question of how to ensure that *Gram Sabhas* are held is clearly important. Policies here could include better monitoring from above or finding means to enhance power of citizens to call *Gram Sabhas*.

Finally, our results call for a better debate about political geography and institutional means to guarantee that villages get an equal share of resources given that the *Pradhan*'s village appears to benefit most of all. This could be in terms of redrawing *Panchayat* boundaries to create more *Panchayats* which contain only few villages or to have a more explicit mechanism for rotating the *Pradhan*'s chair.

It is clear that there is much yet to be learned about how *Panchayats* work and to think of ways of improving the way in which they make policy. However, conducting studies based on large samples of villages seems like an important way forward to enhance the quality of policy making and to understand whether democratic decentralisation is fulfilling its promise.

References

Bardhan, Pranab (2002). "Decentralisation of Government and Development", *Journal of Economic Perspectives* 16(4):185-205.

Bardhan, Pranab and Dilip Mookherjee (2000). "Capture and Governance at Local and National Levels", *American Economic Review* 90(2):135-139.

———. (2003) "Political Economy of Land Reforms in West Bengal 1978-98", *mimeo.* Boston University.

Besley, Timothy, Rohini Pande, Lupin Rahman and Vijayendra Rao (2004a). "The Politics of Public Good Provision: Evidence from Indian Local Governments", *Journal of the European Economics Association*, 2(2-3): 416-426.

———. (2004b). "Decentralisation in India: A Survey of South Indian *Panchayats*". LSE. *mimeo*

Besley, Timothy, Rohini Pande and Vijayendra Rao (2005a). "Participatory Democracy in Action: Survey Evidence from India", *Journal of the European Economics Association.*

———. (2005b). "Political Selection and the Quality of Government: Evidence from South India", *mimeo.*

Chambers, Robert (1994). "Participatory Rural Appraisal (PRA): Challenges, Potentials and Paradigm", *World Development* 22(10): 1437-1454.

Chattopadhyay, Raghabendra and Esther Duflo (2004a). "Women as Policy Makers: Evidence from a India-Wide Randomized Policy Experiment", *Econometrica* 72(5): 1409-1444.

———. (2004b). "Efficiency and Rent-seeking in Local Governments". MIT. *mimeo*

Chaudhuri, Subham and Patrick Heller (2004). "Building Local Democracy: Evaluating the Impact of Decentralisation in Kerala". Paper presented to *Netsappe III.* Paris, June.

Crook, Richard C. and James Manor (1998). *Democracy and Decentralisation in South Asia and West Africa : Participation, Accountability, and Performance*, Cambridge, New York: Cambridge University Press.

Foster, Andrew and Mark Rosenzweig (2001). "Democratisation, Decentralisation and the Distribution of Local Public Goods in a Poor Rural Economy", *mimeo.* Brown.

Government of India (1955). *Report of the States Reorganisation Commission.* Delhi: Manager of Publications, Government of India.

Manor, James. (2004) "Democratisation with Inclusion: Political Reforms and People's Empowerment at the Grassroots," *Journal of Human Development* 5(1): 5-29.

Pande, Rohini (2003). "Minority Representation and Policy Choices: The Significance of Legislator Identity", *American Economic Review* 93(4): 1132-1151.

Matthew, George and Nirmala Buch (2000). *Status of Panchayati Raj in the States and Union Territories of India 2000.* Delhi: Institute for Social Studies.

Verba, Sidney, Kay Lehman Scholzman and Henry E. Brady (1995). *Voice and Equality: Civic Voluntarism in American Politics.* Cambridge Mass.: Harvard University Press.

Part III

Sectoral Perspectives and Interventions

12

Agrarian Reform for a Liberal Pattern of Society?

Karnataka's Land Policy and Poverty Alleviation

RONALD HERRING

Peasants to Farmers: Logics of Land Reform

Critiques of the Karnataka Land Reforms Act of 1974 implicitly centre its irrelevance to a liberal pattern of society under conditions of globalisation (Thimmaiah, 2001). Implicitly, the argument for removing restrictions on agrarian accumulation (land ceilings) and production relations (tenancy laws) assumes that the world has changed from one of peasants to one of farmers.

At Independence, India's agrarian prospect was clouded by the symbolic centrality of the *zamindar*—a figure Jawaharlal Nehru in particular held to be not only useless but an actual drag on economic development. Though Indian land systems in fact varied as much as the continental size and disconnected local histories would suggest, the policy model assumed that democracy and market capitalism were both hindered by remnants of feudal control of terrain and people. Walter C. Neale's justifiably iconic essay was entitled: *Land is to Rule*. The extent to which agrarian reforms on the model of the 1931 Karachi Resolution of the Indian National Congress—"Land to the tiller and power to the people"—and the more specific *Report of the Congress Agrarian Reforms Committee* were legislated and implemented as measures of state-level policy varied significantly.[1] These variations mattered greatly in determining—in a path-dependent way—variations in what John Harriss calls "the balance of caste-class

1. Neale,1969: 3-13; on Congress and land reforms generally, Herring, 1988; in addition to CARC, see Malaviya, 1954.

power," which in turn has been a major driver of variance in poverty alleviation performance across states (2003).[2]

In contemporary policy logic from Delhi, and in developmental discourse internationally, farmers are replacing peasants. In the normative logic of land reforms from both contemporary right and left, this outcome is all to the good. The 'peasantry' connotes an inferior and somewhat homogeneous social estate, politically subordinate, only marginally involved with markets, subject to numerous non-market forms of extraction and dominance. In Barrington Moore, Jr.'s explanation for why India followed none of his normative 'paths to the modern world,' classical agrarian society figured centrally; *Social Origins of Dictatorship and Democracy* was subtitled 'Lord and Peasant in the Making of the Modern World'. As in many nations newly freed from colonial domination, agrarian reforms in India were calculated to address local dependency relations antithetical to freedom and democratic practice *via* mechanisms operating at both ends of the agrarian spectrum: control of people on the land would be diminished by reducing both the concentration of land in few hands *via* ceilings and the institutional terms on which land could be farmed *via* *zamindari* abolition and tenancy reform (Herring, 1983: Ch 8-9). This logic was widely shared—and quite consonant with contemporaneous reforms. In the American occupation forces' land reforms in Japan, classes at the top rungs of the agrarian hierarchy were diminished through ceilings, and control of subordinate individuals and classes was extirpated by abolition of tenancy.[3] This is the logic of land to the tiller.

The assumption of the classic agrarian reform model is that land is scarce, and thus to be rationed in a poor society dependent on agriculture; that dependency is socially dysfunctional—or at least

2. In Delhi's scheme for the states—which are the major arenas for land reform—the symbolically central but analytically amorphous 'abolition of intermediaries' came first, beginning in the early 1950s, followed by ceilings in the mid-1950s, and a lowering of ceilings in 1972. At the time of the 78th amendment to the Constitution, 277 land laws had been incorporated into the Ninth Schedule. The power of central ministries in land reform is limited, except during imposition of President's Rule on a state.

3. This is more or less exactly what the author of those reforms in Japan, Wolf Ladejinsky, told me in Delhi, where he was less successful.

inconsistent with citizenship; and finally that extensive land holdings are farmed too extensively to maximise yields and raise aggregate agricultural production. Uninterested landlords and impoverished tenants combine to depress agricultural investment and thus growth and employment creation. Land reforms could be a lever for creating an agrarian capitalism that was dynamic and consonant with democracy. The abolition of peasant society would create farmers. The historical phasing of land reforms thus becomes critical to their logic.

This temporal interpretation is reflected in contemporary calls for reversal of land reforms in Karnataka. Essentially, critiques imply that the transformative roles of land reforms have been accomplished—the hoary 'abolition of intermediaries.' In this case, new reforms for a new pattern of society make sense. Just as the problematic of the Congress Agrarian Reforms Committee was creating a rural India with agricultural growth and social empowerment, current regimes worry more about the place of India in a global hierarchy of market economies. There are no limits to accumulation in industry: how anomalous it seems to have a ceiling on landed property (Thimmaiah, 2001). If one can rent tractors and apartments, why not land? Barriers to land transactions from the early consensus would seem to create high transaction costs and hinder the efficient allocation of all factors of production in agriculture. More broadly, as the 'socialist pattern of society' hortatory is replaced by acceptance of a liberal pattern of society, the logic of agrarian reform from the Nehruvian consensus is challenged. Thus, G. Thimmaiah (1997: 77) writes in his commentary on land reforms in Karnataka:

> Caste politics and Marxian ideology have lost their relevance and hence their strength. They are politically impotent and socially irrelevant....But a more fundamental ideological issue is that tenancy abolition and impositions of ceilings on landholdings have no justification when such restrictions have been scrapped in the industrial sector...Farmers should demand abolition of land ceilings.

This comment on the irrelevance and impotence of the left, widely shared by public analysts, was made before the left turned in its best performance ever in the Lok Sabha elections of 2004. Nevertheless, the stance is common, and diagnostic. But there is an irony in Thimmaiah's attribution of radical reform to Marxian ideology.

Elsewhere he notes, quite correctly (1997: 62):

> Though this reform measure was vehemently advocated by the Marxists, it received both moral and intellectual support even from those espousing capitalist ideology. This was a curious case of a convergence of ideologies.

The convergence is not so curious, really; there was a consensus that 'feudal elements' were antithetical to modern India, and land was their base. There is nothing particularly Marxist about reforming agrarian systems in favour of small-farmer proprietorships; such policies expand the base of social forces defending private property and conservative politics. Pro-capitalist forces recognise exactly this potential: land reform can be a preemptive strike against the rural left. Some of the most radical reforms in the 20th century were backed by American foreign policy as an antidote to leftist agrarian threats perceived as precursors of communism. Indeed, the vision of yeoman farmers on small plots creating a healthy and industrious society is one endorsed by the founders of the United States in its revolt against British rule, especially in the thinking of Thomas Jefferson. This vision is consistent with Nehru's comment that the *zamindars* were like the fifth wheel of a carriage—not only unnecessary but a hindrance to social progress. Similar views were behind Zulfikar Ali Bhutto's 'anti-feudal' land reforms in Pakistan, pointed toward an elusive 'Islamic socialism' (Herring, 1979). Indeed, agrarian reform may be an essential component of the agrarian bourgeois revolution (Herring, 1983, Ch 4). Specifically, un-encumbering lands and persons of their 'feudal' properties is a necessary condition for land and labour to function as commodities subject to market dynamics. Indeed, lowering the friction of land transactions has been a major component of globally funded initiatives in poor countries for land titling. Better titles, it is held, lower transaction costs and make rural development more vigorous.[4]

---

4. The extreme of this position, though not centered on rural dynamics, is Hernando de Soto's The Mystery of Capital: Why Capitalism Triumphs in the West and Fails Everywhere Else. Concern for rationalisation of land records, for both transparency and ease of transactions, has in Karnataka been undertaken as the *Bhoomi* (land) E-Governance project. The Government claims that 20 million land records of 6.7 million land owners in 176 *taluks* have been computerised, with aid of Delhi and some contribution from the state government.

In sum, land reform for a socialistic pattern of society produces many of the same desiderata as reform for a liberal pattern of society, but with an eye toward lessening rural inequalities. Free-market fundamentalists see the abolition of tenancy as a possible relation of production to be unnecessarily restrictive and the imposition of ceilings on the amount of agrarian capital that can be legally owned as contrary to the logic of accumulation. But in both logics, as we move across policy models from minimal to maximal, poverty alleviation should increase. This follows from the high correlation between landlessness and poverty. Agrarian redistribution should be a major lever for alleviating rural poverty. Karnataka's land reforms have formally followed the radical 'land to the tiller' model of the CARC and Kerala state, rather than the more compromised models of most Indian states, including West Bengal. What can the experience tell us about the relation between agrarian reforms and poverty alleviation?

Land Reforms and Poverty Alleviation in Karnataka

Though agrarian reforms have been extensive in Karnataka, the state has not ranked high in poverty alleviation among Indian states. Kohli's (1987) early work contrasted Karnataka with West Bengal to illustrate how a committed and disciplined left-of-center party could effect poverty alleviation on the ground in ways not possible in states lacking this political resource.[5] Harriss (2003) follows Kohli explicitly in investigating poverty reduction in Karnataka. He uses the Minhas, Jain and Tendulkar rankings from 1991 and the Datt and Ravallion rankings from 1998 to confirm that Karnataka's extent of poverty alleviation as somewhere below the middle for Indian states: 12th of 17 or 11th of 15, depending on data set. In yield performance, Karnataka does well, ranking 5th of 14 states by the calculation of Bhalla and Singh (1997). Harriss (2003: 211) concludes:

> Karnataka is...a middle income state, generally with slightly higher levels of development expenditure and middling agricultural infrastructure (in comparison to other States)...(and) has had a

5. What seems politically rational about the West Bengal reforms is that the politically risky move of making independent landowners of tenants was avoided in favor of making tenants remain tenants, but with privileges dependent on who rules locally and in Kolkata—i.e. the CPI-M. See Herring, 1988; 2001.

> comparatively high rate of growth of farm yields. Yet by all accounts it appears to have been one of the states that has been least successful in reducing poverty.

Harriss writes this conclusion in the 1990s, a period during which poverty measures and realities were—in the words of a prominent protagonist, Angus Deaton—'fiercely debated, politically and statistically.' Karnataka's relatively low ranking, if not a statistical artefact, raises a genuine puzzle: if extensive agrarian reform legislation, comparatively good infrastructure and development expenditure profiles, and fairly rapid agricultural growth do not produce poverty reduction above the mean for Indian States, why not? The 1972 reforms, in form, closely resembled those of Kerala, as both followed the basic pattern of the Congress Agrarian Reforms Committee, but Kerala by all measures has been a leader in poverty reduction (Herring, 2000; Heller. 1999). Does the Karnataka case suggest, contrary to Lipton (1993), that there is little 'evidence against stopping' agrarian reforms as a means of poverty alleviation and rural development?

We can begin to answer this question by disaggregating dimensions of Karnataka's agrarian reforms, beginning with the most critical distinction between the letter of the law and implementation on the ground. Karnataka's reforms are in line with recommended agrarian policy of the national government, which is not true in all states. However, implementation lapses are similar to those of other states. There is here potentially a major caveat: poverty-alleviating effects of land reform have not been adequately tested in Karnataka, as the situation on the ground does not always reflect the objectives in the legislation.

Metrics for assessing land reforms in India are typically derived from legal-rational bureaucratic necessity; percentage of cases 'disposed of' is the dominant comparative empirical referent. This metric reflects the way records are kept, and is thus less costly to employ than alternatives. But cases-disposed does not yield an agronomically or economically useful data base. The reasons are

6. For an argument that much of what we know of the world is driven by convenience of indicators, see Herring (2003a).

simple enough: data are social products, and thus reflect the conditions of their production.[6] The weakest tenants, most dependent on local elites, are least likely to bring cases, for a number of well-understood reasons, centering on embedded production relations (Herring, 1981). Landlords have incentives to hide land, dependents have reasons to collaborate in legal fictions. Bureaucrats are under pressure to show progress.

For penetrating the official numbers of cases to assess changes on the ground, we rely on smaller studies, often of a single village or a small sample in a limited area. From this base, analysts face the problem of scaling up: how representative is the area of study? It is from ethnographic work that we know the biases of official data–though seldom magnitudes of distortion. It is well known that landowners seek to discard the worst land in their holdings; that holding declarations often conceal reality; that *benami* transfers frequently follow reform legislation; that some tenants are not destitute but are instead farmers leasing in land to achieve economies of scale for new capital purchases; that not all tenants know of tenancy provisions or apply for benefits; that some applications by tenants are fraudulent, and so on. Legal categories are confounded on the ground, in the villages, and there is much instrumental obscuring of records.[7] These dynamics run through most detailed micro-level studies of land reforms and are predictable give the political economy of power distribution in agrarian systems, the high stakes in land distribution, and the embeddedness of local bureaucracies in local society.

Keeping these important caveats in mind, we find that by the criterion of 'cases resolved,' Karnataka's reforms have been well administered in comparative perspective. The slippages are remarkably similar to those in other states that have tried reform seriously. By 1997, over 90 per cent of the applications for settlement of tenants had been resolved. Former tenants had received land in the aggregate amounting to 644,000 (6.44 lakh) acres. Under ceiling provisions, the State has declared 275,000 acres surplus—though only 160,000 acres

7. Herring, 1983, Ch. 3, 8. *Benami* is literally 'without name' and connotes fraudulent. For concrete cases and discussion of means of evading ceilings in the Karnataka reforms, Iyer, 1997a.

have been vested in the state, and 115, 000 acres distributed to landless families (2.75 > 1.6 > 1.15 lakh acres, from declaration to vesting to distribution, all discrete stages of administering land reforms). Distribution among scheduled castes constituted well over half of all land distributed by 1993, in accord with stated policy objectives.[8] According to NSS data for 1982, almost a decade after the reforms, large holders (20 ha and above) constituted 3.7 per cent of landholders but held 24.1 per cent of the area; small holders (below 2 ha) constituted 60.5 per cent of landholders but held only 29 per cent of total area (Aziz, 1997:57-58). World Bank data for 1995-96 indicate 42 per cent of holdings less than one hectare, 27.4 per cent between one and two hectares. Together, almost 70 per cent of holdings are less than two hectares, a little higher than the Indian mean. Only 1.7 per cent of holdings exceeded 10 hectares. This skew means that most farmers are unlikely to be financially secure, given the hazards of agriculture on small holdings. Yet the skew is quite minimal in comparison with the norms of corporate capitalism, and is less than the inequality in many agrarian societies, including some in India.

Nevertheless, with more than two-thirds of landholders owning below 2 ha, and only 1.6 lakh acres vested in the state for distribution to the landless, potential for poverty alleviation *via* land reform was quite limited, even in theory. Lowering the ceiling would lower rural inequality, but would add to the numbers of marginal farmers. Moreover, actual performance invariably lags potential. Depending on type of land, such small holdings are typically a weak basis for family prosperity, especially over time, as holdings are divided and re-divided across generations. Finally, the skew of landholdings distribution is typically less important for poverty alleviation than the extent of landlessness: 160,000 acres will not create many secure livelihoods. Landless agricultural workers constitute the most awkward class in agrarian reform. This is true because the coalition that can effect redistribution from large holders depends on a class of farmers that

8. Table 4.2, p.55 of Aziz, 1997. More aggregate data from Krishna, 1997.
9. This is true even in very radical reforms: see Herring, 1980. Consider in parallel the very different scenarios painted by Krishnaji, 1979 and Lerche, 1998, in Kerala and Uttar Pradesh respectively, though the analysis of both would support the text.

would be hurt by the primary mechanism for helping the landless escape poverty: raising rural wages.[9]

Once land becomes available through ceiling legislation, there are both political and economic dilemmas in distribution. Political logic drives distribution to the maximum number of families in the tiniest parcels. Economists have traditionally argued that there should be a minimum size of holding, as tiny plots are 'uneconomic.' In assessing the effect of Karnataka's ceiling reforms, Iyer (1997a: 115) concluded:

> ...allotment of land has increased the social and psychological status of the allottees, and has also partially raised their income. However, they continue to live below the poverty line and continue to work as agricultural labourers. One of the weakest elements is the lack of linkage of financial assistance with antipoverty programmes.

Iyer (1997a: 116) describes the economic effects of ceilings on beneficiaries he studied as 'marginal'.

This finding from Karnataka reinforces a common theme of the limitations of agrarian reform as a poverty-alleviation policy. Recipients who lack credit—or even implements to work the land effectively (e.g. Iyer's case of Belwatigi village in Uttara Kannada)— sell or rent out land they cannot afford to convert to a livelihood. Though ceiling reforms are universally justified in development logic for alleviating the poverty of landless agrarian workers, they almost universally fail to acquire enough land to lift a significant percentage of rural workers into the ranks of peasant proprietors—themselves a precarious class.[10] There is strong political pressure for a mini-max compromise: to minimize the pain inflicted on landed elites by making exemptions to the ceiling, and to maximise the number of beneficiaries by dividing up appropriated land into very small, often sub-viable parcels, often needing extensive investment to be profitably arable (Herring, 1983, Ch 8).

The extent of direct poverty reduction in ceiling reforms is a function of the aggregate land appropriated — reflecting the level of

10. From 1998 onwards, farmer suicides from economic distress became a national concern; on Karnataka, see Vasavi, 1999. The state government's study of farmer suicides indicated, however, that agrarian distress was only part of the picture; understandably, many suicides resulted from personal crises unrelated to production and income (Karnataka, 2002).

the ceiling—and the quality of the land distributed. In the legislation that preceded Karnataka's 1974 Act—the Land Reforms Act of 1961—ceilings were set at 27 standard acres per family. Standard acres were to be calculated in terms of rough productivity equivalents: e.g., one acre of the best irrigated land was counted as equivalent to 8 acres of *barani* land in an area receiving less than 25 inches of rain annually. This ceiling was decreased in 1974 after urgings from the Centre in 1972 for the States to find more land for redistribution. A ceiling that temporally follows a previously generous ceiling will net less land; families have had a chance to rearrange their holdings and they know what is coming. The 1974 Act defined the one standard acre of irrigated land as one unit; a family of five could hold up to 10 units: ie, 10 acres of the best land, or more of inferior land.[11]

Appropriating too little land to make small farms for all the poor does not necessarily mean complete failure. One significant success of the Kerala reforms came through securing land for house-sites for traditionally attached laborers. Similar provisions were legislated in Section 38 of the 1974 Act in Karnataka, though these provisions became operative only in 1979. According to the data of Gowda (1997: 128), about 61 per cent of the cases decided went in favour of the landless, accounting for 15,530 cases covering 2,103 acres. Again, the impulse behind the legislation is radical: ownership of house-sites confers some social standing and autonomy on the weakest rural people, reduces abject dependence on landed elites, raises the reservation wage and offers opportunities for labour-intensive kitchen gardens for better nutrition or cash cropping. Moreover, with the general increases in land values, particularly near urban areas, sale of land may produce a significant sum for underwriting a new livelihood. These house-sites were somewhat larger in Karnataka (averaging 0.135 acres each) than in Kerala, but the aggregate effect was limited by the small scale of redistribution—about two thousand acres.[12]

---

11. See Iyer, 1997a for a lucid description of the technicalities involved in the legislation.

12. Comparable legislation in Kerala typically allowed house-sites for kuddikidappukar only up to 0.1 acre; most in practice were much smaller. My experience is that these plots are very intensively and creatively used, clearly enhancing the autonomy of laborers as well as their cash income and nutrition. With urban expansion, many are sold for very high prices.

Redistributive impact is thus limited by available land, which in turn is a function of legislative compromises and administrative lacunae. Land reforms in Karnataka followed one archetypal path of redistributive reform in general: from radical model to compromised legislation to selectively and partially implemented policy. Abdul Aziz traces the compromises made in legislation to provide comfort to more conservative forces (1997: 54-55)—for example, the familiar exempting of plantation lands, which had been part of agricultural land in an earlier draft, and deletion of strong prohibitions against *de facto* absentee 'cultivation.' Moreover, because of differences in land quality and the small aggregate amount of land available, distributions have per force come in plot sizes that may be too small in many agro-ecologies to yield a livelihood. In these cases, the rational beneficiary may well try to find a way to sell the land as soon as possible.[13] Aziz reports on two small-scale studies, one showing substantial success from reforms, the other a lack of success. Not surprisingly, the difference was the quantity and quality of land. In George's study of beneficiaries in Bijapur and Dharwad districts, occupational mobility of beneficiaries increased and parcels were generally adequate. In Patil's study of Gulbarga, on the other hand, the size of farms distributed was not adequate for a livelihood by local agronomic conditions. Moreover, echoing much of the literature on agrarian reform, the non-land components, especially credit for bunding, levelling and irrigation, as well as extension services for new farmers, were often insufficient. In George's study, cropping intensity among land reform beneficiaries was only 102.7 per cent, compared to an already low 117.4 per cent in the case of farmers who did not receive new land.[14]

We would expect such variation as a function of normal dispersion in a State as large as Karnataka. Moreover, as in all land reforms, existing institutions matter greatly. In this regard, Karnataka, like

13. Or lease it out; see Iyer, 1997a: 115. Aziz argues that at least the SC/ST beneficiaries did not receive on average less land than other beneficiaries, in fact a bit more, but the 3.64 acre average plot may or may not be economically viable.

14. The logical conclusion, drawn by Aziz, is that irrigation made the difference, and absence of credit was a major obstacle for the new beneficiaries in terms of developing irrigation.

Kerala, exhibits significant variation across institutional residues and arrangements on the land. Like Kerala, the state was formed in 1956, on November 1. Karnataka was a combination of Coorg province, Mysore princely state, along with pieces of erstwhile Madras Presidency, Bombay Presidency and Hyderabad province. Land forms vary from the hilly region of the Western Ghats to more arid regions of the Deccan plateau, to the coastal plains. Uniform land law applied to such a varied institutional and agroecological landscape is certain to encounter what one might call the Africa problem of spatial and legal incongruities.

As in much of India, because ceilings seldom yield sufficient land to make very many new farms, tenancy reform has been essential to poverty alleviation where tenants are poor and the rental exactions constitute a very steep tax on production. Tenancy as a form of production has continually declined, from perhaps half of all holdings at Independence. The reasons for decline have much to do with land reform: in anticipation of reform, tenants were evicted, or made *de facto* tenants-at-will off the official records. Other tenants became owners, as the land-to-the-tiller model specified. In theory, the 1974 Karnataka Land Reforms Act entailed a two stage process to confer land to the tiller. First, land held by tenants was vested in the State, with compensation to owners; then, land rights were devolved to the actual cultivator, who may or may not have been the tenant of record. Thus in theory, the myriad of subtenancies and sharecropping arrangements created by subinfeudation were resolved in favour of the lowest rung on the agrarian ladder: whoever was the actual cultivator, title notwithstanding, received the land.[15] This is a radical move on tenancy, particularly in comparison with West Bengal, a state often praised for its redistributive land reforms. Rather than implementing land to the tiller, West Bengal stopped at institutionalising sharecropping by regulating rents and tenure, thus preserving landlordism. With regard to tenancy, Karnataka is closer to Kerala than to West Bengal. Yet conditions vary greatly with regard to tenancy.

In tenancy reform, poverty impact will vary with the percentage of

15. On the complexity of these distinctions, on the ground and in law, see Jannuzi's classic 1974 volume on Bihar, *Agrarian Crisis in India*.

tenanted farms to total and the terms of rental contracts as a reflection of land-labour bargaining power. It is the coastal region of Karnataka (Uttara Kannada, Dakshina Kannada) that comes closest to the Congress Agrarian Reforms Committee's view of agrarian problems of the new nation. Tenanted holdings ranged in coastal Karnataka from 54.4 to 68.2 per cent of all holdings. Resolution of cases was overwhelmingly in favour of the tenants: 77.7 to 81.8 per cent of the applications for tenancy rights were granted. At the other end of the continuum, the Southern Maidan section of Karnataka (Bellary, Tumkur, Mandya, Bangalore, etc.) ranged from 1.5 to 6.2 per cent. In this region, existing rates of tenancy were almost as high as current rates of concealed tenancy (see below). Northern Maidan (Belgaum, Bijapur, Dharwad, Bidar, etc.) was an intermediate region for extent of tenancy. Malnad was mostly on the low end, but Shimoga registered 21.5 per cent of all holdings tenanted.[16]

A sense of this variation can be taken from G.V. Joshi's study of Uttara Kannada district. This was a high-land-pressure, landlord-dominated district before the reforms; a majority of the holdings were tenanted. Effective implementation of tenancy provisions there depended on the peasant movement as a 'vital force.' This force was a function of strong path dependency: the Bombay Tenancy Act of 1946 had 'intensified class conflict' because that legislation had been blatantly pro-landlord. Joshi concludes: "The experiences in this district thus show that half-hearted and defective tenancy legislation intensifies class conflict and reinforces tenants' movement."

This perspective parallels a common generalisation in explaining variation in tenancy-reform success: a ratchet politics in which imperfectly-implemented policy generates social mobilisation for more fundamental reform over time. Such path dependence explains the difference between Malabar and other parts of Kerala in the long struggle to abolish landlordism, and between Kerala and other states in India. 19th century *jacqueries* resulted from severe agrarian structural dislocation: the 'Moplah outrages.' Less-suicidal inheritors of the agrarian radicalism tradition introduced organisational and tactical innovations that more effectively confronted a state increasingly

16. Data from Table 6.1, Rajan, 1997.

willing to negotiate agrarian relations for fear of rural insurrection. The success of the agrarian left was in creating a coalition of diverse social elements with different objective interests around the abolition of landlordism. Representation of landlordism as a social system permitted a tactical integration of grievances across the spectrum of interests, objective and subjective, in the villages. For example, the Malabar Tenancy Act of 1929 gave those tenants who benefited a toehold that mattered for political efficacy and leadership. At the same time, ground-level insecurity in the face of landed power and the exclusion of many kinds of tenants from benefits, sustained and expanded mobilisation on the left (Herring, 1988). Just as Malabar was set apart from other parts of contemporary Kerala, the Bombay act applied only to those areas of Karnataka that came from Bombay in the reorganisation of States by Delhi.

Historical legacies and path dependence thus contribute fundamentally to the uneven development of social forces on the ground that separate effective reforms from dead letters. In Kerala's case, the merger of a radical agrarian movement in Malabar with incipient working-class movements to its south laid the base for the dominance of the Congress Socialist Party in the entire area of Malayalam-speaking people. Agrarian exploitation was clearly a major driver for agrarian mobilization, despite the attempt of some (but not all) colonial officials to blame everything on Islam. Beginning in Malabar in 1836, initially peaking in 1841, and continuing sporadically throughout the 19th century, simmering agrarian tensions exploded in 1921 in a series of encounters known as the Moplah Rebellion, one of the most intense uprisings in Indian colonial history. Leftist success in an especially exploitative agrarian structure is not inevitable, but not unexpected; similar dynamics characterised Thanjavur (Tanjore) district as well (Bouton, 1985; Zagoria, 1971). Under colonial rule, Malabar was but one district of the Madras Presidency, distant from the capital in Madras (Chennai), and from Thanjavur, and isolated from Tamil-speaking middle peasantries that dominated the larger area. Malabar was easy for the Presidency to ignore; the consequence was agrarian revolt and eventually a traumatized state willing to concede on tenurial issues for social peace. After Independence, Malabar was joined to Kerala State, uniting left movements over the entire area in which Malayalam is spoken and adding a more militant agrarian base to Kerala's populace. Thanjavur remained an isolated outpost of agrarian radicalism and electoral leftist voting in the state of Tamil Nadu. This conjunctural reorganisation of political space explains much of the success of radical mobilisation in Kerala and its failure in neighboring Tamilnadu (Herring, 1988). Bases for radical agrarian mobilisation were even more isolated in Karnataka and had even less effect on development of a party system.

In mobilisation for agrarian reform, political and policy talk about 'the peasantry' masks significant conflicts between aspiring tenants and landless labourers. In Kerala, the labourers were kept in the coalition by the argument that the 'rent fund' would be shared out through higher wages after abolition of landlordism. Political conflict over the wage issue ensued between agricultural workers—largely still landless—and former tenants, now relatively wealthy, having become owners of about 42 per cent of the arable land in the state. The institutional outcome was a remarkable piece of legislation—the Kerala Agricultural Workers Act of 1974—that gave labourers a larger share of the bundle of rights in land we call ownership (Herring, 1989; 2001). Workers in Karnataka constituted a smaller demographic and lacked the autonomous organisation qua workers that characterised most Kerala workers in agriculture. Not surprisingly, Chandrashekhara Damle's (1997) study of Dakshina Kannada district concludes that landless labourers were left in need of the most attention.

Central tendencies are inevitably misleading and Indian states are not particularly good units for generalisation. One could multiply examples of variance within Karnataka, as illustrated above, but it is difficult to come to a summary conclusion based on secondary data. Indeed, one of the great difficulties in serious assessment of land reforms is that local data are hard to access, hard to verify, and intensive studies adequate to this task do not easily add up to aggregate pictures. Aggregate data are of dubious validity and lose variance. Nevertheless, generalisations by scholars close to micro-level studies suggest as varied an impact as one would expect from historical and tenurial variance. Iyer (1997b: 198 *et passim*) summarises the tenancy provisions of the land reform act as an "even keel of success/failure...as nearly half the tenants who had filed applications were conferred occupancy/ownership rights and the remaining cases were rejected." Yet in agreement with other studies of similar laws, Iyer found great variance geographically and substantial concealment of tenancy, shifting of plots of *de facto* tenants, and continued debt dependency.[17] Damle (1997: 175) notes that "land reforms and the developmental measures taken by the government had the effect of shaking up rural society but scarcely that of reshaping it on egalitarian lines." In concert with studies of Karnataka and other states, Damle finds that access to institutional credit, differentiated levels of agricultural modernisation and "the failure of governmental reform and legislative measures" have meant the persistence of a concentration of land ownership in the hands of upper caste/dominant class landowners" though such domination rests on somewhat different bases in the modernisation of agriculture. One would hardly expect 'reshaping on egalitarian lines' from ceilings provisions that covered only 3.8 per cent of the land investigated for reform and only 1.1 per cent of net sown area. One does not, then expect remarkable results on the poverty front from the Karnataka land reforms.

Moving Targets and Spreading the Policy Burden

What does Karnataka's outcome on the land reform and poverty question tell us about the place of land reforms in developmental logic for the rural poor? The reforms had pro-poor effects, but often in indirect ways and for small numbers of people. Conceptually similar reforms in Kerala aided in very rapid reduction of poverty. Yet, however important historically, redistribution of tiny patches of land is likely to be swamped by changes in the larger structure of forces that confronts Indian farmers: commodity prices, interest rates, drought, international market rigging. Moreover, as rural welfare increasingly depends on non-farm income (e.g. Lanjouw and Shariff, 2004), might the historical centrality of land reforms become increasingly irrelevant?

Despite what seems a clear case in logic and history, agrarian

17. Concealed tenancy rates varied fairly dramatically by region; Iyer estimates from two to eight per cent of holdings. Yet it is certain that the full extent of concealment is, for obvious reasons, partly hidden even from investigators who set out to find it.

reform has been slighted of late in discussions of pro-poor policy. The developmental paths of South Korea, Japan and Taiwan are widely held to have been enabled by radical agrarian reform. The failure of promised agrarian reforms after the abolition of slavery in the American South during 'Reconstruction' clearly contributed to concentrations of poverty by race that have proved persistent and self-reinforcing (Herring, 2003b: 70-79).

Conceptualisation of agrarian systems as integrated nets of multi-dimensional social and economic control would predict not only compromised policy, but, as important, faulty implementation: power is expressed at all levels of the political system, from agenda setting to administration. Land reforms can fall short in many different ways; some examples from Karnataka in the previous section conform to and reinforce generalisable patterns. Exceptions prove the rule; radical redistributions have depended on rare historical conjunctures—communist revolution (China), external intervention (Japan) or effective social democratic mobilisation of the poor majority (Kerala). When the landless are economically dependent and politically powerless, and sometimes consequently ideologically incorporated, agrarian reform will be unlikely to succeed except under authoritarian auspices. Limited redistribution continually creates veto blocks opposed to further redistribution—an unvirtuous ratchet. Having moved up, substantial farmers want to pull up the ladder after them: a dependent workforce is in their interest, and their own limited prosperity seems paltry in comparison with urban extravagance. Their power *vis-à-vis* governments is structural if not directly political: 'the nation' needs ever increasing production from agriculture; uncertainty about property rights must suppress some investment (Herring, 1983, Chapter 8). Moreover, a political coalition for pro-poor reform is unlikely, for well known reasons: problems of collective action among dispersed actors without resources, economic dependency, multiple cross-cutting political interests among the poor, diffusion of interests by entrepreneurial political parties, hostility of powerful classes with privileged access to state operatives.

The Karnataka case suggests reinforcement for the notion of fairly tight constraints for land reform to have a transformative effect for the bottom of agrarian society—an effect quite limited in contemporary

India, but certainly achieved in Kerala (Herring, 2000; 2001). Atul Kohli's comparison of Karnataka with West Bengal indicates the limits created by absence of a disciplined left party (1987). Perhaps as important as electoral politics, successful left parties often indicate significant class mobilisation in civil society. Such mobilisation energises reforms: uncovering malfeasance, pressing for timely action, intimidating colluding bureaucrats. John Harriss's emphasis on a decisive break with upper class/caste dominance accords with this notion, as landed privilege was highly correlated with social standing in India's version of peasant society. Harriss places Karnataka just outside the range of states with stronger probabilities of state-level regime production of poverty alleviation. He classifies Karnataka in a category with Andhra Pradesh, Gujarat, Maharashtra, and perhaps Punjab as (Harriss, 2003: 215):

> States with middle-caste/class-dominated regimes, where Congress has been effectively challenged but has not collapsed and there is a fairly stable and mainly two-party competition (the politics of accommodation *vis-à-vis* lower-class interests have continued to work effectively, especially in Maharashtra and Karnataka, and least so in Gujarat).

For Harriss, the regimes that have been enabled by a decisive challenge of the dominant class/caste social coalition are Kerala, Tamilnadu, and West Bengal. In these states the umbrella accomodationist Congress lost its dominance at an early period. In Kerala, mass energy in social movements was organized as the Congress Socialist Party (Communist Party after 1942), which eclipsed conservative Congress elements by sheer weight of numbers and activity. Congress hegemony was replaced by a distributive anti-elite populism in Tamilnadu, and by aggressive left coalitions in Kerala (first) and West Bengal (more enduringly). As importantly, I would argue, in Kerala, the Congress and its permutations have been responsive to electoral competition with left forces, particularly on land policy, making the party less conservative than most Congress state units in India (Herring, 1988).

Karnataka has exhibited neither of these paths. Following Manor (1989), Harriss (2003: 219 *et passim*) argues that Karnataka is a State with a 'conservative social order' in which class/caste divisions have not been sufficiently severe as to raise the kind of upheaval one witnesses just to the South, in Kerala. He argues, on the basis of evidence from Crook and Manor, that decentralisation has not "been particularly responsive to 'vulnerable groups,' the poor or marginalised. Parties have been 'weak and factionalized,' with no cohesive left. Even populism as an electoral strategy—which is sometimes helpful for the poor, as in both Andhra Pradesh and Tamil Nadu—is not institutionalised in the party system." Extending beyond Harriss's explicit argument, there is explanatory space for the nature of the party system and resultant state-level regimes. Land reforms are typically driven by factors missing from Karnataka's historical political development: coalitions of disadvantaged classes and class fractions under the leadership of a strong redistributive party (Kohli, 1987; Herring, 1983, Ch 8). The implication is that path dependency is important to policy possibilities and effects, though much current literature in development proceeds otherwise (Herring, 2003b).

So gloomy are the prospects for agrarian reform, and so many are the obstacles to implementation, that market-friendly solutions to poverty largely replaced redistributive policy over time, certainly by the 1980s. In the 1990s, discussion moved away from large-scale political organisations and institutions in general to decentralisation, disaggregated empowerment and institutions of civil society. Land reforms enhance state power, as state builders have always known; powerful states became negatively valenced in neo-liberal orthodoxy.

Within India, the agrarian vision of the CARC has declined in part for reasons of ordinary politics, but resonates with a general silence on redistribution. Yet, even if the analytical core of the vision rings true, its very rootedness in a specifically agrarian political economy suggests reasons for rethinking. Perhaps most obviously, the declining importance of agriculture throughout the poor world reduces the political power of landed oligarchs nationally. Educated youth abandon agriculture in droves. Urbanisation and economic diversification simultaneously reduce the political salience of agricultural land ownership. The necessity of political control of land—and thus suppression of citizenship rights of the landless—was rooted in the absence of economic alternatives for landed elites. Political controversies surrounding agrarian reform and overhanging residues of un-enforced legislation combine with economic change to shift the political salience of land control; it is increasingly prudent, and possible, for agrarian elites to diversify or divest. Yet somehow production must pick up its falling rate of increase.

Because political conditions for radical, transformative agrarian policy are quite constraining, and historically sculpted, pro-poor development policy has turned to easier targets: everything but land. This development is both right and wrong. It is wrong because land ownership still determines a great deal in access to political influence and off-farm opportunity (Lanjouw and Shariff, 2004). It is wrong to expect land reforms to offer panaceas, as the conditions affecting rural development are so varied, but their contribution is often fundamental. Lipton (1993) remains right about the normative reasons for continuing redistributive land reforms after their heyday—"the evidence against stopping" is persuasive on grounds of both economics and social justice.

Nevertheless, turning to alternative pro-poor policies has a valid logic. Too much was expected of land reform, and land is increasingly only one part of the rural story. Technological change in agriculture and changing terms of trade for various crops, and for agriculture as a whole, mean that agrarian systems produce moving targets for policy. Land reform is only one of the many policies that could conceivably help the rural poor, and it is always costly. This concession does not mean that agrarian reforms should be abandoned; social justice is a first desideratum of social systems and there are few economies of scale in high-value agriculture. The specter of "uneconomic holdings" has always been suspect—note what use the house-site recipients make of tiny plots of land in Kerala. Looking ahead, with technological advances in agriculture and increasing incomes in the larger society, the size threshold for viable farms for family livelihoods will almost certainly fall.[18] As consumers demand and can afford more specialised, often labour-intensive, farm products —including 'organic'—returns to small holders can be improved as

18. Biotechnology is certainly one source, and a source much embattled in Karnataka in particular. On the potential, see Herring, 2007. On the battles of the KRRS and what it implies about representation of farmers by NGOs, see Herring, 2005.

non-agricultural jobs expand continuously.[19] Moreover, reforms can be tightened to avoid the *de facto* rentierism that now characterises much land use in India—absentee 'cultivators' holding land for speculation, family footholds, hobby or tax dodge (e.g. Aziz, 1997).

A limitation of the original model of land reforms in India was its historical embeddedness. The vision presented a very accurate portrayal of the transformative task necessitated by historical period and social structure: to make farmers of peasants. It premised more equality, but nothing very socialistic—simply a society of small farmers struggling with markets and weather. But it was a static view. Much like the problem with import substitution industrialization, the difficulty in land reform is to know when to shift strategies—and mustering the political power to do so.

From Landed Assets to Human Outcomes

Discussion of reasons for relative ineffectiveness of agrarian reform is not meant to undermine the wisdom of the policy. Laws against armed robbery are not completely effective, but we would not thereby stop trying to enforce them. Agrarian reforms are not nearly so impossible as those who wish to write them off claim. But, importantly, panaceas are rare: land reforms cannot carry the burden assigned to them by the founders of independent India into the current period. Certainly, breaking the back of exploitative and backward relations of production was necessary for laying the base of genuine and deep democracy (Heller, 1999: 237-248). John Stuart Mill worried that tenants could not be autonomous enough to be allowed to vote, as they were in dependency relations with landlords. Even the barest notion of a liberal pattern of society presumes autonomy on the part of political actors. Agrarian reforms can break long-established patterns of dominance, and in this way create conditions for a liberal society directed by genuinely democratic participation. The implications for the poor vary with the form of society that develops on this base—whether more like Sweden or more like the United

19. Lanjouw and Shariff, 2004 demonstrate that there is great variance across Indian states in the share of non-farm income in rural income. Karnataka falls into the pool of states with very low shares of non-farm income.

States makes a fundamental difference. But agrarian reforms cannot shield the rural poor from insecurity or episodic poverty.[20] Other institutions will have to play this role. Too much has been laid on the plate of agrarian reform; disappointment was inevitable.

This perspective does not write off agrarian reform—far from it—but does suggest limits of time and place. As one considers ancillary policies for the rural poor, it is important to survey the agrarian system by criteria suggested by original thinking about land reform in India by the Congress Agrarian Reforms Committee. Though there are other roads to purposive poverty alleviation, all are subject to distortions induced by social inequality and skewed political power, a major component of which is skewed distribution of landed property. By criteria of directness of results, restructuring of the field of power within which bureaucracies function, positive externalities for governance, and fine-tuned targeting potential, agrarian reform looks better than many of the more fashionable prescriptions. Offering immediate and direct benefit to the rural poor, agrarian reform more importantly can serve both as symbol for mobilisation of powerless people and a means of furthering political development. This argument is buttressed by comparative consideration of the historical experience of the United States. Promised land reforms to rehabilitate former slaves as citizens after civil war in the 19th century were abandoned; the result was an agrarian structure, and attendant political economy, which perpetuated abject dependency. Poverty not only persisted in the population of former slaves over generations, but remains disproportionate. In contrast, Kerala State abolished agrestic serfdom and slavery in a compressed historical time, with notably salubrious effects on human welfare despite experiencing growth rates below the Indian mean (Herring, 2003b).

Whether pro-poor policy promotes more or less state intervention —whether the path is more social democratic or more liberal, in

---

20. Anirudh Krishna's work (e.g. 2005) focuses on instability of poor-non-poor status, the volatility of poverty. In his work, many factors contribute to not-poor becoming poor, and poor becoming not poor; medical emergencies figure prominently in rural India as they do in the United States. See Echeverri-Gent, 1993, on the prospects and problems in alternative methods of reducing vulnerability *via* rural public works. On agrarian distress in Karnataka specifically, see Vasavi, 1999.

Esping-Andersen's (1990) classification scheme—agrarian reform remains one means of restructuring the field of power to which local state functionaries respond, and therefore enables a more effective and responsive state, without which all other anti-poverty options—including growth—are reduced in efficacy. These questions remain of special importance to the most awkward class of all—peasants without land, those for whom the transition to farmer is impossible. Those stuck at the bottom of agrarian systems in India are likely to suffer the multiple disabilities that historically marked off peasants from the rest of society: social denigration, relative lack of education, political marginalisation (Dube, 1998).

The dual contributions of agrarian reform to direct relief of poverty among the landless and democratisation among the oppressed remain real potentials. As Abdul Aziz stresses for Karnataka (1997: 59), reforms are especially critical for those at the very bottom of society, where growth has had the least effects: scheduled castes and tribes. These goals were present at the founding of an independent India. Yet the historical unfolding of the process Corbridge and Harriss (2003) call "Reinventing India" has entailed rejection of many strands of Nehruvian thinking—some cheered by the international community—for example, state planning and autarky—others more ambiguous in their external reception—for example, political formations of left and right rejecting Enlightment values of secularism and science (Nanda, 2003).

Where rethinking the classical theory of agrarian reform may be most needed is in moving from concern with assets and income as measures of development to measures of outcomes. Whatever the size of holding of a rural family, there is no excuse for malnutrition and illiteracy. The problem with land reforms from both the 'socialist pattern of society' and liberal paradigms is the assumption that holding some patch of land alleviates the worst miseries of underdevelopment. The moving-target nature of optimal agrarian institutions is aggravated by globalisation: the pace of change and the range of options and pressures multiply unpredictably (Mehta and Ghosh, forthcoming). The role of just institutions is to ensure that individuals are not crushed in the gears of change. Sheltering the rural poor from forces beyond their control, by providing a base line of basic human needs whatever happens to agriculture on tiny plots, may begin with land reform but must extend beyond it. The evidently increasing volatility of rural poverty means that being non-poor or poor is less a permanent condition, more a function of vectors of change under the control of no one local. Those Pranab Bardhan calls "anarcho-communitarians" believe that the village is the appropriate level for social protection. Looking to real forces in agriculture—shifts in the terms of trade, climatic disasters, infestations of uncontrollable pests or global market rigging by more powerful nations catering to richer farmers—one imagines a re-inventing of the Nehruvian state under globalisation along lines of accountability and strength, not withering away. Universalism would have to replace embedded particularism for this outcome to be feasible (Herring, 1999). De-linking basic human needs from market outcomes—the core of the modern welfare state—may be enabled by the principles of agrarian reform but must quickly move to a recognition that peasants have become farmers, among the most vulnerable groups in globalising low-income market societies.

References

Aziz, Abdul and Sudhir Krishna (1997). *Land Reforms in India*, Vol. 4: Karnataka. New Delhi: Sage Publications.

Bouton, Marshall (1985). *Agrarian Radicalism in South India*. Princeton: Princeton University Press.

Chibber, Vivek (2003). *Locked in Place*. Princeton: Princeton University Press.

Damle, Chandrashekhara B. (1997). "Post-land Reforms Experience in Dakshina Kannada District", in Aziz and Krishna *op. cit.*

Corbridge, Stuart and John Harriss (2000). *Reinventing India*. Cambridge, UK: Polity Press.

Dube, Siddharth (1998). *In the Land of Poverty: Memoirs of an Indian Family, 1947-1997*. London: Zed.

Echeverri-Gent, John (1993). *The State and the Poor: Public Policy and Political Development in India and the United States*. Berkeley: University of California Press.

Esping-Andersen, Gosta (1998). *The Three Worlds of Welfare Capitalism*. Princeton: Princeton University Press.

Frykenberg, Robert E. (ed.) (1977). *Land Tenure and Peasant in South Asia*. Orient Longman.

Government of Karnataka (2002). *Farmers' Suicides in Karnataka: A Scientific Analysis. Report of the Expert Committee for Study on Farmers' Suicides*. Bangalore.

Gowda, K.H. Gopala Krishne (1997). "Tenancy Reforms: The Macro Perspective", in Aziz and Krishna *op. cit.*

Harriss, John (2003). "Do Political Regimes Matter? Poverty Reduction and Regime Differences across India", in Mick Moore and Peter Houtzager (eds.), *Changing Paths: The New Politics of Inclusion*. Ann Arbor: University of Michigan Press.

Heller, Patrick (1999). *The Labour of Development: Workers and the Transformation of Capitalism in Kerala, India*. Ithaca, NY, Cornell University Press.

Herring, Ronald J. (1979). "Zulfikar Ali Bhutto and the 'Eradication of Feudalism' in Pakistan", *Comparative Studies in Society and History* 21(4) (October). Revised version reprinted, with permission in *The Economic and Political Weekly* (Bombay) 15(12) (March 1980).

———. (1980). "Abolition of Landlordism in Kerala: A Redistribution of Privilege", *Economic and Political Weekly* 15(26), June 28.

———. (1981). "Embedded Production Relations and the Rationality of Tenant Quiescence in Tenure Reform", *Journal of Peasant Studies* (London) 8(2), January.

———. (1983). *Land to the Tiller: The Political Economy of Agrarian Reform in South Asia*. New Haven: Yale University Press.

———. (1988). "Stealing Congress Thunder: The Rise to Power of a Communist Movement in South India", in Peter Merkel and Kay Lawson (eds.) *When Parties Fail*. Princeton: Princeton University Press.

———. (1989). "Dilemmas of Agrarian Communism", *Third World Quarterly* 11(1): 89-115 (January).

———. (1999). "Embedded Particularism: India's Failed Developmental State", in M. Woo-Cumings (ed.) *The Developmental State*. Ithaca: Cornell University Press.

———. (2000). "Political Conditions for Agrarian Reform and Poverty Alleviation", *IDS Discussion Paper* No. 375. UK: Institute for Development Studies. Sussex. June.

———. (2001). "Contesting the 'Great Transformation': Local Struggles with the Market in South India", in James C. Scott and Nina Bhatt (ed.) *Agrarian Studies: Synthetic Work at the Cutting Edge*. New Haven: Yale University Press.

———. (2003a). "Data as Social Product", in Ravi Kanbur (ed.) *Q-Squared: Combining Qualitative and Quantitative Methods in Poverty Appraisal*. New Delhi: Permanent Black.

———. (2003b). "The Political Impossibility Theorem of Agrarian Reform: Path Dependence and Terms of Inclusion", in Mick Moore and Peter Houtzager (ed.), *Changing Paths: The New Politics of Inclusion*. Ann Arbor: University of Michigan Press.

———. (2005). "Miracle Seeds, Suicide Seeds and the Poor: GMOs, NGOs, Farmers and the State", in Raka Ray and Mary Fainsod Katzenstein (eds.), *Social Movements in India*. Delhi: Oxford University Press.

———. (2007). "The Genomics Revolution and Development Studies: Science, Politics and Poverty", *Journal of Development Studies* 43(1).

Herring, Ronald J. and Rex M. Edwards (1983). "Guaranteeing Employment to the Rural Poor: Social Functions and Class Interests in the Employment Guarantee Scheme in Western India", *World Development* 11, July 7.

Iyer, K. Gopal (1997). "Implementation of the Land Ceiling Programme", in Abdul Aziz and Sudhir Krishna (ed.) *Land Reforms in India*. Vol. 4: Karnataka. New Delhi: Sage Publications.

Jannuzi, F. Tomasson (1974). *Agrarian Crisis in India: The Case of Bihar*. Austin: University of Texas Press.

Joshi, G.V. (1997). "Implementation of Tenancy Reforms: The Case of Uttara Kannada District", in Aziz and Krishna *op. cit*.

Kohli, Atul (1987). *The State and Poverty in India*. Cambridge: Cambridge University Press.

Krishna, Anirudh (2005). "Poverty Knowledge and Poverty Action in India". Presented at the Institute of Rural Management, Anand. December 6, 2004 and at a workshop on *Understanding Rural Poverty* organised at the India International Centre, New Delhi. February 10.

Krishna, Sudhir (1997). "Land Reforms Debate: An Overview", in Aziz and Krishna *op. cit*.

Krishnaji, N. (1979). "Agrarian Relations and the Left Movement in Kerala", *Economic and Political Weekly* XV, March 9.

Lanjouw, Peter and Abusaleh Shariff (2004). "Rural Non-Farm Employment in India: Access, Incomes and Poverty Impact", *Economic and Political Weekly*. October 2. pp.4429-46.

Lerche, Jens (l998). "Agricultural Labourers, the State and Agrarian Transition in Uttar Pradesh", *Economic and Political Weekly* 33(13): A 29-35. March 28

Lipton, Michael (l993). "Land Reform as Commenced Business: The Evidence Against Stopping", *World Development* 21(4): 641-658.

Malaviya, H.D. (1954). *Land Reforms in India. All-India Congress Committee*, New Delhi.

Manor, James (1989). "Karnataka: Caste, Class, Dominance, and Politics", in Francine Frankel and MSA Rao (eds.) *Dominance and State Power in Modern India: Decline of a Social Order*. Vol. 1. Delhi: Oxford University Press.

Mehta, Aasha Kapoor and Sourabh Ghosh assisted by Ritu Elwadhi, (forthcoming). "Globalisation, Loss of Livelihoods and Entry into Poverty: A Brief Review of Issues Based on Suicides by Farmers", *Alternative Economic Survey 2004-2005*. Rainbow Publishers and Alternative Survey Group.

Moore, Mick and Peter Houtzager (2003). *Changing Paths: The New Politics of Inclusion*. Ann Arbor: University of Michigan Press.

Nanda, Meera (2003). *Prophets Facing Backward: Postmodern Critiques of Science and Hindu Nationalism in India*. New Brunswick: N.J. Rutgers University Press.

Neale, Walter C. (l979). "Land is to Rule", in R.E. Frykenberg (ed.), *Land Control and Social Structure in Indian History*. Madison: University of Wisconsin Press.

Rajan, M.A.S. (1997). "Effects of Land Reforms: What Next?", in Aziz and Krishna *op. cit*.

Thimmaiah, G. (1997). "New Perspectives on Land Reforms", in Aziz and Krishna *op. cit*.

———. (2001). "New Perspectives on Land Reforms in India", *Journal of Social and Economic Development* 3(2): 179-198. July-December.

Vasavi, A.R. (1999). "Agrarian Distress in Bidar: Market, State and Suicides", *Economic and Political Weekly* 34(32): 2263-2268. August 7.

World Bank (2005). "The Political Economy of Gram Panchayats in South India: Results and Policy Conclusions From a Research Project". Washington DC. (July).

Zagoria, Donald S. (1971). "The Ecology of Peasant Communism in India", *The American Political Science Review* LXV: 1 (March).

13

ICT Sector and Economic Development

Evidence from Karnataka State

M.R. NARAYANA

Introduction

Information and Communication Technology (ICT) sector comprises both manufacturing and service activities. On the manufacturing side, it includes computer hardware (i.e. personal computers, notebooks, servers, printers and other peripherals), and telecommunication equipment and networks materials. ICT services include development of software; training of persons for manufacture and operations of computer equipment; use of computers in government, health, education and research, and financial services; use of computer technology for IT (information technology)-enabled services (e.g. call centres and medical transcription services); and telecom services (i.e. basic and value added services on narrow and broad bandwidth by fixed and mobile telephony). Further, ICT and electronics sectors are mutually complementary. Thus, ICT may be broadly defined to include IT, communication and electronics in manufacturing and/or service activities.

India is a federal economy. Industry is in the concurrent list of the Indian Constitution. Hence, both the federal (or Central/Union) and State (or regional) governments have regulatory and promotional/

Grateful thanks are due to Prof. Gopal K. Kadekodi (Former Director, ISEC), Dr. Ramesh Kolli (Deputy Director-General, CSO), Prof. V.R. Panchamukhi (former Chairman, ICSSR), and participants of the Conference for constructive suggestions; Sri Farruq Ameen, General Manager (Operations), Karnataka Telecom Circle (Bangalore), and officials in the Directorate of Economics and Statistics (Bangalore), for providing with updated official data in their respective organisations; and to Mr. M. Kusanna for assistance in data collection. However, the usual disclaimers apply.

developmental functions through industrial policies and programmes, including for ICT industries. The policy making is competitive at the State level in order to attract domestic and foreign investment and business. Further, India being a mixed and open economy, policies for privatisation, international trade, and investment in ICT sector assume special significance. In fact, planning and development, foreign trade, investment and exchange, and pricing policies for the ICT sector are in the domain of the federal government. The role of the State governments is most important in providing with infrastructure facilities, and special fiscal and financial incentives, concessions and assistance for the ICT sector.

Consequent upon the national level economic reforms since 1991, economic structure of ICT sector has been undergoing changes due to privatisation (e.g. allowing entry of private domestic and foreign players into manufacturing and services), regulation (e.g. establishment of Telecom Regulatory Authority of India), corporatisation (e.g. establishment of Bharat Sanchar Nigam Limited), and globalisation (e.g. bringing trade in ICT goods under GATT and ICT services under GATS in the WTO) policies.[1]

Karnataka is the first state in India to announce a separate policy for promotion and development of information technology in the State (i.e. Information Technology Policy-1997) with objectives to increase domestic and export earnings. Over the years, to encourage information technology in educational institutions, government, industry and infrastructure sectors, separate sub-policies are formulated. In addition, incentives and concessions and special assistance are provided. For instance, special assistance package is formulated by development institutions (e.g. Karnataka State Financial Corporation) for equity contribution in small and medium enterprises. Software industries are treated as industrial (not commercial) consumers for tariff purposes and are exempted from pollution control

1. In essence, these changes are the outcome of the Government of India's *National Telecom Policy* 1994 and 1999, and *Internet Service Providers Policy* 1998; and India's Entry into WTO in 1995. An excellent summary of provisions in these policies, and chronology of policy changes, is given by Kathuria *et al.* (2003). Analysis of these national policy reforms is evident in Dossani (2002) and Noll and Wallsten (2004).

acts. Fiscal incentives and exemptions are given to industries with investment on fixed assets upto Rs.100 crore.[2]

Subsequently, the State has announced the Millennium IT Policy in 2000 (called *Mahithi*) (GoK, 2000). The objectives of the policy included important social and cultural aspects. First, to utilise the power of IT technology in the overall goal of the Government of Karnataka in eradicating poverty and empowering women. Second, to promote the usage of Kannada in IT. Third, to encourage business with non-English speaking countries. The important areas for use of IT technology included eradication of poverty and empowerment of women, education, and governance (in the departments of registration, revenue, tax and transport, police and silk).[3] To professionalise the policy making, the Chief Minister's Task Force on IT is set up with globally eminent and successful IT industrialists in the State.[4]

In addition to above public policies and programmes, (a) growth of external market demand, (b) growth and cluster of electrical, electronics and communication technology industries, (c) existence of a large potential domestic demand, and (d) accumulation of a large pool of high skilled, communicative, and low cost technical manpower, are presumed to be the driving factors for growth of ICT industries and services in Karnataka. For instance, with more than 13 universities, 712 general education colleges, 97 medical colleges, 96 engineering colleges, 181 polytechnics, 300 industrial training centres, and several premier institutes of research in pure and applied science, management, and information, manufacturing and foundry technology, the State (popularly called Brain Bank of India) has been providing with technical manpower for growth of ICT sector.[5] Consequently,

2. At present, 30 ICT products and services are taxable at 4 per cent under the VAT. This list of taxable ICT products and services is available on: ***http://www.nitpu3.kar.nic.in/ctax/vat.htm***

3. Details of evolution of State policies and programmes for ICT sector is available on: ***http://www.bangaloreit.com***

4. For instance, the Task Force is chaired by N.R. Narayana Murthy (Chairman: Infosys Technologies Ltd) and includes Azim Premji (Chairman: WIPRO) as a member.

5. In this regard, the role of public and private sectors' investment in providing with high quality and low cost (or subsidised and/or fee regulated) technical education may deserve a special mention in explaining the growth of State's ICT sector.

cont...

most of the 20 top IT companies in the country are located in the State.[6] As Bangalore has shown tremendous progress in attracting national and MNCs in IT sector, it is called Silicon Valley of India and IT Capital of India. This has lead to the emergence of 'New Economy' within the State economy.[7]

In recognition of the important role of the IT sector for generation of income, employment, investment, and exports, and remarkable performance of the sector in the 9th Five Year Plan period, the 10th Five Year Plan of India has set specific objectives and targets (Box 13.1). For instance, the targets for (a) production is Rs.2820 billion by 2006-07 (i.e. Rs.2130 billion for software sector and Rs.690 billion for hardware production); and (b) export of software and IT services is $ 87 billion by 2008 (i.e. $50 billion for export of software and $10 billion for export of hardware). Accordingly, software and IT services industry is targeted to contribute 7.7 per cent of GDP in 2008.[8] On the

...cont...

However, at present, this comparative cost advantage is questionable due to recent changes in pricing policies for professional education (i.e. cost-based pricing policy, as per the judicial decisions).

6. These companies are: TCS, Wipro, Infosys, HP, IBM, Satyam, HCL Tech, Tech Pacific, Intel India, Redington, HCL Insys, Samsung, Ingram Micro, Cisco Systems, Moser Baer, Patni Computer, Microsoft, NIIT, Mahindra BT and CMC.

7. The measures of New Economy include: (a) share of ICT production, exports and employment in nation's total; (b) use of ICT; and (c) size of Internet. The New Economy measures clearly recognise that ICT is an output (or input) from (or into) the ICT-producing (or using) activities (Pohjola, 2002).

8. At the nation level, three recent features of ICT sectors are evident, as reported in Dataquest magazine (2004). First, sales revenue of top 20 Indian IT companies is equal to $7.5 billion (or 49 per cent of total revenues of the IT industry) or Rs.36930 crore in 2002-03. The annual sales (or annual growth in per cent) of PCs are equal to 2.2 million (or 11 per cent), notebooks is equal to 48247 (or 50 per cent), PC servers is equal to 35147 (or 12 per cent) and printers is equal to 1.1 million (or 33 per cent). Second, the domestic market has experienced shrinkage. For instance, in 1998-99, domestic market share was 67 per cent (= hardware 31 per cent; domestic services 18 per cent; packaged software 6 per cent; and others 2 per cent). In 2002-03, the domestic share has been reduced to 49 pe rcent (=hardware 20 per cent; domestic services 13 per cent packaged software 3 per cent and others 3 per cent). Third, the shrinking role of domestic market is replaced by the phenomenal increase in exports of software and services (from 43 per cent to 46 per cent), and BPO (from 0 per cent to 15 per cent). Thus, exports of software and services, and BPO activities shall be dominant in India's IT industry in future. An excellent description of trends in national export of software and IT services is given in Chapter One in NASSCOM (2003).

other hand, the *Report of the Special Group on Targeting Ten Million Employment Opportunities per year over the Tenth Plan Period* (Government of India, 2002) has projected around one million additional employment generation, as direct employment in India's IT sector, at the end of the 10th Plan.

This paper argues that the growth of State's ICT sector is contributory for attainment of the above national objectives and targets. Analysis of the nature, patterns and determinants of growth of ICT sector, under the institutional arrangement for regulation and promotion for ICT sector in India's federal-mixed and open economy framework, is essential to substantiate this argument. Thus, the major objectives of this paper are to: (a) estimate the contribution of ICT sector to Karnataka's State Income; (b) develop a simple empirical framework for estimation of determinants of ICT sector's growth, and implement the framework for Karnataka State; and (c) and derive implications for ICT-driven growth in the State. These analyses and implications are of relevance for regional policy analysis for the ICT industries and services in India in particular, and other developing countries (subject to the comparability of economic structures, however) in general.

Studies on India's ICT sector have focused on national level analysis. This is evident, for instance, in Brunner (1995), Heeks (1996) and Arora and Athreye (2002). On the other hand, regional level studies (including for Karnataka) on ICT sector are a few and do not address the ICT sector in a comprehensive way. This is evident, for instance, in Narayana (2003) with a restricted focus on telecom services. Thus, this paper is contributory to regional empirical and policy analyses of ICT sector in India, especially in setting benchmarks for future studies in Karnataka as well as for comparative studies between Karnataka and other States.

Rest of the paper is organised as follows: Section 2 describes the economic performance of ICT sector in Karnataka State in regard to employment, investment and exports. Section 3 estimates the contribution of ICT sector to national and regional economic growth. In section 4, empirical evidence for the determinant of growth of ICT sector is offered. Section 5 concludes the paper with implications.

Box 13.1

Objectives and Targets for ICT Sector in India's Tenth Five Year Plan

Objectives

- To ensure the sustained growth of software and IT-enabled services and increase India's share in the global market.
- To put in place the basic policy framework for making India a major force in the hardware-manufacturing sector.
- To devise appropriate policy interventions for the greater use of IT for promoting more efficient, transparent and responsive governance.
- To promote the development and use of software in Indian languages to meet local requirements and expand the domestic market.
- To take necessary steps for taking IT to the masses by making it affordable, easy to use and useful in day-to-day life.
- To put in place the required policy framework to improve the quality of manpower, skills and R&D in IT.
- Affordable and effective communication facilities to all citizens.
- Provide universal service to all uncovered areas, including rural areas.
- Building a modern and efficient telecommunications infrastructure to meet the convergence of telecom, IT and the media.
- Enabling Indian telecom companies to become truly global players.

Targets

(i) Production target of Rs.2,82,000 crore by the terminal year of Tenth Plan (2006-07), with the software sector accounting for Rs.2,13,000 crore and hardware production Rs. 69,000 crore.

(ii) Against the current level of $8 billion, software and IT services exports are expected to grow to $87 billion by 2008. While the software export target is set at $50 billion, the target for export of hardware has been kept at $10 billion by 2008.

(iii) Keeping the above growth potential in mind, IT exports are likely to constitute 35 per cent of India's total exports in 2008

Contd...

...Contd...

against the present level of 14 per cent.

(iv) India's share in the overall global software market is expected to increase from the present 2 per cent to 6 per cent by the terminal year of the Tenth Plan.

(v) India's IT spending is about 0.7 per cent of GDP, as compared to 1.3 per cent in Malaysia and 2.5 per cent in Singapore. India is almost five years behind China in terms of the number of PCs, Internet users, cable TV subscribers, fixed telephones, etc.

(vi) The Internet subscriber's base is expected to cross 35 million by 2007 from the present level of four million.

(vii) The IT industry is projected to generate seven million jobs by 2008 (i.e. 4.8 million employment in hardware sector and 2.2 million jobs in software sector and IT-enabled services).

(viii Provision of telephones on demand by the end of 2002-03 and sustain it thereafter.

(ix) Achieve an overall teledensity of 9.91 by 31 March 2007.

(x) Achieve telecom coverage of all villages by December 2002.

(xi) Provide reliable transmission media by the end of March 2003.

(xii) Provide high-speed data and multimedia capability using technologies including ISDN to all towns with a population of greater than 0.2 million by the end of March 2003.

Source: Compiled from Government of India (2003a).

Economic Performance of ICT Sector

Data on registered companies in the Software Technology Park of India (STPI) and Electronic Hardware Park of India (EHPI) is the basis for the following description of economic performance of ICT sector by software and hardware companies:[9] Karnataka has three software

9. *http://www.bangaloreit.com* gives information, among others, on performance indicators on ICT sector in Karnataka State. The following data description draws heavily from this website as on 31 March 2005, as neither the NASSCOM nor the Electronic and Computer Software Export Promotion Council publish State level data on ICT sector. The Visveswaraya Industrial and Trade Centre has been compiling export data from the State, including electronics and computer software, since 1993-94. This data is not used in this paper, as it includes STPI and EHPI data but no disaggregate information.

technology parks (STPs). This comprises one national centre at Bangalore, and two sub-centres at Mysore, Mangalore/Manipal. In addition, Hubli is identified for development as a sub-centre. Development of these sub-centres is a move towards regional dispersal of ICT sector's activities in the State. In general, performance data are presented by these centres and for different years by variables. For instance, data on number of registered software companies is presented from 1999-2000 to 2002-03, and on exports from 1991-92 to 2002-03. Thus, the data for the latest year for each performance indicator is presented in Box 13.2. This implies that Karnataka has much to contribute in accomplishing the production, export and employment targets for the ICT sector during the 10th Plan period.

Contribution of ICT Sector to Economic Growth

Growth and share of ICT sector in the national and State income are important indicators for the sector's aggregate contribution to national and regional economic development. Data for construction and analysis of these indicators in manufacturing and service sectors need to be combined from different sources, as ICT sector's contribution is separately available for the communication and IT sector. In particular, the contribution is explicitly (or implicitly) accounted for communication (or IT) services under the tertiary sector.[10] In fact, this contribution is estimated at the national level and allocated to States (under supra-regional sectors) by the Central Statistical Organisation (CSO).[11] On the other hand, the contribution is not explicitly accounted for manufacturing ICT sector as a whole, or separately by communication and IT sectors. This calls for approximation in determining the sector's contribution from the national and state level data in the Annual Survey of Industries.

---

10. Methodological details of communication and IT services in national accounts are outlined in Government of India (1999).

11. Estimation of national income from ICT sector is based on income method. Allocation for states is based on proportion of workforce in the state to the nation's total.

Box 13.2

Performance Indicators of ICT Sector in Karnataka State

Software Companies—Bangalore STP

- Cumulative number of companies is equal to 1154 with a total investment of US$1.3 billion and employment of 80,000 software professionals (2002-03)
- Composition of 682 companies by their value in US$ million (2001-02): Above 200 million (0.29 per cent); Between 20 million and 200 million (1.91 per cent); Between 2 million and 20 million (13.93 per cent); less than 2 million (36.07 per cent); and less than 0.5 million (47.80 per cent).
- Total value of exports is equal to Rs.12350 crore or US$2.67 billion and annual growth is 25 per cent (2002-03)
- Share in total exports (2002-03): Small and medium enterprises (18.03 per cent), major Indian companies (41.40 per cent), and foreign equity companies (40.57 per cent)
- Annual growth of exports (2002-03): Small and medium enterprises (63 per cent), major Indian companies (14 per cent), and foreign equity companies (22 per cent).
- Highest exports (=Rs.7475 crore) among 12 STPs in India in 2000-01.
- BPO/ITES companies (i.e. banking and financial services, and technical support and insurance claims processing companies) in 2002-03 is equal to 41 (annual growth is 46 per cent) with total investment of Rs.512 crore (annual growth is 23 per cent), employment of 18,000 persons, and exports of Rs.988 crore (annual growth is 275 per cent).

Software Companies—Mysore STP

- Number of companies has increased from 24 in 2001-02 to 26 in 2002-03.
- Total exports are equal to Rs.65 crore in 2002-03 (annual growth is 66 per cent).

Software Companies—Mangalore/Manipal STP

- Number of companies has increased from 13 in 2001-02 to 15 in 2002-03.

Contd...

...Contd...

- Total exports are equal to Rs.330 crore in 2002-03 (annual growth is 36 per cent).

Hardware Companies in EHTP—Karnataka State

- Number of approved companies is equal to 31 in 2002-03 (annual growth is 15 per cent)
- Total exports are equal to Rs.1403.85 crore in 2002-03 (annual growth is 67.50 per cent).

Overall Export Performance

- Electronic and computer software constitute 53.18 per cent in total exports from the State and 25 per cent in total exports from India in 2002-03.

Source: Compiled from the basic data on: ***http://www.bangaloreit.com*** (accessed on March 31, 2005)

Contribution of ICT Services

Communication services include provisioning of postal and telecommunication services. The contribution of telecommunication services (e.g. telephones, telegrams, and overseas communication services) is separable from the postal services (e.g. postal, and money and postal order services) from the details of estimated GDP from within the communication sector. Further, the contribution of public and private sectors can be approximated from this database.[12]

IT services are related to data processing, software development and computer consultancy services.[13] and are implicitly accounted for

12. Two points deserve special mention here. First, in arriving at GDP from the communication services, intermediate consumption is deducted from the gross earning for the sector as a whole. Thus, intermediate consumption is not available separately for postal and telecom services. To overcome this data limitation, intermediate consumption is presumed to be distributed between postal and telecom services in the same proportion as that of the share of postal and telecom services in the gross earnings. Second, private sector (included in the estimation of national income since 1993-94) is dominant in telecom services than in postal services. Thus, private communication services are treated equal to private telecom services.
13. Thus, IT services exclude computer maintenance and service (e.g. maintenance and service contracts for computer hardware and peripherals).

one of the items in business services.[14] The contribution is estimated by the CSO. For state-wise contribution of the IT services, the national level estimate is allocated to the States on the basis of workforce data. In the absence of published data on the contribution of IT services, contribution of business services can approximate the share of IT services in national and State income.[15]

Thus, the sum of contribution of (a) non-postal communication services and (b) total business services in the national and state income is considered below for contribution of ICT services to national and regional economic growth.

Table 13.1 presents the select indicators of contribution of ICT services to national income (i.e. Gross Domestic Product or GDP at factor cost and constant prices) and State income (i.e. Gross State Domestic Product or GSDP at factor cost and constant prices) from 1993-94 through 2001-02.[16] These indicators offer the following evidence:

- Throughout, Karnataka's economic growth has remained higher than the national economic growth, as the annual growth of GSDP is higher than the annual growth of GDP. Thus, the average growth of GSDP (=13.17 per cent) is higher than the average growth of GDP (=6.24 per cent).
- At the national as well as at the State level, the share of tertiary sector has increased. For instance, the share of tertiary/service sector has increased in the national (or State) income from 42.77 (or 38.27) per cent in 1993-94 to 45.78 (or 43.76) per cent in 1997-98 and to 49.30 (or 49.51) per cent in 2001-02.

14. Other business services include services provided on fee or contract basis such as accounting, auditing, bookkeeping, data processing and tabulation, engineering, advertising, commercial art-work and market research activities. In particular, IT services are classified under NIC-892.

15. Financial intermediation services indirectly measured (FISIM) is not separately reported for the business services. Thus, in arriving at the national income from the business services, FISIM is distributed in proportion of business services share in the GDP from the real estate, ownership of dwellings and business services.

16. In the latest published *National Accounts Statistics* (Government of India, 2004a), data on communication services is available up to 2001-02. Hence, the entire analysis is restricted up to 2001-02 to establish comparability between the indicators.

- Throughout, annual growth of tertiary sector in the State income has remained higher at the national level. Average growth of tertiary GSDP (=16.77 per cent) is double than the average growth of tertiary GDP (=8.15 per cent).
- Share of ICT services in GSDP has been higher than in GDP except in 2000-01. For instance, the share of estimated GDP from ICT services in GSDP (or GDP) is equal to 2.26 (or 1.51) per cent in 1993-94, 3.08 (or 2.35) per cent in 1997-98, 4.41 (or 3.23) per cent in 2000-01 and 3.61 (or 4.04) per cent in 2001-2002.
- The annual growth of ICT services has been higher as compared to annual growth of GDP and GSDP as well as the annual growth of tertiary sector in GDP and GSDP. However, the annual growth of ICT services in Karnataka is higher (or lower) than at the national level up to 1997-98 (or since 1998-99).
- Share of ICT services has increased in both tertiary GDP and GSDP, but the share in the GSDP is higher than in the GDP. For instance, the share of ICT services has increased in the tertiary GDP (or GSDP) from 3.53 (or 5.92) per cent in 1993-94 to 5.13 (or 7.05) per cent in 1997-98 and to 9.08 (or 8.39) per cent in 2001-02.
- As the contribution of ICT services is estimated at the national level and allocated to the States, it is plausible to determine the share of State's ICT services in the nation's total. This evidence suggests that the share has fluctuated from 7.89 per cent in 1993-94 to 9.26 per cent in 1997-98 and to 8.01 per cent in 2001-02.
- At the national level, contributions of telecommunication services are further evident in the following indicators. First, the share of telecommunication services in the GDP from ICT services has declined from 72.38 per cent in 1993-94 to 69.11 per cent in 1997-98 and to 65.76 in 2001-02. Alternatively, this implies the increasing contribution of IT services in the GDP from the ICT services. Second, the share of public telecom services remains high (about 90 per cent or above). Nevertheless, since 1995-96, the role of public sector shows a

Table 13.1

Contribution of ICT Services to National and State Income, 1993-94 to 2001-02

	Indicators of Contribution	1993-94	1994-95	1995-96	1996-97	1997-98	1998-99	1999-00	2000-01	2001-02	Average Growth (%)
1.	**National Level**										
1.1.	Gross Domestic Product or GDP at Factor Cost and Constant Prices (Rs. in crore)	781345	838031	899563	970083	1016595	1082748	1148368	1198592	1267833	
1.2.	Annual Growth of GDP (%)		7.25	7.34	7.84	4.79	6.51	6.06	4.37	5.78	6.24
1.3.	Per cent of Tertiary Sector in GDP	42.77	42.71	43.94	43.68	45.78	46.58	48.33	48.85	49.30	
1.4.	Annual Growth of Tertiary Sector in GDP (%)		7.08	10.46	7.20	9.83	8.35	10.06	5.49	6.76	8.15
1.5.	Estimated GDP from ICT Services (Rs. in crore)	11786.32	13912.77	16913.35	19295.23	23882.49	29304.63	37041.70	48468.11	56728.20	
1.6.	Per cent of Estimated GDP from ICT Services in Total GDP	1.51	1.66	1.88	1.99	2.35	2.71	3.23	4.04	4.47	
1.7.	Annual Growth of Estimated GDP from ICT (%)		18.04	21.57	14.08	23.77	22.70	26.40	30.85	17.04	21.81
1.8.	Per cent of ICT Services in Total Tertiary GDP	3.53	3.89	4.28	4.55	5.13	5.81	6.67	8.28	9.08	
1.9.	Per cent of Telecommunication Services in ICT Services' GDP	72.38	72.43	71.42	70.07	69.11	68.25	66.49	65.23	65.76	
1.10.	Share of Public Telecom in Communication GDP-estimated	92.88	93.29	94.30	94.81	94.72	94.47	93.94	89.33	87.82	
1.11.	Share of Estimated Telecom in Combined Communication Services (Post and Telecom) in GDP	90.56	91.61	92.70	92.96	93.96	94.96	95.84	97.03	97.94	

Contd...

...Contd...

	Indicators of Contribution	*1993-94*	*1994-95*	*1995-96*	*1996-97*	*1997-98*	*1998-99*	*1999-00*	*2000-01*	*2001-02*	*Average Growth (%)*
2.	**State Level**										
2.1.	Gross State Domestic Income or GSDP at Factor Cost and Constant Prices (Rs. in lakh)	4107905	4791517	5621456	6517573	7171944	8780738	9530994	10481490	10946407	
2.2.	Annual Growth of GSDP (%)		16.64	17.32	15.94	10.04	22.43	8.54	9.97	4.44	13.17
2.3.	Per cent of Tertiary Sector in GSDP	38.27	39.10	40.24	41.17	43.76	42.46	44.93	45.83	49.51	
2.4.	Annual Growth of Tertiary Sector in GSDP (%)		19.15	20.76	18.63	16.95	18.81	14.86	12.15	12.83	16.77
2.5.	Estimated GSDP from ICT Services (Rs.in lakh)	93029.46	114097.07	145475.74	178600.25	221192.95	265361.09	324771.26	377986.81	454604.53	
2.6.	Per cent of Estimated GSDP from ICT Services in Total GSDP	2.26	2.38	2.59	2.74	3.08	3.02	3.41	3.61	4.15	
2.7.	Annual Growth of Estimated GSDP from ICT Services (%)		22.65	27.50	22.77	23.85	19.97	22.39	16.39	20.27	21.97
2.8.	Per cent of Estimated ICT Services in Total Tertiaty GSDP	5.92	6.09	6.43	6.66	7.05	7.12	7.58	7.87	8.39	
2.9.	Per cent Share of State's Estimated ICT Services in Nation's Total (=GDP from Estimated ICT services)	7.89	8.20	8.60	9.26	9.26	9.06	8.77	7.80	8.01	

Source: Compiled and constructed by using the basic data in Government of India (2003b) and Govenrment of India (2004d).

decline. This indicates an increasing role of private telecom services. Third, share of telecom services in the combined share of postal and telecom services in the GDP has remained high (above 90 per cent), and shows an increase since 1996-97. This indicates a decline in the role of postal services.

In the context of Karnataka State, contribution of IT services within the business services since 2000-01 is accessible from the unpublished records of the Directorate of Economics and Statistics. The evidence for this contribution is presented in Table 13.2. The evidence suggests that the contribution of IT services in the business services has increased from 78.27 per cent in 2000-01 to 84.32 in 2003-04. As a per cent of tertiary GSDP at current (or constant) prices, the share of IT services has increased from 4.21 (or 3.79) per cent in 2000-01 to 6.77 (or 5.73) per cent in 2003-04. In the same way, contribution of IT services as a percentage of GSDP at current (or constant) prices has increased from 1.95 (or 1.70) per cent in 2000-2001 to 3.58 (or 2.95) per cent in 2003-04. These evidences offer support for specific contribution of IT services to Karnataka's economic growth.

Contribution of Manufacturing ICT Industries

Contribution of manufacturing ICT industries is related to production of hardware. In general, production of electronic, communication and computing hardware are accounted for manufacturing ICT sector. This production may be broadly classified under electronic and communication sector, and IT sector. For instance, electronic and communication hardware include the following:[17] (i) consumer electronics (e.g. video and audio equipment, audio visual equipment and consumer electronic items); (ii) instrumentation/control instruments and industrial electronics (e.g. test and measuring instruments, medical electronics equipment, analytical instrument, industrial electronic & automation equipment, process control equipment, power electronic, equipments, and office

17. The following classification is compiled from (a) *Guide to Electronics Industry in India 1999*. Department of Electronics, Government of India, New Delhi; (b) Department of Information Technology's website: *www.mit.gov.in/dbid/*; and (c) Indian Electrical & Electronics Manufactured Association's website: *www.ieema.org/industry/electronics.htm*

Table 13.2

Contribution of IT Services to Economic Growth in Karnataka State: 2000-01 to 2003-04

	Indicators of Contribution	*2000-01*	*2001-02*	*2002-03*	*2003-04*
1.	Gross Valued Added from IT services (Rs.in lakh)				
	At current prices	204331	255467	328091	473885
	At constant prices	119243	142233	173619	237749
2.	Percent of IT services in total GVA of business services	78.27	80.70	81.89	84.32
3.	Percent of IT services in total tertiary GSDP at factor cost				
	At current prices	4.21	4.69	5.36	6.77
	At constant prices	3.79	4.14	4.64	5.73
4.	Percent of IT services in total GSDP at factor cost				
	At current prices	1.95	2.34	2.73	3.58
	At constant prices	1.70	1.97	2.29	2.95

Note: (1) GSDP refers to Gross State Domestic Product.
(2) GSDP data for 2003-04 refers to quick estimates.

Source: Computed by using the basic data in Government of Karnataka (2004) and from the records of the State Income Division, Directorate of Economics and Statistics, Government of Karnataka (Bangalore).

equipment); (iii) data processing systems and other office equipment, excluding computers (e.g. microprocessor based systems); (iv) communication and broadcasting equipment (e.g. switching systems, transmission equipment, terminal equipment, signaling equipment, allied communication equipment, broadcasting equipment); (v) strategic electronics (e.g. electron tubes, semi conductor devices, passive components, electro mechanical components, special components, and electronic components and others); and (vi) electronic components (e.g. mechanical TV tuners, audio-tape deck mechanism, DC-micro motors, magnetic heads, loudspeakers and their parts, transformers, foils, printed circuit boards, black and white picture tubes, semi-conductor devices, and plastic film capacitors). The IT hardware includes: (a) computer hardware (e.g. personal computers, notebooks and servers);

(b) computer peripherals (e.g. printers and UPS); and (c) computer consumables (e.g. printer ribbons and paper).[18]

The ASI 2001-02 (Government of India, 2004b) provides with manufacturing details of products and by-products (NIC-1998 at 3-digit level) in terms of ASICC-1995 (at 5 digit level). Using this information, the Gross Value Added (GVA) of 7 industry groups [i.e. manufacture of office, accounting and computer machinery (300), manufacture of electricity distribution and control apparatus (312), manufacture of insulated wire and cable (313), manufacture of accumulators, primary cells and primary batteries (319), manufacture of electronic valves and tubes and other electronic components (321), manufacture of television and radio transmitters and apparatus for line telephony and line telegraphy (322), and manufacture of television and radio receivers, sound and video recording or reproducing apparatus, and associated goods (323)] are considered for contribution of registered manufacturing ICT sector to gross national and State income at market or constant prices.[19] ASI data before 1998-99, based on NIC-1987, is used for corresponding classification of 3-digit industries except the new industry group: manufacture of computers and computer based systems [367].[20]

Table 13.3 presents the contribution of ICT manufacturing

---

18. This classification is compiled from the following sources. (a) NASSCOM's *Annual Industry Survey 2001-02*; and (b) Department of Information Technology's website: *www.mit.gov.in/dbid/*

19. In all the above 7 industry groups, contribution of products under the ASICC 77 and 78 are particularly considerable for contribution of ICT sector to registered manufacturing production. As GVA for these products under the ASICC is not available in the published form, the product-specific contribution of ICT to registered manufacturing sector in national and State income is not analysed below. In the same way, GVA by sub-class of NIC-98 at 5-digit level [as given in Government of India, 2004c) is not available from the published form. Access to this data in future, however, will facilitate a focused analysis of ICT's contribution with reference to the following sub-classes: 22300, 30005-30007, 31200-31300, 32103, 32107-32109, 32202, 32204, 32208-32209 and 32303. Further, industry group: Reproduction of recorded media (223) is relevant for ICT industries. It is not included in the analysis as it is not relevant for Karnataka (i.e. ASI data is not reported for industry group: 223).

20. This correspondence between (NIC-1998) and [NIC-1987] is as follows: (300) = [358]; (312) = [360]; (313) = [361]; (319) = [362]; (322) = [365]; (323) = [366]; and (321) = [368].

industries (in terms of Gross Value Added (GVA) at constant (1993-1994) prices) to national and regional economic growth from 1993-94 through 2001-02. Two indicators signify this contribution. First, per cent share of ICT industries in the GDP or GSDP. Second, per cent share of ICT industries in total registered manufacturing GDP or GSDP. Karnataka's performance in both the indicators and in all the years is higher than at the all India level. For instance, Karnataka's (or all India) share of ICT industries in the GSDP (or GDP) is equal to 1.52 (or 0.71) per cent in 1993-94, 2.23 (0.77) per cent in 1997-98 and 1.10 (or 0.40) per cent in 2001-02. On the other hand, Karnataka (or all India) share of ICT industries in the registered manufacturing GSDP (or GDP) is equal to 13.86 (or 6.78) per cent in 1993-94, 17.36 (6.64) per cent in 1997-98 and 12.44 (or 3.58) per cent in 2001-02. Most importantly, Karnataka's share of ICT industries in registered manufacturing GSDP has been more than twice than the share of ICT industries in registered manufacturing GDP or NDP in all the years. This signifies a higher growth performance of Karnataka ICT industries that the ICT industries in the country as a whole.[21]

Karnataka's annual share of ICT industries in all India GVA of ICT industries shows wide fluctuations. For instance, the highest share in GVA (= 23.49 per cent) is evident in 1998-99; and the lowest share is evident for GVA (=10.24 per cent) in 1999-2000.

Combined Contribution of Manufacturing ICT Industries and ICT Services

A comparison of contribution of ICT services to GDP and GSDP (in Table 13.1) and manufacturing ICT industries to GDP and GSDP (Table 13.2) reveals the following:

First, in all the years, the contribution of ICT services is higher than that of manufacturing ICT industries in the GDP as well as in the GSDP. Thus, ICT services have a dominant contribution in ICT sector's contribution to the GDP and GSDP in India.

---

21. Further, Karnataka's better performance is evident in higher average growth (1994-1995 to 2001-02) of GVA from the ICT industries as compared to the national level. For instance, the average growth of GVA in Karnataka (or all India) is equal to 0.65 (or 10.39) per cent.

Table 13.3

Contribution of Manufacturing ICT Industries to National and State Income, 1993-94 to 2001-02

Year	*Gross Value Added (GVA) by Manufacturing ICT Industries (Rs. in crore at Constant Prices)*		*GVA by ICT Manufacturing Industries as a Percentage of GDP and GSDP at Constant Prices*		*GVA by ICT Manufacturing Industries as a Percentage Registered Manufacturing GDP and GSDP at Constant Prices*		*GVA by ICT Manufacturing Industries of Karnataka in the Nation's Total (%)*
	India	*Karnataka*	*GDP*	*GSDP*	*GDP*	*GSDP*	
1993-94	5552.74	625.93	0.71	1.52	6.78	13.86	11.27
1994-95	8112.60	1002.29	0.97	2.31	8.66	19.25	12.35
1995-96	7775.12	1095.90	0.86	2.37	7.24	20.26	14.09
1996-97	6754.10	900.21	0.70	1.79	5.67	15.18	13.33
1997-98	7824.56	1198.43	0.77	2.23	6.64	17.36	15.32
1998-99	5898.37	1411.12	0.54	2.33	4.91	16.59	23.92
1999-00	5120.33	524.36	0.45	0.82	4.11	7.47	10.24
2000-01	4941.16	636.45	0.41	0.91	3.68	9.83	12.88
2001-02	5033.33	766.83	0.40	1.10	3.58	12.44	15.23

Notes: (a) GDP and GSDP are measured at factor cost.
(b) Constant prices refer to 1993-94 prices.

Source: Computed by using the basic data on ICT industries in various issues of the Annual Survey of Industries [e.g. Government of India, 2004d), and by using GDP data in Government of India (2004) and GSDP data in Government of Karnataka (2004).

Second, the combined contribution of manufacturing ICT industries and ICT services to the GDP (or GSDP) is equal to 2.22 (or 3.78) per cent in 1993-94, 3.25 (or 5.35) per cent in 1998-99 and 4.87 (or 5.25) per cent in 2001-02. Thus, the ICT sector is more contributory to regional economic growth than to the national economic growth.[22]

Select International Comparisons

Contribution of ICT sector to Karnataka's economic growth is comparable with advanced countries.[23] For instance, Jalava and Pohjola (2002) notes that the ICT goods and services typically constitute between 3 and 5 per cent of total GDP (at current prices) in OECD countries.[24] Cohen *et al.* (2004) notes that the share of ICT sector in total GDP in 1998 was less than 4 per cent in Australia. As compared to these estimates, Karnataka's performance of ICT sector in GSDP in

22. Obviously, our approach has neglected the contribution of unorganised ICT sector to national and State income due to lack of data. However, the Final Report of the III All India Census of Small Scale Industries (SSIs) 2001-02 (Government of India, 2004e) shows that, at the national level, the gross output of registered SSIs in ICT sector (comprising 5 products: software development, data processing computer (PC), monitor (computer display), and electronic components and parts) is equal to rs.20329.8 million. on the other hand, the gross output of unregistered SSIS in ICT sector (comprising 13 products: ISD/STD booths for industries, data processing, internet browsing/setting of cyber cafes, electrical equipment and parts, software development, computer repair/maintenance services, electronic components and parts, batteries, electric supply services, telecommunication exchange, medical/legal transcription using voice/data communication links, computer software development and software service (including computer graphics engineering), and teleprinter/fax services) is equal to Rs.87550.8 million. Thus, if the contribution of unorganised ICT sector's contribution is appropriately added to the national income, the share of ICT sector in GDP would be higher. Further, our analysis neglects the indirect effect of ICT sector. In fact, input-output analysis is a useful technique to estimate both direct and indirect effects of changes in output and employment through forward and backward linkages. At present, lack of input-output table (IOT) for Karnataka State precludes this analysis. At the national level, IOT is available in published form for 1993-94 (Government of India, 2000). In this IOT, sectors like communication equipment, electronic equipments and communication services would account for ICT sector. As major changes in the ICT sector are taking place since 1993-94, this IOT is not useful for the analysis in this paper.

23. At the international level, ICT sector include manufacturing ICT, telecommunications, and other ICT services. The manufacturing ICT includes the following according to the International Standard Industry Classification (ISIC) Revision 3: 3000, 3130, 3210, 3220, 3230, 3312, and 3313. ICT services include 5150, 7123, 6420, and 7200. For details, see for instance, Cohen *et al.* (2004: 18).

24. These estimates are quoted from OECD (2000).

2001-02 is higher, than that of Australia and average for the OECD countries.[25]

Sources of Regional Growth of ICT Sector

Sources of growth of ICT sector are related to determinants of supply of and demand for ICT products and services in the process of regional economic growth. As the use of telephone lines over telephone network is essential for the provisioning and utilisation of ICT services, construction of telecom network, equipment to provide access for users to network, and access to network by users are the preconditions for utilisation or demand for ICT services.[26]

Thus, given the telecom network and access to the network, demand for usage (or usage demand) is the critical determinant of growth of ICT products and services.

In what follows, a framework for estimation of usage demand for ICT services is developed. The framework is implemented for data from Karnataka State to provide evidence for sources of growth of ICT services from the demand side.

Estimation of Usage Demand for ICT Services

Usage demand for ICT services is specific to particular services. Hence, determinants of usage demand will have to be estimated for each ICT service separately. In the absence of data to capture the service-specific usage demand, however, an approximation of usage demand for ICT services as a whole may have to be adopted. This approximation is attempted below by taking total number of metered telephone calls as a proxy for usage demand for ICT services and by taking telecom districts as a unit of analysis.

---

25. To make this comparison robust, the contribution of ICT sector to GDP and GSDP at constant prices was estimated at current prices by multiplying separate deflators for (a) total GDP and GSDP, (b) GDP and GSDP from communication services, (c) GDP and GSDP from IT services, and (d) GVA from ICT manufacturing industries at all India level and Karnataka State. The estimated contribution of the ICT sector to the GDP (or GSDP) was equal to 2.22 (or 3.78) per cent in 1993-94, 1.59 (or 6.25) per cent in 1997-98 and 4.87 (or 5.22) per cent in 2001-02. Thus, Karnataka's performance stands comparable with the OECD countries at current prices as well.

26. This is in line with the argument in Taylor (2003): "telecommunications services are not consumed in isolation. A network is involved...There must be access to the network before it can be used" (p.145).

Framework for Estimation

Usage demand for ICT services at district level is assumed to be influenced by economic variables within the district. To estimate the effects of these variables on usage demand, both cross-section models and panel data models are estimated by linear and log.linear functional forms. The panel data models are (a) Pooled Regression Model (PRM), (b) Fixed Effects Model (FEM), and Random Effects Model (REM). The standard statistical frameworks for estimation of these models are well known. Hence, they are not described here.[27]

Data and Variable Description

Telecom district is used as a unit of analysis. At present, Karnataka State has 19 telecom districts. The estimation period covers three years: 2000-01, 2001-02 and 2002-03. By pooling of these cross-section data for three years, the panel data is generated. The variables used for the final estimations are given in Box 13.3 along with their definitions and data sources.[28]

The sign of coefficient of all the variables is predicted to be positive. First, a positive coefficient on PCI may be interpreted that, other things being equal, an increase in per capita income will have a positive effect on increasing the usage demand for ICT services. Or, income elasticity of usage demand for ICT services is predicted to be positive. Second, a positive sign on STS indicates the effects of structural changes in State's income on usage demand for ICT services. Third, a positive sign on coefficient (and magnitude of coefficient being greater than 1) on TD may be interpreted to mean the presence of network and call externalities in the provision of ICT services in the State.[29]

27. For an excellent description of panel data models, see, for instance, Chapter 14 in Green (1997).

28. To begin with, two more explanatory variables were considered for estimation purposes. (a) Share of primary sector in Net District Income at current prices. (b) Share of secondary sector in Net District Income at current prices. However, in the trial estimations, inclusion of these variables did not yield encouraging results. Hence, they were dropped in the final estimations.

29. Following Das and Srinivasan (1999) "network externality is generated due to the fact that when a new subscriber joins the network, it is not just she who benefits but so do all the existing subscribers who can potentially reach her". Call externality "arises

contd...

Box 13.3

Variables and Data Description

Dependent Variable

- Usage demand for ICT services - Measured by total number of metered telephone calls per capita (TMCPC). That is, total number of metered calls divided by total population as per 2001 census. *Source*: Records of the Office of the Chief General Manager, Karnataka Telecom Circle (Bangalore).

Independent Variables

- *Per capita income* (PCI): Net District Income at current prices divided by total population in the State as per 2001 census. *Source*: Directorate of Economics and Statistics, Government of Karnataka (Bangalore).
- *Teledensity* (TD): Number of telephones per 100 population (TD)=Total number of working connections divided by total population, as per 2001 census, and expressed per 100 population. *Source*: Records of the Office of the Chief General Manager, Karnataka Telecom Circle (Bangalore).
- *Share of Tertiary Sector*: Per cent of Tertiary Sector in Net District Income at current prices (STS). *Source*: Directorate of Economics and Statistics, Government of Karnataka (Bangalore).

Thus, the included independent variables in the model are intended to provide evidence for income effect, effects of structural changes and

...contd...

from the fact that one call leads to further calls from the other party to whom the call is made. Increase in the number of connections per capita by one per cent leads to more than one per cent increase in per capita usage. The magnitude of network externalities tends to get reduced as the telephone density increases". (p.183-184). In the same way, following Taylor (2003), network (or subscriber) externality "arises when a new subscriber joins the network. Connection of a new subscriber confers a benefit on existing subscribers because the number of ports that can now be reached is increased. As this benefit is shared in common by all existing subscribers, the network externality accordingly has the dimension of a public good". On the other hand, "a completed telephone call requires the participation of a second party and the utility of this party is thereby affected. The gratuitous effect, which falls on the second party, represents what is usually referred to as the call (or use) externality" (pp.145-146).

presence of network and call externalities on usage demand for ICT services in Karnataka State.[30]

Description of Data

Table 13.4 presents the descriptive statistic for the variables used in the estimations. Of all the variables, PCI has the biggest mean value. This is followed by the mean values of other variables: TMCPC, TD, and STS. Of the variables, the largest (or smallest) standard deviation is evident in regard to PCI (or TD). However, the range is highest (or smallest) in case of TMCPC (or STS). Further, the simple correlation coefficients of all the variables show that TMCPC is positively correlated with all independent variables. Of all the variables, the highest correlation is evident between TMCPC and PCI (=0.830) and lowest correlation is evident between STS and TD (=0.21).

Results of Estimation

Table 13.5 presents the estimation results of cross-section regression model for three years: for 2000-01, 2001-02, and 2002-03. The results are presented by linear and log.linear functional forms. First of all, all the estimated coefficients have predicted sign and are statistically significant, except the coefficient of TD in log.linear estimation for 2001-02. Second, the magnitude of estimated coefficient on TD is more than unity, and is larger than the coefficients on other variables, in all the linear estimations. This provides empirical evidence for the presence of network and call externalities in the provision of ICT services. This result is in contrast with the log.linear estimations. Third, the income effect has the lowest magnitude in the linear estimations. In case of log.linear estimations, the income effect is greater than unity in all the years. Fourth, the effect of changes in tertiary sector is remarkable in both linear and log.linear estimations.

---

30. In addition, price of ICT services can be an important determinant of the usage demand. Other things being equal, an increase in price of ICT services may be expected to have negative effect on usage demand for ICT services. However, ICT services are a composite of many and different services with service-specific prices. Aggregation or averaging of these prices is not plausible. Hence, price variable is not included to determine the variations in aggregate usage demand for ICT services.

Table 13.4

Descriptive Statistics for Variables Used in Estimation of Determinants of Usage Demand for ICT Services in Karnataka State

1. Summary Statistics

Variables	*Mean*	*Standard Deviation*	*Maximum*	*Minimum*
TMCPC	206.73	190.69	994.18	72.31
PCI	17166.13	5240.52	35207.50	10611.00
TD	4.45	2.58	11.34	1.62
STS	49.00	7.19	69.86	36.95

2. Simple Correlation Coefficients

Variables	TMCPC	PCI	TD	SPS
TMCPC	1.000			
PCI	0.830	1.000		
TD	0.586	0.540	1.00	
STS	0.619	0.543	0.21	1.00

Notes: TMCPC = Total metered calls per capita.
PCI = Per capita income.
TD = Teledensity.
STS = Share of tertiary sector.

Source: Author

This result is supportive for the hypothesis that usage demand is largely affected by the changes in tertiary or services sector, which is relatively more information-intensive. Fifth, the explanatory power of both linear and log.linear models is higher than 85 per cent in all the estimations. In addition, the F-statistic is significant in all the years. This offers evidence for joint significance of all estimated coefficients.

Table 13.6 presents the estimation results of linear and log.linear specification for the panel data models. As in the case of cross section estimation results in Table 13.5, all the estimated coefficients have predicted sign. In terms of statistical significance of estimated coefficients, the log.linear models performs better as compared to linear models. However, estimated coefficient of TD is not supportive of the presence of network and call externalities in the usage demand for ICT services in Karnataka State.

Table 13.5

Determinants of Usage Demand for ICT Services in Karnataka State: Estimates of Cross Section Regression Models

Dependent Variable: Number of Metered Call Units Per Capita

Independent Variables	*2000-01: Linear*	*2001-02: Linear*	*2002-03: Linear*	*2000-01: Log.linear*	*2001-02: Log.linear*	*2002-03: Log.linear*
Constant	-985.722 (6.470)*	-862.743 (5.175)*	-705.372 (4.181)*	-12.640 (7.946)*	-11.854 (4.508)*	-7.297 (3.311)*
Per capita income	0.021 (3.881)*	0.017 (2.728)*	0.014 (2.888)*	1.584 (8.926)*	1.572 (4.969)*	1.089 (4.037)*
Teledensity	21.624 (2.240)**	19.117 (2.133)**	20.015 (2.474)*	0.152 (2.036)***	0.141 (1.129)	0.223 (1.942)***
Per cent of tertiary sector in Net District Income	17.097 (4.520)*	14.273 (3.377)*	10.609 (2.746)*	0.049 (7.170)*	0.309 (2.630)**	0.028 (2.700)**
R^2	0.868	0.858	0.859	0.951	0.762	0.709
F	32.85*	32.26*	30.46*	97.22*	38.57*	32.07*
Sample size	19	19	19	57	19	19

Notes: (a) Figures in parentheses are t-ratios.
(b) *: significant at 1 per cent level or more.
(c) **: significant at 5 per cent level or more.
(d) ***: significant at 10 per cent level or more.

Source: Author.

A comparison of panel data estimation results from linear and log.linear functional forms suggest that, *a priori* specification of a linear or log.linear functional form may lead to divergent evidence on the determinants of usage demand for ICT services in Karnataka State. Thus, the following familiar criteria for models' choice are used to choose an appropriate model on empirical grounds.[31]

31. The details of the following models' criteria (i.e. F-test, Lagrange Multiplier test, and Hausman test) are given, in Chapter 14 in Green (1997). For instance, the F-test is as follows: Let (R^2PRM) be the coefficient of determination from the PRM, and (R^2FEM) from the FEM. Then, the F (n-R, nT-n-R) = [{(R^2PRM) - (R^2FEM)}/(n-1)]/{(R^2FEM) /(nT-n-R)}. If the test is significant, FEM is preferred to PRM.

Table 13.6

Determinants of Usage Demand for ICT Services in Karnataka State: Estimates of Panel Data Models

Dependent Variable: Number of Metered Call Units Per Capita

Independent Variables	*Linear Pooled Regression Model*	*Linear Fixed Effects Model*	*Linear Random Effects Model*	*Log.linear Pooled Regression Model*	*Log.linear Fixed Effects Model*	*Log.linear Random Effects Model*
Constant	-563.567 (6.394)*	- -	-45.393 (0.929)	-11.050 (7.973)*	- -	-10.555 (8.006)*
Per capita income	0.021 (6.090)*	0.001 (0.386)	0.012 (4.715)*	1.540 (9.736)*	0.670 (1.843)***	1.555 (10.433)*
Teledensity	16.583 (2.808)*	9.034 (0.648)	20.666 (3.225)*	0.133 (1.965)***	0.950 (3.666)*	0.140 (2.073)*
Per cent of tertiary sector in Net District Income	6.995 (3.300)*	0.157 (0.112)	0.890 (0.921)	0.021 (7.973)*	0.015 (1.825)***	0.012 (2.989)*
R^2	0.764	0.987	0.764	0.844	0.958	0.844
F	57.31*	128.83*	-	95.84*	38.21*	-
Sample size	57	57	57	57	57	57

Notes: (a) Figures in parentheses are t-ratios.
(b) *: significant at 1 per cent level or more.
(c) **: significant at 5 per cent level or more.
(d) ***: significant at 10 per cent level or more.

Source: Author.

A choice between the linear and log.linear function form, based on the Sargan-criterion, favours for log.linear functional form in all the cross-section and panel estimations.[32] Given this result, a choice between log.linear PRM and FEM, based on the F-test, shows that the FEM is empirically preferred to the PRM.[33] However, Lagrange

32. The criterion is based on a computation formula in Godfrey and Wickens (1981). The formula requires an equation to be estimated by both linear and log.linear functional forms. The residual sum of squares from the log.linear estimation is divided by the product of residual sum of squares of the linear estimation and geometric mean of the dependent variable. If the resultant value of this division is greater (or less) than unity, the data is said to be in favour of log.linear (or linear) functional form.

33. The value of F(18, 35) is equal to 5.296 and significant at 1 per cent level.

Multiplier test for a choice between the log.linear PRM and FEM did not favour for FEM.[34] The Hausman test for a choice between the log.linear FEM and REM favour for FEM.[35] In view of the above tests, the log.linear FEM is empirically preferred to remaining estimated models. The interpretation and implications based on this chosen model is given below:

First of all, the income elasticity of usage demand for ICT services is equal to less than unity. Thus, other things being the same, an increase in per capita income of the district by one per cent will result in about 0.67 per cent increase in usage demand. Second, the magnitude of the coefficient of teledensity is closer to unity. This indicates the absence of network and call externalities.[36] Thus, other things being the same, an increase in teledensity by one per cent will lead to an increase in usage demand for ICT services by 0.95 per cent. Third, the effects of changes in the share of tertiary sector on usage demand are lowest as compared to the effects of per capita income and teledensity. Thus, other things being the same, an increase in the share of tertiary sector in state income by one per cent will lead to an increase in usage demand by about 0.02 per cent.

In short, usage demand for ICT services in Karnataka is determined by changes in per capita income, share of tertiary sector in State income, and benefits of network and call externalities. These determinants constitute the demand-side empirical sources (demand side, however) of growth of ICT services in Karnataka State.

Conclusions and Implications

This paper has focused on the analysis of contribution of ICT sector to regional economic development of Karnataka State in comparison with all India level and estimation of demand-side sources

---

34. The value of Lagrange Multiplier test statistic is equal to 1.51, and is not significant at 10 per cent level or more (degree of freedom is equal to 1).

35. The value of Hausman test statistic is equal to 38.13, and is significant at 1 per cent level (degree of freedom is equal to 3).

36. This result is in contrast with the results in Das and Srinivasan (1999) where the estimated value of the coefficient on teledensity variable exceeds unity and, thereby, indicating the presence of network and call externalities in the usage demand for telecom services in India.

of ICT sector's growth of Karnataka State. This analysis leads to the following conclusions and implications:

At present, contribution of ICT sector is not estimated at the national level by the CSO and at the State level by the Directorate of Economics and Statistics. However, this paper has developed a simple framework for estimation of this contribution from within the available data in the national income and state income accounts. This framework is useful to separate the contribution of ICT sector by manufacturing and service activities (i.e. by telecom and IT services). The results of these estimations offer evidence for the remarkable contribution of ICT sector to national and state income, and higher contribution of ICT sector to State income than to the national income. In the same way, contribution of ICT sector to State income is higher as compared to available estimates for OECD countries. This underlines the importance of ICT sector to the economic development of Karnataka.

Total number of metered telephone calls by telecom districts is used as a proxy for total usage demand for ICT services and its determinants are estimated with respect to changes in per capita income, teledensity, and share of tertiary sector in State income. Of the estimated panel data models, the log.linear fixed effects model is chosen on empirical grounds. The results of the chosen model indicate that the changes in per capita income, teledensity, and share of tertiary sector in State income are empirical determinants of usage demand or sources of growth of ICT services. Of the estimated sources, the changes in teledensity have the biggest magnitude and are followed by changes in per capita income. Thus, from the demand side, the sources of growth of ICT services in Karnataka State is contributed by changes in per capita income, share of tertiary sector in State income, and teledensity.

ICT sector deserves to be further promoted, as its growth has many positive types of fallout. First, growth of ICT sector has lead to the emergence of a 'New Economy' in Karnataka State. This 'New Economy' has been a creator of new jobs for technical persons; major foreign exchange earner through exports; and attractor of foreign investment. These performances are conducive for higher national and regional economic development. Second, indicators of ICT sector are included in construction of indices of competitiveness at the international level. These indices include World Economic Forum's Global Competitiveness Indices, International Institute of Management Development's World Competitiveness Indices, World Bank's Competitiveness Indicators, International Communication Union's Digital Access Index and World Economic Forum and World Bank's Network Readiness Index. Further, growth and widespread utilisation of ICT services are contributory to human development, as evident in UNDP's Human Development Report 2001 [UNDP (2001)]. Thus, growth of ICT sector is contributory to enhance and strengthen the international competitiveness of India as well as Karnataka State.

ICT sector has many indirect effects on economic growth, such as, growth of self-productivity, capital deepening due to high capital investments, and efficiency of ICT-using industries and services. Analysis of these effects require, among others, a disaggregate analysis at the industry and/or firm level.[37] This is an area of future research on ICT sector in Karnataka economy.

Karnataka's experiences in formulation and implementation of policies for ICT in a federal, open and mixed economy framework are of relevance for design of growth-oriented ICT policy in other States in India. In the same way, subject to the comparability of economic structures, Karnataka's policy experiences are of relevance for other developing countries where regional economic growth is driven by ICT industries and services

37. An excellent framework for estimation of ICT sector's contribution at the industry level is available in Chapter 2 in Cohen et al (2004) and in Chapter 3 in OECD (2004). A framework for firm level estimation is available in Chapter 5 in OECD (2004).

References

Arora, Ashish and Suma Athreye (2002). "The Software Industry and India's Economic Development", *Information Economics and Policy* 14: 253-73.

Brunner, Hans-Peter (1995). *Closing the Technology Gap: Technological Change in India's Computer Industry.* New Delhi: Sage Publications.

Cohen, Daniel, Pietro Garibaldi and Stefano Scarpetta (eds.). (2004). *The ICT Revolution: Productivity Differences and the Digital Divide.* New York: Oxford University Press.

Das, Pinaki and P.V. Srinivasan (1999). "Demand for Telephone Usage in India", *Information Economics and Policy* 11: 177-94.

Dataquest (2004). "Industry Datamine", *DATAQUEST*, Vol. XXII(20). Available on *www.dqindia.com.*

Dossani, Rafiq (2002). *Telecommunications Reforms in India*, Asia/Pacific Research Centre, Stanford University. Processed.

Godfrey, L.G. and M.R. Wickens (1981). "Testing Linear and Log.Linear Regressions for Functional Form", *Review of Economic Studies* XLVIII: 487-96.

Government of India (2004a). *National Accounts Statistics 2004.* New Delhi: Central Statistical Organisation, Ministry of Statistics & Programme Implementation.

———. (2004b). *Annual Survey of Industries 2001-02*, Vol.II (Part I & II). Kolkata: Ministry of Statistics & Programme Implementation, Central Statistical Organisation.

———. (2004c). *Updated National Industrial Classification (All Economic Activities) 2004.* Kolkata: Ministry of Statistics & Programme Implementation, Central Statistical Organisation.

———. (2004d). *Annual Survey of Industries 2001-02*, Vol.I. Kolkata: Ministry of Statistics & Programme Implementation, Central Statistical Organisation.

———. (2004e). *Final Results: Third All India Census of Small Scale Industries 2001-02.* New Delhi: Development Commissioner (Small Scale Industries), Ministry of Small Scale Industries.

———. (2003a). *Tenth Five Year Plan 2002-2007, Vol.II, Sectoral Policies and Programmes.* New Delhi: Planning Commission.

———. (2003b). *National Accounts Statistics 2003*, Central Statistical Organisation. New Delhi: Ministry of Statistics & Programme Implementation.

———. (2002). *Report of the Special Group on Targeting Ten Million Employment Opportunities per Year.* New Delhi: Planning Commission.

———. (2000). *Input-Output Transactions Table 1993-94.* New Delhi: Central Statistical Organisation, Ministry of Statistics & Programme Implementation.

———. (1999). *New Series on National Accounts Statistics (Base Year 1993-94).* New Delhi: Central Statistical Organisation, Department of Statistics & Programme Implementation, Ministry of Statistics & Programme Implementation.

Government of Karnataka (2004). *Economic Survey 2004-05: March 2005.* Bangalore: Planning and Statistics Department.

———. (2000). *IT for the Common Man: The Millennium IT Policy.* Bangalore: Office of the Secretary, Information Technology.

Green, William, H. (1997). *Econometric Methods.* New Jersey: Prentice Hall.

Heeks, Richard (1996). *India's Software Industry: State Policy, Liberalisation and Industrial Development.* New Delhi: Sage Publications.

Jalava, Jukka, Pohjola, Matti (2002). "Economic Growth in the New Economy: Evidence from Advanced Countries", *Information Economics and Policy* 14: 189-210.

Kathuria, Rajat., Harsha Vardhana Singh and Anita Soni (2003). "Telecommunications Policy in India", in Aaditya Mattoo and Rebert M. Stern (eds.), *India and the WTO*. New Delhi: Oxford University Press. pp.81-116.

Narayana, M.R. (2003). *Consumer Demand for Telecom Services in Karnataka and Goa*. New Delhi: Economic Research Unit, Department of Telecommunications, Government of India.

NASSCOM (National Association of Software and Service Companies) (2003). *Strategic Review Report 2003*. Mumbai: NASSCOM.

Noll, Roger G. and Scott J. Wallsten (2004). *An Assessment of Telecommunications Reforms in India*, Stanford Centre for International Development and AEI-Brookings Joint Centre on Regulation. Processed.

Pohjola, Matti (2002). "The New Economy: Facts, Impacts and Policies", *Information Economics and Policy* 14: 133-44.

OECD (Organisation for Economic Co-operation and Development) (2004). *Understanding Economic Growth*. Paris: OECD.

———. (2000). *OECD Communication Outlook 2000*. Paris: OECD.

Taylor, Lester D. (2003). "Telecommunications demand", in Gary Madden (ed). *Traditional Telecommunications Networks, The International Handbook of Telecommunications Economics*, Vol.I. Edward Elgar (Mass). pp.145-79.

UNDP (United Nations Development Programme) (2001). *Human Development Report 2001: Making New Technologies Work for Human Development*. New York: Oxford University Press.

14

Social Mobility in the Context of Occupational Health

*The Case of Silk Reeling**

ANAND INBANATHAN

Introduction

Whatever be the means of classifying the poor, absolute poverty is still the condition of about one-third of the Indian population. Bearing this in mind, the need of income generating occupations for the poor (considering their limited education and skills), becomes crucial for their existence. Sericulture has been seen as an activity (or a group of activities) which, in the manner in which it is presently organised, is eminently suitable for people with limited skills and virtually no education. Including such activities as silkworm rearing, reeling, twisting, dyeing and weaving, each occupation is labour-intensive. What is also of some importance is that in various activities associated with sericulture (though not all), men, women and children can be employed in these activities. While child labour is certainly to be discouraged, families of reeling workers consider children as an additional source of income and as such commend silk reeling as an income generating activity. Sericulture has also been a part of anti-poverty efforts of both the state and central governments. However, an important by-product of sericulture is the significant number of people who become victims of health problems (particularly respiratory problems, including asthma). Though silk reeling is considered the most problematic of sericulture activities, this is not to suggest that

---

* This is based on a study on social and health problems of silk reeling workers. Dr. Om Prakash, a physician and specialist in respiratory diseases, carried out the part of the study on health.

dyeing[1] or silkworm rearing also does not have health related problems for those working in them.

Sericulture activities provide income to a large number of people, and though the incomes may not be high for most people, they provide subsistence to people who otherwise would be in dire straits.[2] Having said this, we look at the issue of social mobility as a long-term prospect for the workers. Social mobility is a question being discussed in the context of the present paper, where reeling workers belonged to different groups, with the largest groups being the Scheduled Castes (SCs) and Muslims. While persons of Scheduled Caste background suffer from various disabilities, the poverty that many find themselves in is often exacerbated by their social identity. Economic factors may be considered of greater significance in development but in the activity that reeling workers take up, economic factors are only one aspect of their life. Health problems are also a crucial characteristic of this work for many of the workers. This impinges on their overall lifestyle, and quality of life. Further, it makes it more difficult for them not only to get out of poverty, but they cannot use silk reeling as a means of improving their social status either. To highlight the situation of the Scheduled Castes, comparisons have been drawn with those of other groups, who were also engaged in silk reeling.

The focus of this paper is on reeling, the activity in which silk yarn is unwound from cocoons, and stretched into one long silk thread. Karnataka is the single largest producer of silk in the country. Reeling centres such as Sidlaghatta, Ramnagaram and Kollegal are prominent,

---

1. Some details about the chemicals that are used in dyeing, their effects on the workers who use them, and also on environmental pollution, are available. However, less information appears to be at hand on the health problems that have been encountered in silkworm rearing, particularly through pesticides that are used to prevent silkworm diseases. Rearing is often carried out in the same house/room where people live in, one portion being set aside for this purpose. Since they are in close proximity, there is every likelihood that pesticide use would have some adverse effects on the silkworm rearers' (and their families) health.

2. Large silk reelers have relatively high incomes, but these are confined to a small number of people. Labourers, who are in the majority, are poorly paid, and fall into the category of the poor. Owner-labourers get an income somewhat higher than that of ordinary labourers, but that is only when the units are able to run economically. Otherwise, these owners close the units and take up wage labour in larger units.

with silk produced in Sidlaghatta being considered among the better quality silk. This paper is based on a study which was conducted in Sidlaghatta, in Kolar district of Karnataka. Reeling technology is still of a relatively simple kind, and includes *charka*, filature (or cottage basin), and multi-end reeling units. With modifications, these have remained the mainstay of the reeling enterprises in Sidlaghatta for many years. In recent times, a change has occurred in the number of reeling units that are either charka based or cottage basin based. Earlier, the more commonly used technology was the *charka*, with modifications in technology and design ensuring that it was still in use. That has changed, with more people opting for cottage basins, and thus, there are more of cottage basin units in Sidlaghatta than there are *charka* units (at present there are about 300 *charka*s and 1100 cottage basin units).[3] These different types of technology cost different amounts to set up, with the *charka* units being cheapest and the multi end units the costliest to set up and run. Even those who are not economically very well off can set up *charka* units, and with relatively modest amounts, a small reeling unit can be started up in the home, and run by family labour. Setting up a cottage basin unit is costlier, inasmuch as a minimum is usually of four basins, and only the more affluent can set up these units. While costs vary for different types of reeling units, the physical environment of the reeling units also differs with the type of reeling units as well as the economic standing of the reeling unit owner. For instance, those with less capital establish small *charka* reeling units, and they set them up in one corner of their own homes, while household activities are carried on simultaneously in the other parts of the single room homes. On the other hand cottage basin units are larger, employ more people to run the units, and are usually set apart from the living space of the unit owners. The latter units are larger and better ventilated. These factors are also related to the health problems that will be discussed later in the paper.

A distinction which has also been made is between impairment, which is a "...specific loss of function, such as a decline flow or FEV-1, it is a strictly medical determination. Disability is impairment, such as skill level, education, job availability, etc.; it is therefore based on medical and socioeconomic factors." (Martin, 2000). While the basis

3. Interview with Assistant Director, Sericulture, Sidlaghatta, 15 March 2005.

of the problem that we are considering is the health of the individual, the case of silk reelers is not that of health alone, but other factors, including, predominantly, their poverty, and therefore fits in the category of disability.

Our study had interviewed 229 reeling workers out of which 52 were Scheduled Castes. A few of these were owner-labourers. Muslims are also found among owners of reeling units, and some of the reeling units are relatively large, but they (owners of large units) are not among this sample. Although a few Scheduled Caste people were found among the owners of reeling units, the units that they owned were usually the smallest and based on *charka*s. Our sample had the following distribution:

Table 14.1a

Caste-wise Distribution of Scheduled Caste Reeling Workers

N= 52

	Holeya	*Madiga*	*Tigalaru*	*Total*
Male	4	13	0	17
Female	12	22	1	35
Total	16	35	1	52

Table 14.1b

Distribution according to Religious Group

N=229

	Muslims	*Hindus*	*Christians*	*Total*
Male	62	49	1	112
Female	57	59	1	117
Total	119 (51.97%)	108 (47.16%)	2 (0.87%)	229 (100%)

The reeling workers were usually poorly educated, with 69 per cent of the SC workers being illiterate (comparatively non-SCs have 62 per cent who are illiterate). Women are less educated than the male reeling workers, with almost the same proportion of women of SC background and non-SC background (SC 77 per cent and non SC 76 per cent) being illiterate. The cases of better educated workers, high school educated, or even a degree holder among the SC males, is indicative of the disinclination of workers to move out of Sidlaghatta and look for employment other than silk reeling.

Table 14.2a

Education of SC Workers

N= 52

	Illiterate	*Less than 4 Years of School*	*Primary*	*Middle School*	*High School*	*Pre University*	*Any Degree*	*Total*
Male	9	1	0	2	4	0	1	17
Female	27	0	3	2	2	1	0	35
Total	36 (69.2%)	1 (1.9%)	3 (5.8%)	4 (7.7%)	6 (11.5%)	1 (1.9%)	1 (1.9%)	52 (100%)

Table 14.2b

Education of Non-SC Workers

N= 177

	Illiterate	*Less than 4 Years of*	*Primary*	*Middle School*	*High School*	*Pre University*	*Total*
Male	47	3	9	18	17	1	95
Female	62	0	8	9	3	3	85
Total	109 (61.6%)	3 (2.6%)	17 (9.6%)	27 (15.3%)	20 (11.3%)	1 (0.9%)	180 (100%)

Table 14.2c

Association Between Caste and Educational Level

	Illiterate	*Less than 4 Years*	*Primary*	*Middle*	*High School*	*PUC*	*Any degree*
SC	69.2	1.9	5.8	7.7	11.5	1.9	1.9
General	61.6	1.7	9.6	15.3	11.3	0.6	0.0

Notes: Chi value = 7.013, which is not significant.
Implying no association between caste and educational level.

Reeling and the Health of Workers

Several issues are important in the consideration of the health of workers who are employed in reeling. We begin by considering those whose health was impaired in some manner, whether a chronic problem, or even a disease which afflicted them only for a relatively short while. Respondents were asked whether they had suffered any significant health problem during the past one year (self-reporting). This was not related to their not being able to go to the reeling units for work, since workers chose to work even when they were ill if they thought they can continue to work somehow, and thereby earn their wages for the day. In this connection, their health status was as indicated in table 14.3a. However, 16 workers stated that in the past one year they had stopped work for varying periods due to ill health. Having said this, it should also be noted that none of the workers of Scheduled Caste background indicated that they had any respiratory problem before starting to work in a reeling unit, and only two from the rest of the remaining sample of 177 indicated that they had respiratory problems before starting on reeling work. Now, however, several persons of both the SCs as well as non SCs have respiratory problems after having worked in silk reeling units. In fact, workers of SC groups indicated that they had more of health problems than those of non-SC groups.

Table 14.3a

Health Status of SCs

	Healthy	*With Health Problem*	*Total*
Male	9	8	17
Female	8	27	35
	17	35	52

Table 14.3b

Health Status of Non-SCs

	Healthy	*With Health Problem*	*Total*
Male	53	42	95
Female	40	42	82
Total	93	84	177

Table 14.4

Association between Caste and Health Status

	Healthy	*Have/Had Disease*
SC	32.7	67.3
General	52.5	47.5

Notes: Chi value= 6.34, significant at 5 per cent level.
Implies association exists between the above two variables.

While the association between caste and their health status may appear extraordinary, considering that the workers live in similar conditions, and the work conditions are the same, there is some evidence that they do not have the same income levels. This may suggest that the poorer income levels of SCs has a bearing on their living conditions, and on their health.

Table 14.5

Caste and Income Relation

(Annual Household Income)

	< 6000	*6001–12000*	*12001–24000*	*24001–30000*	*30001+*
SC	1.9	19.2	51.9	15.4	11.5
General	7.3	16.9	32.8	11.9	31.1

Notes: Chi value = 12.2, significant at 5 per cent level of significance.
A good association between caste and income is noticed.

In the context of the health of workers as well as owner-labourers, there is a noticeable difference between the non SCs and the SCs in terms of the proportion of persons who have health problems in relation to their income levels. In the case of the SCs, there is no clear relation between the income levels and their health status, though at the extremes, the highest level of health problems and lowest incomes are related, as also, the highest incomes and lowest levels of health problems are related. With the non-SCs there is a steady reduction in those who have health problems in relation to their incomes, with the incomes above Rs. 24,000 showing that the number of persons without health problems was substantially lower than those who had health problems.

The main health problems that they had indicated include (as shown in Figure 14.1).

Figure 14.1

Share of Workers Facing Health Problems

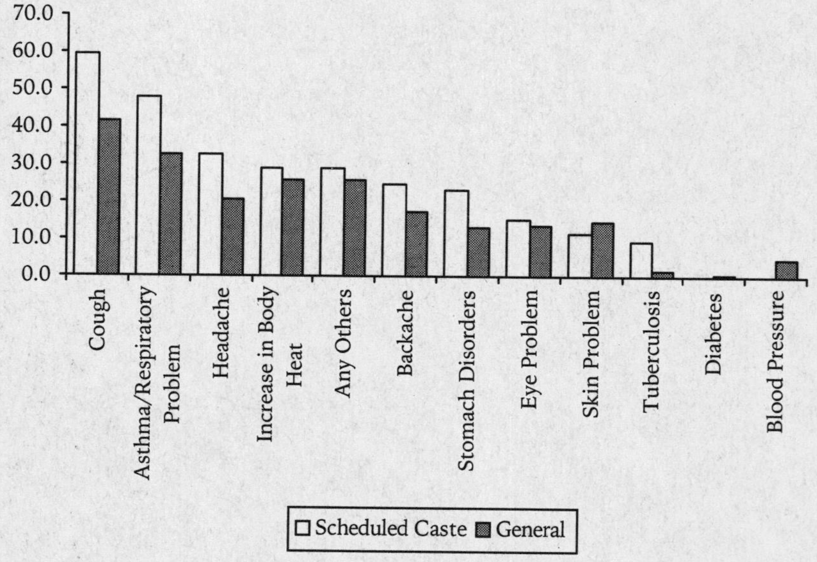

Figure 14.2

Health Status and Income Levels among SCs

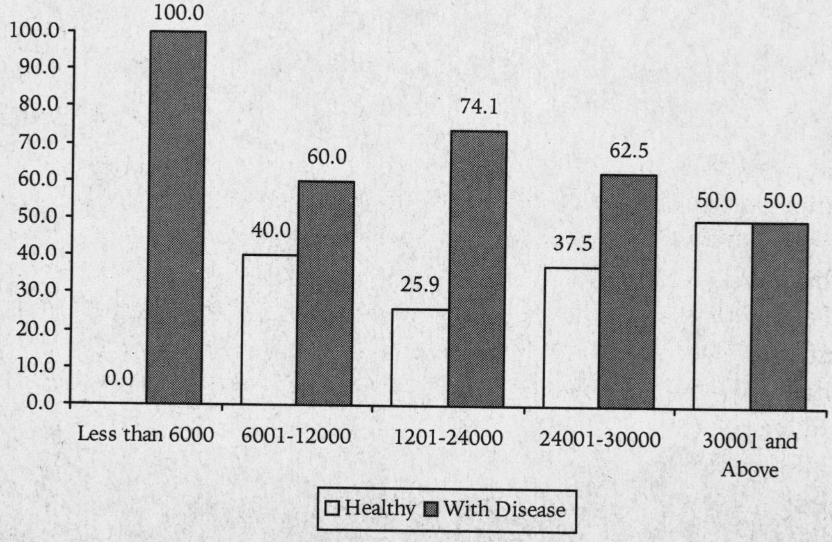

Figure 14.3

Health Status for Different Income Levels among Non-SCs

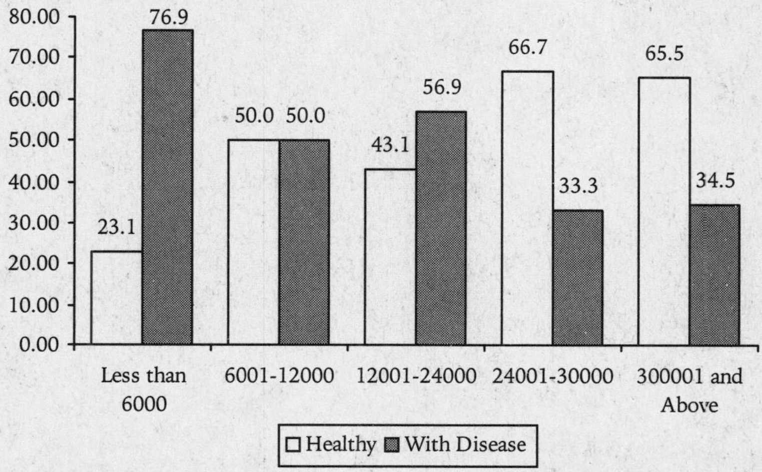

A further contributory factor is that a larger number of the SCs are among hired labourers, while there are more owners among the other caste groups. Hence, the income figures which state that they have a higher income is also because of their being owners of the reeling units too. However, one cannot take this too far, since these owners are not the big unit owners, but owner-labourers, i.e. owning modest units. In these units, the family comprises the labourers; though men tend to work less in the units themselves (as reeling workers) and their family members (particularly women) work as reeling workers. More often, the family incomes differ not only because of individual wages, but according to the number of family members who are earning. Men tend to take up chores which involve going out of the units, to buy cocoons, and later, to sell the silk yarn. Even when women state that they are the owners of the units, it is more often the case that men go out, while the women continue working in the reeling units. Although cocoon markets provide facilities for women to come and buy cocoons, there were very few women who actually went to the cocoon markets. Hence, when we find that owners tend to have less of health problems than those who are hired labourers, there seems a greater likelihood that it is due to the fact that there are more men among owners, who do not continuously work at the reeling (in owner-labourer units) while women actually do the reeling.[4] Another possibility is that with ownership comes a modest increase in income, which could translate into better nutrition and improved health.

Table 14.6

Caste and Ownership

N=229

	Ownership		*Total*
	Reeling Owner and Labourer	Reeling Labourer	
Scheduled Castes	3 5.8%	49 94.2%	52 100%
General	43 24.3%	134 75.7%	177 100%
Total	46 20.09%	183 79.9%	229 100%

Table 14.7

Ownership and Health

	SCs		*Non SCs*	
	Healthy	*Having Disease*	*Healthy*	*Having Disease*
Reeling Owner Labourer	100.0	0.0	69.8	30.2
Reeling Labourer	28.6	71.4	47.0	53.0

It is also necessary to indicate that there is no certainty about what actually makes some people allergic to the silk allergen, and susceptible to health and particularly respiratory problems. Even those who show an allergic reaction to the silk allergen, or even sensitised to the allergen, do not always end with respiratory problems or asthma (see Jarvis and Burney, 2000: 23) The same could be said in relation to the use of biomass fuel—about who would have health problems and who do not. However, in the latter case it seems

4. In the bigger units, the owners are not engaged in reeling work at all, but supervise the work of hired labourers, which however, makes them more susceptible to health problems too, since they remain in the units for much of the day.

probable that those who spend more time in the polluted environment of wood smoke may have a higher likelihood of falling victim to health problems of various kinds. Those working for many years in reeling units may have had more health problems from the pollution caused by burning biomass fuel than those who have worked in reeling units for a much shorter duration.

Table 14.8a

Health Problems and Ownership of Reeling Units

	Owners	*Labourers*
Cough*	37.0	48.1
Asthma/Respiratory Problems**	28.3	38.3
Increase in Body Heat	19.6	28.4
Headache	13.0	25.7
Backache	15.2	20.8
Skin Problem	2.2	18.0
Stomach Disorders	4.3	18.0
Eye Problems	8.7	15.3
Tuberculosis	0.0	2.7
Blood Pressure	6.5	2.7
Diabetes	0.0	0.5
Any Other	23.9	27.3

Notes: *: Persistent cough over the past six months.
**: Chest congestion, breathing difficulty.

Table 14.8b

Association between Health Status versus Ownership

	Healthy	*Having Disease*
Reeling Owner-Labourer	71.7	28.3
Reeling Labourer	42.1	57.9

Notes: Chi value is 12.95 which is significant at 1 per cent level. Implying an association between ownership and health status.

Specific Health Problems

A very large proportion of the workers suffered from respiratory problems, and in the SC groups, included 7 males, 18 females, 25 in all, out of the 52 workers, i.e. 48.1 per cent. In comparison with the total workers, 83 out of 229 had respiratory problems, i.e. 36.2 per cent (among non-SCs alone 32.8 per cent had respiratory problems).[5] It is difficult to say conclusively why there should be any large discrepancy between persons of different social groups, since the reeling workers, regardless of their caste or religious background are not very far so far as their economic conditions are concerned. Living conditions too are the same, and all of them live in poor quarters, slum-like surroundings, and with poor water supply and environment. This is not to be confused with the working conditions, where those working in *charka* units (mostly family owned), work in even worse conditions than in the bigger cottage basin units owned by relatively better off owners. From our study, it was not evident that the technology levels (i.e. *charka* or cottage basin) was significantly related to differing incidence of respiratory problems, although earlier we had surmised that there would indeed be a significant difference. As it turned out, those who had respiratory problems and also worked in *charka* units was 40 per cent, and those working in cottage basin units and had respiratory problems was 36 per cent.

Comparing with a group which did not have any sericulture activities in the neighbourhood of their village (a control group), indicated that in their village, the number of those who had respiratory problems was 12 out of a sample of 86 (i.e. 14 per cent, with an equal number of women and men). There was eight of SC background who had respiratory problems out of a total of 46 members of Scheduled Castes (i.e. 17.4 per cent). Again, we find some difference between the incidence of respiratory problems among the persons of Scheduled Castes and others, though the difference is somewhat modest in comparison with those in reeling work. However, a significant difference in the respiratory problems encountered among reeling workers is that a much larger number of women suffer from respiratory problems than men.

While respiratory problems were the main health problem that reeling workers encountered, the number of those who suffered from

5. The International Union against Tuberculosis and Lung Diseases questionnaire was used, after it was translated into Kannada. Not all the information gathered through this questionnaire have been presented here.

respiratory problems caused by allergic reactions to the silk allergens is much lower than the total number of those with respiratory problems. In the overall sample of 229, roughly 17 per cent suffered from allergic reactions to the sericin and pupal allergens, and they could be classified as suffering from occupational asthma (see also N. Harindranath, Om Prakash, P.V. Subba Rao, 1985). However, others who had respiratory problems were those who could be susceptible to the environment in which they worked. This was particularly with reference to the smoke and dust that was usually found in the reeling units. The fuel that is used in the reeling units is biomass fuel, frequently crop residues such as groundnut husk, which is very cheap to buy. However, this type of fuel emits plenty of smoke, and is harmful to the people who work in the reeling units. A factor that may contribute to the health problems of women is that they not only work the whole day in the reeling units, but also spend substantial time cooking food, using wood as fuel. Most women cook twice a day, starting the day at about 5.30 am, and spending about an hour and a half at each time (i.e. morning and evening). Wood smoke is also harmful when inhaled for hours everyday at work. The cumulative effect of burning wood or biomass fuel in their homes and in the working place appears to have caused more harm to the women than to the men (who, in many cases, do not remain at home while the women are engaged in cooking food). Wood smoke (or from biomass fuel) is also implicated in other health problems that the workers have from time to time. For instance, smoke increases the risk of cataract (see Shalini *et al.*, 1994; A. Saha *et al.*, 2005). While a few workers have indicated eye problems among their health problems, it should also be mentioned that workers, particularly in small reeling units, work in conditions where the smoke as well as poor light make it more difficult to see the silk yarn. A common complaint is also that workers get frequent headaches, which could be related to the conditions indicated above, and the indication that owners have less of a problem (headache) could be that they do not work regularly at reeling (i.e. the men who go out to buy cocoons, etc.). In the context of respiratory problems faced by women, reports of studies elsewhere suggest that women in the reproductive years (15-49 years, which includes the overwhelming majority of women reeling workers) have higher incidence of asthma—compared to men in similar age groups, and also, hormonal factors may be connected with airway behaviour (see Becklake and Kauffmann, 1999; Parikh *et al.*, 1999; Osman, 2003).

While this may be the general condition in most units, it appears that there are some variations between units depending on the technology used. With particular reference to the recently introduced innovations of heat retention through the Tata Energy Research Institute (TERI) designed ovens some changes have been observed. Not many units have started using this design, and even those who have tried it find the initial installation cost high.[6] Further, while the innovations in the design of the oven has reduced the amount of fuel required, and the amount of smoke emitted in the reeling units, the problem of fuel remains, i.e. the fuel used is usually the same as earlier, biomass fuel. So the problem of health may have been reduced, but not eradicated. The observation of a unit owner who had installed the TERI designed oven was that workers who are employed in his unit hardly suffer from asthma, but there have been cases of tuberculosis among the workers.[7]

Income and Economic Factors

Reasons for joining reeling work are essentially related to economic factors. For people who live in areas which are silk reeling centres, this seems to be the most regular and suitable occupation to take up, from the income point of view. Other occupations are either not available, or are not sufficiently income generating, for example, agriculture. Hence, in spite of the health problems, people still opt for silk reeling. In fact, despite several physical difficulties caused by the respiratory problems, their immediate reaction to any enquiry about the main effects of asthma is that they lose wages through not being able to go to work every day.

Workers earn daily wages, even though the unit owners pay them

6. There was a case of a woman who was interviewed, who said her unit was one of those which was given a free trial of the new TERI-designed oven attachment. However, they found it expensive to buy it later, and for the time being have postponed the expenditure.

7. Although cases of tuberculosis were observed elsewhere too during our study, a causal link between silk reeling and tuberculosis has not been established.

once a week. They are paid around Rs. 40 to Rs. 55 a day,[8] and usually work about six to seven hours, and six days of the week. While a rough calculation may suggest that a family of four working in reeling units can earn a reasonable family income, this is not usually the case. The income is not regular, and further, even when they have money in hand, workers (particularly the men) tend to spend a substantial portion on items such as liquor and tobacco. Their health problems also aggravate their already precarious living conditions. Work in reeling units is not continuous over the year, and daily wages are relatively low (compared with wages for agricultural labour, which is available for a shorter period of the year than in reeling). However, on the positive side (in their opinion) silk reeling work does not pay different wages to men, women and children. For the same kind of work, all of them are paid the same, and a child who works as a reeling labourer is paid the same as a man or woman who is engaged as a reeling worker. Reeling is an occupation that has a significant presence of child labour, due in no small measure to the facility of offering avenues of employment for men, women and children. They could be from the same family, and hence it is common to find parents introducing their children to work in reeling units, even when the children are very young. Nearly one-third of the women workers had joined a reeling unit when they were less than 10 years old, and some were just six years old when they started work in reeling units. An additional factor that encourages families to bring their children into reeling work is the practise of owners giving advance against wages. These interest-free loans which have to be repaid over a period of time which is convenient to the reeling workers are in one sense beneficial to the workers (in that they can avail a sum of money with minimum security or collateral, and repay it whenever they can, stretching over years). However, a negative feature of such an arrangement is that the worker is attached to the same reeling units for an indefinite period (until the loan is repaid), and often the entire family is pulled into reeling work so that the money can be repaid.

---

8. Wages are not uniform for all workers, in the sense that they can earn more if they produce more silk yarn. This not only favours the more proficient workers, but also those who choose to work longer hours. Reeling unit owners usually prefer to relate the wages to the quantity of silk yarn produced, rather than just the number of hours worked.

Table 14.9

Age when the Worker Joined a Reeling Unit

	6-10 Years Old	11-15 Years Old	Over 16 Years Old	Total
Male	4	8	5	17
Female	11	5	19	35
Total	15	13	24	52

Notwithstanding the assumption that that there could be a greater likelihood that reeling labourers would fall victim to health problems if they started working in silk reeling units at an earlier age (as several of the workers had done), the statistical indications are that there is no association between the two.

Table 14.10

Association between Joining Age and Health Status

	Healthy	Having Disease
6-10 Years	51.0	49.0
11-15 Years	46.6	53.4
16 and Above	47.6	52.4

Note: Chi value = 0.247, not significant, implies that there is no association between age at joining and health status.

The fact of working in reeling units is of particular importance, since, as our respondents indicated, none of those from SC groups had respiratory problems before they started work in reeling units. The entry of people into reeling work has some clear patterns. Those who had started work in reeling units when they were still very young were introduced to this work by their parents or other members of their families. Those who joined when they were over 16 years, and in the case of women, were those who had moved to Sidlaghatta after getting married, who then started work in reeling.

Despite the knowledge that reeling work causes respiratory problems as well as other health problems, particularly if they work in reeling for a relatively long period of time, there is a substantial number of reeling workers who have followed into this line of work after their parents, and among the SC workers, in two cases this is the third generation in reeling. This is not to suggest that they are eager to enter into silk reeling work. There were several SC workers who emphatically stated that they did not want their children to work in reeling (30, including 7 men and 23 women workers). There is no doubt that when women have more forcefully stated that they did not want their children to work in reeling, they were also reflecting the fact that more women suffer from health problems while working in reeling, than the number of men who do. Intergenerational mobility is low among the workers, and as shown below, several workers have parents in reeling. Even those who do not have parents who were in reeling work, they (parents) had worked as manual labourers. Intragenerational mobility also is not significant, where a worker who joins in a reeling unit moves from a job as 'cooker' and then onto a job as a reeling labourer. The wage difference is not high between these two jobs. A supervisor, which is the highest job that a reeling worker can aspire to in the unit, is paid slightly more than a reeling labourer. Workers indicated an aspiration to be a reeling unit owner, and a few actually manage to set up their small units. However, the success rate of such enterprises is low, and the income and sustainability of such enterprises is not high either.[9] The feeling of being an 'owner', which was among the reasons for setting up these enterprises (in addition to the belief that they can earn more than as a reeling worker), did not last long, since they could not keep the units working throughout the year.

Table 14.11

Generations in Reeling (Scheduled Castes)

N=52

	First Generation	*Second Generation*	*Third Generation*	*Total*
Male	9	7	1	17
Female	20	14	1	35
Total	29	21	2	52

9. We found that practically all such small scale enterprises set up in Sidlaghatta, as well as in Ramnagaram—as also seen in earlier studies, had to stop working frequently, and the owners had to take up wage employment in bigger units (see also Inbanathan 1993). However, a study carried out by Linda Mayoux (1993) in Kollegal suggested that there was some striking success among a few Scheduled Caste entrepreneurs.

Table 14.12

Generations of Workers in Silk Reeling

SC = 52; General = 177

	First Generation	*Second Generation*	*Third Generation*	*Mmore than 3 Generations*	*Total*
SC	29 55.7%	21 40.4%	2 3.8%	0	51 100%
General	82 46.3%	87 49.2%	7 4%	1 0.6%	177 100%
Total	111 48.5%	108 47.2%	9 3.9%	1 0.9%	229 100%

The unfortunate relation between low income and higher health problems makes it much more difficult to get out of this situation. Poverty and health problems feed on each other, impeding social mobility. A factor contributing to health problems would be the amount of food that they are able to get each day. A somewhat simple manner in which the possible nutritional levels were ascertained was through asking how many meals the silk workers were able to get, whether twice or thrice a day. Workers of SC groups were more often found among the workers who had only two meals a day, which even among the reeling workers puts them at a lower standard of living.

Table 14.13

Association between Income and Health Status

	Healthy	*Having Disease*
Less than 6000	20.0	80.0
6001-12000	48.7	51.3
12001-24000	37.6	62.4
24001-30000	58.6	41.4
30001 and Above	63.9	36.1

Note: A good association was established between the above two values, which is established by the chi-value being 15.9, which is significant at 1 per cent level.

Table 14.14

Relation between Caste and Number of Meals a Day

	SC	*General*
Twice a Day	67.3	40.1
Thrice a Day	32.7	59.9

Note: A good association is established between caste and the number of meals per day. Chi value is 11.9, which is significant at 1 per cent level.

Women bear several responsibilities, which also enhance or increase their propensity to suffer from various health problems. Their work in the reeling units entails exposure to both silk allergens which are generated through the steam when cocoons are boiled, and also to the pollution caused by burning biomass fuel in these units. Further, they are also exposed to several hours of wood fuel smoke in their homes while they cook food. Taken together, such exposure faced by the women could cause respiratory problems in some, and aggravate respiratory problems in others. As we observed, women who took time off from reeling work due to their respiratory problems, were often not at the same time able to avoid cooking food at home. During this time, as a woman complained, her main problem was that she could not blow through the pipe to raise the flame for cooking, since she immediately started coughing. Thus, avoiding the cooking of food, and keeping away from the cooking stove, was possible only if they were hospitalised due to acute respiratory problems. Reasons for stopping work from reeling were not only due to health reasons. There were several times when reeling had to be stopped, particularly in smaller units, for example, when the price of cocoons went very high, or higher than what the reeling unit's owner could sustain.

Women are exposed to biomass fuel smoke for much of the day, both at work (as with reeling workers), as well as through their cooking food at their homes (see also Laxmi *et al.*, 2003). Men too face a similar environment that causes respiratory problems, and they work through the day in reeling units as the women workers. There is a feature, however, that is peculiar to the men, and that is, almost all the male reeling workers smoke tobacco. They take several breaks during work to smoke, and smoke after work from reeling too.

However, they do not usually face the smoke from cooking at home. Respiratory problems faced by men are almost always also aggravated by *beedi* smoking (which is considered as even more harmful than cigarettes; see Chhabra *et al.*, 2001).

Figure 14.4

Reasons Given for Stopping Work

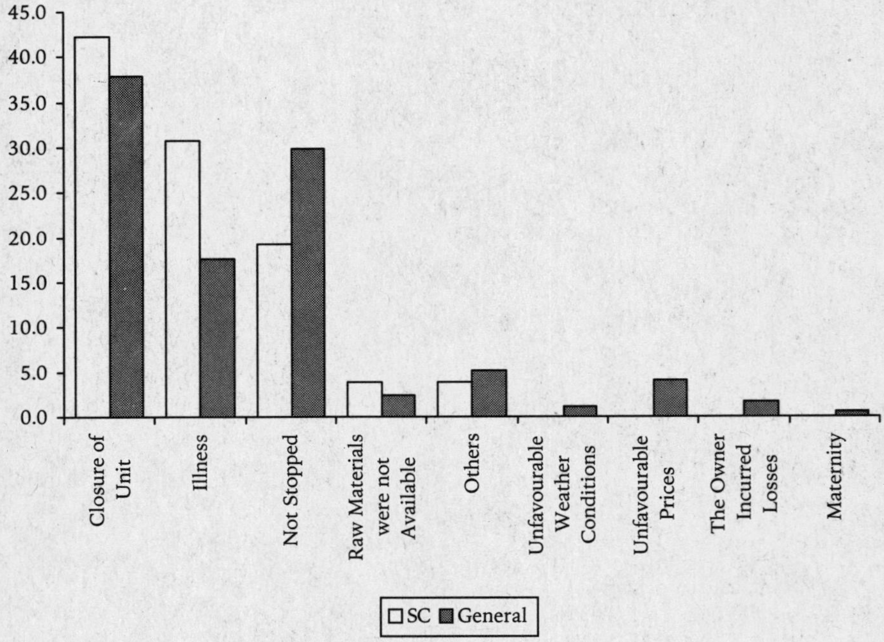

Table 14.15

Needed to be Hospitalised for Breathing Difficulties

N=52 (SC); N=177 (General)

		Yes	*No*	*Total*
SC	Male	5	12	17
	Female	10	25	35
		15	37	52
General	Male	10	85	95
	Female	17	65	82
		27	150	177

The unusual circumstances of the silk reeling is the fact that workers know that health problems may follow from working in reeling. Moreover, even in their perception of the cause of death of those of their families who have passed away, they have implicated asthma as the cause of death in a very significant number of cases. There are no means of ascertaining whether this was indeed so, since it was very rarely that medical doctors were involved in certifying the cause of death after proper clinical investigation. The Registrar's office in Sidlaghatta that maintains the record of births and deaths also had a column of the cause of death. In many cases, the cause of death was listed as asthma (it was usually one of the deceased person's family who filled in the details in the register, or gave the details that were filled in).

Discussion

In a situation of acute poverty, people of Sidlaghatta take up silk reeling as their means to earn a living. However, they face the twin problems of working in an atmosphere that has silk allergens and which cause allergic reactions in some people, as well as asthma. The other condition is one of pollution caused by burning biomass fuel, to boil the cocoons and release the silk yarn. A recurring question in this context is, why do people work in reeling units when they know the conditions of work as well as the consequent health problems. Most families have members who suffer from such problems as acute cough, chest congestion, and difficulties in breathing. On the other hand, there are also several silk reeling workers who do not suffer from breathing or asthma problems. This is what makes them take a chance on the possibility that they would not succumb to the same problems, but would be able to carry on a full working life without such health problems as asthma, or other less debilitating diseases. However, with a very high proportion of workers being victims of respiratory problems, this seems to be a high-risk occupation, which leads to not only health problems but also a lessening of their quality of life.

Workers of Scheduled Caste background share many of the characteristics of the other, non SC workers, in that they are all of almost similar economic condition (though, SC workers' family-incomes are even lower than those of other castes/groups), have similar lifestyles, and by and large suffer from similar problems of health. None of the problems are specific to their castes, but are problems related to the occupation, and the technological levels of the reeling units. As essentially simple technology, which most people can master very soon, and very cheap to install and manage, reeling units tend to have the kind of environment that affects people alike, regardless of their social background. In the social milieu in which they worked, their caste identities were not really a significant problem. Workers were more concerned about their livelihood and employment rather than their castes. Living accommodation was often based on their castes, though this may not have been of their choice, but that of their employers, who gave some form of living quarters for all their workers, which was usually in the same locality. However, some degree of separation between communities was also observed, where for example, SCs chose to live on different sides of the street depending on their caste. For example, *Madigas* lived on one side of the street, and *Holeyas* on the other. But in the working space, none of the workers indicated that they suffered any form of discrimination.

While the problems associated with silk allergens have been confirmed in terms of their causal relationship, and may be classified under occupational asthma, a considerable grey area persists with the remaining and still high proportion that does not show allergic reactions to the silk allergens but do have respiratory problems. In the literature, this has been linked with atmospheric pollution, or indoor pollution, and the burning of biomass fuel for cooking. While the studies reported on their findings of cooking stoves and cooking food, the relationship is almost entirely with women, who do the bulk of cooking in most homes, and are the ones who are near these stoves and face the most of polluted air and smoke. What needs to be emphasised in silk reeling is that women constitute the predominant number of workers, and they are in an environment of both silk allergens as well as smoke from burning biomass fuel, and therefore are the major victims of respiratory problems. That they also cook food at home, is an additional problem that they endure. The literature also gives an indication that children who are less than five years of age also suffer from health problems as a consequence of being in the proximity of wood/biomass smoke. These should be considered along with the problems of the women silk workers, who spend hours in the reeling units and then again in front of their cooking stoves at home. Their children/infants also suffer similar conditions since infants are usually placed in the corner of reeling units, or even on the women's laps, and inhale both the silk allergens as well as the wood/biomass smoke. While no large scale survey which includes a clinical examination seems to have been done to confirm the morbidity among infants of reeling workers, there is every reason to expect that they too suffer from various health problems (see also Celedon *et al.*, 2001, on the situation in China; and Uragoda and Wijekoon, 1991). These are due not only to their own proximity to harmful physical conditions, but their problems may have their origins even before they are born, i.e. while their mothers work in reeling units and also cook food using wood/biomass fuel (on related problems of low birth weight, respiratory tract infections see Mishra, 2003, Mishra *et al.*, 2004).

An additional factor that needs to be discussed in this context is the incidence of health problems among reeling women workers as compared to men who work in reeling. Our data have indicated that women tend to fall sick more often, and also have a higher severity of asthma or respiratory problems than men. We should indicate that men are by no means in robust health (as our clinical tests indicated), considering also their propensity to consume large quantities of alcohol, and they tend to be heavy smokers of *beedis* as well. Despite this, they stated that they were in better health, and were hospitalised less often than women. It appears that the reproductive function, and number of children they bear, may have a bearing on the health of women, in addition to the other factors such as biofuel and silk allergy.

There is always a dilemma associated with the working of the reeling industry. While the people who are poor need work to earn a living, their low skills and virtually no education (most of them are illiterate), make it difficult for them to get jobs elsewhere. The silk reeling technology that is predominantly used is of relatively simple design and technology, making it possible for poorly educated people to work with them. However, the health problems associated with reeling adversely affects their ability to save any part of their income, and makes it less likely that they can move out of reeling, or into better paying and higher skill occupations. This makes it even more likely that most of the reeling workers will remain in reeling for their working life, and their children too, would in many cases, enter and remain in reeling work.

The technological innovations that have been introduced have been with the intention of making silk reeling 'more efficient', and thus, there have been some changes in the design of the reeling equipment, and the ovens that are used in reeling units. Though they are more efficient in using fuel, and also save on the amount of fuel needed, the newly designed ovens have the same drawback as earlier, and i.e. the reeling units still use biomass fuel. There is less smoke than earlier, but smoke still remains a problem in the units, and brought about through burning the same fuel such as groundnut husk, wood chips, other crop residues, and essentially cheap fuel. Health problems associated with smoke from burning biomass fuel is still a major problem in most units. Further, even the units which may use more recently devised technology still have the problem of workers facing steam from hot water in which cocoons are placed, in front of them while they are reeling the silk yarn. Thus, health problems may have been marginally reduced, but still exist.

A disease that a few workers have is often associated with the burning of biomass fuel, i.e. tuberculosis. Tuberculosis has not been confirmed as being 'caused' by smoke from biomass fuel, but has been shown to be associated in some way, i.e. statistically shown to be related to smoke from burning biomass fuel (Mishra *et al.*, 1999). In reeling units, which are relatively small, and with several workers in close physical proximity, someone with TB can spread the disease through coughing, which happens (cough) often in the smoke filled units.

Two important factors impinge on the situation of the workers. The first being poverty, keeps them working in reeling, which uses fuel that is on the lowest rung of the energy ladder. The same fuel is used in their homes to cook food, and this is also a reflection of their relatively low income. The second is a major item of expenditure incurred to try and reduce the impact of their respiratory problems, and that is the use of alcohol. Both men and women consume alcohol, in varying quantities, as a 'medicinal drink'. From clinical reports, it appears that alcohol may in fact have beneficial effects on some individuals (to dilate air passages), and may be used in moderation (Cuddy and Guohua, 2001). However, from information that workers gave, and particularly the men, a significant quantum of their incomes, may be even upto half their daily wages (as several men indicated) is spent on buying alcohol.

Conclusion

Considering sericulture as a means to improve the economic conditions of poor people, including those of the Scheduled Castes, is fraught with problems of another kind. Inasmuch as income is generated through sericulture, and may be seen as a positive outcome, it simultaneously, and as a by-product, causes and is instrumental in health problems in a significant proportion of workers. This is particularly so in silk reeling, which provides employment and income to many, but leads to a poor quality of life due to their ill health. With a substantial portion of their income being spent on medicines and medical treatment, the possibility of effecting any savings is virtually impossible. Further, much of their income is required for basic subsistence, and therefore, very little is left for their children's education. In fact, the children too contribute towards the family income by working in reeling units, and thus, play an adult role even when they are very young (some are less than ten years old). Reeling as a means of social mobility has limitations, and can hardly be considered as an effective means of improving the lives of the workers in the long run. In the short run, it does provide some income, and the possibility of supporting their bare existence.

References

Bajpai, Nirupam and Sangeeta Goyal (2004). "Primary Healthcare in India: Coverage and Quality Issues", Centre on Globalisation and Sustainable Development, *Working Paper* No. 15. New York: Columbia University.

Becklake, Margaret R. and Francine Kauffmann (1999). "Gender Differences in Airway Behaviour over the Human Life Span", *Thorax* 54(12): 1119-38.

Celedon, Juan C., Lyle J. Palmer, Xiping Xu, Binyan Wang, Zhian Fang and Scott Weiss (2001). "Sensitization to Silk and Childhood Asthma in Rural China", *Paediatrics*, Vol. No. 107 (5): e80. *http://pediatrics.aappublications.org/cgi/content/full/107/5/e80*.

Chen, B.H., C.J. Hong, M.R. Pandey and K.R. Smith (1990). "Indoor Air Pollution in Developming Countries", *World Health Statistical Quarterly* 43(3): 127-38.

Chhabra, S.K., S. Rajpal and Raj Gupta (2001). "Patterns of Smoking in Delhi and Comparison of Chronic Respiratory Morbidity among *Beedi* and Cigarette Smokers", *Indian Journal of Chest Diseases and Allied Sciences* 43(1): 19-26.

Cuddy, R. and L. Guohua (2001). "The Role of Alcohol in Asthma: A Review of Clinical and Experimental Studies", *American Journal of Emergency Medicine* 19: 501-503.

Harindranath, N., Om Prakash, P.V. Subba Rao (1985). "Prevalence of Occupational Asthma in Silk Filatures", *Annals of Allergy* 55(3): 511-15.

Inbanathan, Anand (1993). "Scheduled Caste Women in Reeling industry", *Indian Silk* 32(7): 13-21.

Jarvis, Deborah and Peter Burney (2000). "Epidemiology of Asthma", in William W. Busse and Stephen T. Holgate (eds.), *Asthma and Rhinitis*, Edition II: 17-32. New York: Blackwell Science.

Laxmi, Vijay, Jyoti Parikh, Shyam Karmakar and Promod Dabrase (2003). "Household Energy, Women's Hardship and Health Impacts in Rural Rajasthan, India: Need for Sustainable Energy Solutions", *Energy for Sustainable Development* 7(1): 50-68.

Martin, Lawrence (2000). "Occupational Asthma," *http://www.mtsinai.org/pulmonary/occupationalasthma.htm*.

Mayoux, Linda (1993). "A Development Success Story? Low Caste Entrepreneurship and Inequality: An Indian Case Study", *Development and Change* 24: 541-68.

Mishra, Vinod K., Robert D. Retherford and Kirk R. Smith (1999). "Cooking with Biomass Fuels Increases the Risk of Tuberculosis", *National Family Health Survey Bulletin* 13.

Mishra, Vinod, Xiaolei Dai, Kirk R. Smith, Lasten Mika (2004). "Maternal Exposure to Biomass Smoke and Reduced Birth Weight in Zimbabwe", *Annals of Epidemiology* 14 (10): 740-47.

Mishra, Vinod (2003). "Indoor Air Pollution from Biomass Combustion and Acute Respiratory Illness in Preschool Age Children in Zimbabwe", *International Journal of Epidemiology* 32: 847-53.

Osman, M., "Therapeutic Implications of Sex Differences in Asthma and Atopy", *Archives of Disease in Childhood* 88: 587-90.

Parikh, Jyoti, Kirk Smith, Vijay Laxmi (1999). "Indoor Air Pollution: A Reflection on Gender Bias", *Economic and Political Weekly* 34(9): 539-44.

Saha, A., P.K. Kulkarni, A. Shah, M. Patel and H.N. Saiyed (2005). "Ocular Morbidity and Fuel Use: An Experience from India", *Occupational and Environmental Medicine* 62: 66-69.

Schirnding, Yasmin von, Nigel Bruce, Kirk Smith, Grant Ballard-Tremeer, Majid Ezzati and Kseniya Lvovsky (2002). "Addressing the Impact of Household Energy and Indoor Air Pollution on the Health of the Poor: Implications for Policy Action and Intervention Measures". Paper prepared for the *Commission on Macroeconomics and Health*. World Health Organization.

Shalini, V.K., M. Luthra, L. Srinivas, S.H. Rao, S. Basti, M. Reddy, D. Balasubramanian (1994). "Oxidative Damage to the Eye Lens Caused by Cigarette Smoke and Fuel Smoke Condensates", *Indian Journal of Biochemistry and Biophysics* 31(4):261-266.

Shrestha, Iswori Lal and Srijan Lal Shrestha (2005). "Indoor Air Pollution from Biomass Fuels and Respiratory Health of the Exposed Population in Nepalese Households", *International Journal of Occupational and Environmental Health* 11(2): 150-60.

Uragoda C.G and P.N. Wijekoon (1991). "Asthma in Silk Workers", *Journal of the Society of Occupational Medicine* 41(3): 140-42.

Yeh, Ethan (2004). "Indoor Air Pollution in Developing Countries: Household Use of Traditional Biomass Fuels and the Impact on Mortality", University of California, Berkeley.

Youakim, Sami (2001). "Work-related Asthma", *American Family Physician* 64(11): 1839-48.

15

Systematic Hierarchies and Systemic Failures

Gender and Health Inequities in Koppal District

GITA SEN, ADITI IYER and ASHA GEORGE[1]

Introduction

Although Karnataka is among the more socially advanced southern states of India, it lags behind its other southern neighbours, particularly Kerala and Tamilnadu on many dimensions. According to the *Karnataka Human Development Report* of 1999, Karnataka was in the middle among the 15 major states on many dimensions of human development (GoK, 1999). The primary reason for this middling position is that average indicators for the state conceal striking disparities among the districts within it. The northern districts of Karnataka, of which Koppal is one, form a cluster of poorly performing districts that pull down these average indicators.[2]

Koppal is one of the poorer districts in Karnataka where drought periodically takes its toll on the agrarian economy. The lack of income and livelihoods security forces people to migrate or undertake work at great risk to their health. Deprivation is widespread. Public services, including health, exist but are inadequately developed and largely of poor quality. Even private services, because of the widespread poverty of consumers, tend to be thin on the ground, and leave much to be

---

1. This paper is part of work done at the Indian Institute of Management, Bangalore under the Gender and Health Equity Project. We would like to especially thank Chandan Mukherjee for his unstinting willingness to provide statistical and econometric advice and Shon John for competent statistical assistance. We also wish to acknowledge our anonymous reviewer for helpful comments on the first draft of this paper.

2. See the Report of the Nanjundappa Committee (Nanjundappa *et al.*, 2002) for a detailed analysis of the historical and contemporary reasons for these intrastate disparities.

desired in terms of their quality. Belief systems are strongly gender-biased; traditional practices include many that are inimical to women's health and well-being. Poor women's lives are marked by low levels of literacy, inadequate diets, hard labour, below minimum wages, recurring fatigue and illness.

In the midst of these hardships, poor women are also more vulnerable to inferior health outcomes due to denial of their human rights, including their reproductive and sexual rights. Maternal morbidity and mortality are high even as son preference and high infant death rates contribute to repeated childbearing. Reproductive morbidity is common but is often unspoken or taken as a 'natural' part of women's existence. Anaemia is endemic but is only casually—and ineffectively—addressed by public health programmes. Many of these problems have clearly been present over a long period of time. More recently, the threat of HIV infection looms over the region, and infection rates including among women have been going up sharply due to a combination of poor awareness, weak prevention, cyclical out-migration for work, and the denial of women's sexual and reproductive rights. Koppal shows up poorly in many of the health indicators that health administrators and policy makers use.

Health and health care inequities in Koppal reflect systematic hierarchies based on gender, caste, economic class, and life-stage; they also reveal systemic failures in health care services, both public and private. Although over the years, the government has implemented many public health programmes, they appear to have made little difference to girls' and women's health status or health care access on the ground. Three main reasons can be attributed. First, significant gender biases, low levels of health awareness and lack of acknowledgement of certain health problems by families and by health providers have a negative impact on health–seeking behaviour. Second, widespread poverty and, especially recently, rising health costs reduce access even to public health services. Third, government health services have tended to be so top-down in their approach, so gender-biased (or at best gender-blind), so poor in quality and so unresponsive that they have been unable to bridge the gap between service providers and their intended beneficiaries. On the other hand, NGO-implemented projects have tended to be difficult to replicate or scale up.

The unfortunate interplay between systematic hierarchies and systemic failures makes it possible for families and communities on the one side and health providers on the other to exonerate themselves and hold the other side responsible for poor health status and outcomes. Families and communities tend to blame health providers for insensitivity, negligence, and the sheer absence of services; health providers typically hold the view that women and their families are ignorant, superstitious, and careless. Our research reveals undoubted elements of truth on both sides. Nonetheless the 'blame game' diverts attention away from the absence of accountability by both, and the low levels of acknowledgement overall of women's health needs. At the same time, however, changes are also occurring. For instance, whether because of government awareness programmes or not, health seeking by women and their families from private and public providers is far higher than one might anticipate, especially for maternal health. Despite this, preventable maternal deaths continue to be high, and women die in unconscionable numbers from causes related to childbearing.

The paper will present empirical evidence and analysis of health inequities in 60 villages[3] in two *talukas* (sub-districts) of Koppal. It draws on insights gained through research, community mobilisation and institution building efforts for the Gender and Health Equity Project. It will argue that both the systemic and the systematic elements need to be tackled if any policy or programme changes are to really take hold. The research to date has had four main components:

- A health survey of 1920 households.
- A census of private healthcare providers.
- Qualitative research about government service delivery.
- Qualitative enquiry into maternal deaths.

---

3. Fifty-six villages were selected by MSK, four of which have *tandas* large enough to be considered administratively by MSK as separate villages, which leads to the total of 60 villages. A *tanda* is a sub-group of houses populated, in the project site, by a ST group (*Lambanis*).

Koppal District—Human Development and Gender

Karnataka with its population of 52 million accounts for a little over 5 per cent of the population of India (Census of India, 2001). The present Karnataka state was formed in 1956 by combining Kannada language districts from the then states of Madras, Hyderabad, Bombay and Coorg with the former princely state of Mysore. As was true in other parts of India (e.g. Kerala), the area under the princely state of Mysore was better on social and economic indicators at independence than the districts that had been under direct colonial rule. On the other hand, the Northern part of the state belonging to the old 'Hyderabad-Karnataka' which was under the Nizam's rule, tended to be much worse off.

These differences have persisted after independence as noted by the Nanjundappa Committee's Report (Nanjundappa *et al.*, 2002). While many reasons such as the drought-proneness of agriculture, and semiaridity can be adduced for the greater poverty of the northern districts, significant gender inequalities and biases seriously hamper social and economic development in this region. These inequalities are a major reason for the poor health and other indicators of the region. They also come in the way of government health programmes and constrain their effectiveness while providing a ready excuse for government functionaries and even NGOs for their own limitations.

Koppal, a small northern district carved out of the erstwhile Raichur, is a dry district with four *talukas*, a population of 1.193 million, and an overall literacy rate of 55 per cent (IIPS, 2006). Its indicators are near the bottom for the state. Table 15.1 which includes a number of human development indicators places Koppal at or very near the bottom on many of these. Although not uniformly the lowest on all the sub-indicators, this is cold comfort since it lies fairly close to the worst levels for all. Table 15.2, drawn from the All-India District Level Rapid Household Survey conducted in 1998-99 under the Reproductive and Child Health (RCH) programme corroborates this for a number of specific health-related indicators for women.

Additional data from the same source (IIPS, 2006: 48-49; Koppal—Key Indicators) reveals the following: age at first cohabitation among currently married women (ages 15-44) was below 18 in 73.9 per cent

Table 15.1

District-wise Selected Key Indicators of Karnataka

Sl. No.	*Districts*	*Per cent Female Literacy*	*Per cent Girls Married Below 18 Years*	*Per cent Current Users of FP Method*	*Per cent Birth Order 3 & Above*	*Per cent Safe Delivery*	*Per cent Complete Immunisation on*	*Per cent Decadal Population Growth Rate*	*Region*
1	Hassan	59.32	15.20	75.10	19.70	69.70	92.80	9.66	Old Mysore
2	Shimoga	67.24	16.50	69.30	22.80	83.00	92.90	12.90	Old Mysore
3	Kodagu	72.53	22.00	70.60	18.80	79.40	94.80	11.64	Old Mysore
4	Dakshina Kannada	77.39	4.50	63.70	32.00	91.50	86.00	14.51	Old Mysore
5	Uttar Kannada	68.48	15.00	66.00	27.20	86.10	89.90	10.90	Bombay Karnataka
6	Udupi	74.02	4.50	63.70	32.00	91.50	86.00	6.88	Old Mysore
7	Mandya	51.62	37.00	71.70	26.10	61.90	88.00	7.14	Old Mysore
8	Mysore	55.81	47.90	65.40	23.90	69.70	92.70	15.04	Old Mysore
9	Bangalore Rural	78.98	21.05	63.00	16.40	79.10	83.70	34.80	Old Mysore
10	Bangalore Urban	78.98	37.00	60.10	26.10	90.60	77.00	34.80	Old Mysore
11	Chitradurga	54.62	30.05	59.90	34.40	53.80	88.40	15.05	Old Mysore
12	Tumkur	57.18	27.10	61.30	27.30	63.50	88.00	11.87	Old Mysore
13	Dharwad	62.20	36.50	61.20	37.40	65.30	74.80	16.65	Bombay Karnataka
14	Chamraj Nagar	43.02	47.90	65.40	23.90	69.70	92.70	9.16	Old Mysore
15	Chikkamagalur	64.47	37.00	71.40	26.10	78.00	83.50	11.98	Old Mysore
16	Kolar	52.81	33.50	57.10	29.70	59.20	90.60	13.83	Old Mysore
17	Gadag	52.58	36.50	61.20	37.40	65.30	74.80	13.14	Bombay Karnataka
18	Belgaum	52.53	55.80	61.80	36.70	68.60	64.80	17.40	Bombay Karnataka
19	Haveri	57.60	36.50	61.20	37.40	65.30	74.80	13.29	Bombay Karnataka
20	Bellary	46.16	44.20	50.40	48.60	54.00	52.60	22.30	Hyderabad Karnataka
21	Davangere	58.45	35.50	59.90	34.40	53.80	53.80	14.78	Old Mysore
22	Bijapur	46.19	64.80	47.10	43.00	50.10	53.20	17.63	Bombay Karnataka
23	Bidar	50.01	67.60	50.60	52.90	52.50	50.30	19.56	Hyderabad Karnataka
24	Raichur	36.84	57.10	45.40	52.80	48.00	37.20	21.93	Hyderabad Karnataka
25	Gulbarga	38.40	47.70	39.20	53.70	47.70	25.30	21.02	Hyderabad Karnataka
26	Bagalkot	44.10	64.80	47.10	43.00	50.10	53.20	18.84	Bombay Karnataka
27	**Koppal**	**40.76**	**57.10**	**45.40**	**52.80**	**48.00**	**37.20**	**24.57**	**Hyderabad Karnataka**

Source: GoK, 2003: 10.

of the cases; 41 per cent of them had illiterate husbands; and 51.4 per cent of girls married during 1999 (until the survey) were below 18.

Table 15.2

Range of RCH Indicators in Karnataka

	Indicators	*Minimum*		*Maximum*		*Koppal*
1	Girls married below 18 (%)	2.2	Kodagu	59.4	Raichur	51.4
2	Illiterate eligible women (%)	19.9	B'lr urban	74.9	Raichur	66.8
3	Total fertility rate	1.37	Mandya	2.98	Raichur	2.77
4	Birth order 3 and above (%)	11.9	B'lr urban	51.0	Gulbarga	48.2
5	Infant mortality rate (per 1000 live births)	16.3	B'lr urban	88.7	Koppal	
6	Knowledge of any modern family planning methods (%)	97.3	Raichur	99.8	Gulbarga	98.5
7	Current use of modern FP methods (%)	40.3	Gulbarga	73.5	Mandya	42.4
8	Full antenatal check-up (%)	12.8	Gulbarga	49.8	Bangalore rural	24.4
9	Safe delivery (%)	41.2	Gulbarga	95.7	Bangalore urban	52.8
10	Full immunisation (%)	48.1	Gulbarga	95.2	Bangalore urban	50.2
11	Eligible women aware of HIV (%)	37.7	Raichur	89.2	Kodagu	41.4
12	Use of govt. health facilities for antenatal care (%)	7.2	Uttar Kannada	60.6	Kodagu	19.4

Source: IIPS, 2006.

For women in Koppal, in addition to a life of hardship shared with poor men, gender power takes the form of curtailed autonomy and domestic violence. Women are married into their in-laws' households while very young, making it harder for them to have a voice of their own. Once married there is tremendous pressure to bear children, especially sons. The health implications of having closely spaced pregnancies at a young age further exacerbate existing malnutrition, anaemia and the risks of future maternal morbidity and mortality.

Apart from son preference, high fertility in northern Karnataka (Sekher *et al.* 2001), is also a counter to high neonatal and infant mortality with the trade off being women's reproductive well being. It is not considered unusual for a woman to have repeated miscarriages or abortions. The reasoning being that if a pregnancy is lost, a woman can always get pregnant again (Umamani & Yogananda 2003). Yet such attitudes hold significant risks for women's health, especially considering existing levels of unrecognised but high reproductive morbidity. Maternal deaths, however, represent only the extreme end of a continuum of underlying maternal morbidity. Not only are the risks to women of maternal mortality and morbidity undervalued, but so are their direct linkages to neonatal well being and survival.

Such risks to women's and newborn health are heightened by the hazards of poverty as has been documented in various studies in different parts of south India. In Andhra Pradesh, all of the women dying from pregnancy and obstetric complications were reported to have been working as labourers for subsistence reasons (ANS, 2001). In Tamilnadu, many women who had uterine prolapse ascribed their condition to heavy manual labour within a week or fortnight following delivery, possibly explaining why the mean age for developing symptoms was 26 years (Ravindran *et al.* 1999). In southern Karnataka, women continued to undertake strenuous work until late in their pregnancy (Mathews *et al.* 2001). When pregnant and postnatal women are forced to do heavy manual labour in order to survive, health education messages asking them to 'take rest' while pregnant have little relevance to the hard reality of their lives.

Methodology

Our research uses both quantitative and qualitative methods to study the patterns of systematic hierarchy and system failures in health-seeking behaviour and access to health care. The quantitative data are based on a cross-sectional survey designed to document intra- and inter-household inequities in health care-seeking during sickness and pregnancy. It also sought to elicit household level attitudes to education of girls, attitudes to gender power, and domestic violence. A household census conducted prior to the survey in 60 villages enumerated 15,358 households and 82,901 individuals. A unistage-stratified sampling design was adopted with households as the sample units. The project villages under each PHC were grouped, and each group treated as a separate stratum. With eight PHCs in the project area, there were thus eight strata. A sample was drawn from each stratum to the extent of 12.5 per cent of all the households within it leading to 1920 households.

Systematic Hierarchies

Our broad starting hypothesis was that intersecting hierarchies of economic class, caste and gender (as well as the individual position in the life cycle) would affect attitudes to her health needs, and health seeking behaviour. In this paper we do not go into the details of all these intersections, but only focus on the ways in which gender affects health seeking behaviour. Nonetheless it is impossible to avoid commenting on the class and caste realities that permeate and define people's lives, their perceptions, and their behaviour because of their possible interactions with gender hierarchies.

Economic Class and Caste

The economic position of a household is largely defined, in this poor and largely unirrigated agricultural district, by relationship to land, which in turn defines the extent of the household's dependence on sending out its members as casual wage labourers. As Koppal is a dry and drought prone region, agricultural productivity depends not merely on the amount of land owned but also on the possibility of ground water irrigation. Bore wells and 'pump sets' are important assets for this reason. In our survey, most households (84.1 per cent) owned some land, but only 24.3 per cent owned pump sets. The overall share of landless and small (< 5 acres) unirrigated farm-owning households was as high as 51.8 per cent. 23.9 per cent of households owned unirrigated land equal to or above 5 acres. Households owning irrigated land constituted only 24 per cent of all households.

Our survey did not undertake a detailed study of the quality of irrigation, but this is obviously important in determining the extent to which a household can rely on income from self-employment versus sending out family members as wage labourers. Overall, the major source of income for most households was through self-employment (53.4 per cent), followed by casual wage labour (39.8 per cent). Regular wage employment was rare, as only 5.2 per cent of the households derived their income from it. This picture varied considerably by the household's landholding.

Landless households depended mainly on casual wage labour (61.6 per cent) and artisanal work such as basket or pot making (21.1 per cent). Among unirrigated landholding (< 5 acres) households, only 36.1 per cent managed on self-employment; 57.9 per cent of these also depended on casual wage labour. By contrast, self-employment without resort to casual wage labour characterised the larger unirrigated landholding (equal to or > 5 acres) households (70.1 per cent), as well as the irrigated landholding households whether small (72.8 per cent) or large (91.1 per cent). Nevertheless, it is clear that owning a plot of land larger than 5 acres or owning a small irrigated plot does not insure almost 30 per cent of such households from casual wage labour.

Most families (78.3 per cent) owned the houses they inhabited. However, only 29.1 per cent of the owned houses were *pucca*[4] structures. Around one-fourth (or 22.7 per cent) were semi-*pucca* structures but 48.1 per cent were *kuccha* structures. While electricity was not uncommon, very few of even the *pucca* houses had piped water (15 per cent) or toilets (4.2 per cent). Government-allotted housing was only 14.3 per cent of the total (much less than the 26.7 per cent population share of SC/ST households for whom such housing is meant), not all of which was *pucca*, and only 57 per cent of which had electricity while none had toilets or piped water supply.

Caste variations tend to follow the economic class patterns[5] as can be seen from Table 15.3. Upper castes have more large irrigated holdings than the average; while they also have more landless households than the middle castes, this may reflect the fact that almost 9 per cent have regular employment as the major source of income. Middle caste landholding is near the average for all households although they have less irrigated landholding above 5 acres

4. Adopting the NSS definition, we defined *pucca* houses as those that had *pucca* roofs and *pucca* walls. Semi-*pucca* houses were those that had *pucca* roofs but *kuccha* walls, or *kuccha* roofs but *pucca* walls. Kuccha houses were those that had *kuccha* roofs and *kuccha* walls.

5. A detailed enumeration and checking of caste groups was undertaken; details are available in Annexure 3 of Iyer (2005).

than the average. SC/ST households have higher proportions of landless and casual wage labourers.

Table 15.3

Caste, Class and Landholding

	Per cent Landless	*Per cent Owning less than 5 Acres of Unirrigated Land*	*Per cent Owning 5 or more Acres of Unirrigated Land*	*Per cent Owning less than 5 Acres of Irrigated Land*	*Per cent Owning 5 or more Acres of Irrigated Land*	*Per cent Casual Wage Earning Households*	*Per cent Distribution of all Households*
Upper castes	13.3	28.6	29.1	8.5	20.2	24.7	28.3
Middle castes	11.4	35.2	28.0	9.8	15.6	36.9	37.8
SCs /STs	20.9	45.8	14.3	11.7	7.2	59.2	26.7
Muslims	29.6	31.2	17.1	8.5	13.6	39.9	4.1
All households[1]	15.9	36.0	24.0	9.8	14.3	39.8	100.0

Note: [1]: 3 per cent belong to other castes.

Source: Gender and Health Equity household survey.

How do these variations in the economic and social status of households translate into health-seeking behaviour? Are there significant differences across households and within them by gender, age or life-cycle status?

Healthcare Needs and Gendered Health Seeking

The survey classified illness by its duration—short-term (lasting < 3 months) or long-term (> 3 months), and by its severity.[6] Self-reported morbidity was high overall, with 82 per cent of households reporting at least one sick person during the reference period. Considerable care was taken in designing probes to overcome the well –known biases in self-reported morbidity, although this may not have been completely successful because our interviewers were local people who were trained by us but were relatively inexperienced. Treatment seeking for illness was also high—almost 90 per cent of illnesses

6. Severity for short-term sickness was measured in terms of difficulty in eating normally, in doing regular work in—and outside—the house, and being able to go outside the house. For long-term sickness, severity was measured in terms of difficulty in going to school, doing housework or other work, and in income-earning.

reported for girls/women, and over 90 per cent for boys/men were treated.[7]

Within this overall picture, health-seeking behaviour varied along a number of dimensions, such as gender within the household, and also by the economic class of the household, and the duration and severity of the illness. Economic class in this analysis is represented by per capita household consumption expenditure quintiles.[8]

The analysis below first presents some cross-tabulated data for short- and long-term illnesses. For short-term illnesses the responses were classified into two categories based on whether the person ever received treatment. For long-term illnesses, the responses were classified into three categories based on whether the person ever received treatment, and whether the treatment was discontinued. Multinomial logit regressions were also run on the data to check for the nature and statistical significance of interactions among economic class and gender.[9]

Table 15.4.1 shows that, for short-term sickness, the proportions of girls/women who were never treated[10] was significantly higher than the same proportions of boys/men within every expenditure quintile. However, there is not much variation across the expenditure quintiles per se; treatment levels generally appear to be high regardless of household economic class.

---

7. The high levels of treatment-seeking in our survey may be affected by two factors: the confounding of illness with treatment, wherein people only acknowledge illness as such if it is treated; second, the fairly broad definition of treatment-seeking used in the survey. Nonetheless, even our qualitative and in-depth inquiry into the circumstances of maternal death reveals the same phenomenon of high-levels of health seeking.
8. The plausibility of these self-reported consumption expenditure data has been crosschecked by examining the distributions and also comparing the corresponding National Sample Survey data.
9. There are clearer hypotheses about how and why gender and class might influence health-seeking than there are for caste. Caste is likely to affect the choice of provider and quality of care obtained, but not the decision of whether or not to seek treatment. Our analysis of gender and caste *vis-à-vis* health seeking for short-and long-term sickness shows that caste per se does not discriminate among households when it comes to discontinued, or non-treatment. Interactions based on caste are part of our ongoing work but not explored in this paper.
10. We refer to sick persons and sicknesses interchangeably while discussing Tables 15.4.1 and 15.4.2, because most persons (73.9 per cent) in fact reported only one sickness.

Table 15.4.1

Health-seeking by Gender and Economic Class

Gender-based Groups within Per Capita Consumption Expenditure Quintiles	*Short-term Sicknesses*				
	Ever Treated (%)		*Never Treated (%)*		*p value*[1]
Quintile 1 (poorest)					
Female	1488	(89.0)	184	(11.0)	0.000
Male	1334	(96.5)	48	(3.5)	
Total	2822	(92.4)	232	(7.6)	
Quintile 2					
Female	1385	(84.5)	255	(15.5)	0.000
Male	1285	(94.1)	80	(5.9)	
Total	2670	(88.9)	335	(11.1)	
Quintile 3					
Female	1587	(89.5)	187	(10.5)	0.000
Male	1201	(94.9)	64	(5.1)	
Total	2788	(91.7)	251	(8.3)	
Quintile 4					
Female	1304	(93.7)	87	(6.3)	0.000
Male	1179	(97.4)	32	(2.6)	
Total	2483	(95.4)	119	(4.6)	
Quintile 5 (richest)					
Female	1170	(89.1)	143	(10.9)	0.000
Male	942	(98.3)	16	(1.7)	
Total	2112	(93.0)	159	(7.0)	

Notes: Totals are population estimates.
Percentages are over the total number of sicknesses within each quintile & sex group.
[1] Chi-squared test, degrees of freedom = 1.

Source: Gender and Health Equity household survey.

Table 15.4.2 suggests that for long-term sickness, there were both gender and economic class differences (in the expected directions) among those with continued treatment. There were also significant gender differences in all the quintiles for those who were never treated. Girls/women were more likely to never be treated for long-term illness in all households. However, when treatment was discontinued, it appeared to vary both by economic class and by gender. Furthermore, these gender differences are not uniform across the quintiles, indicating the presence of interactions between gender and economic class, which we tested further with the regression analysis.

Table 15.4.2

Health-seeking by Gender and Economic Class

Gender-based Groups within Per Capita Consumption Expenditure Quintiles	*Long-term Sicknesses*			
	Continued Treatment (%)	*Discontinued Treatment (%)*	*Never Treated (%)*	p value[1]
Quintile 1 (poorest)				
Female	632 (49.1)	465 (36.1)	190 (14.8)	0.000
Male	494 (59.5)	296 (35.7)	40 (4.8)	
Total	1126 (53.2)	761 (35.9)	230 (10.9)	
Quintile 2				
Female	638 (50.8)	466 (37.1)	151 (12.0)	0.000
Male	654 (71.9)	216 (23.7)	40 (4.4)	
Total	1292 (59.7)	682 (31.5)	191 (8.8)	
Quintile 3				
Female	789 (56.7)	421 (30.3)	181 (13.0)	0.000
Male	631 (70.3)	182 (20.3)	84 (9.4)	
Total	1420 (62.1)	603 (26.4)	265 (11.6)	
Quintile 4				
Female	798 (65.0)	309 (25.2)	120 (9.8)	0.001
Male	543 (67.6)	219 (27.3)	41 (5.1)	
Total	1341 (66.1)	528 (26.0)	161 (7.9)	
Quintile 5 (richest)				
Female	812 (66.9)	283 (23.3)	119 (9.8)	0.000
Male	546 (73.1)	169 (22.6)	32 (4.3)	
Total	1358 (69.3)	452 (23.0)	151 (7.7)	

Notes: Totals are population estimates.
Percentages are over the total number of sicknesses within each quintile & sex group.
[1]: Chi-squared test, degrees of freedom = 2.

Source: Gender and Health Equity household survey.

The foregoing discussion suggests that the lower and more insecure the household's economic status, the greater the chance that health seeking will be rationed within the household, and this is borne disproportionately by girls and women. This suggests that greater economic security (and higher income levels) may reduce the rationing phenomenon, and with it some but not all of the health-seeking differences between women and men. However a caveat is in order. While we may be tempted to assume that the improvement is because of income security, economic vulnerability may not be the only reason; other factors such as educational status may play a role as well.

Logit regression analysis with interaction terms for gender and economic class (using two models—Model 1 for the aggregate sample, and Model 2 with dummies for male versus female and poor versus non-poor) presented results that corroborate those above, and extend our understanding.[11] For short-term illnesses, Model 1 suggests that the likelihood of not being treated is significantly higher if the person is older, female, or poorer, or if the illness is less severe. Children and the young may be more likely to be treated (in an area with higher than average infant and child mortality rates) because of concerns about their greater vulnerability; it may also be the case that in this poor region, older people are less likely to take time away from work for short-term ailments. This requires further qualitative investigation. Gender bias clearly discriminates against all women whether poor or non-poor. However although the aggregate sample suggested significant economic class differences, Model 2 only showed some economic class differences among men (10 per cent significance level), and not among women.

For long-term illnesses, Model 1 showed that the likelihood of continued treatment is higher the more severe the illness, or if the person is male, the head of the household, or belongs to the top two expenditure quintiles. Whether the person was an income earner or not in the household was also highly significant but in an unexpected direction suggesting that income earners were less likely to be continuously treated. Our tentative explanation for this is that there

---

11. While the cross tabulations have been presented by quintile, we believe that there is variation even within the poorest and the better-off quintiles. This variability is being explored in our on-going work. For the purposes of this paper, the regressions were run using a fairly standard dichotomy between poor (bottom 3 quintiles) versus better-off (top 2 quintiles).

is a trade-off between earning income and receiving treatment (possibly because of the time and distance involved in seeking treatment) and therefore income earners may never be treated or may discontinue treatment.[12] Model 2 showed that gender differences in continued treatment were strong (1 per cent significance level) in the poorer groups but not among the better off. There were also significant differences (1% significance level) between poorer and better-off women, but not between poorer and better off men. Thus poorer women were less likely to receive continuous care for long-term illness than better-off women, and also compared to poorer men. The test for the interaction between gender and economic class showed that gender differences in the likelihood of continued treatment were also significantly different between the poor and the better-off.

There were some differences in the variables affecting complete non-treatment versus discontinuation of treatment. In Model 1 a person was more likely to never be treated for a long-term illness if the illness was less severe, but also if the person was female or from a poorer household (only 10 per cent significance level), or an income earner. Model 2 showed significant gender differences (1 per cent level) within both richer and poorer households. There were significant class differences among women (5 per cent level) but not among men. Gender is clearly a more important discriminator than income when it comes to never being treated and economic class also impacts more strongly among women than among men.

On the other hand, treatment was more likely to be discontinued (Model 1) if the person was from a poorer household, was not the head of the household, and was an income earner. These effects were not however uniform for men versus women. Model 2 with interactions showed some gender differences among poorer households (10 per cent significance level), but no gender differences among richer households. But economic class was a more important discriminator among women than among men as there were no economic differences among men, but strong differences between richer and poorer women.

12. This runs counter to received wisdom and further exploration is clearly warranted.

These results suggest that gender and economic hierarchy operate at different levels and interact in important ways. If we think of being treated at all versus never being treated as the first level, it is gender that discriminates more between people, and even economic class differentiates poor from non-poor women, but does not differentiate between men. Once people begin to receive treatment, it is economic class that seems to be more important than gender per se, but even here class appears to operate specifically for women and not for men. The disaggregated Model 2 provides far more nuance to our understanding of the interactions than the aggregate Model 1. These 'layered' interactions are explored further in our ongoing work.

An examination of the reasons given for lack of treatment throws some more light on basic gender power differences. For both females and males, the major reasons for never treating or discontinuing treatment were only a few: either the illness was not considered serious by the patient or the family, or the treatment was too expensive, or the patient felt s/he was not getting cured. Short-term illness among men was also not treated because they said they didn't have the time for treatment. However the relative importance of the reasons given by women and men varied. Never treating either short or long-term illness because they thought it was not 'serious' was the most important reason for women. For men, expense was the dominant reason for never treating illness. Expense was an important barrier to treatment for women as well but lack of acknowledgement of illness (as reflected in the statement that it was not serious) was the more salient barrier. This barrier has its roots in powerfully ingrained gender norms that instil in women from an early age a lack of confidence or self-worth, a lower recognition of their needs, and a value to suffering in silence. Men have few such internalised norms of behaviour.

Both women and men gave 'not getting cured' as a major reason for discontinuing treatment for long-term illness. More detailed analysis of the evidence shows that women tended to give up treatment more quickly.

Table 15.6

Per cent Distribution of Main Reasons for Non-treatment of Sicknesses

Main Reason for No Treatment	*Short-term Sicknesses*		*Long-term Sicknesses*			
	Never Treated		*Discontinued Treatment*		*Never Treated*	
	Female N=856	*Male N=240*	*Female N=1944*	*Male N=1083*	*Female N=760*	*Male N=237*
I did not know what to do	6.4	0.0	1.5	0.7	9.6	3.4
I did not think it was serious	39.1	23.3	11.1	12.6	42.6	29.1
Family did not think it was serious	11.9	10.0	1.2	2.2	12.5	6.8
No one to accompany me	2.8	3.3	0.7	0.0	3.2	3.4
I didn't have the time	2.8	10.0	1.6	0.0	0.9	3.4
Too expensive	23.1	46.7	20.0	21.6	17.6	40.5
Health provider unavailable	1.9	3.3	1.6	3.7	0.0	3.4
Health provider unhelpful	0.0	0.0	1.2	0.0	0.0	3.4
Medicines make me ill	0.9	0.0	0.0	0.0	1.1	0.0
Not getting cured	3.6	0.0	43.4	30.0	5.1	6.8
Other	7.4	3.3	4.7	5.8	7.4	0.0
No response	0.0	0.0	13.0	23.4	0.0	0.0
Total (%)	100.0	100.0	100.0	100.0	100.0	100.0

Notes: Totals are population estimates.
Source: Gender and Health Equity household survey.

Our discussion in this section highlights the fact that systematic hierarchies of economic class and gender play an important role in structuring the health-seeking behaviour of households. While it is noteworthy that the extent of health-seeking overall is high, there are also important ways in which it is distributed across different groups. Such rationing appears to happen both because of economic constraints, and also on the basis of deeply ingrained gender norms.

Systemic Failures

The systematic hierarchies within communities and households that limit health-seeking behaviour favouring women, are compounded by major failures of the health system. These failures are discussed in this section with a particular focus on maternal health. Systemic weaknesses have been documented in our research through a census of private health providers that was undertaken in the 60 villages, as well as in the surrounding larger villages and towns within the district. Information was collected about the characteristics of traditional birth attendants, spiritual and traditional healers, provision stores selling tablets, private doctors, rural medical practitioners (RMPs)[13], medical stores and laboratories. Detailed qualitative information of the government health services was also obtained through in-depth observation and interviews.

In addition to this survey research, we documented the experiences of 12 women with obstetric complications, 9 of who died despite seeking care from health providers from primarily one *taluka*. These data provide compelling information that highlights how poor women in need of obstetric services interact with plural, unaccountable, and unregulated health systems in Koppal.[14]

Government Health Provision

The Karnataka Government has established an extensive network of health facilities structured according to a hierarchy of services based in theory on population norms.[15] Facilities have proliferated due to the preference of elected representatives for sanctioning PHCs and hospitals in their own constituencies and due to the availability of budget lines for infrastructural development. Several PHCs had new labour rooms constructed with funding from the Reproductive and Child Health programme and foreign funding supported infrastructural improvements of secondary level hospitals, with the aim of improving referral.

In Koppal, this investment in infrastructure has not translated into comprehensive emergency obstetric care as none of the higher-level

13. RMPs stands for rural medical practitioners. They are also sometimes called registered medical practitioners, although the Medical Council of India no longer registers them. They are usually men who primarily practice allopathy despite not having any formally recognised medical qualifications. We considered all those private doctors who did not hold current formally recognised medical degrees (MBBS, BAMS, BHMS, BUMS, BYNS, BDS) as RMPs.

14. Detailed analysis is available in George, Iyer and Sen (2005)

15. CHC, PHCs and sub-centres are supposed to cover populations of 100,000, 30,000 and 5,000 respectively. In 2001, PHCs and sub-centres in Karnataka were catering, on average, to smaller populations than specified by national norms: 20,817 and 4,285 respectively. CHCs, on the other hand, were dealing with larger population loads than envisaged—1,40,117 persons (GoI, 2004).

government facilities have all the required specialists or critical supplies. Neither policy makers nor implementers have addressed the lack of technical inputs for emergency obstetric care (including abortion) by ensuring the availability of specialists, upgrading the emergency skills of existing personnel and ensuring their access to critical supplies such as blood, anti-epileptic and haemorrhage drugs.

Even if the logistics of ensuring emergency obstetric care through appropriate inputs, supplies and staffing were addressed, there still remain large managerial barriers to improving the effectiveness of maternal health care services. A key contribution of the Karnataka Task Force on Health and Family Welfare was to highlight the need to address vacancies at the primary health care level (GOK, 2001). Medical officers, lab technicians, nurses and male junior health assistants (MHWs) were recruited within the district on a contract basis, while junior female health assistants (ANMs) were selected for training and recruitment at the state level. Although staff postings are biased against equity considerations through corruption, vacancies in primary health care service delivery in Koppal have substantially improved.

However progress on the more systemic problems identified by the Task Force (corruption, neglect of public health, distortions in primary health care, lack of equity, implementation gaps and weak ethical imperatives) has been more difficult to achieve. These cannot be addressed through managerial reforms alone. They require strategies to combat the political pressures that sustain such inequitable features of health systems.

Private Health Providers

In addition to the government health system, a large number of informal providers including spiritual and traditional healers, shopkeepers selling tonics and tablets, traditional birth attendants and RMPs exist at the village level. Our provider survey interviewed 548 providers working in the 60 villages covering a population of about 82,000 people. This included 35 spiritual healers, 133 traditional healers, 178 traditional birth attendants, 47 RMPs, 1 qualified Ayurvedic doctor, 152 provision stores and 2 medical shops. Although there are a few private specialists in the largest towns, the rural reality of Koppal is defined by a health care market dominated by informal providers. The district capital in contrast was where we interviewed 65 per cent of qualified private doctors[16], 41 per cent of medical shops and 50 per cent of laboratories. The 4 largest commercial towns surrounding the project area, including the district capital, accounted for 36 per cent of 90 RMPs, 93 per cent of 43 private doctors, 84 per cent of the 70 medical shops and all the 8 laboratories interviewed through our census.

The end result of the combination of an unaccountable government health system and an unregulated private health system is that women have few qualified providers who can handle obstetric complications. In an emergency, women and their families are forced to run from one provider to the next, often back and forth between government and private providers, all too often without being assured of the services they desperately need.

This forced pluralism is reflected in health seeking behaviour during delivery. In terms of assistance during childbirth, according to our household survey the main provider who helped women during normal deliveries were: traditional birth attendants (60 per cent), RMPs/private doctors (14 per cent), relatives (18 per cent), ANMs and lady health visitors (6 per cent) and government doctors (0 per cent). When there was a complication during labour some women did seek more 'skilled' providers by turning to RMPs/private doctors (26 per cent) and government doctors (8 per cent). Nonetheless 45 per cent of women with complications still sought the help of traditional birth attendants as a main provider.

Apart from their dominant role in assisting women during delivery, traditional birth attendants, unlike other health providers, play an important role in cleaning, massaging and bathing both mother and child for several days after delivery. Traditional birth attendants also take ritual care of the placenta. They are trusted and familiar village level confidantes, who assist women with home deliveries in the customary squatting positions to which women are accustomed. But, despite being so responsive to women's needs, it is a concern that

16. This includes practitioners with degrees in Dental sciences, Ayurveda, Unani, Homepathy and Allopathy. Out of 43 private doctors, 13 (30 per cent) were allopaths.

only 36 per cent of traditional birth attendants in the project area reported following 4 of the 5 'cleans' needed for a safe delivery.

Unlike traditional birth attendants, RMPs are less involved in the time-consuming work of assisting women during the long hours of delivery and the hard work of caring for mothers, their babies and placentas after birth. Yet RMPs are more literate and command more social status than traditional birth attendants. RMPs are perceived by communities to be much more responsive than government health workers, although they have fewer qualifications (or none at all). Unlike government health workers they will make house visits regardless of the time of day, live in the village and can always be relied upon to provide injections and tablets. Indeed during and after delivery an RMP's primary role is to provide oxytocin, tetanus toxoid and vitamin B injections. However, the irrational use of oxytocin, especially in injection form, can lead to a higher risk of uterine rupture, higher fetal distress and maternal morbidity. In addition to providing and charging for injections, RMPs also seem to play an important role in mediating access to health care for poor, often illiterate families, unfamiliar with larger towns and formal health care institutions.

Women's experiences of child-bearing in Koppal have to be seen in the context of the weaknesses of these plural health systems. Our research shows that women and their families made heroic attempts to seek health care prior to and during delivery. These iterative efforts by families and women result in ineffective outcomes because health systems fail to acknowledge women's requests for help and are not held accountable for the systemic failures that continue to allow women to die. It is our argument that these gendered failures in acknowledgement and accountability are responsible for the multiple delays that prevent women from accessing the effective care that could save their lives.

Family planning, antenatal care and a stress on institutional deliveries are critically important, but when they are not integrated into a continuum of care, they are not sufficient to save women's lives. All the maternal deaths we documented in Koppal did receive antenatal care and live within accessible distance of a subcentre or

PHC. And they made serious efforts to seek out health providers, both private and public. Yet despite all their efforts, the women died.

Gender Biased Services

Gender bias serves to devalue, and worse, stigmatise women's experiences, their bodies and biological processes. For example, in southern Karnataka, pregnancy is seen as a time during which 'dirty' or 'bad fluids' are accumulated in the body, bleeding after delivery is considered important as it drains the body of this bad blood. Delivery is also a ritually polluting process, after which a long period of cleansing and penance is required. During this post partum period, elders enforce restricted mobility, diets and fluid intake for newly delivered mothers (Kilaru *et al.*, 2004). These biases directly interfere with the recognition of obstetric complications, like haemorrhage, as well as inhibit healthcare seeking in the postnatal period.

Health professionals also delegitimise women's point of view. One reason why women are not able to get effective care despite physically accessing government facilities is due to the lack of agreement between women and health providers about what their health needs are. Although women seek help for labour pain, medical officers diagnose them with lower back pain or 'false' labour pain. This disjuncture between women's experiences of labour pain and its medical diagnosis indicates several problems in communication and care seeking. Women might be misinterpreting their experiences or health providers may be misunderstanding the situation. Social bias may also be at play by inhibiting women from speaking freely about their intimate reproductive health concerns with health providers from a different gender, class, educational and caste background. At the same time, health providers may have social biases that invalidate women's experiences. Finally, biases may exist in the technical understanding of what constitutes labour pain. Due to these factors, the process of seeking care and advice may be quite complex in practice.

Access to government facilities for institutional delivery once successfully negotiated does not mean an end to marginalising experiences. It is not just that cleanliness is not assured, but that the treatment received by women can be dehumanising. Women and their families are often left in labour rooms by themselves. They have to trust health workers who are strangers, often having to seek them out from other wards or their quarters. Women are expected to deliver in a position that is different from what they are used to at their homes and which helps the health worker more than it helps them. Even for normal deliveries, medical rituals involve shaving the pubic area, administering IV drips, repeated deep vaginal examinations and episiotomies. Health workers learn their skills in hospital wards giving orders to women in labour who are allowed little control over their situation. Yet if complications arise, health workers tell families, who are neither informed nor in control, to be prepared to face the consequences (Caleb Varkey, 2004).

Women with poor entitlements within families and in health systems tolerate high levels of pain, discomfort and humiliation. Not only are their rights to protest weakened by their unequal access to resources, including finances, expertise, and authority, but also because of the shame that surrounds women's bodies and the 'normalisation' of many women's reproductive morbidities. Explicit gender bias thus operates to disenfranchise women objectively through unequal status, and also normatively through disempowering normative local traditions and medical frames of knowledge.

Conclusion

Our experiences based on the Gender and Health Equity project in Koppal have highlighted the interplay of systematic hierarchies and systemic failures in determining health outcomes for poor women. Government providers of services often blame communities for their ignorance and superstition, while people accuse providers of bias, neglect and irresponsibility. What our research shows is that there is partial validity on each side but neither is true by itself.

A striking finding of our quantitative and qualitative research and field level interactions is that, whether for general illnesses (short or long-term) or maternity, women and their families invest considerable effort and resources in many instances in seeking health care. Yet the combination of poverty, biased gender norms, and unresponsive and unregulated health systems results in this investment going to nought.

The result is that disproportionately women suffer illnesses and die from entirely preventable causes.

While our research has focused on two *talukas* of a single district, we can probably extrapolate our findings to much of northern Karnataka. What should be obvious is that these systematic and systemic factors underwritten by gender bias and underpinning gender biased outcomes must be addressed urgently if the state is to fulfil its development potential.

References

ANS (Academy of Nursing Studies & Women's Empowerment Research Studies) (2001). *Study of Factors Contributing to Maternal Death in Andhra Pradesh: Report of a Study in Medak and Mahaboobnagar Districts*. Hyderabad: ANS.

Caleb, Varkey L. (2004). Presentation made on the National Consultation on Linking Home to Referral Hospital. Organised by Centre for Health Education, Training and Nutrition Awareness (CHETNA-Ahmedabad) and Academy for Nursing Studies (Hyderabad). May 5. Ahmedabad.

George, A., A. Iyer and G. Sen (2005). "Gendered Health Systems Biased Against Maternal Survival: Preliminary Findings from Koppal, Karnataka, India", *IDS Working Paper* 253. Brighton: Institute of Development Studies.

GoI (Government of India) (2004). *Health Information of India 2004*. New Delhi: Central Bureau of Health Intelligence, Directorate General of Health Services, Ministry of Health and Family Welfare. Statistics derived from tables accessed on 15 June 2005 from *http://cbhidghs.nic.in/HII2004/content1.asp*.

———. (2001). *Census of India*. New Delhi: Office of the Registrar General.

GoK (Government of Karnataka) . (2003). *Karnataka State Integrated Health Policy*. Bangalore: Department of Health and Family Welfare.

———. (2001). "Task Force on Health and Family Welfare", *Karnataka: Towards Equity, Quality and Integrity in Health. Focus on Primary Health Care and Public Health*. Bangalore: Government of Karnataka.

———. (1999). *Human Development in Karnataka 1999*. Bangalore: Planning Department.

IIPS (2006). *Reproductive and Child Health District Level Household Survey (DLHS 2) 2002-2004*. Round 2 Phase 1. Koppal. Mumbai: International Institute for Population Sciences.

Iyer, A. (2005). *Gender, Caste, Class and Health Care Access: Experiences of Rural Households in Koppal District, Karnataka*. Trivandrum: Achutha Menon Centre for Health Science Studies, SCTIMST.

Kilaru, A., Z. Mathews, J. Ramakrishna, S. Mahendra and S. Ganapathy (2004). "She has a tender body: Postpartum care and care-seeking during bananthana in rural South India". in Unnithan-Kumar M. (ed.) *Reproductive Agency, Medicine and the State: Cultural Transformations in Childbearing*. Oxford: Berghahn Books.

Mathews, Z., S. Mahendra, A. Kilaru and S. Ganapathy (2001). "Women in Waiting: Antenatal Care, Care Seeking and Morbidity in Rural Karnataka. Results of a Prospective Study", *Asia Pacific Population Journal* 16(2): 11-29.

Nanjundappa, D.M., A. Aziz, B. Seshadri, G. Kadekodi and M.J.M. Rao (2002). *Report of the High Power Committee for Redressal of Regional Imbalances in Karnataka*. Bangalore: Government of Karnataka.

Ravindran, T.K.S., R. Savitri and A. Bhavani (1999). "Women's Experiences of Utero-Vaginal Prolapse: A Qualitative Study from Tamil Nadu, India", in *Safe Motherhood Initiatives: Critical Issues*, (eds.) M. Berer, TKS Ravindran, Reproductive Health Matters/Blackwell Science, Oxford.

Sekher, T.V., K.N.M. Raju and M.N. Sivakumar (2001). "Fertility Transition in Karnataka: Levels, Trends and Implications", *Economic and Political Weekly* 36(51): 4742-52.

Umamani, K.S. and C. Yogananda (2003). *Place of Delivery and Delivery Practices in Rural Karnataka.* Bangalore: Population Research Centre, Institute for Social and Economic Change.

Annexure 15.1

Results of Logit Regressions—Estimates of Odds Ratios

Independent variables[2]	Short-term sicknesses: Logit Regression, Non treatment=1, Otherwise=0		Long-term sicknesses: Logit Regression, Continued treatment=1, Otherwise=0		Long-term sicknesses: Multinomial Logit, Continued treatment=1: Discontinued treatment=2		Non-treatment=3	
	Model 1[1]	*Model 2*[2]	*Model 1*[1]	*Model 2*[2]	*Model 1*[1]	*Model 2*[2]	*Model 1*[1]	*Model 2*[2]
Age	1.017 ***	1.017 ***						
Sex (dummy: female=1)	2.703 ***		0.667 ***		1.153	4.170	***	
Income earner (dummy: non-earner=1)			1.668 ***	1.658 ***	0.632 ***	0.636 ***	0.496 ***	0.498 ***
Household head (dummy: others=1)			0.690 **	0.688 **	1.764 ***	1.773 ***	0.714	0.714
Severity	0.811 ***	0.809 ***	1.119 **	1.114 **	0.936	0.939	0.767 ***	0.769 ***
Economic class (dummy: non-poor=1)	0.622 **		1.453 ***		0.696 ***		0.658 *	
Male, Poor (dummy: d1)			2.349 *	0.945		1.041	1.129	
Female, Non-poor (dummy: d2)			3.908 ***	0.924		0.817	3.180 ***	
Female, Poor (dummy: d3)			5.610 ***	0.528	***	1.448 *	5.505 ***	
Sample Size								
Tests								
Coeff.(d1)=Coeff.(d3)			***		***	*	***	
Coeff.(d2)=Coeff.(d3)			***		***	**		
Coeff.(d3)-Coeff.(d1) =Coeff.(d2)[3]					**	*		

Notes: Notations: * significance at 10% level, ** significance at 5% level, *** significance at 1% level
Definitions: Economic class: Poor: bottom 3 quintiles, Non-poor: top 2 quintiles
Severity: Number of difficulties due to sickness

[1] Model 1 tested the independent effects of the explanatory variables on treatment-seeking outcomes

[2] Model 2 tested interactions using non-poor men as the reference group, and dummies for poor men, non-poor women and poor women. Economic class and sex were dropped to avoid multi-collinearity.

[3] The test was modified for continued treatment of long-term sicknesses to Coeff.(d1)-Coeff.(d3)=Coeff.(d2) because apriori coeff(d2)>coeff(d1)>coeff(d3)

16

Choosing 'not' to Participate

Evidence from Drought Prone Area Programme (DPAP) in Chitradurga, Karnataka

G. ANANDA VADIVELU

It is pointless to expect development agencies to 'correct' their mistakes in any meaningful sense. Rather, we should expect 'failing' projects to receive renewed funding precisely because they are succeeding in a broader sense, in depoliticising such key issues as the distribution of land or the extension of bureaucratic power in contested zones of governance. What seems like failure is success by another name. (Kumar and Corbridge, 2002: 94-95)

Introduction

The main purpose of the Drought Prone Areas Programme (DPAP), which comprises a core component of projects implemented as per the GoI (1994) guidelines, is to restore ecological 'balance' through soil and moisture conservation on a watershed basis. However, the Technical Committee (GoI, 1994a) has noted that watershed projects were "implemented in a fragmented manner by different departments through rigid guidelines without any well-designed plans prepared on watershed basis by involving the inhabitants" (GoI, 1994a: i). Therefore, the result has been that the programmes initiated were

I am thankful to Prof. D. Rajasekhar, Prof. R.S. Deshpande, Prof. K.V. Raju, Prof. Kadekodi, Dr. Vijayendra Rao, Dr. Anirudh Krishna, Dr. Priya for their support. Dr. Ajit menon has been a great source of support from the very early stages of this work. Dr. Sivakami spent quite a bit of her time in helping me code the data. Dr. Madeshwaran and Dr. Venkatachalam provided crucial support during a critical stage of the work. Venugopal facilitated my initiation into qualitative response models. Balraja and Srinivas were of great support during data collection, while Sushma and Manjula provided computational assistance. Last, but not the least the farmers who *choose* to spend their time in talking to me. The usual disclaimer applies.

unable to arrest the overall process of ecological degradation. The Technical committee has noted that based on 'successes'[1] achieved that this has been possible due to—"planning on watershed basis through the participation of people at all stages, active involvement of the voluntary organisations and coordinated effort by the administration" (GoI, 1994a: i).

The lacunae in the implementation of the programme in terms of the nature of participation are clearly noted—"Except in rare cases, the participation of the people was conspicuous by its absence either in the preparation of plans or in their implementation. The people were found to be *passive at best and skeptical and even hostile at worst* (*emphasis mine*). In quite a few cases, the structures created by the departments were demolished by the farmers, as, for example, in certain areas as many as 25 per cent of the bunds laid on the fields were demolished" (GoI, 1994a: 13).

The attempt of the State to transform the governance structure of the watershed programmes implemented by the Ministry of Rural Development through the Common Guidelines (GoI, 1994) has therefore been characterised as being revolutionary in nature by Shah and Memon (1999) for three reasons, pertaining to the design of the institutional mechanism: (a) devolution of decision making and financial allocation directly to the district and then to the village level, (b) creation of a partnership between the Government, Non-Governmental Organisations (NGOs) and communities and (c) evolution of flexible mechanisms regarding the technical and financial norms. The changes that are occurring in terms of Government bureaucracies trying to reform are part of wider changes wherein there is move towards 'depoliticisation' of development through the crafting of single purpose user committees (water user committees, watershed development committees, health committees, forest protection committees, etc.).[2] In this paper, we have a limited

1. The cases of success cited in the report are from Ralegaon Sidhi and Adgaon in Maharasthra, certain Tribal areas of Pancahaml in Gujarat, Mittemari in Karnataka and Jhabua in Madhya Pradesh.

2. These attempts to 'depoliticise' development is rightly argued to be based on the unrealistic and flawed assumption that these groups are apolitical in nature, a critique of this 'second wave' of decentralisation is beginning to emerge (Manor, 2004).

purpose and we only examine the constraints that farmers face in participating in the programme of somebody else—'the government'.

The paper is organised as follows: In section one, we discuss the framework adopted for the study and state our normative position and locate the enquiry in the participatory development discourse. In section two, we briefly discuss the 'failure' of the DPAP, which provides a backdrop to understand the historical baggage under which current programme constraints are encountered. In section three, we introduce the study area and specify the methodology adopted for the field enquiry. In section four, we present the evidence and in the last section, we conclude by raising certain policy issues in the context of our findings.

Framework to Examine Participation

The typology of Cohen and Uphoff (1980) provides a useful framework for discussing participation. The three dimensions of participation outlined are: what kind of participation is under consideration, who is participating in it and how is participation occurring?. With respect, to What, they are: (a) Participation in decision-making; (b) Participation in implementation; (c) Participation in benefits; and (d) Participation in evaluation. To answer the, *what* question, we have to examine as to what are the levels in which participation can occur. The three types of decisions are—initial decisions, ongoing decisions and operational decisions. An important issue relates to Resource contribution (cash, labour and raw materials) —"It is particularly important to know as to *who* is contributing and *how* their contributions are made, whether they are voluntary, remunerated or coerced, the degree to which they are provided on an individual basis and whether they occur on an intermittent or continual basis" (Cohen and Uphoff, 1980: 220). The next question that has to be answered is–Who participates? The study analyses the differential levels of participation of farmers (small, medium and large) located across the upper and lower reaches of the watershed, regarding certain key variables relating to the planning and implementation of the intervention.

Participation in the watershed context is usually defined as 'communities' being involved in the analysis of the soil and water conservation problems and 'jointly' arriving at strategies to alleviate them. The aspects critical for such processes it is argued are the ability of members to participate 'as community' or to have 'collective' voice (Kolavalli and Kerr, 2002). We argue that the problematisation of participation by seeing it in terms of the all-inclusive notional concept of 'community' is too simplistic for the following reason. The 'community' consists of heterogeneous individuals and their perceptions and incentives to be involved in processes of planning, implementation and cost sharing differ based on various factors. The interaction of the 'individual'—the farmer with a variety of stakeholders ultimately results in some collective decision-making. The 'participation' of the individual farmer, therefore, needs to be understood in a disaggregated manner, which would enable us to understand the differential roles that various stakeholders play and viewpoints that emerge before collective decisions are taken.

Constraints in Participating—Choice between 'Voice' *vis-à-vis* 'Exit' Options

Appadurai explains, "poor people have a deeply ambivalent relationship to the dominant norms of the societies in which they live. Even when they are not obviously hostile to these norms, they often show forms of *irony, distance,* and *cynicism* about these norms...and what they often seek strategically (even without a theory to dress it up) is to optimise the terms of trade between recognition and redistribution in their immediate, local lives" (*emphasis mine,* Rao and Walton, 2004: 65). Breaking this *status-quo* is not a easy proposition and in contrast, it is observed, that the rich have a more fully developed capacity to aspire "because they have a bigger stock of available experiences of the relationship of aspirations and outcomes, because they are in a better position to explore and harvest diverse experiences of exploration and trail, because of their many opportunities to link material goods and immediate opportunities to more generic possibilities and options" (Rao and Walton, 2004:68).

Development projects, typically have the mandate of breaking such a *status quo* situation; however, this is not an easy proposition because of the constraints involved including the incentives structures of the 'street' level bureaucrats whose mandate is to break such status-quo scenarios. Appadurai explains certain way of changing such scenarios:

> "any development project or initiative, however grand or modest in scope, should develop a set of tools for identifying the cultural map of aspirations that surround the specific intervention that is contemplated. This requires a method of placing specific technologies or material inputs in their aspirational contexts for the people most affected by them. This will require careful and thoughtful surveys, which can move from specific goods and technologies to the narratives within which they are understood and thence to the norms which guide these narratives" (Rao and Walton, 2004: 83).

The challenges that development projects face is to change the mentality and *status quo* situation wherein people often choose the 'exit' option rather than the 'voice' option in their engagement with development interventions that are facilitated by governmental organisations or NGOs.

Normative Position

The normative stand that we hold is, participation in itself is important, only to the extent that it facilitates the realisation of 'desirable' outcomes. These outcomes are increase in crop production and productivity, groundwater recharge, reduced rates of migration, etc.

We believe that the intrinsic value of participation as an empowering' exercise is a 'second-best' solution and the logical outcome of 'better' participation would be realisation of desirable outcomes. If this does not happen, the 'value' of participation is 'limited' in nature.

Locating the Study in the Participatory Development Discourse

The central importance of community based development is based on the principle that a more inclusive process of planning and implementation can lead to better outcomes in terms of the efficiency of the intervention in achieving its desired goals. This facilitates a greater possibility that the communities sustain the intervention since they have played an integral part in planning and implementing the programme. Better "participation is expected to lead to better designed projects, better targeted benefits, more cost effective and timely delivery of project inputs, and more equitably distributed projects with less corruption and other rent seeking activity" (Mansuri and Rao, 2004: 6).

The empirical constraints involved in achieving such idealised objectives are the following based on the review of Mansuri and Rao (2004):

First, the basic constraint is that individuals have opportunity costs in exercising 'voice' as there are implications in terms of the time lost or the financial loss incurred due to such participation. Second, mainstreaming participation is used simply as a means of cost-effective delivery or low-cost maintenance rather than as a vehicle for social transformation. Third, it is argued that it would be naïve to expect participatory exercises to transform the attitudes and implementation style of authoritarian bureaucracies.[3]

Some of the insightful studies, which have examined participatory projects, are Mosse (2003), Kumar and Corbridge (2002) and Baviskar (2004), (see Mansuri and Rao (2004) for an over-arching review of the empirical literature). Based on an investigation of the various 'doubts' that have begun to be asked about the participatory development 'project', certain keen observers have asked and attempted to answer the following question - whether participation is the 'new tyranny'? (Cooke and Kothari, 2001). The various authors in the above volume argue that participatory processes undertaken 'ritualistically' have turned out to be 'manipulative' in nature and has 'harmed' those it was supposed to empower. The questions examined are—(a) Do participatory facilitators override existing legitimate decision-making processes? (b) Do group dynamics lead to participatory decisions that reinforce the interests of the already powerful; and (c) The third question relates to the nature of the participatory method itself. Our study is an effort in examining the above questions, in particular question-(c).

---

3. This is based however, on the qualifier that concerted efforts do lead to the required results but more strategic attempts have to be made (See Thomson, 1995).

Historical 'Failure' of DPAP (1973-74 to 2002): A Brief Picture of State Inertia

The DPAP was initiated in 1973 covering 947 blocks of 155 districts in 13 states. The programme is a centrally sponsored scheme with the expenditure being shared equally by the Centre and the States. By April 1995, a total area of 74.6 million hectares had been treated under the programme. The financial implication of this intervention was Rs. 2,195 crores. The results however have not been satisfactory and the Report of the Comptroller and Auditor General[4] states that the "drought conditions and ecological conditions had shown no perceptible improvement" and the "drought prone areas had increased from 55.3 million hectares in 1973-1976 to 74.6 million hectares in April 1995". However in defense, the Ministry of Rural Areas and Employment stated in January 1999 that this increase was due to a refinement in the criteria adopted for identifying a drought prone area and as a reason the programme was extended to 74.6 million hectares. It was also stated that the meager allocation meant that efforts to drought proofing was restricted to only a few confined pockets and there was a need for enhanced allocation to ensure effectiveness of the programme. However, the CAG report found that this explanation by the ministry untenable as "the impact of the DPAP was not monitored and the Ministry had no information on the magnitude of the drought proofed area after a quarter of century of the implementation of the programme" while recognising that insufficient fund allocation was a contributory factor for the poor results. The Mid Term Appraisal by the Planning Commission for the 1997-2002 period states in very clear terms the contributory factor for the poor performance which include issues related to poor participation, incentive of the staff, insecurity about funding, lack of impact assessment, etc. (See GoI, 2002: 250-51).

We now proceed to examine the evidence emerging from our study sites.

---

4. *www.cagindia.org/reports/civil/1999-book3* accessed on 7th March, 2005. The report of the Comptroller and Auditor General (GoI, 1998) includes a review of the programmes of the Ministry of Rural Areas and Employment including the DPAP and is a severe indictment of the programme. The Audit was conducted in 60 districts of 14 states, including Karnataka from April 1998 to June 1998.

Study Area and Methodology

Chitradurga district falls under the Central Dry Agro climatic zone, which comprises 17 *taluks* of the districts of Chitradurga and Tumkur. The total geographical area is 19,98,509 ha and the Gross cropped area is 10,9169 acres. The major crops grown in the district are: Ragi, Rice, Jowar, Pulses and Oil seeds. The district falls under the Krishna basin and two major rivers Vedavathi and Tunghabhadra drain the district. The mean annual rainfall for the 1901 to 1990 period was 565.mm. The projects in the II phase were selected as they were the earliest available to examine projects implemented as per GoI (1994). The *taluk* has faced consecutive crop 'failures' from 2000 to 2003 period, especially during the *Kharif* (rainy season crop) period. There had been lack of interest in agriculture due to the uncertainties prevailing and the more urgent need of the small and medium farmers was for wage-labour. Under such a backdrop the DPAP intervention was undertaken in the *taluk*. Certain basic information on the study villages has been provided in Table 16.1, while Table 16.2 provides a snapshot picture of the village's response to the intervention.

Table 16.1

Profile of the II Phase Villages—DPAP (1999-2003)

Sl. No.	Name of the Village	Number of Households	Total Area (ha)	Watershed Area (ha)	Dry land (ha)	Irrigated (ha)	CW[5] (Ha)	NAC[6] (Ha)
1	Bommadevarahalli	210	1,029.94	307.00	568.03	4.86	92.46	34.92
2	Rajapura	180	1,059.07	360.47	762.75	28.32	70.91	34.56
3	Devasamudra	428	1,476.43	526.52	408.61	177.83	356.21	77.15
4	Vithalapura	51	379.98	375.34	54.33	25.97	25.97	2.94
5	Venkatapura	301	374.38	370.01	219.28	88.04	40.18	26.88
6	Oorthalu	81	563.03	501.28	342.24	301.04	27.95	43.32
7	Muthugarahalli	208	1,543.49	496.64	426.58	30.0	26.49	153.23

Source: DPAP project documents (Number of Households and Watershed area) and the rest from GoI (1991).

5. Culturable Waste.
6. Area not available for cultivation.

Table 16.2

Locating the Differential Village Level 'Responses' to the Watershed Intervention

Name of the Village	*Characterisation of the Village*
Devasamudra ('Head-end' Village).	Local power structures are centralised in the village; attempt have been made to appropriate the maximum resources within the village; in 'tail' end villages, resources get spent—'adjusted' based on some sort of 'patron-client relationship'. Conflict between the *Panchayat* (controlled by the Congress) and the Watershed Development Committee (controlled by the Janata Dal); The current *Panchayat* President's predecessor was his father who had been the *Panchayat* Chairman for 36 years continuously. Decision on (a) whether the land has to be treated, (b) what sort of treatment to be done, to a large extent, is influenced by whether a farmer has alliance is to the Congress or the Janata Dal. The effective 'control' of the programme was exercised by the Z.P. member's husband. The Agricultural assistant before he proceeded to the plots to plan and implement the treatment used to visit the Z.P. member's house and based on his 'instruction/ authorisation' the work proceeded.
Venkatapura and Vithalapura ('Tail-end' Villages)	Lobby to ensure that there is only one WDC and not WDCs in each village so that resource 'appropriation' by Devasamudra can be minimised. WDC members representing the tail end villages lobby (with the MLA at the *hobli*[7] and Agricultural assistant) to ensure that the power exercised by the influence of Devasamudra WDC members is minimised.
Bommadevarahalli (Passive Village)	Strong indigenous 'corporate 'organisation of the Temple Committee, which is involved in various activities. Although there is this strong indigenous set up, government is in the realm of the 'other' and the designated person '*Sarkarada Manusha*' represents largely any 'interaction' that needs to be undertaken with the '*Sarkara*' (Government)
Muthugarahalli (Passive Village)	Decisions taken by the Agricultural assistant, the WDC chairman is a 'rubber stamp' to the Agricultural assistant, certain amount of 'elite capture' takes place (ex: Boulder removal being done in *Lingayat* (a forward caste) plots while not in others, which is not an authorised activity under the DPAP programme)

7. Unit of administration below the *Taluk* level.

Sampling Procedure

The study involved data collection from five DPAP villages from the following strata of households after the list of the treated plots were prepared during the transact undertaken from the upper to the lower reach of the watershed.

(a) Upper Small.

(b) Upper Medium.

(c) Upper Large.

(d) Lower Small.

(e) Lower Medium.

(f) Lower Large.

Small is defined as those farm households, having less than 5 acres. Medium is defined as households owning between 5 to 10 acres and large are those households having more than 10 acres. One acre of irrigated land is considered to be equivalent to 2 acres of dry land. Totally, 150 households were interviewed from the above six strata. We now examine the processes in the study villages.

Preparation of "Master Plan and Action Plan" Document

The basic flaw in the planning process has been that the activities relating to SHG formation were made only after the action plans were prepared and submitted. The Participatory Rural Appraisal (PRA) exercise as envisaged by the architects of the Common Guidelines in terms of a 'learning sharing and contestation' exercise did not take place. If anything which had a semblance of a PRA exercise, the following took place—The Agricultural assistant undertook the transact with the assistance of the 'key person' in the village. The person could be a NGO staff (who had been shortlisted to get a contract for the 'software' part of the work) or a farmer who potentially became an 'assistant' to the Agricultural assistant in the village. The transact lead to the identification of treatment plans for the entire designated watershed area and the preparation of year-wise action plan. The Agricultural assistant solely made this exercise based on his one-two days visit to the village and one-week of number crunching in his calculator, in between his trips to the line departments for data collation. Having done so, the Master plan was finalised and submitted to the *Zilla Panchayat* in Chitradurga.

Self Help Groups (SHGs)

The process of being a part of the SHGs is a 'learning' and in some sense, empowering exercise for the members. By collectively managing the credit activities, this provides some sort of a 'ground' wherein higher-level objectives in terms of building up other village level organisations could be embarked upon (Fernandez, 1994). The basic flaw in the intervention process has been that the process of building rapport and the initiation of SHGs is considered as the 'software' part of the intervention and "NGOs were supposed to have comparative advantage to do this."[8] This work was 'contracted out' to them. This was contradictory to what the Guidelines envisages. These processes initiated by the government staff, which was supposed to be a 'learning experience' (initiation of SHGs, conduct of PRA exercises). But all these had not happened, the effort was in terms of getting the 'real thing done'—fulfillment of work targets prepared in the action plans.

Even the 'second–best' option of contracting the work to NGOs which was exercised, was plagued with problems, as there was no commitment on the part of the district level authorities to ensure that these efforts were supported adequately. The NGOs were basically one-two men teams. Effort was put by the organisation SAHANA in the four villages of Devasamudra, Venkatapaura, Vithalapura and Bommadevarahalli in terms of initiating SHGs. However, no proper follow up was undertaken, as the NGOs were not paid regularly for their efforts. This meant that some of the SHGs had become defunct (one of the reasons was that these groups which are formed with the expectation of getting 'loans' lost interest when they realised that their chances of getting the loans were low). In at least two of the above four villages, efforts were put in terms of 'creating' 'area groups' which basically consisted of households following a particular

8. Interview with the *Taluk* Agriculture Officer (Team leader of the Watershed Development Team), on 3rd March, 2004.

occupation—pottery, for example. However these area groups remains only on "paper" (in the NGO records) as further efforts were not put in terms of training, facilitating the evolving of income enhancement strategies, etc.[9]

Only 8.5 per cent of the respondents belonged to those SHGs initiated by the NGOs which were providing support to the programme, with the majority (91.5) being member of other initiatives independent of the watershed intervention (see Table 16.3). Although it is clearly evident that the effort put in organising these groups was 'limited' in nature, the more serious issue pertains to the lack of effort of the Government staff to 'engage' with already existing organisational capital to create some sort of 'interest' in the programme (Table 16.4). Lack of effort has implications in terms of poor processes, which are evident in the later stages of the project cycle.

Table 16.3

Membership of Self-Help Group

(in Percentages)

Strata	*Not a Member*	*Member of Some SHG*
Upper Small	46.2	53.8
Upper Medium	65.4	34.6
Upper Large	50.0	50.0
Lower Small	47.1	52.9
Lower Medium	59.1	40.9
Lower Large	50.0	50.0
Average	52.7	47.3

Attendance of the First Meeting in the Village before the Initiation of the Watershed Development Committee (WDC)

The initial meeting was held in only three of the five villages. The meeting was not held in Venkatapura and Vithalapura villages as all the meetings were centralised in Devasamudra. Only 23 per cent of the farmers stated that they had attended the meeting. In terms of

9. Interview with the Team leader of SAHANA on 1st June, 2004 who admitted that lack of financial support prevented him from taking any further initiative.

Table 16.4

Membership—Type of Group

(in Percentages)

Strata	*NGO Providing 'Software' Support to the Watershed Programme*	*Others*[10]
Upper Small	7.1	92.9
Upper Medium	0.0	100.0
Upper Large	10.0	90.0
Lower Small	11.1	88.9
Lower Medium	11.1	88.9
Lower Large	9.1	90.9
Average	8.5	91.5

reach, their distribution was almost equal, while upper reach farmers represented 53 per cent, lower reach was 47 per cent. The distribution of farmers who attended the meeting was skewed, a significant proportion of the farmers belonging to the politically 'vibrant' environment of Devasamudra (41 per cent), followed by the tail-end village of Venkatupura (22.72).

Table 16.5

Attendance at the First Meeting in the Village

(in Percentages)

Strata	*Not Aware of the Meeting*	*Aware, but did not Attend. As Busy in Agricultural Work*	*Aware, but did not Attend for Other Reasons*	*Attended*
Upper Small	53.8	11.5	15.4	19.2
Upper Medium	69.2	3.8	7.7	19.2
Upper Large	40.0	30.0	5.0	25.0
Lower Small	61.8	8.8	5.9	23.5
Lower Medium	54.5	13.6	9.1	22.7
Lower Large	36.4	27.3	4.5	32.1
Average	54.0	14.7	8.0	23.3

10. These SHGs were started by the Department of Women and Child Development (Stree Shakthi), through the World Bank support (Swashakathi) and other NGOs, which were operating, independent of the watershed intervention.

Table 16.6

Attendance at the First Meeting—Village-wise Distribution Across the Strata

(in Percentages)

Village	Not Aware	Busy in Agri. Work	Other Reasons for not Attending	Attended
Devasamudra	33.3	16.7	6.7	43.3
Vithalapura	55.2	17.2	3.4	24.1
Venkatapura	41.4	27.6	10.3	20.7
Muthugrahalli	66.7	0.0	6.7	26.7
B.D. Halli	71.9	12.5	12.5	3.1

Awareness About the Existence of WDC Chairman

The disheartening finding is that 66.7 per cent of the farmers were not able to identify as to who the WDC chairman was. Expectedly, this proportion was higher among the small farmers as compared to the medium and large farmers in both the upper reaches (Table 16.7). There is a clear pattern that emerged in the inter-village analysis with a very high proportion of farmers in the politically stronger (76.7 per cent) village of Devasamudra being aware of the existence of the WDC Chairman as compared to the 'passive' villages, where it is as low as 23.3 per cent for Bommadevarahalli and 15.6 per cent for Muthugarahalli. The 'tail end' villages fall in between these two, with Vithalapura at 75.9 per cent and Venkatapura at 62.1 per cent (Table 16.8).

Table 16.7

Identification of the WDC Chairman—Five Villages across Strata

(in Percentages)

Strata	Cannot Identify the Chairman	Can Identify the Chairman
Upper Small	84.6	15.4
Upper Medium	61.5	38.5
Upper Large	50.0	50.0
Lower Small	76.5	23.5
Lower Medium	68.2	31.8
Lower Large	50.0	50.0
Average	66.7	33.3

Table 16.8

Village-wise Identification of the WDC Chairman across Strata

(in Percentages)

Village	*Cannot Identify*	*Can Identify*
Muthugarahalli	86.7	13.3
Bommadevarahalli	84.4	15.6
Vithalapura	75.9	24.1
Venkatapura	62.1	37.9
Devasamudra	23.3	76.7

Contribution

The norm as per the GoI (1994) was that farmers were supposed to pay 10 per cent of the costs for the treatment in the private land. The *taluk* had been facing crop failures for the past three years preceding the intervention. When the staff got information from the elite that farmers would be unwilling to pay the required contribution, there was no serious attempt made to ensure that the contribution was collected. Therefore, the evidence was not surprising. 92 per cent of the farmers were never asked for their mandatory 10 per cent contribution towards the costs. Only a certain section of the farmers were asked if they would be willing to contribute. These were the farmers in the 'medium' (11.5 per cent) and 'large' farmer category (10 per cent). Surprisingly, none of the farmers from the lower reach were asked and there is some evidence, at least in terms of their stated preference, that there was willingness to pay some contribution for the treatment undertaken in their plots, if somebody had asked them. This was stated by 4.5 per cent of the respondents in the Lower Medium strata and an equivalent proportion among the Lower Large strata. The 'easy way' for the staff to 'mobilise' the contribution was in the form of the 'adjustments' that they did—compromise in the quantum and quality of work. These compromises ensured that such 'savings' made could be shown as farmer's contribution. Having got a sense from the 'elite' of the village that the farmers would not be paying the contribution, the Devasamudra WDC Chairman took the stand that the work should be done without any contribution from the farmers.[11] (See Chootray, 2004 and Kolavalli and Kerr, 2002: 235 for evidence from elsewhere in the country).

Table 16.9

Reasons for not Paying the Contribution

(in Percentages)

Strata	*Nobody asked me*	*Asked we told that we could not pay*	*If they had asked us, we would have contributed*
Upper Small	92.3	7.7	0
Upper Medium	88.5	11.5	0
Upper Large	85.0	10.0	5.0
Lower Small	97.1	0.0	2.9
Lower Medium	90.9	4.5	4.5
Lower Large	95.5	0.0	4.5
Average	92.0	5.3	2.7

Table 16.10

Village-wise Reasons for not Paying the Contribution

(in Percentages)

Strata	*Nobody asked me*	*Asked we told that we could not pay*	*If they had asked us, we would have contributed*
Bommadevarahalli	87.5	9.4	3.1
Muthugarahalli	96.6	3.4	0.0
Vithalapura	93.1	3.4	3.4
Venkatapura	96.6	3.4	0.0
Devasamudra	93.3	3.3	3.3
Average	92.0	5.3	2.7

Awareness of the Existence of the Agricultural Assistant

46.7 per cent of the farmers were unaware that the agricultural assistant existed, and surprisingly this ratio was the highest among the large farmers in both the reaches (Upper Large: 55 per cent,

11. While he took such a stand he expected the Agricultural Assistant to come to the village every day during the programme implementation phase to ensure proper implementation.

Lower Large: 54.5 per cent), while it was the least among the upper medium strata (34.6 per cent) (Table 16.11). The village-wise evidence was on expected lines, with the proportion of farmers unaware about the agricultural assistant being highest in the passive villages—Bommadevarahlli (65.6 per cent) and Muthugarahalli (60 per cent) with the least in the 'head end' village of Devasamudra (30 per cent). The proportion of the farmers being unaware of the agricultural assistant was quite high in the tail-end village of Vithalapura (62.1 per cent) which reflects that the village had a few farmers who actively lobbied, this coexisted with a majority who were unaware of the existence of the agricultural assistant. Similarly in Venkatapura, close to half the farmers (48.3 per cent) were unaware of the existence of the agricultural assistant (Table 16.12)

Table 16.11

Awareness of Existence of Agricultural Assistant

(in Percentages)

Strata	Yes	No
Upper Small	57.7	42.3
Upper Medium	65.4	34.6
Upper Large	45.0	55.0
Lower Small	52.9	47.1
Lower Medium	50.0	50.0
Lower Large	45.5	54.5
Average	53.3	46.7

Table 16.12

Village-wise Awareness of the Existence of the Agricultural Assistant

(in Percentages)

Village	*No*	*Yes*
Bommadevarahalli	65.6	34.4
Muthugarahalli	60.0	40.0
Vithalapura	62.1	37.9
Venkatapura	48.3	51.7
Devasamudra	30.0	70.0

A majority of the farmers were unaware that an agricultural assistant existed (52.7 per cent) with this proportion being the highest among the 'small' farmers—upper reach (57.7 per cent) and lower reach (52.9 per cent). Although the visibility of 'adjustments' was low, only 8.7 per cent of the respondents have stated that the quality of the work is poor and the staff is corrupt (Table 16.13), the data on the quality of the treatment reveals 'problems' due to the compromise on the quantum and quality of the treatment undertaken.[12] The proportion of farmers stating that 'good' work was done was expectedly higher in Devasamudra (40 per cent), where most of the resources got 'appropriated' and spent. In the same village, 30 per cent of the farmers stated that they were not aware of the Agricultural assistant, indicating the differential processes that were underway in the same village.

Table 16.13

Perception by the Farmers on the Agricultural Assistant

(in Percentages)

Reach	*Do not Know*	*Corrupt & Quality is Poor*	*Did not do as I wanted-Did as per Estimates*	*Fought with him to get the Work Done*	*Met me and took consent*	*Good Work Done*
Upper small	57.7	11.5	1.0	1.0	0.0	23.1
Upper Medium	65.4	7.7	0.0	3.8	0.0	23.1
Upper Large	40.0	5.0	10.0	5.0	5.0	35.0
Lower Small	52.9	11.8	8.8	0.0	23.5	2.9
Lower Medium	50.1	9.1	9.1	0.0	0.0	31.8
Lower Large	45.5	9.1	9.1	4.5	0.0	31.8
Average	52.7	8.7	6.7	2.7	1.3	28.0

Decision Making on the Treatment in the Plot

The findings for the five villages on the aggregate are that 30 per cent of the farmers were never consulted, while 24 per cent of them were consulted and consent was taken. In 36 per cent of the cases, the farmer made a request, while active lobbying was done by 10 of per

12. A detailed discussion on this is beyond the scope of this paper.

cent of the farmers. The disaggregated strata-wise inference (Table 16.14) clearly shows that the proportion of households, which were not consulted, was higher among the small farmers in both the upper and lower reaches (38.5 and 35.3 per cent respectively), while the proportion was the least among larger farmers (20 and 18 per cent respectively for the farmers in the upper and lower strata). This proportion was lower in the case of 'large' farmers because they themselves were actively involved in lobbying to get the desired treatments.

This was more so the case of lower reach farmers (18.1 per cent) than the upper reach (10 per cent). These farmers largely took the initiative to meet the Agricultural assistant and request the required treatment. For, the Agricultural assistant too, such farmers were more 'easily' accessible whenever he decided to visit the village, while it was more difficult to meet the 'small' farmers whose livelihoods depended not only on the crops that they cultivate, but also on wage employment for which they frequently had to go to the neighbouring villages.

Table 16.14

Decision Making on Treatment in the Plot

(in Percentages)

Strata	*Treatment Done without Consultation*	*Farmer's Consent Taken*	*Farmer Stating His Request*	*Farmer Undertaking 'Proactive' Action*
Upper Small	38.5	15.4	46.1	0
Upper Medium	34.6	23.1	26.9	15.4
Upper Large	20.0	35.0	35.0	10.0
Lower Small	35.3	20.6	32.3	11.8
Lower Medium	27.3	36.4	31.8	4.5
Lower Large	18.2	18.2	45.5	18.1
Average	30.0	24.0	36.0	10.0

The disaggregated village-wise analysis is on predictable lines, with the proportion of 'no consent' treatments highest among the 'passive' villages of Bommadevarhalli, which had the highest proportion of households falling under this category (53.1 per cent), followed by

Muthugarahalli (43.3 per cent), while the politically 'dominant' Devasamudra had the least proportion of households (10 per cent). The proportion in the tail-end villages fell between the two extremes with Venkatapura having 17.2 per cent of households, while Vithalapura is 24.1 per cent (Table 16.15).

Table 16.15

Decision Making in the Plot across the Villages

(in Percentages)

Village	*Treatment Done without Consultation*	*Farmer's Consent Taken*	*Farmer Stating His Request*	*Farmer Undertaking 'Proactive' Action*
Bommadevarahalli	53.1	21.9	21.9	3.1
Muthugarahalli	43.3	40.0	16.6	0.0
Vithalapura	24.1	24.1	31.0	20.7
Venkatapura	17.2	10.3	55.2	17.2
Devasamudra	10.0	23.3	56.7	10.0
Average	30.0	24.0	36.0	10.0

Econometric Analysis

The objective of the econometric analysis is to examine the causative factors for the 'differential' decision making process regarding the treatment undertaken in the farmer's plot. The farmer is either aware or unaware of the 'processes' underway (formation of SHGs, Watershed Development Committee, preparation of an action plan for the treatment) before reaching a stage wherein a decision has to be taken on the nature of treatment that has to be undertaken in the farmer's plot. If the farmer is unaware, then the decision is made:

(a) without taking the farmer's consent, or

(b) by taking his consent.[13]

If aware, he either:

(c) requests or

(d) lobbies.

13. This initiative of the Agricultural Assistant in meeting the farmer is the 'first' and probably only indication to the farmer that the DPAP programme is underway in his village.

Since, the dependant variable has four sets of responses, multinomial logit is an appropriate model to analyse the data. The Model is based on unordered choices. Each of the responses are *not* close substitutes and the choice made by the farmer is a conscious one and each of the events is a mutually exclusive event. Therefore Hausmann test is not required to test the IIA property.[14] In the Multinomial Logit Model (MNLM), we specify each nominal outcome as a nonlinear function of the independent variables x's. Once the model is identified we express this nonlinear probability model as linear of the log of odds.

The general form of the decision making on the treatment model equation is

$$In\frac{P(Y_i=1)}{1-P(Y_i=1)}=\beta_0+\beta_1 REACH+\beta_2 TOTALLAN+\beta_3 IRRIEXE+\beta_4 YEARSCHO+ \beta_5 ADUMALAG+\beta_6 AWARAGRICULTURALASSISTANT+ \beta_7 AWAWDCC+\in_i \quad (1)$$

The dependant variable for our analysis represents the choice made by an household in either 'passively' giving consent or in making more active attempts in terms of either requesting or lobbying for treatment. The most undesired process of decision making is undertaking of the treatment by the Agricultural assistant on his own without taking the consent of the farmer. This forms our base category as it represents the reference point as compared to other forms of decision-making. Hence the objective of the model is to know the probabilities of households under each of the set of the responses. The set of explanatory variables have been presented in Table 16.16 and their expected signs in Table 16.17.

Regression Estimates

Multinomial logit models have been estimated for the equation (1) based on the survey data. Maximum likelihood estimation has been

14. The multinomial logit specification imposes the restriction that the odds (ratio of the probabilities) of choosing the jth alternative over the ith depend only on the characteristics of the two alternatives. In other words, the choice of any other alternatives in the choice set has no influence on the odds between the ith and jth alternatives. This feature is called the independence from irrelevant alternatives (IIA) property.

Table 16.16

Description of the Variables

Variable	Description	Mean
Dependant Variable		
Decision made without consent	1 if no consent was taken, 0 otherwise	27.3%
Consent taken	1 if consent was taken, 0 otherwise	25.3%
Farmer requested	1 if farmer requested, 0 otherwise	37.3%
Farmer lobbied	1 if farmer lobbied, 0 otherwise	10%
Explanatory Variables		
a. Endowment Variables		
Reach	1 is lower reach while 0 is upper reach	53%
Totallan	Total land holding of the farmer (in acres)	9.92
Irriexe	Proportion of land that is irrigated (per cent)	5.8
Yearscho	Years of schooling for the head of the household	4.45
Adumalag	Number of adult males involved in agricultural labour as secondary occupation	1.53
b. Mode Level Variables		
Awaraa	1 if aware of the existence of the Agricultural assistant, 0 otherwise	47%
Awawdcc	1 if aware of the existence of the Watershed Development committee, 0 otherwise	34%

Table 16.17

Explanatory Variables and Expected Signs

Variable	*Description*	*Expected Signs*		
		Agricultural Assistant Decides and Consent of the Farmer is Taken	*Farmer Requested*	*Farmer Lobbied*
REACH	Location of the plot, upper or lower reach (binary)	+ -	+ -	+ -
TOTALLAN	Farm size in acres (continuous)	+	+	+
IRRIEXE	per cent of total land holding that is irrigated (continuous)	+	+	+
ADUMALAG	Number of adult males in the household involved in agricultural labour (continuous)	-	-	-
YEARSCHO	Years of schooling for the head of the household	-	+	+
AWAWDCC	If the farmer is aware of the existence of the Watershed Development Committee or not (binary)	-	+	+
AWARAA	Whether the farmer is aware of the existence of the Agricultural assistant or not (binary)	+	+	+

used to estimate the coefficients, which have been reported in Table 16.18. The likelihood test rejects (at less than 1 per cent significance level) the hypothesis that all the coefficients of the explanatory variables (except the constant) are zero. The coefficient of each of the variables reflects the effect of change in each of the variables on the probability that a certain mode of decision making took place relative to the decision made without consent of the farmer. The Pseuedo R^2 is 0.150.

Table 16.18

Multinomial Logit Regression Estimates for the Decision Making on Treatment Model

	Farmer's Consent Taken		*Farmer Requesting*		*Farmer Lobbying*	
Variable	*Coeff (S. error)*	*Odds Ratio*[15]	*Coeff (S. error)*	*Odds Ratio*	*Coeff (S. error)*	*Odds Ratio*
Constant	-.201 (.501)		-.798 (0.672)		-3.74 (1.04)	
Reach	-.009 (.0323)	0.81	-.474 (.493)	0.62	0.264 (.697)	1.02
Totallan	.010 (.0195)	0.99	.0156 (.0295)	1.01	.0293 (.0316)	1.02
Irriexe	.110 (.060)	1.01	-.000 (.0199)	0.99	.005 (.022)	1.00
Yearscho	-.258*** (.266)	1.11	.136** (.0650)	1.14	.166*** (.087)	1.18
Adumalag	1.248 (.541)	0.77	-.228 (0.260)	0.79	.362 (.329)	1.43
Awaraa	2.544** (.806)	3.48	1.264** (.532)	3.54	1.800** (.969)	6.07
Awawdcc	-.611** (0.683)	5.23	2.544* (.806)	12.73	1.800*** (0.969)	6.05

N = 150 Likelihood ratio test = 58.80 Pseudo R^2 = 0.150

Notes: *** Significant at 10 per cent level

** Significant at 5 per cent level

* Significant at 1 per cent level

The coefficients of three of the seven explanatory variables included in the model have been found to be significant. The coefficient of years of schooling (YEARSCHO) was estimated to be positively signed and as expected has been found significant at either 10 per cent or 5 per cent level. The Odds Ratio of 1.11 for the farmer consent taken group indicates that a farmer with an additional one year of schooling would lead to a 11 per cent higher probability that the agricultural assistant would consult the farmer before deciding on the treatment

15. The odds ratio in multinomial logistic models is referred to as Relative Risk Ratio (RRR). Like the odds ratio, a relative risk equal to 1 implies that the event is equally probable in both groups. A relative risk greater than 1 implies that the event is more likely in the first group. A relative risk less than 1 implies that the event is less likely in the first group.

on his land. Similarly, the Odds Ratio of 1.14 for the farmer requesting group indicates that an additional year of schooling of the farmer increases the the probability of the farmer taking the initiative and making a request to the agricultural assistant on the desired treatment required for his land by 14 per cent. The Odds Ratio of 1.18 for the farmer lobbying group indicates that an additional one-year of schooling would increase the probability by 18 per cent of the farmer making proactive attempts to lobby.[16]

The coefficient of awareness of agricultural assistant (AWARAA) was estimated to be positively signed and as expected was found to be significant at the 5 per cent level. The Odds Ratio of 3.48 for the farmer consent taken group indicated that an 'effort' by the farmer to 'recognise' that the agricultural assistant existed meant that the probability that the staff would consult the farmer increased by more than 3 times. The Odds Ratio of 3.54 for the farmer requesting group similarly increased the probability by 3 times of the 'effort' the farmer would put in making a request to the agricultural assistant. For the farmer lobbying category, the Odds Ratio of 6.05 indicated that an awareness of the existence of the agricultural assistant increased the probability by six times that the farmer would lobby to influence him (either directly or indirectly).

Contrary to the expected positive sign, the coefficient for the consent taken group showed a negative sign (-.61) for the awareness of the existence of the watershed development committee variable (AWAWDCC). (in comparison the expected positive sign is met for the other two groups). This finding clearly indicates that the consent taken was largely based on a one-to-one interaction between the agricultural assistant and the individual farmer and the awareness or unawareness of the existence of the WDC did not play a role in the decision making process involved between the individual farmer and the staff. This 'arrangement' was unproblematic for both the farmer (his consent was taken) and the staff (consultation was done although not through the mandated route of the WDC playing a role in that consultation process).

---

16. This can be either the Agricultural Assistant being influenced one-to-one by the farmer or through the MLA or the ZP member's husband. This pertains to the head end village of Devasamudra and tail end villages of Venkatapura and Vithalapura.

The Odds Ratio of 12.73 for the farmer making a request category indicates that the awareness of the existence of the Watershed Development Committee (WDC) increased by more than 12 times the probability that the farmer would take the 'effort' to request the desired treatment, while the Odds Ratio of 6.07 indicated that such an awareness would increase by more than 6 times the probability that the farmer would put in the required 'effort' to lobby to garner the required benefits.

The causative factors for certain independent variables being not statistically significant were the following. Regarding, the REACH variable, we hypothesised that that the farmers in the lower reach would have a better interest to participate in the programme (due to their better initial endowment- higher quality soil, higher proportion of irrigated land) because of their more optimistic assumptions about the benefits that could be derived from the various soil and water conservation treatments, the project offered. However, this was not found to be true, as the lower reach farmers similar to the upper reach farmers were pessimistic about the programme. This was because the failure of the rains in the past three years predominantly dominated their thinking about the utility of the programme whose benefits were contingent on good rainfall. The occurrence of a large number of borewell failures was another reason for them to loose faith in the possibilities that agriculture offered. Therefore, the variable regarding irrigation (IRRIEXE) also was insignificant.

For the variable, land holding (TOTALLAN), the qualitative inference clearly showed that differential modes of decision making occur based on the extent of the land owned. The econometric result has not substantiated the qualitative finding due to the nature of the econometric exercise wherein due to the effect of various other variables, land holding is not significant, while this has not been the case in the qualitative inference as we establish a one-to-one relationship between the variables. The same argument holds true for the variable-Adult Males involved in agricultural labour (ADUMALAG).

Central Argument of the Paper

The farmer's option to choose the 'exit' option (passiveness and deliberate choice to 'exclude' themselves from the processes) was due to a combination of various factors. First, when the *taluk* was facing three consecutive crop failures, the mode of operation of the DPAP programme did not factor in the major concern which a majority of the farmers (small and medium) had: need for wage labour creation. Instead of meeting this concern, the programme was largely implemented using machinery. Such a programme did not prove of interest to the farmer, as their expectation of the outcome of the programme (in terms of higher output and yield) was not positive. Therefore, a programme of wage labour generation, through a Food for Work Programme (FFW) would have been of interest to them as at least in terms of meeting their 'immediate' concern.

Second, a 'mode' level factor is the lack of conditionalites or "no negotiables" not being there. When farmers could get their land treated without attending meetings, without making a contribution, without knowing who the WDC Chairman or Agricultural assistant was, why would they take the 'trouble' of going though all this processes, which the architects of the national guidelines expect them to do? (GoI, 1994). The staff also found this as non-problematic as they had alternative mechanisms—'adjustments' to meet the requirements of the national guidelines. Since the auditor did not undertake a verification exercise, to see what is happening in terms of the guidelines, the targets were met, the projects get completed and the staff gets busy with the 'new' project—the SUJALA Watershed Project[17] funded by the World Bank or various other projects, underway.

To conclude, the 'exit' option exercised by the farmer and the behaviour of the bureaucrat to be 'inefficient' (not follow the norms prescribed by the guidelines (GoI, 1994) proved to be a win-win situation for both the farmers and the staff as they could finally achieve something which was desired by both. For the farmers, they

---

17. The supervision norms apparently were quite 'strict' in this project and was a greater source of 'pressure' as better processes had to be initiated in the 'ground' to ensure upward accountability.

could get their land treated, without having to 'waste' their time in 'unnecessary' processes, while the bureaucrats could mange to get their projects completed without having to undertake various tasks involved in putting the processes in place.

Policy Implications in the Context of the Policy Discourse

The policy initiative in terms of the funding envisaged for the Watershed programmes in the country involves a total outlay of Rs. 76,000 crores to be spent over a 25 year period which would lead to a treatment of 63 million ha. This is as per the Perspective Plan prepared by the Planning Commission. The Government intends to do this by merging various employment guarantee schemes in the dry land and by shifting a part of the allocation from irrigation and water resource. However, the evidence in the context of an important programme—the Drought Prone Areas Programme (DPAP) has been extremely unsatisfactory. This is based on two important policy documents—(a) Report of the Comptroller and Auditor General (CAG) on the programmes of the Ministry of Rural Areas and Employment, and (b) Mid term appraisal for the 1997-2002 period of the Planning Commission. The evidence from our field sites substantiates the findings of the above policy documents and documents, the lacunae in the programme and provides certain causative factors for such a situation to exist.

Since the Planning Commission is well aware of the lacunae in the programme the question that needs to be answered is: How does one proceed further in terms of design of the programme? Joy and Parajape (2004: 120-126) have suggested mechanisms to restructure the programme, which needs to be seriously considered by the policy makers. It is pointed out that the current time span of projects of five years is not sufficient and there is need for increasing the project duration to a range of seven to ten years. It is envisaged that the programme would proceed from one phase to another based on the condition that funding for each phase would be tied to the performance of the previous phase. An assessment would be carried out after the end of the period and that would decide as to how much proportion of the assistance would have to be treated as a loan vis-à-vis how much as a grant based on the performance criteria (that needs to be evolved). It is beyond the scope of this paper to discuss the nitty-gritty's of the components of each of the phases. However based on our findings, our concern relates to the need to build in strong conditionalites on the various components of participation for each of the phases. In this context, an important contribution to the debate is the contribution of Shah (2005) who has worked out certain modalities under which the existing subsidy regime in the watershed context needs to be reworked.

Considering that droughts are going to persist in the near future too, the current modes of implementation are quite 'naïve' and 'insensitive' to the concerns that farmers have. If such, sensitivity does occur, Food For Work (FFW) programme would emerge as a major 'mode' of implementation strategy (particularly in such distress situations) to address the concerns raised in this paper. If serious thought on these issues is not given, we would end up replicating and scaling up 'failures' and not 'successes'. The implications of this is not only the 'loss' of Rs. 76,000 crores to be spent over the next twenty five years but also of the lost opportunities for us to demonstrate that dry land development programmes *do* deliver.

References

Appadurai, Arjun (2004). "The Capacity to Aspire: Culture and the Terms of Recognition", in Vijayendra Rao, and Michael Walton (eds.), *Culture and Public Action*. New Delhi: Permanent Black.

Baviskar, Amitha (2004). "Between Micro-politics and Administrative Imperatives: Decentralisation and the Watershed Mission in Madhya Pradesh, India", *European Journal of Development Research* 16(1): 26-40.

Chhotray, Vasuda (2004). "The Negation of Politics in Participatory Development Projects, Kurnool Andhra Pradesh", *Development and Change* 35(2): 327-352.

Cohen, John M. and Norman Uphoff (1980). "Participation's Place in Rural Development: Seeking Clarity though Specificity", *World Development* 8: 213-235.

Cooke, Bill and Uma Kothari (2001). *Participation: The New Tyranny*. London: Zed Books.

Fernandez, A.P. (1994). *The Myrada Experience: The Interventions of a Voluntary Agency in the Emergence and Growth of People's Institutions for Sustained and Equitable Management of Watersheds*. Bangalore: MYRADA.

Government of India (1991). "Census of India 1991", *Series 11-Karnataka, District Census Handbook, Chitradurga District, Part XII-A, Town and Village Directory*. Bangalore, Director of Census Operations.

———. (1994a). *Report of the Technical Committee on Drought Prone Areas Programme and Desert Development Programme*. Ministry of Rural Development, April

———. (1994b). *Guidelines for Watershed Development*. New Delhi: Government of India.

———. (2002). *Mid-Term Appraisal–Final Document (1997-2002)*. New Delhi: Planning Commission.

Joy, K.J. and Suhas Paranjape with A.K. Kiran Kumar, Rohini Lele and Raju Adagale (2004). *Watershed Development Review: Issues and Prospects, Technical Report*. Bangalore: Centre for Interdisciplinary Studies in Environment and Development.

Kolavalli, L., Shashi and John Kerr (2002). "Mainstreaming Participatory Watershed Development", *Economic and Political Weekly*, Vol. XXXVII (3): 225-242, January 19.

Kumar, Sanjay and Stuart Corbridge (2002). "Programmed to Fail? Development Projects and the Politics of Participation", *The Journal of Development Studies* 39(2): 73-103.

Maddala, G.S. (1983). *Limited Dependant and Qualitative Variables in Econometrics*. Cambridge: Cambridge University Press.

Manor, James (2004). "User Committees: A Potentially Damaging Second Wave of Decentralisation", *The European Journal of Development Research* 16(1): 192-213.

Mansuri, Ghazala and Vijayendra Rao (2004). "On Community-Driven Development", *The World Bank Research Observer* 19(1): 1-39.

Mosse, David (2003). "Good Policy is Unimplementable? Reflections on the Ethnography of Aid Policy and Practice", Paper presented at the *EIDOS Workshop on Order and Disjuncture: the Organization of Aid and Development*, 26-28th September. London: SOAS.

Rao, Vijayendra (2002). "Experiments in 'Participatory Econometrics' Improving the Connections between Economic Analysis and the Real World", May 18, *Economic and Political Weekly* 37(20): 1887-1891.

Shah, Amitha (2005). "Economic Rationale, Subsidy and Cost Sharing for Watershed Projects: Imperatives for Institutions and Market Development", Paper Presented at the *2005 IWMI-TATA Water Policy Program Partners Meet*.

Shah, Amitha and Gani Memom (1999). *Watershed Development Project in Gujarat—A Quick Review*. Vadodara: Gujarat Ecology Commission.

Thomson, John (1995). "Participatory Approaches in Government Bureaucracies: Facilitating the Process of Institutional Change", *World Development* 23(9): 1521-54.

17

At Times When Limbs May Fail

*Social Security For Unorganised Workers in Karnataka**

D. RAJASEKHAR, J.Y. SUCHITRA,
S. MADHESWARAN and G.K. KARANTH

Introduction

The unorganised sector in India, comprising about 92 per cent of the working population, makes significant contributions to the national wealth; yet, workers in this sector do not have access to sufficient and reliable statutory social security.[1] Social security benefits (pensions, family and maternity benefits, etc.) provided to them by the government is limited in terms of both coverage and benefits.[2] Faced with persistent deprivation associated with general low standards of living and socio-economic insecurity, unorganised workers are forced to adopt informal mechanisms such as borrowing at usurious interest rates, distress-sale of assets, etc., and their continued dependence on such mechanisms renders them highly vulnerable.

Governments find it challenging to formulate and implement social security schemes for unorganised workers, who are illiterate, poor and

---

* This paper is culled out from the research study on "Design and Management of Social Security Benefits for Unorganised Workers in Karnataka" undertaken by the Institute for Social and Economic Change, Bangalore, and supported by GTZ and the Department of Labour, Government of Karnataka.

1. Of 376 million workers in the country in 2004, only 8 per cent belonging to organised sector, had access to statutory social security benefits.

2. These social security schemes (pensions, etc.) have been targeted at the general poor in India. Since the poor in the country almost certainly belong to the unorganised households, this seems reasonable. But it is also inadequate. This is because poverty in India is benchmarked using the poverty line criterion, and only those households which fall below the line are eligible to avail of these benefits, leaving a large number of households out of even such minimal social security cover (Rao, Rajasekhar and

vulnerable, for the following reasons: First, the employer-employee relationship in this sector is either absent (in the case of the self-employed) or loosely defined (in the case of the wage-employed). Second, the sector is characterised by the temporary, seasonal and changing nature of employment often resulting in long periods of unemployment, the failure of wages to meet minimal requirements, poor work environment, long working hours, irregular incomes, etc., which contribute to the poor employment security of the workers. Third, notwithstanding the expectation that economic reforms initiated in India would increase employment in the formal sector and reduce the size of the informal sector,[3] there has been increasing casualisation and informalisation of labour, without corresponding improvements in basic livelihood security and social security in the informal sector. Fourth, workers in certain sectors like the *beedi* industry in Karnataka, who were initially benefiting from statutory provisions such as minimum wages, provident funds, etc., have chosen to become 'unorganised' by way of withdrawing from their accumulated provident funds to meet their life-cycle needs (Rajasekhar and Sreedhar 2002). This raises the question of policymakers' awareness of the social security needs of the unorganised workers. Finally, a severe resource crunch not only disables the governments from introducing social protection programmes but also induces them to question the need to start, for instance, universal health insurance schemes when free health care services are provided through public health centres.

The following questions are thus of great interest and relevance. What are the priority social security needs of these workers? What mechanisms (formal and informal) do they adopt to meet these needs? These questions are addressed in this paper with the help of data collected from 910 unorganised workers from four agro-climatically different districts in Karnataka—Mysore, Bangalore, Dakshina Kannada and Gulbarga. Three sub-sectors—agricultural labourers, construction workers and domestic workers are covered.

---

3. Although the terms 'formal and informal' sector and 'organised and unorganised' sector connote slightly different things, we use them interchangeably in this paper, and this seems to be the popular trend in almost all the literature on this issue.

The paper is presented in five sections. In Section 2, we summarise the main debate over social security for the unorganised sector and locate our research questions in this larger framework in the literature. In Section 3, the social security needs of the workers are analysed. A methodological point to be noted is that in our analysis of the social security needs of the workers, we refer only to the 'protective' social security needs of the workers, using the International Labour Organisation's (ILO) concept. Although in Section 2, we discuss 'promotion' as an important paradigm in social security literature, an analysis of this element is beyond the scope of this paper.[4] Here, we also provide evidence on the different emergency situations faced by workers and their households using the Social Risk Management (SRM) framework (see, Section 2). An interesting insight we get is that the workers routinely face highly debilitating emergency needs such as accidents, health-related needs, social functions and obligations, etc. However, what they perceive as priority social security needs in response to overt questions are not these, but rather those related to their current and future livelihoods.

In Section 4, we analyse the mechanisms that unorganised workers and their households employ to meet their priority social security needs. We also continue to employ the SRM framework and analyse the means by which they overcome the household and work-related risks.[5] We find that for meeting all types of needs, owing to minimal access to formal mechanisms, there is extreme dependence on the informal mechanisms. Section 5 concludes the paper.

---

4. For a detailed analysis of the promotional social security needs of the unorganised worker households, see Rajasekhar *et al*, 2006.

5. 'Risk', in our analysis, is representative of a large gamut of emergency needs faced by households, and not merely the 'unpredictable' events as indicated by the conventional definition of the term 'risks'. For vulnerable sections of the population such as the unorganised sector households, even predictable events are just as shattering as unpredictable events. For instance, a drought situation is a risk because of its unpredictable character, but so is the arrangement of the wedding ceremony of a daughter. For these households, the expenses incurred on such occasions, and more importantly, the sources through which they finance these occasions, render them even more vulnerable than they already are. We therefore use the terms 'risk', 'crisis' and 'emergency/emergency need' interchangeably.

Conceptualising Social Security

Protection and Promotion

The two dominant paradigms in the social security literature are Protection and Promotion. Protective Social Security is the name given to the ILO's definition of social security as, "The protection which society provides for its members, through a series of public measures, against the economic and social distress that otherwise would be caused by the stoppage or substantial reduction of earnings resulting from sickness, maternity, employment injury, unemployment, invalidity, old age and death; the provision of medical care; and the provision of subsidies for the families with children" (ILO, 1984).

This definition presupposes that the members of society have already reached an acceptable standard of living and that the main aim of social security is to protect them from a fall in their standard of living. Implicit in this is the understanding of social security as a concept whereby the core of income and welfare is assured through regular participation in work and production, leaving only specific contingencies to be tackled through public policy. While this type of social security succeeds in developed countries, its applicability in and adaptability to developing countries are found to be questionable given the large unorganised sectors in these countries.

The need for a broader concept of social security, therefore, has been felt in developing countries, as protective social security does not take into account the high degree of deprivation and vulnerability of a majority of the population (Dev *et al.*, 2001). Dreze and Sen (1989) first articulated the broader concept of social security as "...social means to prevent deprivation and vulnerability to deprivation." Known as promotional social security, this concept has the twin objectives of enhancing the normal living conditions of households and dealing with the regular and often persistent deprivations that they face. In other words, promotional social security refers to the need to ensure that households have adequately met their basic entitlements, i.e., food, education, employment, housing, health and drinking water security. It is, in a sense, more ambitious, in wanting to eradicate problems that have persisted for thousands of years, and this ought to be the ultimate end of any social security programme (Dreze and Sen, 1991: 3).

There have been several debates on the two aspects of social security[6], but one thing is clear: while the objectives of protection and promotion are distinct, the pursuits of these objectives are not entirely independent of each other. Nor is the importance of one independent of the achievement of the other. Dreze and Sen argue that success with the promotional objectives is likely to make protection easier—eg: individual insurance may be less difficult when one's normal level of prosperity is higher. It can also make protection less intensely crucial. For example, a decline from a higher standard of living may cause hardship but not the kind of starvation and extreme deprivation that a fall from a lower and more precarious level would entail. There are therefore, crucial links between the protective and promotional elements of social security.

Social Risk Management

More recently, the provision of social security has also been analysed in the Social Risk Management (SRM) framework (Holzmann and Jorgensen, 2000). The main idea behind SRM is that all individuals, households and communities are vulnerable to multiple risks from different sources, whether they are natural (earthquakes, floods, etc.) or human-made (unemployment, environmental degradation, war, etc.). These shocks hit the individuals, communities and regions in unpredictable ways, and cause and aggravate poverty. This implies increased vulnerability since the poor are typically more exposed to risk while they have limited access to risk management instruments. Therefore, the provision and selection of appropriate SRM instruments become important in order to reduce vulnerability and poverty. SRM, thus, clubs both the promotional and protective aspects of social security, and is useful in analysing mechanisms adopted by the unorganised sector workers.

Holzmann and Jorgensen refer to three types of arrangements—formal, market-mediated and informal, and three types of strategies—

6. These debates have been well summarised in the papers in Dev *et al.* (2001) and Etisham et al (1991). See also van Ginneken (2003) for a brief and concise summary of the debate over the concept of social security.

prevention, mitigation and coping. Formal arrangements typically refer to government-initiated programmes, savings and insurance with private or public sector financial institutions, etc. Under informal arrangements such as sharecropping arrangements, borrowing from employers, moneylenders or relatives, sale of assets, etc., promises of reciprocity cannot be enforced due to lack of legally binding commitments. Market-mediated arrangements refer to programmes such as microfinance and micro-insurance.[7] Prevention strategies are employed before a risk occurs, the idea being to reduce the probability of a downside risk. Mitigation strategies are also used before the risks occur; but the main aim of mitigation is to reduce the adverse impact of a future risk. Coping strategies are used after the risk has occurred, when there is no other option.

When do Limbs Fail?—Social Security Needs of Workers

We have regrouped the nine protective needs identified by the ILO into five main categories, namely, old age, employment injury, unemployment, death and sickness. For women workers in the reproductive age, maternity has also been included. The exercise on the identification of priority needs was done using participatory techniques. Being shown pictures on the five/six types of protective needs, each respondent was asked the following questions. Did s/he think that these needs were relevant to them? If yes, to which one of them did s/he assign the greatest priority and why?

Of the 910 sample workers, 840 were willing to express their perceptions on the protective needs and identify the priority need.[8] In Table 17.1, we show the preference matrix of the three categories of workers.

Across worker categories, the two social security needs ranked as the most important were old age pensions (OAP) and unemployment benefits (UB). Among the construction workers, another equally important need was for insurance against employment injury. We now

7. Microfinance in India, however, is clubbed with the informal arrangements since microfinance programmes are less dependent on the market forces.

8. The rest were unwilling to assign ranks to the protective social security needs for a variety of reasons.

look at each of these needs and identify some of the key reasons that these workers felt them to be important or otherwise.

Table 17.1

Preference Matrix of Workers for Social Security Needs

Social Security Needs	*Agricultural Workers*	*Construction Workers*	*Domestic Workers*
Unemployment	164 (32.48)	90 (29.90)	26 (25.00)
Sickness	48 (9.50)	37 (12.29)	12 (11.54)
Employment injury	39 (7.72)	69 (22.92)	6 (5.77)
Old age pensions	180 (35.64)	75 (24.92)	38 (36.54)
Death	26 (5.15)	20 (6.64)	11 (10.58)
Did not rank	48 (9.51)	10 (3.33)	11 (10.57)
Total	**505**	**301**	**104**

Note: The figures within the parentheses are percentages and represent the proportion of workers in each category who indicated the first preferences for the five needs, and also those who did not express their preferences at all.

Old Age

The most important factor for the high priority towards OAP was the workers' fear of being unable to work in their old age. Many workers indicated that traditional kinship ties were fast getting eroded and feared that their children would not take care of them or would not like aged people living with them. A few stated they did not want their children to suffer on account of having to take care of the elders.

An interesting correlation was found between the age of workers and their prioritisation of OAP—as the age increased, the proportion of workers assigning the first priority to pensions also increased. This implies that for the workers in the unorganised sector, their immediate day-to-day needs are the most important ones to be met. Only after these are adequately met do they even consider long-term needs such as OAP. For the younger workers, therefore, OAP was not the most important need simply because old age was a period in life that was distant and yet unreal. It was not the most relevant need for their current lives.

For the older workers, the rationale for the top priority given to OAP was obvious. For these workers, old age was a current and the most immediate need to address. Without the pension, these workers would be unable to lead their day-to-day existence. A considerable number of middle-aged workers also gave the highest priority to pensions since these workers had their elders living with them and were, therefore, able to appreciate the problems of old age. This was also the period when old age began to look like a reality to the workers. They realised that old age was not all that distant, and it would be useful for them to be prepared to face it.

Unemployment

As a category under the protective social security needs, 'unemployment benefits' posed considerable problems methodologically. First, unemployment was not really a contingency to most of the workers. The state of unemployment, rather, was a norm and an accepted way of life for these workers. However, by including it as one of the protective needs, we were able to get excellent insights into the workers' perceptions on how they value these protective needs. In Box 17.1, we present a summary of the unorganised workers' notion of 'unemployment benefits'—we find that it coincides more with the concept of simple employment guarantee rather than with the payment of 'doles'. In the context of the unorganised workers, therefore, it is worth questioning whether this social security need is really a protective or a promotional need.

The reasons why nearly 33 per cent of the agricultural workers gave the highest preference towards UB are as follows. Given the seasonal nature of agriculture, the employment available to agricultural workers is dependent on two factors: 1) the occurrence of the monsoons, and 2) the number of farmers with irrigated land in the villages, who usually have a greater demand for agricultural labourers, notwithstanding the monsoons. In those villages where there were larger tracts of irrigated land,[9] the workers tended to give much less importance to UB, as compared to the dry land villages.

---

9. As also in villages in Dakshina Kannada, where a majority of the agricultural workers were employed as permanent workers in plantations.

Box 17.1

Unemployment Benefits—Promotional or Protective?

In the context of the importance accorded by the unorganised workers to 'unemployment benefits', we may note that what the workers expected in terms of unemployment benefits were not really unemployment 'doles' as the conception is in developed countries. For this would be unthinkable and impractical in the context of these workers, given that for them, the state of being without employment was more the norm than an exception. When the unorganised workers said that they preferred unemployment benefits over and above the other needs, they really meant that they needed the *assurance of continuous employment*. Several workers even clearly articulated that the reason they gave top priority to security against unemployment was that if the state was able to assure them continuous employment, then the workers were willing to take the responsibility of providing for the other needs themselves. The implication is that for the unorganised workers, the concept of 'unemployment benefits' coincides with the concept of 'employment security', i.e., primarily the guarantee of continuous employment (Rajasekhar and Suchitra, 2006).

A greater proportion of construction workers gave the top priority to UB than to OAP, but on comparing across categories of workers, this proportion was still lower than the proportion of agricultural workers who gave UB the top priority. The preference mapping of the construction workers as in Table 17.1 also shows that these workers expressed a more diverse set of needs as compared to the agricultural and domestic workers.

A majority of the construction workers having sporadic employment through the year gave top priority to UB. This behaviour cuts across the income and skill levels of the workers. The data shows that an equal proportion of skilled[10] and unskilled construction workers felt that unemployment was the most serious constraint to

10. Among construction workers, in all, 47 unskilled workers were interviewed, while the sample of 168 skilled and semi-skilled workers belonged to various trades such as masonry, electrical, painting, bar-bending, etc.

their livelihood security, and therefore gave this the first priority. An important reason for this is that akin to the intense competition among the unskilled construction workers, there is severe competition among the skilled labourers in different trades. Given the high in-migration of skilled workers from different parts of the country, many native skilled workers felt extremely insecure about their employment.

For the domestic workers, unemployment was the second most important contingency. Even though they had employment throughout the year, the incomes they earned were quite meagre and not sufficient to meet even the basic needs. While this was not a constraint in households where the domestic worker's income was only supplementary to the principal earner's income, in the cases where the domestic worker herself was the principal earner, it was a serious constraint.

Employment Injury

Table 17.1 shows that insurance against employment injury was considered the most significant need by nearly quarter of the construction workers (as against 7 and 5 per cent of the agricultural and domestic workers respectively). It is well established that construction is high-risk work and that construction workers face work-site risks such as accidents, chronic health problems due to the nature of the work, general illnesses that get exacerbated as a result of the work they undertake, etc. Insurance against employment injury thus becomes an important protective need for these workers. Our data shows that the high preference towards this need was related to the incidence of work-related risks among the workers. A majority of the workers who accorded the highest priority to insurance against employment injury had experienced work related risks of different kinds and degrees during the reference period (one year).[11]

---

11. We should note, though, that among the construction workers, one would never find that just because a worker had never experienced an employment injury before, s/he was likely to give a lower rank to the insurance against this eventuality. These workers were always aware of the fact that the probability of occurrence of such risks was quite high, and given a chance, that they would like to insure themselves against it. Therefore, we find that even among workers who had not experienced work related risks before, a large percentage of workers accorded a higher preference towards insuring themselves against it.

Particular Needs of Women Workers

Given the increasing feminisation of labour (especially agricultural labour) in the recent years, it is essential to identify the special needs of the women workers. An important social security benefit necessary for women is maternity benefit (MB). All women workers in the reproductive age were, therefore, asked to rank, in addition to the five general protective needs discussed above, maternity as a social security need.

There were 335 women in the entire sample of workers—inclusive of all domestic workers, 225 agricultural workers and 6 construction workers. Among them, more than half had assigned the zero rank[12] to maternity benefits. The handful of women who ranked MB in the top four priorities (around 6 per cent of women respondents) were newly married women, women in confinement at the time of the interview and women desirous of having male children in the future as they only had girl children till then.

Shockingly, however, 35.22 per cent of the women opined that MB was the least important social security need. This has to be understood, perhaps, in the light of the fact that these women were asked to rank MB along with other gender-neutral social security needs such as OAP, UB, etc. Most of them gave it the last rank because 'compared' to other needs this did not seem to be very important. Some women said that maternity was neither a situation that came suddenly nor could it be classified as a long-term need. It was only for a brief duration of time and they would somehow manage their lives. Many women said that they did not want to have any more children, and therefore, MB obviously was unimportant for them.

---

12. As mentioned earlier, some workers were unwilling to participate in the exercise of prioritising the social security needs. Even among those who did participate, there were many who expressed the ranking for a few needs, usually the first two ranks, and not the others. Such needs that were not given ranks by the workers were given the 'zero rank'. In the case of maternity benefits, the zero rank was used to include not just women workers who were unable to/unwilling to rank the needs, but also those not in the reproductive age, widowed women and divorced/separated/deserted women. Effectively, therefore, only around 45 per cent of the women workers were asked to take into consideration maternity benefits while ranking the social security needs.

Sickness and Death

A surprising finding from Table 17.1 is that across worker categories, sickness and death emerged as relatively insignificant contingencies, i.e., health and life insurance were given low priority by the unorganised workers. In the next section, we show that a majority of the risks faced by the workers and their households were related to these two needs, but nonetheless, in the workers' perception, these were not the most important needs. An analysis of this dichotomy between the 'perceived' and the 'actual' is necessary here.

Death

The proportion of those who gave the greatest importance to life insurance did not exceed around 10 per cent among all worker categories. The reason for this may be found in their perception of such a contingency. Most of these workers lived day-to-day, and for them, death was a very distant and almost unreal phenomenon. They did not consider it very important in the context of their here-and-now problems.[13] Also, some workers tended to get offended when 'death' was mentioned as an eventuality. An interesting trend was that some of the more pragmatic and practical workers who had taken out life insurance policies (see, Section 4 for details on insurance coverage) tended to give this need much less importance, since they were already covered for such a contingency.

Sickness

With respect to health insurance, around 12 per cent of the domestic workers accorded this need the highest importance, but this proportion in the case of agricultural and construction workers was lesser than 10 per cent. This may be understood as follows: since the workers were asked to *rank* the needs, they tended to give continuous and persistent problems more importance. Unemployment, for instance, was a pressing problem for them almost all through the year. However, events like ill health were also serious but short-term

---

13. Many workers even declared that given their current state of existence, death was perhaps the best thing that could happen to them. Although such responses were more in an emotional strain, they are still important to take into consideration to understand how these workers regard and cope with various contingencies.

occurrences, the fall-outs of which might not last long enough for the workers to perceive them as being *as* important as the continuous needs.

Household and Work-related Risks

Here, we present the risks faced by the unorganised workers and their households. We categorise them under household and work related crises.

Household Crises

The extent of risk-proneness of a household is primarily indicated by the occurrence of risks during the reference period,[14] and the frequency of occurrence of risks. Table 17.2 shows that households of all worker categories had faced some or the other emergency situation in the reference period, the incidence being more than 40 per cent in the case of the agricultural and construction worker households.

Table 17.2

Occurrence of Household Level Risks

Category of Worker	*Risks faced in the last three years (per cent)*	
	Yes	No
Agricultural	41.39	58.61
Construction	41.86	58.14
Domestic	35.58	64.42

Only 25 out of 910 households had experienced more than one crisis. Across the categories of workers, the risk with the highest incidence was health emergencies (Table 17.3), followed by 'death of a household member' and the arrangement of marriages and other social functions/obligations, which typically involved large expenditures.

14. The reference period was taken as the last 3 years.

Table 17.3

Different Crises Faced by Households

Worker Categories	*Death of Household Member*	*Health Emergency (including Operations)*	*Marriages and Other Festivities involving Large and Compulsory Expenditure*	*Accident*	*Other*	*Total Number of Crises*
Agricultural	53 (23.77)	105 (47.09)	37 (16.59)	26 (11.66)	2 (0.90)	223
Construction	20 (14.60)	67 (48.91)	27 (19.71)	22 (16.06)	1 (0.73)	237
Domestic	6 (15.79)	20 (52.63)	9 (23.68)	3 (7.89)	0(0.00)	38

Note: * The figures within parentheses are percentages and represent proportion to the total number of crises faced by households.

Work Related Crises

Risks are equally likely occurrences at the workplace as well, more so in the context of the unorganised workers. Some types of work are, by their nature, more risk-prone than others—for instance, construction. We now proceed to look at the risks faced by the workers in their respective work contexts during the reference period.[15]

The overall proportion of workers who faced risks at the work-site was quite low (13.7 per cent). It was marginally higher among the domestic workers as compared to the agricultural and construction workers.[16] Although we categorise the various risks into accidents, prolonged illness,[17] etc., all of them are in one way or another related to health issues.

15. The reference period taken for the work-related risks was one year.

16. In the next section, we will however, show that the risks faced by domestic workers were less severe and much less expensive to treat as compared to those faced by the construction and agricultural workers.

17. Work-related health hazard is differentiated from prolonged illness due to the nature of work, in the sense that the former is a short-term problem, while the latter is a chronic one. For example, many domestic workers faced chronic back problems because of their work. Short-term health hazards would be cold and fever on account of working with water continuously.

Table 17.4

Types of Work-related Risks Faced by the Workers

Worker Categories	*Types of Work-related Risks Faced*				
Agricultural	*Accident while using Implements*	*Health Problems related to Chemicals Used*	*Prolonged Illness due to Nature of Work*	*Other*	*Total Number of Crises*
	18 (37.50)	16 (33.33)	7 (14.58)	7 (14.58)	48
Construction	*Accident at Work Site*	*Work-related Health Hazard*	*Prolonged Illness due to Nature of Work*	*Other*	*Total Number of Crises*
	29 (52.73)	19 (34.55)	7 (12.73)	0 (0.00)	55
Domestic	*Health Problem due to Nature of Work*	*Prolonged Illness*	*Other*	*Total Number of Crises*	
	19 (86.36)	3 (13.64)	0	22	

Note: The figures within parentheses are percentages and represent the proportion to the total number of crises faced by each worker category.

Table 17.4 shows that in absolute terms, the incidence of work related risks was highest on the construction workers. A majority of these risks were accidents and health hazards like breathing problems, allergies, etc. Agricultural workers also faced accidents such as snakebites, and other health problems. As for the domestic workers, most of their work related risks were health problems due to the nature of work, such as colds and fevers, swollen feet, skin allergies due to detergents used, etc.

This section thus shows clearly while that workers perceive some needs as important, they, however, fail to acknowledge the kinds of emergency situations that they have actually faced in the recent past as equally important. The overall implication, therefore, is that the perceptions of the workers regarding the priority protective needs should not be taken at face value for policy purposes. If that were to be the case, then health and life insurance would not be important needs for them. But the actual occurrence shows that these are also equally important. This necessitates the creation of a social security package for them, which covers all these contingencies.

How are Failed Limbs Healed?—Formal and Informal Risk Management Mechanisms

In this section, we analyse the mechanisms adopted by the workers and their households to meet the priority social security needs, as well as the risks faced at the household level and work places. Formal mechanisms refer largely to the government-initiated schemes of social security. Predominant among these is the National Social Assistance Programme (NSAP)—including the National Old Age Pension Scheme (NOAPS), National Family Benefit Scheme (NFBS) and National Maternity Benefit Scheme (NMBS). The government of Karnataka also has some social security schemes for the unorganised workers—these include old age pensions, maternity benefit, destitute widow pensions and pensions for the physically handicapped. The performance analysis of these schemes over the last decade shows that they are all characterised by minuscule coverage and very low amounts of benefits, and therefore, grossly inadequate.

Formal mechanisms also include both public and private sector savings and insurance services available to the workers. These are usually classified as 'formal mitigating strategies' in the SRM framework. The objective of mitigating strategies, as mentioned earlier, is to minimise the adverse impact that the potential risk is likely to have. Here, we present briefly the savings and insurance behaviour among the unorganised sector workers.

Savings

Overall, the proportion of workers who had savings in some source was over 33 per cent. However, we find that with respect to savings, the dependence of unorganised households was not as much on formal sources such as banks, post offices, etc., as on less formal sources such as microfinance Self Help Groups (SHGs). Table 17.5 shows that the single most popular agency for savings among these workers was SHGs, where around 60 per cent of the workers chose to save money.

The access to formal destinations of savings such as banks and post offices was lowest among the agricultural workers and highest among the construction workers. This is easy to understand as the incomes of the latter were much higher, and the urban localities where these workers are concentrated facilitated greater access to such formal institutions.

Table 17.5

Agencies for Savings

(Per cent to Total Workers with Savings)

Type of workers	*Banks*	*Post office*	*SHG*	*Chit fund*	*Employers*	*Others*	*Total Workers with Savings*
Agricultural Workers	11.21	8.41	71.96	5.14	1.87	1.40	214
Construction Workers	18.58	12.39	41.59	23.01	0.88	3.54	113
Domestic Workers	12.00	12.00	48.00	28.00	0.00	0.00	25
Total	**13.64**	**9.94**	**60.51**	**5.40**	**8.52**	**1.99**	**352**

Given the rural setting of the agricultural workers and the more localised networks, and given the marginal savings that they were capable of, they depended more on SHGs. While SHGs were also popular among the construction and domestic workers as well, these workers also had savings in other sources such as chit funds.

Insurance

Janashree Bhima Yojana (JBY) is a social insurance policy introduced by the central government for several categories of unorganised sector workers.[18] None, however, among the sample workers, had taken up this policy, and in fact, the awareness of this policy was only around 2 per cent. This is surprising, because the JBY is a policy that is specifically meant for the unorganised sector workers, and we found that instead, workers had taken out other policies.

18. This group insurance scheme, which covers death and partial disability, is meant for the Below Poverty Line (BPL) households, and is operationalised through the Life Insurance Corporation (LIC) of India. The premium amount is Rs.200 per annum, half of which is borne by the government and the other half by the worker. As of 2004-2005, there were around 18.9 lakh beneficiaries of this policy in the country.

The results on the insurance coverage show that overall, just 18.2 per cent of the total sample workers had any coverage. Table 17.6 shows that the construction workers had a higher incidence of insurance coverage than the other two. The lowest coverage was among domestic workers, not surprisingly, since all of them were women and subject to severe gender bias. However, the domestic workers had the highest 'active' insurance coverage. This is due to two factors—a) domestic workers had continuous and steady employment throughout the year, and therefore, a regular source of income, notwithstanding the fact that the income was quite low, and b) where the domestic workers' incomes only supplemented that of the principal earning member of the household, it was easier for them to keep aside amounts of money regularly for such payments.

Table 17.6

Workers with Insurance Coverage

(Per Cent to Total Workers)

Type of Workers	*Ever Insured*	*Active Policies*
Agricultural workers	17.23	82.76
Construction workers	23.26	84.29
Domestic workers	8.65	88.89

More than 90 per cent of those without any insurance coverage responded that they could not afford it, or were unaware of any such schemes. Even among those insured, a large number had no clear knowledge of what specific insurance they had subscribed to, which was the agency that provided the scheme, or how the scheme worked.

Having established that the access to formal risk management mechanisms was very low among the unorganised workers, we now focus on each of the social security needs and analyse the means by which workers and their households met them.

Old Age Pensions

The findings from the primary data show that old age pension was obtained by only 25 per cent of the eligible workers. In the absence of pension, most of the older workers were forced to work and foresaw that they would continue to work as labourers for many more years, notwithstanding the lack of physical strength, health problems, etc. Second, they depended on their children/relatives. Third, they resorted to borrowing every now and then. The dependence, therefore, was on informal mechanisms.

Even among workers who were getting pensions, many complained that the payment was quite irregular. A few complained that they had to incur expenses in going to the *Gram Panchayat* several times before getting the pension, etc. It is thus clear that access to the old age pension scheme was very limited among sample workers, and even where it existed, it was not in smooth operation. In addition, the BPL criterion specified by the policies left out a large number of highly vulnerable (but not classified under the BPL category) out of the pool of benefits.

Unemployment Benefits

Employment opportunities for the agricultural and construction workers are seasonal in nature. Domestic workers, though employed throughout the year, are a largely underpaid lot, and therefore, are often on the lookout for more employment opportunities and alternative employment. Our results show, however, that among the agricultural workers and rural-based construction workers, awareness on state employment generation schemes like the Sampoorna Grameen Rozgar Yojana (SGRY) and the Swarnajayanti Gram Swarozgar Yojana (SGSY) was very poor—around 90 per cent of the workers were *unaware* of such programmes, and none of the sample workers had availed of the benefits of either programme. The urban-based workers did not have awareness of or access to 'any' formal schemes by which they could ensure themselves basic employment security.

A related point is the payment of stipulated minimum wages. Nearly all the sample workers were unaware of the minimum wages law. The construction workers were marginally better off, since, despite unawareness, quite a few skilled workers were found to be getting at least as much as the minimum wage stipulated for their category of work.

None of the domestic workers knew or got minimum wages

specified for their occupation, despite the announcement of the Act in 2004. These workers, in general, had employment throughout the year; however, they always had the fear of discontinuity of this security due to sudden termination from work, etc. Only those workers who had the luxury of having worked at one or two employers' houses for many years, and who had built a reasonably strong bond of trust with their employers did not face this problem. While the closer contact between the employer and the employed in the case of some domestic workers allowed these workers greater patronage from their employers, among the highly vulnerable workers, such luxury was rare. Many lived in the eternal fear that they would render themselves jobless by seeking any sort of help from the employers.

Risk Management in the Face of Household Crises

Table 17.7 shows the different sources of expenditure that the households depended on to overcome the household crises. The most important source was borrowing from moneylenders at high rates of interest. The construction workers, being in general, significantly higher-income groups as compared to the agricultural and domestic workers, their dependence on own sources was higher than among the other two categories. Relatives are also an important source of borrowing for the households during the crises, especially for the domestic workers. Dependence on employers and sale of assets are also important sources for the expenditure on the household crises.

Table 17.7

Sources of Expenditure (Per cent) on Household Crises

Category of Workers	*Own Sources*	*Borrowing from Money-lenders*	*Relatives*	*Bank*	*Employer*	*Sale of Assets*	*Other Source*	*Total Expenditure (in Rs.)*
Agricultural worker	18.06	54.92	12.21	0.86	8.49	2.79	2.67	2,684,600
Construction worker	25.32	48.29	12.17	4.33	4.26	3.04	2.59	2,795,100
Domestic worker	18.65	50.79	17.28	5.43	2.61	3.62	1.63	552,650

An important phenomenon that remains concealed in this Table is that it shows only how the households faced the crises through dependence on some source or the other. There were also some households who had faced risks of varying degrees, but they were unable to do anything about them, and were therefore, forced to carry on with life as though nothing had happened. For example, many health problems would go untreated by these households because they would not have the resources to address these problems at that juncture. It is in this context that the dependence on borrowings is significant. While borrowing from moneylenders or others at high rates of interest may seem to be the most wretched and disabling form of coping with risks, even worse is the eventuality that the inability to borrow puts the households in.

Non-borrowing is, thus, of two types. One category of households does not depend on borrowings, or depends to a lesser degree on this source to meet the requirements. This is the category that is reflected in Table 17.7, i.e., the households who alternatively depended on sources such as savings, own sources, etc. The even more vulnerable category is that comprising of households who not only do not have the luxury of sources other than borrowing, but also cannot borrow from any sources since they are sure they can never repay the amounts. The same applies to dependence on sale or pledge of assets. Many households do not depend on these sources since there is no necessity, but very many households cannot afford to depend on them since they are so vulnerable that they do not possess any assets.

The dependence on borrowing imposes on the unorganised sector workers heavy costs in the form of interest rates. Borrowing from relatives is also a costly mechanism for these workers even though not always monetarily. While relatives usually do not demand any interest on the amount lent, such borrowing and lending is always based on the principle of 'balanced reciprocity',[19] which could render them helpless and more vulnerable in the future.

In the case of borrowings on interest, on many occasions, these workers pay interest amounts for years together without having

19. Balanced reciprocity means that for any 'gift', there is the inevitable strong assumption that at some time in the future, there will be a counter gift.

returned any of the principal amount borrowed. Table 17.8 shows that the domestic workers were the most vulnerable with respect to the rates of interest they paid. Some workers had even paid more than 100 per cent of the amount borrowed merely by way of interest, indicating a situation of absolute vulnerability.

Table 17.8

Distribution of Households (Per cent) by Rates of Interest Paid on Borrowings

Worker Categories	*Rates of Interest (per cent per annum)*			
	<25	*25 – 50*	*50 – 100*	*>100*
Agricultural	16.46	37.34	37.34	8.86
Construction	13.59	43.69	33.98	8.74
Domestic	6.90	27.59	34.48	31.03

Table 17.9 shows that costs incurred by the workers in the form of interest payments were substantial. Although more than 75 per cent of the workers in all the categories had paid interest amounts less than 50 per cent of the amount borrowed, there were workers who had paid more than they had borrowed just by way of interest. This was particularly evident in the case of domestic workers where 14.29 per cent of them had repaid more than 100 per cent of the principal just as interest. The construction workers were relatively better off, as almost 85 per cent had paid only less than 50 per cent of the principal amount as interest.

Table 17.9

Distribution of Households (Per cent) by Proportion of Interest Amount Paid to Principal Amount

Categories of Workers	*<50 per cent*	*50–100 per cent*	*>100 per cent*
Agricultural Worker	76.43	15.71	7.86
Construction Worker	84.95	10.75	4.30
Domestic Worker	75.00	10.71	14.29

Risk Management in the Face of Work-related Risks

It is in this context that protective social security is all the more important because it can be argued from a 'rights' perspective that the employer has a legal as well as moral obligation to provide for care and expenses towards treating health risks of workers while at work or those occurring as a result of the nature of work undertaken, and the role of the state is imperative in ensuring the same. In general, the expenditure on such risks was greater for the construction workers (in the range of an average of Rs.3,000) than for the agricultural workers. The domestic workers' expenditure was much lower—over 50 per cent of their expenditure on work-related risks was less than Rs.500, and only around 7 per cent was greater than Rs.1,000.

The extent to which such expenditure affected the workers and their households is shown markedly in Table 17.10, representing the proportion of expenditure to the monthly per capita income of the households. We take the expenditure on these risks as 'at one point in time' expenses, i.e., when the expenditure is incurred, it is likely to have an adverse impact on the household 'at that particular period of time'. We take this period to be a month.[20]

Table 17.10

Distribution of Workers (Per cent) by Proportion of Expenditure to Average Monthly PCI

Categories of Workers	*<100 per cent*	*100–250 per cent*	*>250 per cent*
Agricultural	22.92	29.17	47.92
Construction	41.82	25.45	32.73
Domestic	72.27	22.73	0.00

The domestic workers' expenditure was not very hard-hitting to their households. The agricultural workers were the worst off as nearly 48 per cent of them bore the brunt of more than two and a half

20. It is likely that the expenditure was not incurred 'at a point in time' but was a continuous process, for instance in the case of prolonged illness. But the incidence of prolonged illness was shown to be quite low among all categories of workers. Besides, we took an entire month as the reference point to gauge the impact of the expenditure.

times their monthly per capita income, and almost 30 per cent spent 100–200 per cent of the same. The construction workers were relatively better off in terms of the extent of impact the expenditure had during that particular period. The implication of this table, overall, is that when the unorganised workers were encountered with the kind of crises that involved expenditure to this degree, they were forced to draw upon other sources, at times draw upon their household consumption, etc., to meet these needs. At times, they might have to compromise on other more basic needs to fulfil these needs.

Table 17.11

Sources of Expenditure on Work-Related Risks

Sources of Expenditure	*Agricultural Workers*	*Construction Workers*	*Domestic Workers*
Assistance from family and friends	20.72	15.85	20.91
Falling back on savings	16.64	9.56	17.73
Borrowing	30.40	66.30	42.73
Sale of assets	2.40	5.76	8.64
Employer covered expenses	27.52	2.52	10.00
Other	2.32	0.00	0.00

Note: * The figures in the table are percentages, representing the proportion to the total expenditure on work-related risks.

Table 17.11 shows that in the event of expenses concerning work-related risks, sale of assets was minimum. At least about 15 per cent of the workers in each category reported that they depended on family and friends to meet the expenses over such risks. Although this was a relatively less depended-on source, it signals the fact that the family and kinship relations, though declining, have not altogether disappeared as a source of help. As noted in the case of sources of financing household risks, borrowing is the single most important fall-back option for all the categories of workers to fund the expenditure on work-related risks.

Importantly, evidence on the employers covering the expenditure on work-site risks is the least in the case of the construction workers, for whom the expenditure was the highest. Domestic workers had some support from the employers, but such support was considerable in the case of agricultural workers. We find, however, that this was the case largely in Dakshina Kannada district, where many workers were permanent and attached to particular estates, and therefore, the relationship they shared with their employers was quite different from what the casual labourers faced. The implication, thus, is that the employers, who are in part responsible for the welfare of their workers, seldom take interest in this. There is no support forthcoming from the state in this respect either. The unorganised workers, who contribute much to the economy, are in effect left to their own defences, and are rendered increasingly vulnerable.

Conclusion

The unorganised workers are currently in receipt of some social security benefits such as old age pensions, maternity and family benefits. However, these schemes suffer from the twin problems of low coverage and small amounts of benefits. The workers are, therefore, forced to depend on informal mechanisms, which, however, impose high costs in the form of usurious interest rates, vulnerability to bondage, balanced reciprocity, etc. Continued dependence on such mechanisms makes the workers and their households more vulnerable.

In the context of increasing casualisation and informalisation of labour, and the absence of reliable statutory social security benefits for the unorganised workers, we have examined the social security needs of these workers and risk management mechanisms they adopt. The workers perceive continuous and persistent problems such as unemployment and old age to be the most important social security needs. Even though they do not perceive health emergencies and death to be significant needs, most of the worker households faced crises relating to these two contingencies. The introduction of a social security product covering all these contingencies is likely to be the most rewarding for the workers. A considerable proportion of unorganised workers would be willing to contribute towards such a scheme when introduced (Rajasekhar *et al,* 2006).

References

Dev, S.M., P. Antony, V. Gayathri and R.P. Mamgain (2001). "Towards a Holistic Perspective of Social Security", in Mahendra Dev *et al.* (eds.), *Social and Economic Security in India*. New Delhi: Institute for Human Development.

Dev, S.M., P. Antony, V. Gayathri and R.P. Mamgain (2001). *Social and Economic Security in India*. New Delhi: Institute for Human Development.

Dreze, J. and A. Sen (1989). *Hunger and Public Action*. Oxford: Clarenton Press.

———. (1991). "Public Action for Social Security: Foundations and Strategy", in E. Ahmad *et al.* (eds.), *Social Security in Developing Countries*. New Delhi: Oxford University Press.

Etisham, Ahmad, Jean Dreze, John Hills and Amartya Sen (1991). *Social Security in Developing Countries*. New Delhi: Oxford University Press.

Gayatri, V. (2001). "Security for Women Workers", in Mahendra Dev *et al.* (eds.), *Social and Economic Security in India*. New Delhi: Institute for Human Development.

Holzmann, R. and S. Jorgensen (2000). "Social Risk Management: A New Conceptual Framework for Social Protection and Beyond", *Social Protection Discussion Paper*.

ILO (1984). *Introduction to Social Security*. Geneva: International Labour Office.

Rajasekhar, D. and G. Sreedhar (2002). "Changing Face of Beedi Industry in Karnataka", *Economic and Political Weekly*. September.

Rajasekhar, D., J.Y. Suchitra, S. Madheswaran and G.K. Karanth (2006). "Design and Management of Social Security Benefits for the Unorganised Sector Workers in Karnataka". New Delhi: GTZ.

Rajasekhar, D. and J.Y. Suchitra (2006). "Employment Security for the Unorganised Sector Workers in Karnataka". *ISEC Working Paper*, No.169. Bangalore: Institute for Social and Economic Change.

Rao, V.M., D. Rajasekhar and J.Y. Suchitra (2006). "Unorganised Workers: Deprivation, Social Security and Policy Implications", *Economic and Political Weekly* XLI (19). May.